Object-Oriented Programming With C++

2nd edition

David Parsons

David Parsons has lectured in both further and higher education, and is currently a senior lecturer in the Systems Engineering faculty at Southampton Institute. He has a BA from the University of Sussex, a Certificate in Education from Garnett College (London) and an MPhil from the University of Southampton, faculty of Engineering and Applied Science. His current research interest is in enhancing the extensibility of object-oriented systems, particularly in the area of schematic capture for electronic circuit design.

Continuum
London • New York

Acknowledgements

Many people have had an influence on the second edition of this book, but some deserve special mention. I would particularly like to thank my colleagues Mark Cranshaw, Rob Callan and Ian Court with whom I have taught many courses on object-orientation and C++. Their insight and experience has been invaluable. I am also grateful to Tom Kazmierski for his consistent support for my research. Thanks are also due to the hundreds of students who have endured my lectures and the thousands(!) who bought the first edition of the book. I would also like to thank the many people who provided constructive comments on the first edition, either directly or via the publisher's questionnaire. I have tried to take as many of your comments into account as possible in preparing this edition. Finally, I would like to thank my wife and daughters: Di, Jenny, Katie and Abbie, who (almost) prevent me from going insane.

David Parsons
Email: dave.parsons@solent.ac.uk
home page: http://www.solent.ac.uk/syseng/sef9027.html

A CIP catalogue record for this book is available from the British Library

ISBN 0 8264 5428 3
Copyright D. Parsons © 1997

First edition 1994
Second edition 1997
Reprinted 2000

Typeset by Elizabeth Bennett, St Albans, Herts

Printed in Great Britain by
Ashford Colour Press, Gosport

Continuum
The Tower Building, 11 York Road, London, SE1 7NX
370 Lexington Avenue, New York, NY 10017-6550

Contents

Preface

Background

Now that the various aspects of object technology are firmly in the mainstream of computing, the principles and practices of object-orientation have become increasingly important to students on university and college computing courses. Object-oriented languages such as C++ and Java have found wide popularity in the workplace, and new methodologies such as the Unified Modelling Language (UML) have been developed to encompass object-oriented design and analysis. As higher education courses adapt to the changing technology, more and more students are finding the need for a simple introductory text to object-oriented concepts, programming, analysis and design.

Aim

The aim of this book is to demystify the rather forbidding terminology used in object-orientation, and to present each aspect of the approach in a simple form, using C++ as the example language. The guiding principle is that concepts can only be learned by practical 'hands on' experience.

Need

Most texts on object-orientation tend to fall into one of three camps.

1. Books about programming in a particular language, or a particular company's version of a language, with the emphasis on syntax. The underlying concepts of object-orientation are often relegated to a few paragraphs.

2. Purely conceptual texts, extremely complex for the beginner to grasp with no concrete coding examples.

3. Books specifically tied to a particular design or analysis methodology, and therefore, whilst in many cases including good general introductions, they tend to contain much information inappropriate to a more general understanding.

In many cases, complex terms are interpreted differently by different authors, and there is little entry level material available for the student.

Approach

This book assumes that the reader has a practical knowledge of the basic principles of computer programming, though not in any particular language. Experience in traditional procedural languages such as BASIC or Pascal should stand the reader in good stead. A simple subset of standard C++ as described by its inventor Bjarne Stroustrup in his book 'The C++ Programming Language' [Stroustrup, 1995] is used for the examples in the book, and no syntax is used without explanation. The intention is that all examples should be easily assimilable and lead to working programs as soon as possible. They should also be portable across the various C++ compilers with little or no modification.

Each chapter deals with a particular aspect of object-orientation, firstly dealing with the general concepts and terms, and then demonstrating them separately with simple examples in C++. The intention is that the text can be used as a reference for the concepts alone, but can also be used as a learning tool for object-oriented programming in C++. Object-oriented programming skills are developed incrementally, building on what has gone before.

In-text questions (with answers) enable the reader to stop and reflect, and at the end of most chapters there are programming exercises; some have answers provided at the back of the book.

Overview

The book begins with chapters on the background to object orientation and C++, outlining their development. Bjarne Stroustrup has this advice about books on object-orientation: *"My rule is: look to see if there is a history section, and look to see if there is a lot of hype about object-oriented programming at the beginning; and if there's no history and there's object-oriented hype - don't touch it!"* [Stroustrup in Watts, 1992 p.36]. In Chapter 1, there is some history and just a little object-oriented hype!

This is followed by a basic introduction to the syntax of C++ (including data types, operators, selections, loops, functions and simple I/O syntax). It is not intended that this should provide an in-depth knowledge of C++, but simply that it should provide a basic level of knowledge appropriate to understanding the examples used in the book and tackling the initial programming exercises. In the following chapters, object-oriented concepts such as classes, objects, inheritance and polymorphism are introduced in the context of previous material. Later chapters cover relatively advanced topics such as building container classes, multiple inheritance, object persistence and approaches to object-oriented analysis and design.

Organisation

The book is organised so that the material can be delivered in discrete units in one semester (or supplemented with other material for longer courses if required). Most chapters are appropriate to one week's lecture and workshop material, though some shorter semantically related chapters can be combined. For a 15 week semester, the following gives a good balance of material:

Week no.	Chapter	Material Covered
1	1, 2	Introductory object-orientation/C++
2	3	C/C++ syntax
3	4	Classes
4	5	Objects
5	6	Object lifetimes
6	7	Metaclass
7	8	Inheritance
8	9	Association and aggregation
9	10, 11	Introductory polymorphism/operator overloading
10	12	Parametric polymorphism
11	13, 14	Polymorphic methods
12	15	Container classes
13	16	Multiple inheritance
14	17	Persistent objects, files and streams
15	18	Analysis and design

A mid-semester assignment may be given around week eight, when enough of the fundamental concepts have been covered to produce a reasonably object-oriented program. An example program is provided after chapter nine to give some idea of the kind of application that might be appropriate, and to give students a frame of reference.

Experience suggests that being able to teach a full fifteen weeks in a semester is often impossible where a period for exams is required. In these circumstances, more specialist areas such as some aspects of polymorphism, multiple inheritance and analysis and design can be left out, perhaps as directed learning for the students to pursue individually.

Resources available on the internet

The source code for all the example programs in the book, along with those exercises that have answers provided in the appendix is available from the Letts Educational website at:

> http://www.lettsed.co.uk/parsons.htm

Other complementary materials will also be made available via this site as they become available.

Lecturers' supplement

A supplement is provided free of charge to lecturers recommending the book as a course text, including suggested answers to those exercises not included in the appendix. A diskette is also available containing both the files from the website and those from the lecturers' supplement. Application should be made to the publishers on departmental headed notepaper.

Dave Parsons
May 1997

1 What is object-orientation?

Overview

In this chapter, we look at what is meant by the term 'object', and how it reflects our natural view of the world. The general characteristics of the object-oriented approach are described, and some key terms are introduced. The development of object-orientation is traced through previous developments in languages and methodologies, and the object-oriented and procedural programming paradigms are compared. Finally, some current issues in object technology are discussed.

Objects in software

The field of object-orientation (or 'object technology' as it is often called) is a large and growing one, and what it entails can to some extent depend on the context. For example, the facilities of the programming languages vary widely; some languages are more 'object-oriented' than others. Generally, however, object-orientation is about trying to represent the 'objects' that we find in the real world (or at least that part of it which our programs address) in software. These 'objects' may be of various types, ranging from the physical (aircraft in an air traffic control application for example) to the more conceptual (some sort of container for other objects perhaps).

Shlaer and Mellor [1988, pp.15–16] in their object-oriented analysis method identify five types of objects:

1. *Tangible Things*   Physical objects, e.g. 'car', 'bar code reader'
2. *Roles*   Of people or organisations, e.g. 'account holder', 'employer'
3. *Incidents*   Something happening at a particular time, e.g. 'flight', 'transaction'
4. *Interactions*   A link between objects, e.g. 'electrical connection', 'contract'
5. *Specifications*   A definition of a set of other objects, e.g. a description of a particular type of stock item

While this is only one approach to analysis, clearly some objects are more 'real' (in the sense of physically existing in the real world) than others! A more general distinction in terms of object-oriented programming is made by Stroustrup [1995, p.402] when he identifies two kinds of object:

1. Those that directly represent the ideas used to describe the application.
2. Those that are 'artifacts of the implementation' – objects used as programming tools to implement the code.

We may make a distinction then between objects that are part of an application such as banks, petrol pumps and customers, and others that are programming tools such as data structures (stacks, queues etc.) which allow us to implement the application objects.

What is an object?

Having said object-orientation is about representing 'objects' in software, we must ask ourselves two questions:

1. What is an object?
2. Why use objects in programs?

We may answer the first question by saying that, in essence, objects are the elements through which we perceive the world around us. We naturally see our environment as being composed of 'things' which have recognisable identities and particular behaviours. All objects have these characteristics of identity (what we call an object) and behaviour (what an object does) which enable us to recognise them as discrete things. They also exhibit 'state', which means that we can describe what an object is, as well as what it does and what it is called. Another key element in the object-oriented model is that objects can be classified into types, again a natural response to our environment. It is instinctive to classify individual objects according to their common characteristics; we recognise for example that all cats are of a single 'type'. Although we may also identify individual differences between specific cats, our perception is that all individual cats belong to a general 'class' which we call 'Cat'. We 'know about' all cats because we recognise what they have in common.

We are also able to recognise that some objects are composed of other objects, or contain other objects. A 'house' object is composed of other objects such as bricks, windows, doors, tiles etc. A shopping trolley full of groceries is an object in its own right and a container of other objects. All these human responses to the world are elements of the object-oriented approach.

The basic philosophy of using objects in programs is a simple one – that the world is composed of interacting, classifiable and identifiable objects, and therefore programs, too, can usefully be structured in this way. Since all software applications serve people living in the real world, then that software should mirror the real world as closely as possible, both in its workings and in its underlying design. Simply, object-oriented programming is a more 'natural' way to program.

Question 1.1   Is an object a concrete 'thing'?

Some objects in software represent concrete things in the real world (though they are not themselves concrete). Other objects are more abstract, and do not represent 'things' which can be touched or seen.

Object = (private) data + (public) processes

What is perhaps most important (and different) about the object-oriented approach to software is that it unifies inside 'objects' two things that have traditionally been separated in programming paradigms:

1. Data
2. Processes

The linking of these two aspects of programming is known as 'encapsulation', and allows the implementation of 'information hiding' – restricted access to the internal representations of objects. Objects have a 'private' part of hidden internal detail (state data and internal processes), and a 'public' interface which clearly defines the set of possible behaviours of the object (the messages to which it can respond). This separation of the public interface of an object and its internal implementation allows us to treat the two as separate parts of the programming process. An object's private implementation details can be defined without reference to other objects or a particular application context, and then the object may be used in an application that utilises only the object's public interface.

Both the public and private part of an object are defined in an 'abstract data type' which defines the common aspects of all objects in a particular 'class', i.e. objects that we classify as one type.

Relating to existing paradigms

Although object-orientation gives us new tools and a new approach to software, it is an evolutionary rather than a revolutionary approach. The following sections discuss the development of approaches to software engineering and the many parallels between this and other paradigms.

Functional and data decomposition

All large programming projects have to be 'partitioned' in some way if they are to be managed at all, since there has to be some way of allocating programmer tasks and assembling their work into a cohesive unit. Before the coming of object-oriented methods, serious programs had been generally developed using one of two general approaches, or 'structured methods' (these are encompassed by several different methodologies).

1. Process Driven (Functional Decomposition)
2. Data Driven (Data Decomposition)

In functional (or 'algorithmic') decomposition, a programming problem is 'decomposed' into constituent processes, each of which should be a coherent and simple module. The structure of the data which these modules process is a secondary consideration, meaning that data tends to be generally spread across a system with little logical organisation.

In the data driven approach, sets of data are used to design the program, so that the internal structures of data are used to organise the processes that take place. Here, we may find large amounts of data being processed in a way dictated by an arbitrary file or database structure that may be used in many different applications. The fixed structures of global data held in files or tables tend to cause difficulties when a particular process does not easily match the existing data structures.

Both of the above approaches have their disadvantages, and some of the problems that arise when using them are because they are both computer-oriented paradigms – one based on the organisation of computer processes, the other based on the organisation of data files. When either of these is applied to a real situation (which tend to be rather less clear cut than computer systems) there can be a lack of connectivity between reality and the attempted solution.

Question 1.2   Structured methods are used to decompose programming problems. Why is this necessary, and what may be used to drive the decomposition?

Programming problems of any size must be decomposed to be successfully managed, particularly for large teams of programmers. There are two approaches to decomposition in structured methods, which may be either data driven or process driven.

The 'software crisis' and the 'silver bullet'

The process and data driven approaches to structured methods were, in part, responses to the 'Software Crisis', a term coined in 1968 by the NATO Software Engineering Conference which maintained that contemporary software production methods were inadequate for the developing needs of the defence and data processing industries. Subsequent methodologies were an attempt to find the 'silver bullet' that would overcome the software crisis. The term 'silver bullet' comes from a 1986 article by Fred Brooks comparing software projects with werewolves – 'because they transform unexpectedly from the familiar into horrors' [Brooks, 1986 p.10]. Werewolves, as Hollywood teaches, can be killed by silver bullets.

If software implementation had been successful in the decades since 1968, then there would be no need to look for new approaches. However, there is still plenty of evidence to suggest that many software projects still come in over time, over budget and under specification, despite the proliferation of analysis and design methods. We are all familiar with traditional engineering projects which cost much more than they were supposed to, are completed late and are substandard, but the sheer degree to which this happens in software engineering suggests an even more serious problem.

Code re-use versus code salvage

One primary reason for the problems of software production has been that, despite good intentions, it is very difficult to reuse code generated from traditional approaches. As Ed Yourdon, an influential author on both structured and object-oriented techniques, says, 'Reusability is, of course, a Boy Scout virtue like loyalty, thrift, and bravery, but no-one is quite sure how to practice it' [Yourdon, 1990 p. 258]. However general a module of functionally decomposed code might appear to be, it tends to be either too implementation specific to reuse, or too general to be of use in a different specific context. Instead of code reuse, only code salvage (dismantling and reconstructing) seems possible using existing techniques, unless the module's function is very trivial. The non proximity between processes and data in traditional systems means that processing modules are over dependent on external data stores.

In contrast, the modular unit in object-orientation (the 'abstract data type', which provides the blueprint for objects of a specific type) encapsulates both data and process. Because abstract data types hide their internal information behind a consistent 'public' interface, they can be easily ported from one application to another. These units therefore provide the reusability absent from other methods in that not only can they be used in many applications without modification, but they can also be extended, without corrupting what already exists. Once we have true reusability, we have the tools for the 'Software Industrial Revolution' [Cox, 1990 p.210], by which the assembly of software from prefabricated components becomes as easy and commonplace as it is for traditional engineering.

True modularity through object-orientation

Object-orientation is not so much a radical new approach as an evolutionary development in the maturation of software engineering. Many ideals that have been sought in functional (and data) decomposition can be achieved via object-orientation. What in essence it provides is true 'modularity', in which software modules (objects) provide the ultimate in:

1. *Low (data) Coupling*   Coupling is the extent to which different modules rely on one another and/or external data in order to function.

2. *High (functional) Cohesion*   Cohesion is the extent to which a programming module makes sense as an entity.

A module which exhibits 'low coupling' is not tied to a particular environment in order to function. The external interface of an object is clearly defined in terms of the operations that object can undergo, and any external inputs that affect the object's behaviour. Its coupling to other objects is through flexible 'message passing' mechanisms, and it is only the uses of these message passing mechanisms that will tend to vary widely between applications. Therefore an object is easily 'decoupled' from a particular application and 'coupled' to another.

Cohesion is to some extent a matter of semantics – what the 'meaning' of a particular module is. A 'highly cohesive' module is therefore one that has a clearly defined role. The ideal type of cohesion in functional decomposition is 'functional cohesion', by which a module performs one problem-related task. Object-orientation can go further than this and encapsulate together functions related to data representations of real world objects. The semantics of a module then becomes the same as the semantics of the real world – if we can understand something as an object in reality, then we can model it as a cohesive module in software. Not all objects have 'real world' parallels, but 'computational objects' such as stacks, queues and lists exhibit the same characteristics of modularity as cars, stereos and dogs, since their role in an application is defined by their external behaviours, not by their internal workings.

Benefits of modularity

Because object-orientation provides modularity, it also provides the generally assumed benefits of modularity, namely:

1. *Reusability*   Programs can be assembled from pre-written software components that can be used in many different applications.

2. *Extensibility*   New software components can be written or developed from existing ones without affecting the original components.

Meyer (the creator of the 'Eiffel' object-oriented programming language) gives five criteria for modularity [Meyer, 1988]. These criteria may be applied to any type of system, but are difficult to achieve using functional decomposition:

1. *Decomposability*   Breaking a system down into manageable units
2. *Composability*   Modules may be freely combined into other systems
3. *Understandability*   Understanding the part contributes to understanding the whole
4. *Continuity*   Small changes to the system imply small changes to behaviour
5. *Protection*   Exception and error conditions are confined to the module in which they occur, or affect only closely related modules

All these criteria are met in an object-oriented system by virtue of objects reflecting semantically cohesive units with simple interfaces, hiding their internal implementation.

In summary, modularity is easier to achieve using object-oriented techniques, and it is therefore easier to take full advantage of its benefits.

Question 1.3   What differentiates a 'module' from an 'object'?

A module is a 'functionally decomposed' piece of code which performs a particular process or set of processes. An object is a unit of software comprising both data and process which provides some meaningful behaviour.

Areas of object technology

The general field of object technology can be seen as falling into four areas of application:

1. Object-Oriented Programming (OOP)

2. Object-Oriented Design (OOD)

3. Object-Oriented Analysis (OOA)

4. Object-Oriented Databases (OODBs)

All these necessarily interact in some way, particularly object-oriented analysis and design – many methodologies have been proposed, but we can see common elements between them. Object-oriented databases are a very important field because traditional forms of data storage do not sit easily with the object-oriented approach, and more appropriate and flexible ways of storing objects on disk need to be used. While this book introduces object-orientation primarily as a programming methodology, later chapters introduce the areas of object-oriented analysis, design and databases.

A brief history of object-orientation

There have been a number of milestones on the road to object-orientation, both theoretical developments and language implementations. The following table shows some of the most important:

1968:	Simula67 – the first object-oriented language
1972:	David Parnas' seminal paper on 'Information Hiding'
1970s:	Graphical User Interfaces (GUIs) developed using object-orientation
1980:	First version of Smalltalk
1983:	First version of C++
1988:	First version of Eiffel
1990s:	Object Oriented Analysis and Design methods
1995:	First version of Java

Although there has been a claim that the designers of the 'Minuteman' missile used rudimentary object-oriented techniques as early as 1957 [Graham 1992 p.2], the 'birth' of object-orientation came in 1968 with Simula67 – the first object-oriented language, and an extremely influential one. One only has to consider that the key personalities behind three of the major object-oriented languages – Bjarne Stroustrup (C++), Alan Kay (Smalltalk) and Bertrand Meyer (Eiffel) – all had backgrounds in Simula to realise its influence. Simula was developed in Norway as a discrete event simulation language, and was the first language to introduce the key object-oriented concepts of classes and inheritance.

Many people have been influential in developing the theoretical basis of object-orientation, but perhaps the most influential single paper was published by David Parnas, who introduced the idea of 'information hiding'. Parnas' principle was that a programming module should 'reveal as little as possible about its inner workings' [Parnas, 1972 p.147]. This basic idea is crucial to the way that objects hide their internal implementations behind a public interface.

Throughout the 1970s and 1980s, a great deal of development using object-oriented techniques went on at various research centres. At Xerox PARC (Palo Alto Research Centre), Smalltalk was developed, an object-oriented language that comes with its own WIMP (Windows, Icons, Menus and Pointers) interface. Its interface style in particular has had a strong influence on the subsequent growth in the development of GUIs (Graphical User Interfaces) for many applications. Other languages also appeared in the 1980s, notably C++ (a 'hybrid' language based on C with object-oriented extensions) and Eiffel (like Smalltalk, a 'pure' OO language). In the early 1990s object oriented analysis and design methods proliferated, and in 1995 Java became the language of choice for programming on the Internet.

Clearly, object-orientation has had a long development path, which has taken off only in recent years partly because the programming languages are very demanding on hardware resources. Another reason for its recent growth has been the popularity of the GUI, which has become the norm for all types of applications. Since the user interface has become increasingly more sophisticated, the advantages of the object-oriented approach, particularly in terms of reuse, have seen it become the standard method for coding GUIs. Other areas that have grown in importance in recent years are those of concurrency and rapid prototyping, both of which can benefit from the object-oriented approach. Design methodologies such as the 'Unified Modelling Language' [Rumbaugh, Booch and Jacobsen, 1997] provide us with tools for designing concurrent systems using objects, while languages such as C++ and Java allow multithreaded programs. In the area of rapid prototyping, the modular nature of an object-oriented program means rapid reuse and modification without compromising robustness or reliability. This is particularly useful in applications where there are new and unknown problems to be solved – it is possible to test various approaches quickly and efficiently when we can easily assemble and disassemble software objects in prototype systems. In addition, the fields of object-orientation and knowledge based systems seem likely to grow closer together as they increasingly find common theoretical and practical ground [Harmon, 1990].

Basic terminology and ideas

The various aspects of object-orientation will be covered in detail throughout the book, but the three key features of the object-oriented approach are often quoted as:

1. Abstraction / encapsulation
2. Inheritance
3. Polymorphism

Abstraction/encapsulation

Abstraction is the representation of all the essential features of an object, which means its possible states and behaviours. These are 'encapsulated' into an 'abstract data type' which defines how all objects in a class (type) of objects are to be represented and how they behave.

Encapsulation is the practice of including in an object everything it needs, (both data and processes) hidden from other objects in the system. The internal state of an object is not directly accessible from outside, and cannot be altered by external changes to the application. Similarly, changes to the internal implementation details can be made without affecting the external interface.

Inheritance

Inheritance means that one class inherits the characteristics of another class as part of its definition. Inheritance is appropriate when one class is 'a kind of' other class (e.g. A is a kind of B – 'text window' is a kind of 'window'). These types of hierarchies are fundamental to object-oriented programming. Some classes may inherit from more than one other class, and this is known as 'multiple inheritance'.

A 'classification hierarchy' shows the inheritance relationships between classes, based on the similarities between different classes of objects. Inheritance has two complementary roles:

1. To allow a class to be extended so that its existing functionality can be built on for new applications.
2. To allow similar objects to share their common properties and allowed behaviours.

Polymorphism

Polymorphism means 'having many forms', and there are many forms of polymorphism! The general description of polymorphism is that it allows different objects to respond to the same message in different ways, the response specific to the type of object. This is achieved by various types of 'overloading' – allowing a symbol (an operator like '+', or a function name like 'show') to have more than one meaning depending on the context in which it is used. Polymorphism is particularly important when object-oriented programs are dynamically creating and destroying objects in a classification hierarchy at run time, so that it is not possible when compiling to predict the number or classes of objects which will receive messages when the program is running. We therefore have to defer decisions about the meaning of a particular symbol until run-time, a practice known as 'dynamic binding'. 'Run-time' polymorphism of this kind is one of the most useful aspects of object-oriented programming.

These three main ideas (encapsulation, inheritance and polymorphism) tend to build on each other, so that once we have encapsulation, then we can build classification hierarchies of inheritance, and from these we can really begin to use the power of polymorphism.

Aggregation

In addition to the three concepts mentioned above (which apply to classes) there are also 'aggregation' relationships (which apply to objects). These apply when objects of one class are composed (at least partially) of objects of another class (e.g. A is a part of B – 'engine' is a part of 'car'). Aggregations of this kind are more flexible than inheritance because they can be more readily reorganised. Objects which contain other objects (but are not composed of them) are also forms of aggregation.

Behaviour and message passing

The most important aspect of an object is its behaviour: 'by their ways shall ye know them' [Graham, 1991 p.9]. The behaviours of an object (the things it can do) are initiated by sending the object a 'message'. In practice, an object-oriented program is a set of objects sending messages to each other and responding accordingly via their 'methods' (also called 'operations' or 'services'). A 'method' is the mechanism by which an object can receive and process a particular message. The set of messages to which an object can respond via its methods is sometimes called its 'protocol'.

Question 1.4   Reuse is said to be a 'boy scout virtue'. In what ways can the various aspects of object-orientation described above contribute to reuse?

There are various contexts in which reuse is possible: Encapsulation allows us to reuse an abstract data type to create multiple objects, and inheritance allows classes to be reused in the definition of other classes. Polymorphism means the reuse of symbols (operators and names) to apply to different object behaviours, while aggregation reuses existing classes to provide components for larger objects.

Object based, class based and object-oriented

Because there is some separation between the different object-oriented concepts, we find some languages have more facilities than others for object-orientation, and some texts make a distinction between three types of programming, depending on the facilities available:

1.   Object based
2.   Class based
3.   Object-oriented

Object based programming involves some aspects of encapsulation inside 'objects', which can be created from a specified set of existing classes, but does not provide mechanisms for creating new classes. Class based programming includes facilities for creating classes, but these classes cannot be organised into a classification hierarchy in order to implement inheritance (or, therefore, full polymorphism). However, the semantic differences between these two types need not further concern us here. The key point is that a truly object-oriented language has all the facilities for encapsulation, inheritance and polymorphism.

It is in fact possible to make many distinctions between the facilities of different object-oriented languages, and to say that one is more or less object-oriented than another. Wegner [1989, p.249] identifies no less than six 'language classes' with different levels of 'object-orientedness' but, by most standards, C++ provides all the crucial elements for applying the object-oriented paradigm.

Object-oriented programming

There are in essence two elements to object-oriented programming

1. *Making Classes:*   Creating, extending or reusing abstract data types
2. *Making Objects Interact:* Creating objects from abstract data types and defining their relationships over time

The key to reusability in object-orientation is that when we come to a new application, we do not begin by reinventing the wheel, but by looking to see if we can reuse any existing abstract data types in our new program. Some may be reusable directly. Others may need to be extended by using inheritance to add extra functionality. Others again may need to be created from scratch. 'Domain analysis' is a term used to mean (among other things) looking at an application area and identifying commonality between the new application and existing applications of a similar type. Common abstract data types can then be identified for reuse or extension.

Once all the abstract data types are identified or coded, then the program can be created by making and destroying objects and defining the messages that are passed between them over time.

The way in which a program is approached will depend partly on the language used. In C++ we can use as much or as little of the object-oriented facilities on offer as we like. In a wholly object-oriented language there is no such option. The intention of this book is to take as much of an object-oriented approach as possible, given the constraints of working with a hybrid language.

Comparing approaches

What similarities can we identify between the types of programming elements we know from procedural programming, and what we have in an object-oriented program? As the following table shows, there are several aspects that can be equated [adapted from Wirth, 1990 p.13].

Procedural	Object-oriented
Data type	Abstract data type / Class
Variable	Object / Instance
Function / procedure	Method / Operation / Service
Function calls	Message passing

All the aspects of the procedural paradigm may also be present in an object-oriented program to a greater or lesser degree, but object-orientation provides extensions to the facilities we already have. As well as existing data types, we can define our own 'abstract data types' which describe all objects of a class. In addition to variables of simple data types, we can create instances of our abstract data types, called 'objects'. Instead of functions and procedures existing apart from data and other procedures, they become part of particular object classes – encapsulated inside abstract data types (where they are known as 'operations', 'methods' or 'services'), and their calling mechanism is known as 'message passing', since objects communicate with each other by calling each others' methods via 'messages'. The internal workings of an object are no different in many ways to the internal workings of a module in a procedural program, so many skills learned using other programming paradigms can be usefully employed in object-oriented programming.

Question 1.5	A traditional procedural program might be implemented by first writing and testing a series of modules, and then linking them all together into an overall system using function calls to manage the various modules. How is an object-oriented program implemented?

Like a procedural program, the components of an object-oriented system are built and tested first, and then integrated. In the case of object-orientation, however, it is not modules which are built but classes, and objects of these classes are created and tested. Finally, the objects are combined into a system which allows the objects to pass messages to one another.

Object technology: present and future

Object technology has established itself as the leading paradigm for component based programming (particularly for Graphical User Interfaces) and programming for the Internet, using Java. It has also made major inroads into more general applications development. Object-oriented languages, methodologies and software tools have developed a large user base, such that object technology is now very much part of the mainstream of software engineering.

However, there are a number of areas where object technology still has much scope for development. These include:

1. *Object persistence*

   An object's natural environment is in RAM as a dynamic entity. This is in contrast to traditional data storage in files or databases where the natural environment of the data is on external storage. This poses a challenge when we want objects to persist between runs of a program, even more so between different applications, perhaps widely distributed. Development of object-oriented databases has had to compromise in many cases, because of substantial past investment in, and support for, existing relational databases.

2. *Reusability*

   The engineering of reusable software components has been proven at the level of programming components such as Graphical User Interface libraries and Container Class libraries. However, the development of larger scale reusable 'business objects' is a more difficult task and has much scope for development. Reusability of non-code components has attracted much interest, for example, the reusable 'design patterns' of Gamma, Helm, Johnson and Vlissides [Gamma et al, 1995].

3. *Distributed systems*

   Because objects tie data and process together, designing object-oriented distributed systems raises questions about where the objects reside and how their distribution is managed. Initiatives such as the Object Management Group's Common Object Request Broker Architecture (CORBA) have attempted to standardise distributed object protocols, while the platform independent nature of Java has demonstrated the power of distributed 'Applets'.

The way ahead for object technology remains full of challenges, but as the technology matures and develops, it becomes more and more pervasive in all aspects of computing, to the point where it will become impossible to ignore. As Ed Yourdon says:

'No turning back. Object-orientation is the future, and the future is here and now.'

[Yourdon, 1990 p.263]

Summary of key points from this chapter

1. The object-oriented approach reflects our natural perceptions of the world as being composed of objects, classifiable into general types.

2. Objects comprise private data and public processes.

3. 'Structured methods' were developed as a response to the 'software crisis'.

4. Object-orientation effectively addresses many of the same problems encountered by structured methods.

5. Object-orientation enhances modularity and reusability.

6. Object technology encompasses the fields of analysis, design, programming and databases.

7. Object-orientation dates from the development of Simula in 1968, but has become established primarily due to the popularity of GUIs.

8. The key ideas are abstraction (encapsulation), inheritance and polymorphism.

9. Object-oriented programming is a two stage process, first identifying and creating classes, and secondly creating objects of these classes and defining the messages that pass between them over time.

10. Some aspects of procedural programming have near parallels in object-orientation, and many of the same techniques can be applied.

11. Challenges for object technology include object persistence, reusability, and distributed systems.

2 What is C++?

Overview

In this chapter, the history and development of C++ is explained in the context of a number of other languages which had an influence on it, principally C and Simula 67. The way in which C++ programs are composed of functions (including library functions) is introduced, and the C++ philosophy is compared to that of 'purer' object-oriented languages such as Smalltalk, Eiffel and Java.

C++, a better C?

C++ has been called 'a better C', but that is not the whole story. C++ is not the next version of C but a separate language which has been developed using C as the basis for its syntax. C++ in fact has an interesting history, which does begin in some senses with the development of C in the early 1970s, but has other roots too. The 'genealogy' of C++ is shown in Fig. 2.1.

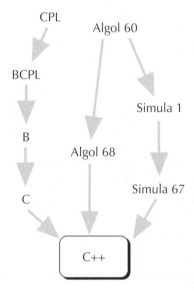

Fig. 2.1: The languages from which C++ has been developed

C, Unix, BCPL and B

The story of C begins back in 1968 when two Bell Laboratories programmers (Ken Thompson and Dennis Ritchie) were developing an operating system written in assembler on a DEC PDP–7 computer. This was the birth of the first version of the now widely used Unix operating system. In order for Unix to be more easily portable to other computers, it was necessary to replace the assembler with a higher level language, since assembly languages are very much tied to particular processors. The first non assembler Unix language was called 'B', (with a virtual memory version called 'vb') and based on a 1967 British computer language called BCPL (Basic CPL), itself based on an earlier language called CPL (Combined Programming Language) developed by Oxford and

13

Cambridge Universities (1962–7). However, since B was interpreted rather than compiled, its performance was inadequate for Unix and it became a tool for writing an assembler for the more powerful PDP–11 to which Unix development was transferred in 1970. One of the key characteristics of BCPL and B is that they are 'typeless' languages. Instead of dealing with a range of data types, they only address a 'machine word'. In order to improve the execution speed of B, Ritchie produced a compiler which was able to deal with types, overcoming inefficiencies caused by the 'typelessness' of B which meant complex operations identifying machine addresses: C was born! Unix was rewritten in C in 1973 and the rest, as they say, is history.

Because C was developed as a tool for driving an operating system, it had certain characteristics such as speed, compactness and some very low level elements (C is in some senses a high level assembly language). This made it popular with programmers for many applications which had nothing to do with Unix, and it became widely used, although an ANSI standard for C was not completed until 1990. The definitive C text is 'The C Programming Language' by Brian Kernighan & Dennis Ritchie [Kernighan & Ritchie, 1988], but you don't need to know any C to read this book.

Question 2.1   What differentiates the data representation facilities of C from its predecessors BCPL and B?

BCPL and B are 'typeless' languages, which means they are only able to address 'machine words' of memory. In contrast, C includes the ability to define different data types with different storage representations.

Simula 67

Whilst C made a major contribution to the syntax of C++, the Norwegian language 'Simula' is equally important for its contribution of object-oriented concepts. Simula was the first ever object-oriented language, developed during the 1960's by Kristen Nygaard and Ole Dahl as an extension of Algol 60 (ALGOrithmic Oriented Language – an early competitor of Fortran and incidentally the first language to be formally defined using BNF – Backus Naur Form – not that this need concern us here!). Their philosophy of a computer language included some key aspects of object-orientation:

1. Dynamic instances of program elements (Objects)

2. The linking of data and operations (Encapsulated Classes)

3. Similarities between processes (involving both data and actions) should not need to be repeated (Inheritance)

4. Dynamic memory management to remove dynamic instances which are no longer needed (this last concept borrowed from LISP).

The first (early 1960s) version of Simula was Simula I, but the final definition of the language was delivered in May 1968 (though it had already been optimistically christened Simula 67!). Simula 67 gave us the crucial object-oriented concepts of classes, dynamic objects, encapsulation and inheritance which will be investigated in detail in subsequent chapters. Simula was primarily developed as a tool for simulation (hence its name, though it seems to have also reverse engineered its own acronym – 'SIMple Universal LAnguage'), and this remains one of the most appropriate application areas for object-oriented techniques.

C++

C++ was developed by Bjarne Stroustrup in 1983 (version 1.0 became commercially available in 1985, version 2 in 1989 and version 3 in 1992) at the AT&T Bell laboratories, and is basically a superset of C, though there are one or two inconsistencies. Stroustrup became interested in the object-oriented approach whilst studying for his PhD at Cambridge University, using Simula 67 to write a distributed systems simulator. However, he had major problems with the resources required by the simulator, and had to write the final version in (interestingly enough) BCPL. In the light of this rather difficult experience, Stroustrup decided that a proper programming tool was needed for complex projects and that such a tool should:

1. Help with complexity (use classes)

2. Ensure correctness (have strong type checking)

3. Be affordable in terms of hardware and resources

4. Be open – easy and cheap to integrate existing software libraries and facilities

5. Be portable

The language he developed was first called 'C with classes' (in 1980) and later C++. The name derives from the 'increment' operator in C, which is '++'. The effect of the increment operator is to add one to the operand (C++ means something like C plus 1). Therefore the name suggests that C++ is an incremental development of C – an extension to the existing syntax – as opposed to a separate language. In fact Stroustrup suggests another root for the name; 'Newspeak' (the language of English Socialism) in George Orwell's novel '1984'. Two quotations may help to elucidate this. Firstly, one which refers to the third vocabulary of Newspeak, the 'C' vocabulary (the others are the 'A' and 'B' vocabularies, for everyday and political usage respectively – all 3 vocabularies are tightly defined and unambiguous).

> 'The C vocabulary was supplementary to the others and consisted entirely of scientific and technical terms' [Orwell, 1949 p. 322]

The second refers to the meaning of 'doubleplus':

> 'any word ... could be strengthened by the affix plus–, or, for still greater emphasis, doubleplus–.' [Orwell, 1949 p. 315]

C++ derives directly from C in terms of its syntax, but also owes much in terms of its facilities to Simula 67 and also Algol 68 (a considerable extension of Algol 60).

Stroustrup used C as the basis for his new language because, despite feeling that some aspects of C were problematical, it was good enough as a computational language, and it would enable existing C tools to be used in its development. No doubt another crucial factor was that he was working at AT&T Bell, the home of C, and had access to the C compiler and associated software. Also, since this was a commercial rather than academic project, it was not practicable to built a new language entirely from scratch. C's deficiencies 'are in the area of program organisation and support for good design and programming – those then became my areas of work' [Stroustrup in Smith, 1989 p.13]. The combination of C's low level programming power and run-time efficiency, plus the higher level constructs added with C++, mean that C++ is able to span a wide spectrum of programming applications. Despite the fact that C++ was developed 'on the cheap', it has proved extremely successful, with many former C applications migrating to it.

Indeed some future development in the Unix operating system may well be developed in C++ rather than C. The ANSI standard C++ is based on Stroustrup's book 'The C++ Programming Language'. The most recent (1995) edition includes a number of resolutions of the ANSI committee.

C++ is in many ways a 'better C', and is primarily important for its addition of object-orientation. C++ can be used to write procedural code just like C, but its real value lies in the ability to write object-oriented programs. In this sense it is a hybrid language, able to produce both traditional procedural and object-oriented programs, or pretty much anything in between. From this point of view it is useful as a tool for an incremental approach to object-oriented programming.

C code can be written in such a way as to be virtually unintelligible, even to the programmer who wrote it. This rather unfortunate characteristic is also evident in C++, but it does have a number of improved syntax elements which make it easier to read and write whether or not the object-oriented facilities are used, and clarity of code is largely dependent on common sense. There is not much real gain in writing on one line what can be written much more lucidly on three.

C++ has come in for a lot of criticism from object-orientation 'purists' (such as Bertrand Meyer [Watts (2), 1992]) who regard its hybrid approach as clumsy and inadequate. However, Stroustrup counters such criticisms by stressing that it is a practical approach, allowing flexibility for working programmers to learn the concepts incrementally if necessary without losing all the power and efficiency of C code. He is quoted as saying 'It is not right to be pure. It is right to serve your own and others' needs. Diversity of approaches has been shown to work. There's not just one right way, and anyway I have a problem with the word 'pure', because it makes me think of Stormtroopers.' [Stroustrup, in Watts (1), 1992].

Question 2.2   What is the relationship between C and C++?

C++ is a development of C, providing an additional set of object-oriented facilities on top of the existing syntax.

C++ keywords and functions

A keyword is a word which the compiler recognises as being part of the language's built in syntax. A function is a set of source code which is defined by a name. That name is not a keyword since it is not part of the compiler's instruction set.

C++ has a small set of keywords (about 60, depending on version and implementation) and some of those are not used very much (the dreaded 'goto' for example!). Compare this, for example, to COBOL with its vast and ever growing collection of reserved words. C++ achieves its power not just through a fixed set of keyword syntax but through extensibility; the facility for a programmer to extend the language with ease. Most parts of a C++ program rely on the use of 'library functions' which are external to the compiler itself. These library functions are in effect C++ source code which is available to the programmer to incorporate into his / her own programs. It is possible to continuously build on existing functions to create code at a higher and higher level, so that apparently very simple programs can be written, calling functions (or in the case of object-oriented programs, creating objects) that do all the serious work invisibly behind the scenes. Indeed, it is very much part of the philosophy of the object-oriented approach that the implementation details of an object in a program are not seen, only its external behaviour. A well written object-oriented program should be extremely easy to follow, even if the underlying code which defines a library object's behaviour is very complex indeed. Although there are only a few library functions defined as part of the standard language, the vendors who provide particular implementations of the C++ compiler tend to provide large function libraries for a wide range of applications including graphics, hardware–specific functions and screen interface designs, among many others. These will of course vary widely in their contents and syntax.

Library functions and header files

Library functions are defined in 'header files'; source code text files which define the facilities of a particular set of functions. A header file has a standard '.h' extension, so that one of the few standard C++ libraries is called, for example, 'iostream.h'. To use the functions contained in a header file we must ask the compiler to include the file in our program. This is called a 'preprocessor directive' (that is, it tells the compiler to do something before compiling the rest of the program) and looks like this:

#include <iostream.h>

Nearly all C++ programs will begin with at least one '#include', since there is very little you can do without library functions. In some cases, the header files do not contain all the appropriate source code, and your program will also need to be linked to some other associated library file. However, since the detail of this is implementation dependent, you will need to refer to the appropriate manuals for your own compiler.

What has this got to do with extensibility? The key point is that as well as including functions which are in the C++ library provided with your compiler, you can include functions you have defined yourself, and utilise those in your programs too. In effect, you can extend the language as much as you like by defining more and more functions to do what you want.

In object-oriented programs, we can use the 'preprocessor directives' to include libraries of object classes which we can create for ourselves and/or acquire from third party suppliers.

Question 2.3 Why is it necessary to include header files in C++ programs?

Because the syntax of C++ is relatively small, much of its functionality comes not from the use of keywords but from predefined functions stored in libraries. These are accessed by including the appropriate header file in the source code. As well as functions, object classes may also be defined in header files.

C++ and other OO languages

How does C++ compare with other object-oriented languages? There are a number of object-oriented languages available with their own particular characteristics (some of these languages are listed in Fig. 2.2, but this is a very partial set – ref [Booch, 1994 pp.472 – 490]). One thing which characterises C++ is its hybrid nature, as an orthogonal extension of C. 'Orthogonal' is a commonly used term which strictly speaking means something to do with right angles, but in this context is used to mean that the object-oriented extensions do not affect the existing syntax. C++ is (with a few minor exceptions) orthogonal to C, and it shares this characteristic of being a direct extension of another language with CLOS (Common Lisp Object System), which is based on Lisp with object-oriented facilities. Previous 'object-oriented Lisps' included 'Loops' and 'Flavors' but CLOS has superseded these.

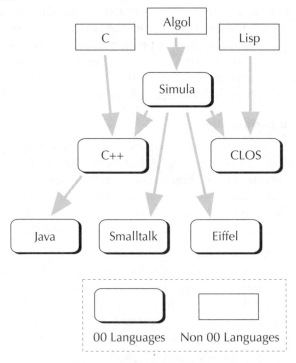

Fig. 2.2: Some object-oriented languages and their ancestors

Extended procedural languages contrast sharply with 'pure' object-oriented languages such as Smalltalk and Eiffel which are not based on pre-existing sets of syntax (though there has been some cross-fertilisation between LISP, CLOS and Smalltalk). In Smalltalk 'everything is an object', and the language is fully integrated with its graphical user interface (GUI). It is impossible to write a Smalltalk program independent of its environment, which comes in two main versions – 'Smalltalk–80' and 'Smalltalk/V'. A Smalltalk program is only executable within that environment and is not portable beyond it, which means something of a processing and cost overhead for those wishing to use a Smalltalk application. It is not really possible to learn object-oriented concepts incrementally in Smalltalk; rather one has to go in at the deep end and sink or swim!

The Eiffel language is named after the French engineer and the tower he built, which serves as an analogy for object-oriented software construction – 'It is built of a few small, simple parts which you combine' [Meyer in Watts (2), 1992 p.29]. It was originally developed by Bertrand Meyer in 1985 (though like C++ is under constant development) and is described in Meyer's book 'Object-Oriented Software Construction' [Meyer, 1988]. Eiffel is, like Smalltalk, entirely based on the implementation of object-oriented concepts and is not an extension of an existing procedural language syntax (though it owes a lot to Simula in concept). It contrasts with it, however, in not being dependent on a graphical environment. Executable Eiffel programs are as portable as those generated by C++.

In the software marketplace, it seems that the close similarity of C++ with an existing commonly used language has been something of an advantage, in that former C programmers are more willing to learn the additional syntax than to learn a completely new language from scratch. The ability to either learn or convert to the object-oriented syntax elements incrementally seems to be an aid to the transition to object-orientation for many programmers, though it often leads to rather odd programming practices during the transition which are neither one thing nor the other (neither procedural nor wholly object-oriented). Nevertheless, Stroustrup wholly endorses this approach of taking on board object-oriented syntax one step at a time – 'You don't expect things to happen in one step … It takes a little time but it always happens … going in at the deep end is just asking for failures'. [Stroustrup in Watts (1) p.34]. This should be a good maxim to bear in mind as you read this book!

More recently, Java has benefitted from its similarity to C++, providing a simple learning curve to a pure object-oriented language for existing C++ programmers. Java has been described by its creator, James Gosling, as 'C++ without the guns, clubs and knives', because it builds on the best features of C++ while removing some of its more complex syntax.

Question 2.4   Is C++ an object-oriented language?

C++ is a procedural language (C) with object-oriented extensions. Whether that makes it a 'true' object-oriented language depends on your point of view – some would claim that only languages such as Smalltalk and Eiffel are object-oriented because they are not based on an existing procedural language. Java sits somewhere between the two, as a language based on C++ but with most non object-oriented characteristics removed.

Approaching C++

In order to learn C++, some elements of C syntax have to be understood. Without the 'nut and bolt' components of a program – data types, arithmetic and assignment expressions, loops and selections – the larger scale 'objects' cannot be built. However, to learn C++ as an object-oriented language is conceptually different from learning C++ as 'a better C'. The approach of this book is to introduce the syntax of object-orientation as soon as possible, with the minimum amount of C syntax. To this end, the next chapter covers the basics of syntax common to C and C++ as a basis for implementing the object-oriented examples which follow.

Summary of key points from this chapter

1. C++ is derived primarily from two other languages – C and Simula 67.

2. C++ is a 'hybrid' language since it is a procedural language with facilities for object-orientation 'orthogonally' added. This contrasts with 'pure' object-oriented languages such as Smalltalk, Eiffel and Java.

3. A C++ program is based on keywords and libraries of functions. These function libraries may be written by the programmer or be supplied with the compiler. In an object-oriented system, libraries contain classes for the creation of objects. The use of libraries is what makes C++ an easily extensible language.

4. C++ may be learned as a procedural language (a 'better C') or as an object-oriented language. In either case, much of the underlying syntax is the same, but the programming approach is different.

3 Getting to grips with C++

Part 1 Data types, operators, functions and I/O

Overview

In this part of the chapter, enough of the essential syntax of C++ is outlined for simple programs to be written. The areas of syntax covered here are largely those directly inherited from C, since they cover the basic programming concepts of data representation, arithmetic and functions. However, some aspects of syntax (for example 'pass by reference', comment notation and empty function parameter lists) apply to C++ only. Similarly, the I/O library used is exclusive to C++. Like C, C++ is case sensitive, and all C++ keywords must be written in lower case. In this book, all variable (and object) names also appear in lower case, while function names are in lower case but with embedded capitals (see later examples).

The basic requirements

In order to approach the object-oriented facilities of C++, it is vital to understand how to create the fundamental building blocks of any program, object-oriented or not. The purpose of this chapter is to introduce enough of the syntax of C++ for the ensuing examples and exercises to be understood. It is by no means meant to be exhaustive.

Data types

The fundamental building blocks of any language are the data types it can handle, since a program has to represent data in order to do any useful processing. These data types are used in all languages to declare variables (or constants) which will contain values when a program is running. As you may recall from the last chapter, C is a derivation of a 'typeless' language called BCPL, but one of the key differences between them is that C (and C++) do have a range of data types. The data types which we can use to declare variables and constants in C++ are listed in the following table. Since implementations of these data types vary, the ranges and sizes of each type may also vary. The specific examples used here are typical but not defined as part of the standard language.

Type	Range		Bytes	Represents
	From	To		
char	−128	127	1	characters
unsigned char	0	255	1	characters
short	-32,768	32,767	2	whole numbers
unsigned short	0	65,535	2	whole numbers
int	−32,768	32,767	2	whole numbers
unsigned int	0	65,353	2	whole numbers
long	−2,147,438,648	2,147,483,647	4	whole numbers
unsigned long	0	4,294,967,295	4	whole numbers
float*	3.4×10^{-38}	3.4×10^{38}	4	fractional numbers
double*	1.7×10^{-308}	1.7×10^{308}	8	fractional numbers
long double*	3.4×10^{-4932}	3.4×10^{4932}	10	fractional numbers

* Positive ranges only shown. There will also be a range for negative numbers.

While this might seem like a long list, there are actually (as the table indicates) only 3 fundamental types of data which are being represented here, with variations according to the likely maximum size of number which may need to be stored in a particular context:

The three basic data types

1. Single (ASCII or EBCDIC) characters (letters, digits and punctuation characters), are represented by the 'char' data type.
2. Whole numbers: 'short', 'int' and 'long' types (all 'unsigned' if required – if only positive numbers need to be stored). The 'short' data type is usually the same size as 'int' – normally two bytes – and the two are interchangeable for all practical purposes, though the 'short' type is not often used.
3. Numbers including decimal fractions: 'float', 'double' or 'long double'.

There is also a data type called 'void', which means no data type at all! The use of such a data type will become clear when we look at functions. You may have noticed that there is no built in 'string' type in C++. This means we have to handle strings in a rather indirect fashion, as will be explained later. The ANSI standard also includes a 'bool' type which can have two values, either false (zero) or true (non-zero).

Choosing data types

When choosing data types to represent something in a program, think about the likely data range which the variable will need to hold. For example, if a variable is to hold student exam scores out of 100, then an int type will be more than sufficient. However, if the variable is to hold, for example, the population of Britain (some 55 million or so), then the integer type will be too small, and a long data type will be required. Unsigned variables are useful if we know there will never be a negative value. If the variable records how many students are on a course, then the value can never be less than zero, so an unsigned variable may be used. This only becomes an issue if we want to make the most out of the potential storage, since an unsigned variable roughly doubles the maximum positive number which can be stored. Of course, there is no real problem with using a data type which is too big, though it may use unnecessary storage.

Any variable which is likely to contain decimal fractions will of course have to be at least a float, as will a variable which is required to handle very large numbers. Although it only takes up the same storage space as a long, the storage method of a float is different so the potential data range is much greater. Accuracy as well as size is an important consideration – generally speaking, the larger the storage of the data type, the higher its precision will be. For programs dealing with astronomy for example the 'long double' data type would probably be necessary to deal with large numbers and accuracy requirements.

The char type is an interesting one, since according to the table, it holds numbers, but is usually used to represent characters. Which particular character each number represents will depend on the conversion table being used by your compiler, typically ASCII (American Standard Code for Information Interchange) but maybe EBCDIC (Extended Binary Coded Decimal Interchange Code). Both tables work on the basis that each character is represented by a number which can be stored in binary code in a single byte (i.e. 8 binary digits), and the number of characters in the table is 127 (because that is the maximum storage of a char data type; 1111111 in binary – 7 bits plus the sign bit). The unsigned version of the char data type gives us 255, (no sign bits, so 11111111 in binary) which is known as the extended character set. This includes lots of occasionally useful symbols such as greek letters and simple text based graphics characters. A char can be assigned either a numeric value (the code number of a character), or the character itself, surrounded by apostrophes. For example, (using ASCII code) the number 65 and the character 'A' are equivalent values for a char data type, since 65 is the ASCII code for a capital 'A'. Data such as 'A', or any other single character between apostrophes, is known as a 'character constant'.

The 'escape sequence' characters

A character constant in a C++ program may also be an 'escape sequence' if preceded by the backslash character (\). Although these may appear to contain two characters, they still represent single 'chars'. This is because the escape sequences are references to numbers on the character table. For example, '\n' represents the newline character (ASCII number 10). The escape sequences are:

newline	\n	bell	\a
horizontal tab	\t	backslash	\\
vertical tab	\v	question mark	\?
backspace	\b	single quote	\'
carriage return	\r	double quote	\"
form feed	\f	integer 0	\0
octal number	\ooo	hex number	\xhhh

Most of these are applicable to formatting output. Note that since the backslash is the escape character, it has to have its own escape sequence to be usable in another context.

For example, a DOS directory path normally looks like this:

A:\topdir\subdir\anotherdir

but in a C++ program would have to be defined as:

A:\\topdir\\subdir\\anotherdir

Octal or hex numbers may be used to represent any character in the table as an alternative to the character itself or its decimal equivalent. The '½' character for example can be represented by any of the following:

decimal: 171
octal: '\253'
hexadecimal '\xAB'

Question 3.1   What would be appropriate data types to store the following:
1. Someone's height in metres
2. An exclamation mark (!)
3. The number of students in a university

1. *A float, because it will contain a decimal fraction.*
2. *A char, because it's an ASCII character.*
3. *An int, or more appropriately an unsigned int, since there will never be a negative number of students.*

Declaring variables in a program

Variables are declared in a C++ program by following the type name with the variable name, for example:

```
char a;
int b;
float c;
```

These declarations give us a char variable called 'a', an int variable called 'b' and a float variable called 'c'. Note the use of the semicolon – every C++ statement ends in a semicolon. Extra white space and line feeds are ignored by the compiler, so it is ok to split statements over more than one line or to pad code with spaces to improve layout.

Assignment

Once we know what data types can be used in a program, we need to be able to assign values to them. This is simple in C++, since it just involves the equals (=) sign, known as the 'assignment operator'. For example, if we want to assign the value 4 to an integer called x.

```
int x;
x = 4;
```

Or we can both declare and assign in one line.

```
int x = 4;
```

Remember that of course you only declare a variable once, so to assign another value to 'x' later it would not be re-declared:

```
int x = 4;
x = 2;
```

Constants

As well as declaring variables in a program, we may want to declare and assign constants – those values which must remain constant throughout the execution of a program. This is done with the keyword 'const' as follows:

```
const float PI = 3.141;
const int CHARBUFFER = 80;
```

A 'const' cannot have its value altered, and it is common practice to write constant names in upper case to differentiate them from variable names which are typically in lower case. Note that C++ is totally case-sensitive, so that 'pi' and 'PI' would be regarded as different variables by the compiler (as indeed would 'Pi' and 'pI'!).

Arithmetic operators

Assignment alone is not very useful in a program – it is generally used in association with some kind of arithmetic. C++ has the four familiar arithmetic operators which are common to most programming languages, plus a 'remainder' operator:

```
add          +
subtract     -
multiply     *
divide       /
remainder    %
```

You should be familiar with the usage of the four principal operators in other languages, and the order of precedence is the usual one – multiply and divide are evaluated before add and subtract e.g.

```
int x = 4 + 2 * 3;
```

Since the multiplication will be executed before the addition, the result would be 10. Again, C++ follows other languages in the use of brackets to alter the order in which parts of an expression are evaluated. To force the addition to be executed first we can write:

```
int x = (4 + 2) * 3;
```

As you would expect, this gives the result of 18, since the addition is performed before the multiplication.

The remainder operator has equal precedence with multiply and divide. Operators of equal weight (e.g. add and subtract) are evaluated left to right. For example:

```
int x = 5 + 3 – 4;
```

will evaluate the addition before the subtraction.

The remainder operator works quite simply as follows:

```
int x = 5 / 3;
int y = 5 % 3;
```

While 'x' would contain 1 (the result of dividing 5 by 3) 'y' would contain 2 (the remainder from dividing 5 by 3).

Unary operator shorthand

C++ parts company with most other languages in that it has some arithmetic shorthand which makes some expressions less clumsy when using 'unary' operators (those which have one operand). In fact they convert what would be 'dyadic' expressions (more than one operand) to unary. The most 'famous' must be the increment operator, since it appears in the name of the language! This is the '++' operator which adds one to a variable as follows:

```
int counter = 1;
counter++;
```

In this example, the integer variable 'counter' would be incremented to hold the value 2. We can see that the increment operator is simply a shorthand for the following:

```
counter = counter + 1;
```

There is also a decrement operator, which logically enough is '--' and subtracts one from a variable:

```
counter--;
```

This would subtract 1 from the current value of 'counter', and is shorthand for:

```
counter = counter – 1;
```

Other expression shorthands

Both the increment and decrement operators are only appropriate when we need to add or subtract 1 from the existing value of a variable. However, we also have a shorthand for changing the value of a variable by arithmetic on its existing value. In this syntax outline, '?' means any one of the 5 arithmetic operators:

In general terms: **variable_name = variable_name ? n**

can be replaced with: **variable_name ?= n**

Therefore to add 5 to 'counter' we could replace:

```
counter = counter + 5;
```

with:

```
counter += 5;
```

Variables can be decremented similarly, so to subtract 4 from 'counter' we could write:

```
counter -= 4;
```

Similar examples for the other operators might be:

counter = counter * 2;	is equivalent to	counter *= 2;
counter = counter / 2;	is equivalent to	counter /= 2;
counter = counter % 2;	is equivalent to	counter %= 2;

These modifying shorthands are to some extent useful in simplifying code, though they still lack the COBOL simplicity of 'ADD 1 TO Counter'!

Question 3.2 Why do we have two forms for some types of arithmetic in C++?

In some circumstances, shorthand versions of simple expressions (inherited from C, which needed to be concise when used for writing Unix) are available. These provide for more succinct code, and since they only work with a fixed set of simple expressions they need not lessen readability if applied with discretion.

Prefix and postfix notation

The examples of the increment and decrement operators above both used 'postfix' notation (i.e. the '++' or '--' appears after the variable). We may also use 'prefix' notation (the operator appears before the variable):

| postfix notation: | **counter++** | or | **counter--** |
| prefix notation: | **++counter** | or | **--counter** |

This makes no difference if the operator is not used as part of a larger expression, but can be significant if it is. If one of these operators is used in prefix notation, then the operator will execute before the rest of an expression, but if postfix notation is used then it will be executed afterwards. For example, if the value of our 'counter' variable is to be assigned to another variable in the following expression:

```
int counter = 1;
int x = counter++;
```

The value of x will be 1, because the increment operator (which adds 1 to counter) will be evaluated after the assignment of the value of 'counter' to 'x' (postfix notation). With prefix notation, the value of 'x' will be 2:

```
int counter = 1;
int x = ++counter;
```

To avoid confusion, the increment and decrement operators will not be used as part of larger expressions in this book, and the postfix notation will be adopted in all cases.

Because of the different meanings of prefix and postfix notations, it has been suggested that '++C' is a better name for the language than 'C++'! [Stroustrup, 1995 p.4] (Ponder that at your leisure).

There are a number of other operators for various uses in C++, many of which are beyond the scope of this book. For a full listing, see 'The C++ Programming Language' [Stroustrup, 1995 pp.89–90].

Functions

Before attempting a program, we have to look at the format of C++ functions. C++ programs are basically just a series of functions which are able to call each other. A function has 4 features:

1. *A Name*
2. *A Body*
3. *A Return Type*
4. *A Parameter List*

The name must be a unique name (though what constitutes a unique name is more flexible than you might think).

The 'body' means the actual C++ code which defines how the function works. This is surrounded by braces {} (also known as curly brackets). Braces are very important in C++ because they define 'scope' – any variable declared within the scope of a set of braces is only 'visible' (useable) within that scope. i.e. it is only visible between its declaration and the closing brace of its scope.

The 'return type' is the type of the single variable which the function is able to return to whatever other function called it.

The parameter list contains any values which the function needs to use from outside itself in order to do what it has to do. This list is enclosed in ordinary round brackets ( ). This, then, is the general format of a C++ function:

```
return_type function_name(data_type parameter1, data_type parameter2...)
{
    function_body
}
```

The return type of a function is 'int' by default, so if no return type is declared, the compiler expects the function to return an integer. It is not good practice to use the default type, since it lessens the readability of the source code. The return type should always be declared, even if the type is 'int' (the default). If no data is to be returned from the function, then its type is declared as 'void'.

The parameter list may also be 'void', when there are no parameters to the function. The brackets may be left empty if this is the case.

i.e   **(void)**   means the same as   **()**

If there is more than one parameter, then they should be separated by commas. Each parameter must be defined by both a data type and a (local) name.

In the following example, a function called 'square' takes an integer parameter (with the local name 'value_in') and returns the square of that value. The return type is therefore 'int'. Any function which is not 'void' must contain a 'return' statement as the last state-ment in the function. In this case, the function returns an 'int', and the last statement in the function body is 'return squared' – 'return' is the keyword for returning a value from a function, and 'squared' is the name of a temporary integer variable used to hold the result of the expression.

```
int square (int value_in)
{
    int squared = value_in * value_in;
    return squared;
}
```

The 'return' statement may return the result of an expression directly instead of via a variable. We could therefore rewrite the above function as follows:

```
int square (int value_in)
{
    return value_in * value_in;
}
```

Pass by value and pass by reference

By default, most types of function parameter are passed 'by value', which means that the function makes a copy of each parameter which is passed to it, and the original data is unaffected. C++ also has a simple 'pass by reference' syntax, which allows the actual variable rather than a copy to be passed to a function. This is an example of C++ being 'a better C' – C does not have this simple form of a pass by reference mechanism. One of the key advantages of this is that it allows more than one value to be derived from a function. With pass by value, we can only return one value from a function. With pass by reference we can change more than one value directly. The syntax for a 'pass by refer-ence' parameter is to add the ampersand character (&) to the end of the data type, which makes the name of the parameter an 'alias' for the actual variable, not the name of a temporary copy. If we wanted the above ('square') example to square the original data parameter directly, the function would look like this:

```
void square (int& value_in)
{
    value_in = value_in * value_in;
}
```

Note that we no longer need to return a value from the function, since 'value_in' is directly accessed and altered. Therefore the return type is 'void'. A useful example of 'call by reference' is a function which swaps the values of two variables as follows (note the use of commas to separate multiple parameters):

```
void swap (int& first, int& second)
{
    int temp;
    temp = first;
    first = second;
    second = temp;
}
```

In effect we are deriving two values from one function, since the original variables (the 'actual parameters') represented by 'first' and 'second' (the 'formal' parameters) are both directly changed by the function.

Pass by reference does not necessarily imply that the parameters are to be changed. It may be used simply to avoid the overhead of making a copy of the parameter. In cases like this, the 'const' prefix is often used to indicate that, although a parameter is being passed by reference, it should not be changed by the function. We could rewrite the first 'square' function like this:

```
int square (const int & value_in)
{
    int squared = value_in * value_in;
    return squared;
}
```

In this version 'value_in' is passed by reference rather than by value, but still cannot be changed by the function.

Question 3.3   What happens to the two parameters used by the following function?

void aFunction(char& a, char b)

The first parameter (a) is passed by reference, which means that the actual variable will be accessed by the function. The second parameter (b) is passed by value, which means that the function only has access to a copy of the data held in the original variable.

Calling functions

Functions are 'called' (made to execute) by their names, followed by the appropriate parameter arguments. A function called 'addToCount' for example would be called as follows, assuming in this case it takes no parameters, and returns no values (i.e. it is a 'void' function with a 'void' parameter list):

```
addToCount();
```

A void function called 'addToTotal' which takes an integer parameter might be called as follows (either with a literal number or a variable – 'n' in this example):

```
addToTotal(30);     OR     addToTotal(n);
```

If a function gives a return value, then it should be called so that the return value is used (if the return value is not used, then you would probably get a warning from your compiler). If a function called 'getUserOption' returns an integer, then we would need to do something with that return value such as putting it into a variable as follows:

```
int x;
x = getUserOption();
```

The 'main' function

If functions are called by other functions, where does a program start? The answer is a special function called 'main', which is where all C++ programs start executing (there are exceptions to this which need not concern us here), and 'main' is called by the operating system when the name of the program is typed at the operating system prompt. Like all other functions, 'main' can take parameter arguments, and return a value (though this is returned to the operating system rather than to another function). Since we very often don't want to pass any parameter arguments to main, and do not want to return a value, it frequently looks like this:

```
void main(void)
{
    ...
}
```

Notice the use of the return type 'void' here. As we know, whenever we have a function which does not return any values, the type of that function is void. This applies to 'main' just the same as for all other functions. If there is no parameter list, then that is also void. In C++, a void parameter list is usually indicated by empty brackets, which means the same thing as '(void)'

```
void main()
{
    ...
}
```

This convention of using an empty list rather than '(void)' will be used for the remainder of the examples in this book.

Function declarations, definitions and prototypes

Every function in a program must have a function declaration (which tells us about the function's name, return type and parameters) and a function definition (the implementation of that function). These may appear together as a single unit of code, as in our earlier example of the 'square' function:

```
int square(int value_in)
{
    int squared = value_in * value_in;
    return squared;
}
```

In this case the first line of the function (sometimes known as the 'declarator') gives us the appropriate declaration of return type, name and parameters (including their local identifiers) for the function call.

Static type checking

C++ will not allow a function to be used before it has been declared, and the reason for this is so that the compiler can perform 'static type checking', which checks that the data types used in all function calls are appropriate to the actual function requirements. For example, it would ensure that our 'square' function (above) could not be called with an inappropriate argument type, or the wrong number of parameters. In practice, numeric data types are often interchangeable when used with functions because the compiler is able to make implicit temporary conversions between similar types. It would be perfectly acceptable to the compiler to call 'square' with a float argument for example, since the conversion to an integer is straightforward (if not exactly accurate!). However, the compiler would certainly complain if we tried to call the function with more than one argument, as in this example:

```
int a = 3;
int b = 4;
int c = square(a, b);
```

The function call would be flagged as an error by the compiler for having more arguments than the function's parameter list allows.

In any case we should beware of allowing the compiler to make temporary type conversions when calling functions.

Prototyping functions

In some cases, the declaration of a function may need to appear separately in the source code some time before the definition. If we have a function call occurring after the definition of that function, then static type checking is not a problem, since the compiler is 'aware' of the data requirements of the function, but what if we need to include a call to this function before the declarator has been 'seen' by the compiler? This is often the case in, for example, larger programs consisting of more than one separately compiled source file. It may be that our 'square' function needs to be called in a section of code which is compiled before the function itself is compiled. In these circumstances, we need to use a function declaration (or 'prototype') before the function. In this example, assuming that 'square' is to be called before its definition, we would have to prototype the function before the call as follows:

Declaration (Prototype):   **int square(int value_in);**
...
Function call: **void main( )**   (or some other function)
   {
   ...
   int a = square(10);
   ...
   }
Declarator: **int square(int value_in)**
   {
   //... function definition
   }

The prototype, then, is simply the declaration of the function's name and data types so that the compiler can ensure that any calls to the function are made with appropriate values.

Question 3.4   What does the following function prototype mean, and what purpose does it serve for the compiler?

char aFunction(int x, float& y);

The function called 'aFunction' has a return type of 'char' which means that when it is called, its return value should be handled as a 'char' (or compatible) data type. Its parameter list contains an integer which is passed by value (i.e. the function processes a copy of the original variable) and a float which is passed by reference. This means that the original variable is processed directly by the function, not a copy of its data. The compiler uses this information provided by the prototype to statically type–check any calls to the function.

Note that the prototype does not have to name the parameter(s), and indeed may even use a different identifier to that used in the declarator without the compiler flagging an error, since it ignores any identifiers on the prototype. Our declaration above might equally have appeared as:

int square(int);   (no identifier)

or

int square(int a_value);   (a differently named identifier)

However, to aid readability, it is good practice to use a consistent identifer in both the prototype and the declarator.

A simple program

So far we know how to declare a variable of a particular type, how to assign values and what the basic arithmetic operators are. We also know that a program has at least one function in it, and that the first function to be executed is always called 'main'. We know too that a C++ statement ends in a semicolon, so let us write a program which adds the assigned values of two integer variables ('x' and 'y') and puts the result in a third integer variable ('z'). In other words, it adds two numbers together...

```
void main()
{
    int x;
    int y;
    int z;
    x = 4;
    y = 2;
    z = x + y;
}
```

So far so good. You could even compile, link and run this program, but it won't do anything very exciting because we can't see any output, or enter any input. What we need is some syntax to achieve some simple keyboard/screen input and output.

Simple I/O

Unfortunately C++ has no I/O syntax! At least, there are no keywords built into the language to allow I/O. Therefore we have to use a library – like much of C++, we use functions which are defined elsewhere and included in our program by the use of header files.

C++ has its own set of I/O library syntax which is very easy to use. This is defined in a header file called 'iostream.h', which we must include in our program before 'main'. The syntax for including a library file is, as we know, the 'hash' sign (#) followed by the word 'include', followed by the name of the appropriate header file in pointed brackets (<>)

#include *<headername>*

To use the 'iostream.h' header file, then, we would start our program with:

#include <iostream.h>

What does this allow us to do? Well in fact it gives us access to a large object-oriented library of I/O functions, but at this stage, we don't need to know anything other than the simple I/O syntax.

Output

To output data onto the screen, we use the word 'cout' (pronounced see out), followed by the 'insertion' (or 'put to') operator, which is two 'smaller than' symbols: <<. This, for example, would output the contents of variable 'x' to the screen:

cout << x;

We can use this syntax to output any type of variable, or string literals enclosed in speech marks:

cout << "This is a string literal";

Any function which returns a value can also be put into a 'cout' statement. If we assume that a 'getAge' function returns a value, we could display that value:

cout << "Age is: " << getAge( );

As this example shows, a series of items can be output in one 'cout' statement by separating them with insertion operators as follows (note the inclusion of spaces):

cout << "Value of x is: " << x << " Value of y is: " << y;

These will all display on one line. If 'x' has the value 10 and 'y' the value 3 for example then it will display the following:

Value of x is: 10 Value of y is: 3

What if we want to force a line feed in our output? there is a simple way of doing this: 'endl' (end line).

Whenever 'endl' is put into a 'cout' statement, it forces a line feed, so this will put the two variables on different lines:

cout << "Value of x is: " << x << endl << "Value of y is: " << y << endl;

The output from this (given our previous example values) would be:

Value of x is: 10
Value of y is: 3

In fact 'endl' is virtually identical in function to the escape sequence '\n', and the two are interchangeable for all practical purposes (your compiler may not have 'endl' defined in 'iostream.h' but '\n' will do just as well. Alternatively, you will probably find 'endl' defined by another header file called 'iomanip.h').

Let us modify our addition program to output the result on the screen. We will also make another simple modification. If more than one variable of a single type is to be declared, then they can all be declared in one statement by separating the variable names by commas. Here, instead of declaring the integer variables x, y and z separately, they are all declared in one statement. We also include 'iostream.h' so that we can use 'cout':

```
#include <iostream.h>
void main( )
{
    int x, y, z;
    x = 4;
    y = 2;
    z = x + y;
    cout << "Value of z is: " << z << endl;
}
```

We will now see some output from our program, namely:

Value of z is: 6

Input

To input data from the keyboard, we use the word 'cin' (pronounced see in), followed by the 'extraction' (or 'get from') operator, which is two 'greater than' symbols: >>.

The following will wait for a value to be entered at the keyboard and (when enter is pressed) will put that value into the variable 'x':

```
cin >> x;
```

We can use this syntax to accept data into any type of variable. Similarly to 'cout', a series of items can put into one statement by separating them by extraction operators as follows:

```
cin >> x >> y;
```

However, this form is rarely used as it is a potential source of error – the two inputs have to be separated by a space. Usually, a 'cin' statement is only used to accept a single value at a time.

Unlike 'cout', 'cin' automatically forces line feeds, so 'endl' is not applicable to 'cin'. A series of 'cout' / 'cin' statements will all by default be paired on separate lines, the input following the output on the same line, followed by a line feed as follows:

```
...
cout << "enter a number ";
cin >> x;
cout << "enter another number ";
cin >> y;
...
```

sample output/input:

enter a number 7

enter another number 8

Sometimes we may want to force at least one line feed before a 'cout' statement rather than at the end of it. The 'endl' may therefore be used at the beginning of a 'cout' statement, as below:

```
cout << endl << "Enter a number ";
```

Now we know how to input and output data, here is a final version of our program, which now adds the values of two variables entered at the keyboard and outputs the result on the screen. This example uses 'endl' at the beginning of 'cout' statements to leave blank lines between output:

```
#include <iostream.h>
void main( )
{
    int x, y, z;
    cout << "Please enter an integer ";
    cin >> x;
    cout << endl << "Please enter a second integer ";
    cin >> y;
    z = x + y;
    cout << endl << "Total is: " << z << endl;
}
```

An example test run:

> **Please enter an integer** 12
> **Please enter a second integer** 4
> **Total is: 16**

Simple though it is, the example above illustrates the fundamental building blocks of any C++ program – a 'preprocessor directive' (including a header file), a 'main' function, input, output, assignment and arithmetic.

Question 3.5   What must come before 'main' in any program which uses keyboard and screen for I/O?

In order to use 'cin' and 'cout' for I/O, we have to include the standard C++ header file 'iostream.h', since the compiler does not have any integral I/O syntax. The header file must be included outside 'main' before any of the syntax is used, as follows:

```
#include <iostream.h>
```

Comments

Before proceeding further, the syntax for comments in C++ source code needs to be introduced, since it is used in many of the examples in the second part of this chapter. There are two ways of writing comments in C++, one inherited from C, and one taken from BCPL.

The C style comment is as follows

/* This is a comment */

Everything in the source code between a '/*' and a '*/' is ignored by the compiler, regardless of how many lines the comment spans.

```
/******************************************************
 *
 *    This is a multiple line comment
 *    using the syntax which is also
 *    available in C
 *
 ******************************************************/
```

You can also use the style of comment introduced into C++ from BCPL, which is as follows:

```
//    This is a comment
```

Note that while the comment has a beginning symbol, the '//', there is no terminating symbol. This is because this style of comment is terminated by the end of a line. Therefore such a comment cannot span more than one line.

```
//    This is a multiple line comment
//    using the C++ syntax.
//    Note how we need a '//' on every line
```

Summary

With the syntax covered so far, you should be able to write simple C++ functions and programs which manipulate simple variables and allow user I/O. However, in order to write programs of any complexity, we will need to look at the handling of strings of characters as well as simple numbers, and the syntax for control structures (selections and loops). These topics are dealt with in part two of this chapter.

Exercises

1. Using shorthand forms of the expressions as appropriate, make the following code as concise as possible (note that this is an exercise in comprehension, not a recommendation for programming style!).

```cpp
#include <iostream.h>
void main( )
    {
        int x;
        x = 1;
        x = x + 1;
        x = x * 5;
        int y;
        y = x - 1;
        x = x - 1;
        cout << "x = " << x;
        cout << endl;
        cout << "y = " << y;
        cout << endl;
    }
```

2. Using the appropriate escape sequence, write a program to output the following line on the screen:

    C++ is an "Object-Oriented" language

3. Write a program to test the two versions of the 'square' function described in the text (one passing a parameter by value, the other by reference). The values to be squared should be input from the keyboard. Remember that the functions must be either fully declared or prototyped before the main function to allow static type checking to take place.

    What happens if we pass data types other than an integer to the functions (e.g. a float)?

Part 2 Arrays, strings, pointers and control structures

Overview

This part of the chapter describes C++ syntax for handling more complex data types such as arrays and strings, and looks at the use of pointers. Implementation of control structures (selections and loops) is also outlined.

Arrays

If you have programmed before, you should be familiar with the concept of an array. It is basically a data structure representing a set of values of the same type which have the same name but are identified by an index number (subscript). In C++, arrays are declared and accessed by the use of square brackets, as follows:

Declaring an array ('number_array') of 10 integers:

```
int number_array[10];
```

Note that in common with many other languages, the 0 index is used, so that we have access to 10 elements of the array in this range:

```
number_array[0]...number_array[9]
```

'number_array[10]' therefore does not exist. However, C++ has no 'bounds checking', so the compiler will let you refer to array elements even if they are outside the declared range. For example, we could refer to 'number_array[20]' in a program, even though the array only goes up to subscript 9. If you do this, dreadful consequences could result, since the memory location of 'number_array[20]' could contain anything!

The moral is, be very careful never to use an array element which has not been explicitly declared as part of the allowed range.

We may if we wish have arrays of more than one dimension. The following example shows the declaration of a two dimensional array of floats:

```
float another_array[10][5];
```

Initialising arrays

We may put values into any individual element of an array using the assignment operator, as in the following example which puts the value '99' into element 4:

```
number_array[4] = 99;
```

However, when declaring an array we may also wish to initialise its values, and we can assign these in one statement by surrounding them in braces, separated by commas, as shown here:

```
int number_array[10] = {99, 67, 3, 5, 7, 2, 34, 4, 98, 1};
```

In fact we can omit the array size if we wish, since the compiler can automatically size the array from the number of values provided:

```
int number_array[ ] = {99, 67, 3, 5, 7, 2, 34, 4, 98, 1};
```

A characteristic of arrays is that the array identifier in fact references a constant address which may not be altered. In the example above, 'number_array' refers to the address of the first element of the array ('number_array[0]') and this cannot be changed at run time. If we try to display a numeric array using 'cout' (i.e. 'cout << number_array;') then we will see that what is displayed is the address of the first element of the array.

Arrays and functions

Arrays are always implicitly passed by reference to functions, never by value. One implication of this is that they cannot be used as the return type of a function. To demonstrate that arrays are passed by reference to functions, the following example shows a function ('setArraySize') which takes two parameters; an integer representing the size of an array, and an array of integers. The size value is put into the first array element ('array_in[0]') by the function. Note that it is the original array which is passed to, and modified by, the function, so that when we display the first element of 'an_array' it has in fact been altered by the function, because 'array_in' is a local 'alias' for 'an_array' – they are one and the same thing. Note that an array parameter can be denoted by empty square brackets in the parameter list (we cannot of course always anticipate the size of any arrays which might use the function).

```
#include <iostream.h>
// definition of the function 'setArraySize'
void setArraySize(int size, int array_in[ ])
{
    array_in[0] = size;
}
void main( )
{
// a constant for the array size
    const int ARRAY_SIZE = 15;
// declare an integer array
    int an_array[ARRAY_SIZE];
// call the function
    setArraySize(ARRAY_SIZE, an_array);
// display the first element of the modified array
    cout << "First element is " << an_array[0];
}
```

The output from this program is as follows:

First element is 15

Pointers

Pointers are an important part of C++, and are a crucial mechanism for object-oriented programming because they are used to control the creation and destruction of 'dynamic' objects in a program. A pointer is a simple concept – it points to a memory location which contains data of a particular type. The contents of a pointer therefore is not data but the address of some data. A pointer is declared by the use of an asterisk after the data type as follows (in this case a pointer to an integer):

```
int* number_pointer;
```

The data type defines what may be stored in the address to which the pointer is directed, so that 'number_pointer' above will contain the address of an integer-sized area of memory. This typing of pointers is important since a pointer is a variable which can undergo certain arithmetic operations such as '++' which moves a pointer to the next item of data. Since different data types occupy different sizes of memory block, the data type of the pointer defines how many bytes the pointer must be incremented.

Unlike arrays, pointers may be used as the return type of a function. However, when pointers are used as function parameters or return types remember that they contain addresses, and it is the memory address which is passed or returned, not the contents of the address.

One very common application of both arrays and pointers is the representation of strings of characters. Pointers also have a key role to play in referencing objects in object-oriented programs.

Handling strings in C++

Unlike some other languages, there is no 'string' data type in C++ (though there is a string 'class' in the standard library, which will be described later). This is one of the most difficult areas for those new to the language, since we can only represent strings of characters in two rather indirect ways:

1. As arrays of type char
2. By pointers of type char

Neither of these approaches offers a complete solution to the representation of strings, so in practice elements of both are often necessary. First, we will examine the use of arrays of type char to represent strings of characters.

An array of type char

As indicated previously, arrays in C++ are declared and accessed by the use of square brackets. An array of 10 characters called 'astring' would be declared thus:

char astring[10];

Since this contains 10 characters (from element 0 to element 9), we can use it to contain (short!) words. In fact the maximum string which we could contain in this array would be 9 characters long, since all strings must be terminated by the 'escape sequence' character '\0' (from the table in the first part of this chapter we can see that this represents 'integer 0'). Although this character is automatically and invisibly appended to strings of characters in most contexts, if it is lost then strange results can ensue. Fig. 3.1 shows the contents of 'astring' when it contains the string 'hello'. Note that the sixth element of the array contains '\0' to terminate the string. If 'astring' was to contain a 10 character string (e.g. 'characters') then the terminating '\0' would be lost. Any attempt to display or copy this string would cause problems since the string has an undefined length, and the program would simply display or copy the contents of all the memory locations after the string until a '\0' was encountered.

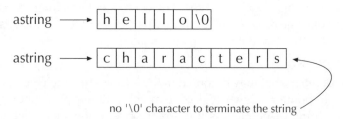

**Fig. 3.1: All arrays of type char must be terminated with the '\0' character.
A 10 element char array can therefore only safely contain 9 characters.**

Initialising character arrays

If we want to initialise a character array with a string literal, then we can use the assignment operator ('='), and speech marks round the string:

```
char astring[ ] = "hello";
```

This is a more compact syntax than that which is used with other data types, where the array element values are separated by commas.

However, this is the only context in which the assignment operator can be used to put literal strings into character arrays. We cannot, for example, assign a string literal to a character array after it has been declared – this can only be done one character at a time:

```
void main( )
{
    char astring[4];      // Note size - 3 chars + '\0'
    astring = "abc";      // This will not compile!
    astring[0] = 'a';     // This is ok
    astring[1] = 'b';
    astring[2] = 'c';
}
```

Likewise, if we want to make one array of characters equal to another, then unfortunately the assignment operator cannot be used, and we have to use the functions available in a standard C header file called 'string.h' which should be available in some form in all compilers. (This means putting '#include <string.h>' at the beginning of our programs).

For example, we might want an array of characters called 'bstring' to have the same contents as the array 'astring'. We CANNOT say:

```
bstring = astring;       // not allowed
```

If 'astring' and 'bstring' are character arrays then this will not work in C++. We have to use a function such as the ANSI C 'strcpy' function which is defined in 'string.h' (or its equivalent)

it works like this:

```
strcpy(destination, source);
```

so to copy the contents of 'astring' into 'bstring', we would write

```
strcpy(bstring, astring);
```

This would copy the contents of 'astring' into 'bstring', including the terminating '\0' character.

An alternative standard function is 'strncpy', which takes an extra parameter indicating the number of characters to be copied. This makes the copying a little safer, since we can then avoid the possibility of putting too many characters into the array. If 'bstring' is an array of 10 chars, then we might write the function as:

```
strncpy(bstring, astring, 9);
```

Remember that we need to reserve the last character position for the '\0' terminating character if required. This may be explicitly added:

```
bstring[9] = '\0';
```

The following program demonstrates the use of 'strncpy' in safely copying a string from one array to another. It also demonstrates the use of 'cin' and 'cout' with arrays – note that the array of characters is, in effect, treated as a string. The allocation of the terminating character ('\0') to the last element of the array is an 'insurance policy' – if the string being copied is longer than 9 characters then there will be no terminating character, so we have to provide our own. Remember that it is perfectly all right to assign single characters to single elements of an array using the assignment operator:

```cpp
#include <iostream.h>
#include <string.h>
void main( )
{
    char astring[20];
    char bstring[10];
    cout << "Enter a string (up to 19 characters!): ";
    cin >> astring;
    cout << astring << endl;
// strncpy will truncate any string longer than 9 characters
    strncpy(bstring, astring, 9);
    bstring[9] = '\0';
    cout << bstring << endl;
}
```

This example run shows a long string truncated by the program

Enter a string (up to 19 characters!): Superconductivity
Superconductivity
Supercond

Using pointers to strings

From the above it is clear that using arrays of type 'char' to represent strings has a number of drawbacks, since arrays are difficult to manipulate and cannot, for example, be used as the return type of a function. A complementary approach is to use a pointer to reference a string of characters. To declare a pointer to a string it must be of type 'char'. As we know, a pointer is defined by an asterisk between the data type (in this case 'char') and the name of the variable, as follows:

```cpp
char* string_pointer;
```

This declares a pointer of type char called 'string_pointer', which is able to point to the first character of a string of characters!

We can use a char pointer to reference an array of characters quite easily:

```cpp
void main( )
{
    char string[11] = "char array";
    char* string_pointer = string;
    cout << string_pointer;
}
```

The assignment operator directs the pointer to the address of the first character in the array, and the above program will display the text 'char array' using the pointer.

It is also easy to assign literals at declaration, similar to arrays:

```cpp
char* string_pointer = "A string";
```

However, this is not a particularly safe way to create strings, since any attempt to assign a longer string to the same pointer can cause other data to be overwritten. This is a similar problem to going beyond the bounds of an array.

Another contrast between the syntax for arrays and pointers is that the assignment operator may be used at any time after declaration to make one char pointer equal to another. The following program demonstrates that attempts to assign one array to another, or to assign a string literal to an array after its declaration will lead to compiler errors. In contrast, both of these processes are legal with pointers:

```
void main()
{
    char a[10] = "spring";
    char b[10] = "summer";
    char* c = "autumn";
    char* d = "winter";
    a = b;                  // WRONG!! (will not compile)
    a = "printemps"         // WRONG!! (will not compile)
    c = d;                  // will compile
    c = "fall";             // will compile
}
```

Being able to assign char pointers to each other is obviously useful, but there is a potential problem. This is because using the assignment operator with two pointers will not copy the data itself, but the address of the pointer. In the following program, two strings are assigned to two pointers of type char, and then the assignment operator is used to make them equal. The effect of this is that the two pointers end up pointing to the same memory address:

```
void main()
{
    // declare two 'strings' with initial values
    char* a = "summer";
    char* b = "winter";
    // assign a to equal b
    a = b;
}
```

Fig. 3.2 shows the contents of a and b before the assignment. When they are initialised they will be pointing to separate strings in separate memory locations.

$$char* \ a = "summer";$$

$$char* \ b = "winter";$$

a $\longrightarrow$ | s | u | m | m | e | r | \0 |

b $\longrightarrow$ | w | i | n | t | e | r | \0 |

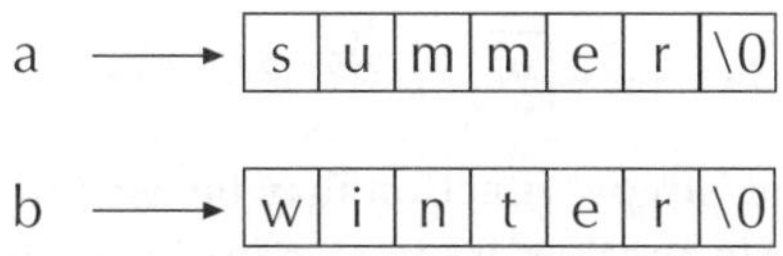

Fig. 3.2: The two pointers initially point to separate strings of characters at separate addresses.

Fig. 3.3 shows what happens when we execute the assignment statement 'a = b'. In fact the address to which 'a' is pointing is changed so that both 'a' and 'b' are pointing to the same memory location. When we redirect pointers like this, we should be aware that there is no protection against changes being made to the string of characters we are pointing at, and it may even cease to exist if the original pointer which referenced it acts upon it in another part of the program. Generally speaking, using the assignment operator with char pointers should only be used for short term processes. For safe storage of strings, arrays are more reliable.

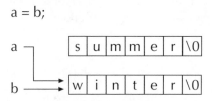

Fig. 3.3: Using the assignment operator with pointers simply redirects them by copying the address contained in one pointer to the other.

It is possible to use 'strcpy' (or 'strncpy') with character pointers to copy data rather than addresses. Fig. 3.4 shows that 'strcpy' will alter the data which char pointer 'a' is pointing at rather than the address it references. However, this is not a recommended approach since we may overwrite data in subsequent memory locations. This will happen if we declare a character pointer to point to a string of one length and then copy a longer string to it, or attempt to allocate a string of characters to a predeclared pointer. Since a character pointer only points to the address of one character, what may be in the subsequent memory locations is unpredictable, and using only pointers to handle strings may therefore lead to obscure errors.

```
char* a = "summer";
char* b = "winter";
char* c;
strcpy(a,b);
```

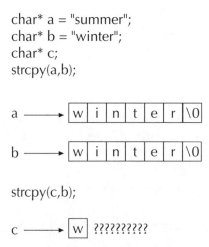

```
strcpy(c,b);
```

Fig. 3.4: Although the 'strcpy' function may be used to copy data from one character pointer to another, it can also lead to memory corruption.

In Fig. 3.4, the use of 'strcpy' with 'a' and 'b' does not cause a problem because the two strings are the same length. However, any attempt to copy a string to 'c', which has been declared as a pointer without a string literal will overwrite memory.

A strategy for strings

In practice, we can see that although pointers provide a flexible means for string manipulation, they can lead to 'unsafe' practices in some contexts. Therefore we are better served by using arrays to store strings, but may use pointers to manipulate them. Alternative approaches might be to use the facilities provided by vendor–specific library functions which may be provided with your compiler or by a third party supplier, or to use dynamic memory to store strings. Dynamic memory management will be dealt with in a later chapter.

Here is an example of combining arrays and pointers to provide string functionality. The important point is that the parameters can be passed as arrays or pointers, copied and returned (if necessary) as a pointer. The conversion is implicit between the constant array address and the pointer variable which is returned:

```
char* truncateString(char short_string[ ], char string_array [ ])
{
    strncpy(short_string, string_array, 9);
    short_string[9] = '\0';
    return short_string;
}
```

Declaring multiple pointers

Incidentally, you may find examples in other text books of the asterisk in a different position. In fact, the asterisk can come next to the type (as above), next to the pointer name or even between the two, separated by spaces. All three of these statements would have the same effect:

```
char* t;    or    char *t;    or    char * t;
```

The only circumstance in which this might cause confusion is if you declare more than one variable in the same statement, since the asterisk will only apply to the first variable in the list – it is not 'transitive'. Take the following for example:

```
char x, y, z;
```

We know that this declares 3 variables of type 'char'. What about this?

```
char* x, y, z;
```

Is this 3 pointers of type 'char'? In fact it is not. it is one pointer of type 'char' ('x') and two variables of type 'char' ('y' and 'z'). Three pointers of type 'char' would have to be declared as this:

```
char* x, * y, * z;
```

The main lesson to draw is that of seeking clarity. The above set of pointers is much better declared as:

```
char* x;
char* y;
char* z;
```

Whilst this may appear long winded, its main advantage is that it is perfectly clear, and also less likely to cause errors if changes are made to the declarations.

De-referencing pointers (numeric data types)

You should be aware that the asterisk has another application in relation to pointers, which is to 'de-reference' a pointer. This simply means that we can access the data which a pointer is referencing by preceding the pointer name with an asterisk. Remember that the pointer itself contains an address rather than data, and if we display a pointer (of a numeric data type) then we will see a memory address, not the data in that address. In the following program an integer pointer is assigned to the address of an integer variable. The address of any variable can be obtained by using the ampersand (the 'address of' operator) before the variable name, in a very similar manner to the 'pass by reference' syntax. In this example, the address of the variable 'x' is obtained by this operator, i.e. '&x'. The pointer is displayed (an address will appear), and then the pointer is de-referenced to show the data which is in that address:

```
#include <iostream.h>
void main( )
{
// x is an integer variable
    int x = 4;
// y is a pointer to an integer, assigned the address of x
    int* y = &x;
    cout << "variable is: " << x << endl;
    cout << "pointer is: " << y << endl;
    cout << "dereferenced pointer is: " << *y << endl;
}
```

The output might be as follows (of course the actual address shown will vary)

```
variable is: 4
pointer is: 0x8f8f0ffe
de-referenced pointer is: 4
```

De-referencing character pointers

Pointers of type char (i.e. strings) behave in a rather different manner to numeric types. Firstly, there is an implicit conversion when one is displayed using 'cout', so that the string rather than the address is displayed. Secondly, if you de-reference a 'char' pointer which you are using to represent a string you will get the single character which the pointer is addressing. In this example program a string ('C++') referenced by a character pointer is displayed complete, and then the first character ('C') is de-referenced. Then the increment operator is used on the pointer (this is an example of 'pointer arithmetic'). This moves the pointer to the next character in the string ('+'), so that the complete string when displayed is missing the first character. The dereferenced pointer then shows the second character only.

```
#include <iostream.h>
void main( )
{
    char* x = "C++";
    cout << "string is: " << x << endl;
    cout << "dereferenced char pointer is " << *x << endl;
    x++;
    cout << "string after incrementing is " << x << endl;
    cout << "dereferenced char pointer is now " << *x << endl;
}
```

In this case, we get the output:

```
string is C++
de-referenced char pointer is C
string after incrementing is ++
de-referenced char pointer is now +
```

Question 3.6   What are the main differences between representing a string as an array of characters or by a character pointer?

The primary difference is that an array refers to a constant address and a pointer is a variable whose contained address may vary. This means that the syntax for handling the two representations of strings is different. The assignment operator may not be used with arrays, but may be used with pointers, though this only redirects the pointer, it does not copy the value. Arrays are passed to functions by reference and therefore may not be used as the return type of a function, but pointers may be both passed to and returned from functions. In general terms, both char pointers and arrays of chars are necessary for successful string manipulation.

Constructing larger programs

In order to begin writing object-oriented programs in C++, it is first necessary to know how to use the simple programming constructs which apply to traditional programming as well as object-orientation. The three fundamental components of any program (defined by Bohm and Jacopini in 1966) are:

1. *Sequence* one statement following another
2. *Selection* making a choice between at least two alternative courses of action
3. *Iteration* repeating a section of code zero or more times

Although these components are to some extent masked by the object-oriented approach, they still underlie the construction and use of objects.

Sequence

The order in which program statements are executed in C++ is the same as for most other languages – from top to bottom of the source code. As demonstrated in our example programs, the compiler recognises the semicolon as representing the end of one program statement. Apart from selections and iterations (below) there are occasions when control may pass to a different line other than the next sequential statement, such as 'goto' (which is discouraged in all languages since it leads to unstructured programming), 'break' and 'continue'. Both 'break' and 'continue' relate specifically to control within structured blocks of code, and are, in a sense, examples of a 'structured goto'.

Selection

In order for a program to behave differently in different circumstances, it has to be able to evaluate conditions and select alternative courses of action accordingly.

In C++ we have two ways in which selections may be made:

1. The if statement
2. The switch statement

The 'if' statement follows similar rules to the 'if' statements in other languages, which is to say that it contains two (and only two) different courses of action and a condition. Which of the two courses of action is taken depends on whether the condition is true or false. One course of action may be, in fact, to do nothing.

The *if* statement

The general format of the if statement is:

```
if(condition)
    ....
else
    ...
```

with the 'else' part being optional. If there is more than one statement in the 'if' or the 'else', then braces must be used to define the scope of the statement.

As an example, we might use an 'if' statement to find out if a variable ('x') has a value greater than zero. Braces are used here, though they would be optional in this case since there is only one statement in each part of the selection.

```
if(x > 0)
{
    cout << "greater than zero";
}
else
{
    cout << "less than or equal to zero";
}
```

Testing for equality

When writing selection statements, we need to express various conditions which compare variables using 'relational operators'. In C++ the following symbols are used:

Condition	Relational Operator	Example
equal to	==	if(x == y)
not equal to	!=	if(x != y)
less than	<	if(x < 0)
greater than	>	if(y > 10)
greater than or equal to	>=	if(x >= 9)
less than or equal to	<=	if(y <= 100)

To evaluate more complex conditions we need to use the logical operators to combine the simple relational operators above. There are three logical operators in C++:

Logical Effect	Logical Operator	Example
Logical AND	&&	if(x > 0 && x < 10)
Logical OR	| |	if(x == 1 | | y == 1)
Logical NOT	!	if(!x)

When evaluating Boolean (true/false) conditions, all expressions return either 0 (false) or non–0 (true). For example, the NOT operator (!) is used above in the expression if(!x). The expression will evaluate to be true if x is 0 (i.e. if x is false, then 'not x' is true!).

The *switch* statement

The general format of the switch statement is

```
switch(variable)
{
    case value: <action> ; [... ;break;]
}
```

This is an appropriate construct when a number of possible states for a variable have to be evaluated at one time.

This example assumes that different (void) functions are called by a user input:

```
int x;
cout << "Enter choice";
cin >> x;
switch(x)
{
    case 1: addCustomer( ); break;
    case 2: removeCustomer(); break;
    case 3: editCustomer( ); break;
    default: errorHandler( );
}
```

Note the use of the 'default' if the case is not found. This is an optional part of the switch statement. The 'break' clause acts like a 'structured goto' in that it sends control to the end of the switch statement without evaluating any other cases. There is of course no point in including a 'break' after the last option since it has no effect. It is important to use 'break' after preceding options, since without it the switch statement will not function correctly.

Iteration

Iteration can be achieved in three slightly different ways

1. *The 'for' loop*
2. *The 'while' loop*
3. *The 'do...while' loop*

In each case, there will be a condition which allows the loop to terminate. Which one to use depends on a number of factors, and each will be explained in terms of examples.

The *for* loop

The 'for' loop has three principal elements:

1.   The start condition
2.   The terminating (while) condition
3.   The action which takes place at the end of each iteration

The format is as follows:

```
for(start condition; 'while' condition; action)
// followed by a statement, or a block of statements in braces
```

Note that the three parts of the statement are enclosed in brackets following the word 'for' and that they are separated by semicolons.

The following example uses a 'for' loop to print out the squares of the numbers 1 to 10. The square is evaluated here in the 'cout' statement, though it could of course be evaluated separately, and the result displayed. Note that the terminating condition is a 'while' condition – the loop finishes when it becomes false.

```cpp
int i;
for(i = 1; i <= 10; i++)
{
    cout << "The square of " << i << " is " << i * i << endl;
}
```

Remember that 'i++' is simply a shorthand form of 'i = i + 1'. Another aspect of the 'for' loop is that we can declare the initial variable inside the statement itself, so that rather than declaring 'i' before the loop, as we did in the above example, we might equally have written:

```cpp
for(int i = 1;...
```

In this context, the scope of 'i' remains exactly the same as if it had been declared outside the 'for' statement.

The *while* and *do...while* loops

These loops are very similar in that both execute until a given condition is false (i.e. while it is true), but there is one key difference between them. the 'while' loop tests for a precondition, which is to say that the condition for executing the loop is evaluated at the beginning of each loop. In contrast, the 'do..while' loop tests for a postcondition, so that the condition is evaluated at the end of each loop. This means that the 'do..while' loop executes at least once, whereas the 'while' loop may not execute at all if the condition is already false. The 'while' loop therefore is a true iteration (i.e. it executes 0 or more times) whereas the 'do...while' loop is a repetition (it executes 1 or more times). Which one you choose in a particular application depends entirely on the context.

The *while* loop

The 'while' loop has the following syntax:

```cpp
while(condition)
    statement(s)...
```

As with all block structures, if there is more than one statement then braces must be used. The following example uses a 'while' loop to display the numbers 1 to 10 using the increment operator (++)

```cpp
int x = 1;
while(x <= 10)
{
    cout << x << " ";
    x++;
}
```

The *do...while* loop

Similarly, the 'do...while' loop has this syntax

```
do
{
    statement(s)
} while (condition);
```

Note the semicolon which must follow a 'do..while' statement.

A similar example to that used for the 'while' loop looks like this:

```
int x = 1;
do
{
    cout << x << " ";
    x++;
} while(x <= 10);
```

In this case, the two loops are interchangeable in terms of output, but if we had set the initial value of 'x' to 11 before each loop, only the 'do...while' loop would have executed, since the 'while' loop would already have evaluated the condition as false before the first iteration.

Question 3.7   What criteria would you apply in deciding which of the three forms of loop to use in a program?

The choice between a 'while' and a 'do...while' loop depends on whether a true iteration is required (the loop executes 0 or more times) or a loop which will always execute at least once. A 'for' loop is appropriate where the number of iterations is known beforehand, and/or where it is appropriate to have an integral counter.

An example program

The first part of this chapter finished with a simple program which added two numbers. This program draws together a number of the features covered in the second part of the chapter, namely an array of characters, an 'if' statement and 'for' and 'do...while' loops. By calling a function which identifies characters relating to digits in the ASCII table (i.e. the characters 0 – 9), it counts the number of digits in a string.

```
#include <iostream.h>
// Define a function which returns true (1) if the parameter character
// is in the ascii range 48 to 57 (ie a digit), false (0) if it is not
int isADigit(char c)
{
    if(c >= 48 && c <= 57)
    {
        return 1;
    }
    else
    {
        return 0;
    }
}
// main tests the function
void main()
{
// declare variables
```

```
        char buffer[80];
        int digit_count;
        char answer;
    // loop until the user terminates the program
        do
        {
            digit_count = 0;
            cout << "Enter a string of characters ";
            cin >> buffer;
    // loop through the string, counting digits
            for(int i = 0; buffer[i] != '\0'; i++)
            {
                if(isADigit(buffer[i]))
                {
                    digit_count++;
                }
            }
    // display the result
            cout << "Total number of digits in string = " << digit_count << endl;
            cout << "Try another string (Y/N)? ";
            cin >> answer;
            cout << endl;
        } while (answer != 'n' && answer != 'N');
    }
```

An example test run follows:

Enter a string of characters Abcd4r5
Total number of digits in string = 2
Try another string (Y/N)? y
Enter a string of characters 999
Total number of digits in string = 3
Try another string (Y/N)? y
Enter a string of characters C++
Total number of digits in string = 0
Try another string (Y/N)? n

Summary

The two parts of this chapter have covered all the basic tools needed to build C++ programs. With this syntax knowledge, you should be equipped to deal with the examples and exercises in this book. Other elements of C++ syntax, particularly those specific to the application of object-oriented programming, will be introduced throughout the forthcoming chapters. However, there will be many aspects of the language not covered here, and you may wish to pursue your C++ knowledge further with a more comprehensive syntax reference. There are many books on the market designed to provide an in-depth reference to C++, for example Stroustrup's definitive 'The C++ Programming Language' [Stroustrup, 1995]. However, you may also find it useful to look at books written for particular compilers which will cover issues such as graphics functions and interface class libraries. Since these are vendor-specific they are beyond the scope of a 'standard C++' text.

Exercises

1. Use the 'swap' function (below) to sort an array of 10 integers. Size the array with a constant.

```
void swap (int& first, int& second)
{
    int temp;
    temp = first;
    first = second;
    second = temp;
}
```

2. Write a program which will accept a string of up to 10 characters from the keyboard, and count the occurrences of each of the 5 vowels in the string. The output should be in a (tabbed) format similar to this example:

> *Vowel counts are as follows:*
>
> | *A* | *E* | *I* | *O* | *U* |
> |---|---|---|---|---|
> | *0* | *1* | *0* | *0* | *1* |

Remember that a 'string' in C++ is terminated by the '\0' escape sequence character.

3. C++ includes an operator called 'sizeof' that returns the size (in bytes) of a data type. For example:

```
char c;
cout << sizeof(c);
```

will display the size of a 'char' variable.

Write a program to test the sizes of the data types listed on p.21. Try 'sizeof' with an array of ten chars, and an array of ten integers. What is the difference and why?

4 Modelling the real world

Overview

This chapter is about how we can build abstract models in programs of things in the real world. It discusses how encapsulation links together data and processes, how information hiding limits external access to internal data and processes, and what an abstract data type is. It explains that the three components of an abstract data type are a unique name, attributes and methods. The syntax for the C++ class is outlined with examples.

Encapsulation

The most important aspect of an object-oriented software system is that it links together data and the operations that are performed on that data. The reason why this is seen as an advantage in programming is that it reflects objects in the real world and, after all, it is people in the real world that programs are intended to serve.

Any 'real world' object we choose to investigate can be described in terms of what it is called (its identity), what it is (its state) and what it does (its behaviour). If we pick up a coffee cup, we might say that it has a name ('coffee cup'), a state (it may be white, hot, full etc.) and has certain fixed behaviour (it can be manufactured, filled, drunk from, carried, washed and broken, for example). These elements are all 'encapsulated' into one object – we cannot divorce any one from the others. For example, the state of being full is irrevocably linked to the behaviour of being filled – we cannot separate the two. If the cup has not been filled then it cannot be full. It is this kind of link between data ('what it is') and operations ('what it does') that things in the real world have that we are seeking to reflect with object-oriented software.

Question 4.1   What two aspects of an 'object' are linked together by encapsulation?

Encapsulation is based on the linking together of an object's state and behaviour.

Information hiding

We have defined the term 'encapsulation' as meaning that we represent in software some kind of unit which, like real world objects, has both state and behaviour. This integration of state and behaviour allows us to implement 'information hiding' (a term first coined by David Parnas in 1972). Which means that encapsulation hides private elements of an object behind a public interface. This separation between the public and private parts of an encapsulated object has two aspects – protection of the object's state from unforeseen external influences, and hiding of the implementation details used to define an object's behaviour.

Firstly, then, 'information hiding' means that an object's state cannot be altered except by its fixed methods of behaviour. This is crucial, because we are trying to protect the state data inside an object from being changed by unpredictable external influences. If we take the coffee cup example (Fig. 4.1), we can say that it has a state of 'fullness' (how much coffee is in the cup). Unless we resort to conjuring tricks, this state can only be affected by specific operations: being filled (from kettle, jug etc.) or being emptied, (drunk or spilled). No other external effect can change the state of 'fullness'. The protection of state data is something which object-orientation provides us with in software. In effect, when programming we need the security of knowing that data in our program won't suddenly change state because of some apparently unconnected external event, with the same conviction that we know our coffee cup won't suddenly turn from white to black because the sun has gone behind a cloud.

Fig. 4.1: A coffee cup encapsulates both its state and its behaviour. This one may be full and cold. An appropriate behaviour in this state may be to be emptied down the sink!

Question 4.2   In the above example, a coffee cup is used as an example of a simple object with state and behaviour. Can you suggest states and behaviours which might apply to a retractable ball point pen?

Possible states might be: full, empty, nib out, nib in etc. Possible behaviours might be: write, refill, retract, propel, leak down front of shirt etc.

This protection of state data behind a 'fire wall' of fixed behaviour makes the life of the programmer easier because it means that the behaviour of software is predictable and less prone to error. It enhances reusability and maintainability because we only have to be aware of an object's interface, not its internal structures.

The second aspect of information hiding is that we do not need to know how behaviour happens, only that it does. In software, what goes on inside the programming unit which represents an object is not relevant to the user. We don't need to know how the manufacturer made our coffee cup white – we only need to know that it is white so that it will match our kitchen. This 'public' view of the cup would be unaffected by any change in the manufacturer's process which is 'private' – hidden from the user. In the same way, the behaviour of a software 'object' should be unaffected by changes in its internal implementation.

The way in which encapsulation allows information hiding to be applied is often described in terms of a 'doughnut' diagram (Fig. 4.2) – the private state is hidden behind the surrounding public interface, which represents that behaviour which is externally visible. From 'outside' the object, we cannot see the private, internal elements. What constitutes the public interface is defined in the 'abstract data type' (below). In fact, a jam doughnut is a better analogy than a ring, since its internal state is hidden!

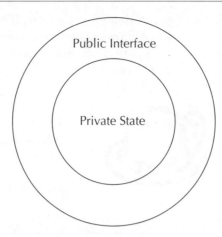

**Fig. 4.2: 'Doughnut' diagram of a hidden,
private state behind the public interface.**

Question 4.3   What is being hidden when we talk about information hiding?

We can make a distinction between two kinds of information which is being hidden by information hiding. One is the hiding of state data behind a 'public' interface of fixed behaviour, which is made possible by encapsulation. The other is the hiding of implementation details from the user. As well as state data, these include the data structures and algorithms used to create a software 'object's' behaviour.

Abstract data types

When using the coffee cup as an example of an object, we assume that we are looking at a particular coffee cup, and are evaluating its particular state and behaviour. However, we are able to identify it as a coffee cup because it is one of many which we recognise as being of a particular type of object. We know the possibilities for the state and behaviour of a particular coffee cup because in fact it shares these with all other coffee cups. It is this commonality of possible states and behaviours which allows us to 'classify' objects as belonging to particular groups, or 'classes', and when we try to model objects in software, we do so by defining the possible states and behaviours of all objects of a particular type. The vehicle for doing this is the 'abstract data type'.

Anyone who has any degree of programming experience will understand what is meant by the term 'data type'. It defines the type of data which a particular variable can hold – it may be an integer, a character, a float, or any of a range of simple data storage representations. However, when we build object-oriented systems, we use more complex data types, known as 'abstract data types', which represent more realistic (more worldly) entities. Whereas the 'integer' data type defines how all integer numbers are handled in a program (how they are stored and what operations they can undergo), we might be interested in representing a 'bank account' data type, which describes how all bank accounts are handled in a program (again, how they are stored and what operations they can undergo).

Abstraction is about reducing complexity, ignoring unnecessary detail. An abstract representation of something is supposed to contain the essential features of what is being represented. A realistic painting contains all the details seen by the eye, whereas an abstract painting intends to reflect the essential features of what is being seen. Unfortunately that meaning is not necessarily communicated to the viewer of the picture! A more appropriate example might be a map. Only the essential features of an area are shown on a map – it is not just an aerial photograph. Important elements are clearly shown, unimportant ones are ignored.

| **Question 4.4** | What do you think are the essential features of a 'Person' which we might include in an abstract data type? |

Given that an abstract data type should represent the essential features of something, we might concentrate on those which are most commonly used to identify individuals on official forms etc. These generally include name, address, age, sex and occupation among others. On the other hand, we might look at it in the context of what makes a person physically distinct, such as height, hair colour, skin colour, weight etc. Since we are always ignoring unnecessary detail, an abstract data type is often shaped not only by the objects it represents but by the context in which they are being used.

Another key point about an abstract data type is that it represents what is common between all examples of that particular 'thing', not just an individual example. An abstract data type for 'coffee cup' would be a representation of all the things that are common to all coffee cups, not just a particular one. This means that an abstract data type contains no values, it only defines the types of data or data structures which together will define the state of any object of that type.

Objects and classes

We have already referred to 'objects' as things in the real world, and used the example of a coffee cup as a particular type of object. We instinctively classify objects in terms of what we see as their types (e.g. a type of cat, a type of apple) based on the attributes and behaviours they have in common. The term 'classify' gives us the idea of the 'class' – all objects belong to a particular class of object. The common elements of a set of objects which allow us to classify them are those which we try to encompass in an abstract data type. Indeed C++ uses the word 'class' to describe an abstract data type.

Attributes and methods

If we are to build an abstract data type in a program, we have to identify three things:
1. The abstract 'thing' we are trying to represent
2. The data which represents the state of that 'thing'
3. The behaviour of that 'thing'

The 'thing' will be the name of the abstract data type (in our example above, 'coffee cup'). It may be worth stressing here that the 'thing' we are trying to define is not the object, but a class of objects (the common aspects of all objects which we classify as being of a particular type). The class will define the common attributes and methods for all objects of the class (Fig. 4.3).

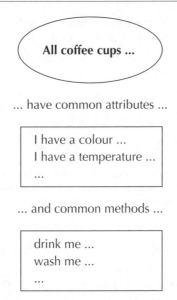

... have common attributes ...

I have a colour ...
I have a temperature ...
...

... and common methods ...

drink me ...
wash me ...
...

Fig. 3.3: **All coffee cups have common state**
attributes and behaviour methods.

Attributes

Having decided what our abstract data type is going to represent, we have to identify what elements go to make up its state. These are known as 'attributes' in object-oriented terminology, but in programming terms are variables and/or data structures (e.g. arrays, lists etc.) It is important to note that when we identify attributes, we are not specifying values for them. For example, we might decide that our data type must have the attribute of 'colour', but we do not predetermine what that colour might be for any individual coffee cup, only that all coffee cups will have a colour of some kind. This is exactly analogous to deciding the record structure of a file or database table. When we define fields in a record structure, we only specify their names and types, but the data held in each field may be different for each actual record.

Methods

The behaviour of our 'thing' is going to be defined by its 'methods' (sometimes called 'operations' or 'services'), which are processing routines related to the data type. In an abstract data type, the methods act as the only path between the user and the state data – it is normal practice to limit access to the data so that it can only be accessed via these methods ('information hiding').

There are several types of method, but two in particular are relevant here:

1. 'selector' methods
2. 'modifier' methods

A 'selector' method is a 'read' method, one which allows access to the state of an object, but does not allow that state to be altered. This is analogous to the traditional idea of a function (data is unaffected by executing a function). It is also known as a 'get' method. A 'modifier' method is a 'write' method, allowing state attributes to be altered. This is analogous to the traditional idea of a procedure (data is changed when a procedure is executed) and is also known as a 'set' method.

It is up to the designer of the abstract data type to decide which attributes may be read by selector methods, and which may be altered by modifier methods. If an attribute has no selector method, then to all intents and purposes it is 'invisible' from outside the abstract data type. If it has no modifier method then its state cannot be altered. In practice most attributes will have both 'get' and 'set' methods as a matter of course.

Modifier methods are not confined to setting individual attributes. Any method that changes the state of an object, such as moving a window across a screen or starting a timer, is a modifier.

Meyer [Meyer, 1988] uses the example of a simple 'black box' machine to highlight the external (public) interface of an object, and the different types of method. Indeed the idea of an object as a '(finite) state machine' is often used in object-oriented terminology. The machine has two types of button – 'command' (modifier) buttons and 'query' (selector) buttons. Pushing a query button returns some state information from the machine, but does not change the state. Therefore if the button is pushed ten times in a row, the same result will be returned 10 times. Pushing a command button changes the state, so that the next query about that state will produce a different result.

The example (Fig. 4.4) shows a 'number box' object which contains a collection of numbers. Our (rather limited) selector methods which display the current state of the object on the output screen will return either the current count of numbers in the machine (the 'count' button), or the mean average of those numbers (the 'mean' button). Neither of these methods will affect the data inside the machine. The two modifiers allow numbers to be added to the set via the numeric keypad (the 'add' button) or will delete all the numbers, leaving the box empty (the 'delete' button).

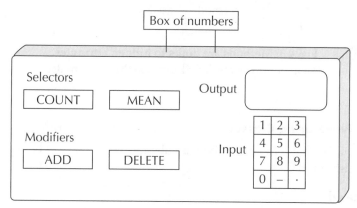

Fig. 4.4: A 'Number Box' object seen as a state machine, with selector and modifier operations.

Question 4.5   What type of method is able to alter the state of an object?

A 'modifier' method can alter the state of an object. In contrast, a 'selector' method may only return the value of an object's attributes without altering its state.

The most important concept which the 'black box' machine demonstrates is that the interface of an object is all that we see – only the methods are at our disposal. What happens inside the box is irrelevant to us. The object is seen as a hardware component – unaffected by other hardware components save for messages passed to and from it. An object-oriented software component has the same discrete nature – you can 'plug it in' to a program and use it as you would plug an integrated circuit board into a computer. Indeed, this analogy is the basis for the Brad Cox's use of the term 'software IC' [Cox, 1986].

Having discussed the attribute and method aspects of an abstract data type, it may be useful to return to our 'doughnut' diagram (Fig. 4.2) and think of it in terms of the methods providing controlled gateways or doors to the attributes (Fig. 4.5).

When we come to look at the syntax for creating an abstract data type in C++, we are aiming to achieve both a model of the type via its attributes and methods, and also to ensure the correct relationship between them. Methods provide the tools for programs which use the abstract data type to gather or manipulate data. Without methods, there is no useable interface to the private attributes. In the coding examples which follow, we will see that many of the external methods are derived naturally from the internal attributes.

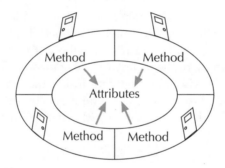

Fig. 4.5: Methods are doors to hidden attributes.
We may only access attributes via these methods.

C++ Syntax

Abstract Data Types Using Classes

This section of the chapter explains how an abstract data type can be represented using the 'class' construct in C++.

Syntax introduced

In these examples, the following syntax is introduced which allows the creation of abstract data types:

1. The 'class' keyword for defining a class (abstract data type).
2. The 'private:' keyword, which defines the 'hidden' part of the class.
3. The 'public:' keyword, which defines the visible interface of the class.
4. The 'scope resolution operator' – a double colon (::) used to link together classes and the definition of their methods.

The class in C++

In C++ we model an abstract data type by using the 'class'. The class has two parts; 'private' and 'public'. The private part of a class contains any elements which are to be hidden from public access. The public part of the class defines the 'behaviour' (methods) of any object of the class. In a program, a behaviour means a process which the object is able to perform or undergo.

It is normal practice to put attributes into the private part of the class, where they can only be accessed via methods. Methods themselves appear in the public part of the class so they can be accessed externally and provide the interface to the class. It is possible (though not usually appropriate, since it undermines the principles of encapsulation) to put attributes in the public part of the class. It is also possible to put methods in the private part of the class. This is useful for methods which are used by other methods of the same class, but not appropriate as part of the external interface. In the following examples, attributes are private and methods are public.

The syntax of a class (here called 'ExampleClass') in C++ is as follows:

```
//   first, the keyword 'class' is used, followed by the name of the class,
//   then the opening brace as used for all block structures in C++
class ExampleClass
{
//   the keyword 'private' is used to define the subsequent attributes as private
private:
//   a private attribute is declared (a single integer called 'i')
    int i;
//   the keyword 'public' is used before the methods
public:
//   a public method called setValue which sets the value of the
//   attribute 'i' using an integer parameter
    void setValue(int value_in)
    {
        i = value_in;
    }
//   a public method called getValue which returns the attribute 'i'
    int getValue()
    {
        return i;
    }
};
```

Notes

- A class definition is terminated with a semicolon, unlike a function definition.
- The members of a class are private by default, so the keyword 'private' could be omitted. The integer variable 'i' is private and therefore inaccessible from outside the class, except indirectly via the 'setValue' and 'getValue' methods.
- Methods are usually known as 'member functions' in C++. The member functions 'setValue' and 'getValue' are defined 'inline' (inside the class definition) in this case. 'setValue' is of 'void' type because it has no return value. 'getValue' is of 'int' type because it returns the value of the integer attribute.

Classes – declaring methods

In the above example, the definitions of the two methods appear inside the body of the class. This makes them 'inline' methods, which in practice means that the implementation code (the body of the method) will be duplicated for every object we create of this class. While this is perfectly acceptable for simple methods, it is not appropriate to define them inline when they are more than two lines long because of the potential memory requirements. In fact the compiler will not allow anything other than very short and simple methods to be defined inline. In most cases, methods must be prototyped (declared) inside the class, with their definitions given outside the class using the double colon 'scope resolution operator' (::) as follows:

```
return_type Class_name :: method_name(parameter list...)
```

The scope resolution operator tells the compiler that the method belongs to the named class, even though it has been defined outside the class body.

The effect of this is that only one version of the method exists at run time, accessible to all objects of the class. When defining methods out of line, the return type of the method appears to the left of the class name. The previously described class is defined here with its methods out of line:

```
//   the class body is defined, including method prototypes but not
//   definitions
class ExampleClass
{
private:
    int i;
public:
//   only the 'function prototypes' of the methods appear in the class body
    void setValue(int value_in);
    int getValue();
};
//   outside the class itself, the 'setValue' and 'getValue' methods are defined
void ExampleClass::setValue(int value_in)
{
    i = value_in;
}
int ExampleClass::getValue()
{
    return i;
}
```

Note that the method definitions, unlike the class definition, do not end in a semicolon.

The 'ExampleClass' shows the essential features of the syntax, but does not provide a useful abstract data type. All we could do with it would be to set and return the value of an integer. As a more realistic example, we will create a class called 'BankAccount' which will have the following attributes:

```
account number
account holder
current balance
```

It will have the following methods:

Selector methods:

get account number
get account holder
get balance

Modifier methods:

set account number
set account holder
deposit
withdrawal

We might usefully put these together into a simple diagram typical of object-oriented design notations (e.g. those used by [Coad/Yourdon, 1990] and [Rumbaugh et al, 1991]). This contains the name of the class, followed by its attributes and finally its methods, using a divided rectangle:

Bank Account
account number account holder current balance
get account number get account holder get current balance set account number set account holder deposit withdrawal

The class might be implemented in C++ as shown below.

Note the following:

- The attributes must have types (int, char* and float in this case)
- The methods must also have return types. Selector methods usually have a specific return type, whereas modifier methods are often void.
- It is good practice (though it makes no actual difference to the compiler) to group selector operations, followed by the modifier operations, as shown here.

```
#include <string.h>        // for the 'strncpy' library function
class BankAccount
{
//   the private attributes come first
private:
    int account_number;
    char account_holder[20];
    float current_balance;
//   followed by the public methods
public:
//   selector (get) methods
```

```
          int getAccountNumber();
          char* getAccountHolder();
          float getCurrentBalance();
//    modifier (set) methods
          void setAccountNumber(int number_in);
          void setAccountHolder(char* holder_in);
          void deposit(float amount);
          void withdrawal(float amount);
};
//    now we define the function bodies for each of the methods;
//    getAccountNumber returns the integer account number
int BankAccount::getAccountNumber()
{
     return account_number;

}
//    getAccountHolder returns the name of the account holder
char* BankAccount::getAccountHolder()
{
     return account_holder;

}
//    getCurrentBalance returns the current account balance (a float)
float BankAccount::getCurrentBalance()
{
     return current_balance;

}
//    setAccountNumber sets the account number from the integer parameter
void BankAccount::setAccountNumber(int number_in)
{
     account_number = number_in;

}
//    setAccountHolder sets the name of the holder from the char* parameter
void BankAccount::setAccountHolder(char* holder_in)
{
     strncpy(account_holder, holder_in, 19);
     account_holder[19] = '\0';

}
//    deposit allows a parameter value to be added to the current balance
void BankAccount::deposit(float amount)
{
     current_balance = current_balance + amount;

}
//    withdrawal allows a parameter value to be subtracted from the balance
void BankAccount::withdrawal(float amount)
{
     current_balance = current_balance – amount;

}
```

With the BankAccount class we have modelled a simple bank account as an abstract data type, providing the attributes and methods necessary to hold and update state data for any bank account created using this data type. However, so far we have not done anything beyond the definition of the abstract data type – it has not been 'used in anger'. We have not as yet created anything which could be regarded as a program. We have, rather, created the definition of a data type which could be used to make objects in any number of programs. In order to do this effectively, we will need to store it in a header file (i.e. a '.h' file, for example 'bankacct.h') which may be included in subsequent programs which process bank accounts. We could put both the class definition and a program into the same file (and indeed many of the examples in this book are written this way), but putting the class into a separate header file is necessary if we need to use it in more than one program.

Whenever we create new abstract data types and store them in header files, we are adding to a potential library, allowing us to create objects of any predefined class. However, user-created header files are usually included in a program using a different syntax to that used when including header files provided with the compiler. When including header files in previous examples, we used the following syntax:

```
#include <header_name.h>
```

Examples seen so far are:

```
#include <string.h>
#include <iostream.h>
```

In contrast, user-defined header files are usually included using the following syntax:

```
#include "header_name.h"
```

The only difference is in fact to do with the location of the files. The compiler expects to find header files enclosed in " " characters in a local drive, whereas those enclosed in < > characters it will look for in its usual library directory. In theory, either syntax will work for any type of header file, but sometimes in practice this is not the case (for example over a network). To include our bank account header file in a program we might therefore have something like the following at the beginning of our source code:

```
#include "bankacct.h"
```

In the next chapter, we will see how the bank account class can be included in this way in a simple program to create bank account objects and test their behaviour.

Summary of key concepts from this chapter

1. Encapsulation is the combination of state and behaviour into a software 'object'.

2. 'Information hiding' is the division of an object into private and public parts. The public part provides the external interface. The private part (and all internal processes) are 'hidden' inside the object.

3. An abstract data type defines the attributes (state) and methods (behaviour) of all objects belonging to a particular 'class'.

4. We may make a distinction between 'selector' methods (which access attributes but cannot change them) and 'modifier' methods (which are able to change the state of attributes).

5. In C++, we use the 'class' to model abstract data types. The keywords 'public' and 'private' are used to define the class interface and hidden part respectively. The scope resolution operator (double colon) is used to link member functions (methods) to the class.

Exercises

Put your answers to these exercises in header files (with a '.h' extension). To test them, read Chapter 5 up to the example program on page 71 and use this as a model for your test programs.

1. Consider the attributes and methods suggested for the coffee cup in the preceding chapter. Using the notation previously shown (the divided rectangle), list the name, attributes and methods which would apply to a 'coffee cup' abstract data type. Add any you can think of which have not already been mentioned.

2. Suggest attributes and methods for a 'wallet/purse' abstract data type. Think about what you need a wallet or purse for (what its behaviour is) and what internal attributes relate to these behaviours. Bear in mind that there is no single 'right answer' for this kind of abstract exercise.

3. Question 4.4 referred to a 'Person' abstract data type. Create a C++ class to represent a person with attributes of name, year of birth and height in metres. Define methods to get and set these three attributes. Add a method which will return a person's (approximate) age when given a year as a parameter. Add another method which will return their height in centimetres. These values may be derived from the given attributes. Do not add extra attributes to the class.

4. Create a C++ class for a 'StockItem' abstract data type. It should have the attributes of stock level (an integer) and unit price (a float). Define methods to return the values of these two attributes and to set them using parameters. Add two more methods to allow stock receipts, and stock issues, updating the stock level as appropriate.

5 Classes and objects

Overview

In this chapter we will look at the differences between classes and objects. We will examine what is meant by the three elements of an object, namely identity, state and behaviour. Instantiation of objects is demonstrated in C++, along with the use of the various types of constructor method. The syntax for sending a message to an object (i.e. using a method) is outlined.

What is a class, what is an object?

In the previous chapter, we began by discussing a specific object, (a coffee cup) and ended by describing an abstract data type (for a bank account) which defined the class to which all 'BankAccount' objects belong.

What then is the relationship between a class (described by an abstract data type) and objects of that class?

The role of the class is to act as a kind of blueprint for all the objects of that type. A class defines the types of state data appropriate to the class (the attributes), and also its set of allowed behaviours (the methods). The class is in effect an 'object factory' which allows us to create new objects of the class, each one of which follows an identical pattern of attributes and methods. A single abstract data type is used to create as many instances of the class as we wish, in the same way that a single simple data type (such as the type 'integer') can be used to create many instances of that type.

Question 5.1   What are the similarities and differences between a simple data type (like integer) and an abstract data type (like bank account)?

Both simple and abstract data types define the behaviours of a single set of data. However, for the integer there is only one attribute (the integer value) and a limited set of behaviours (adding, subtracting etc) defined by the language syntax we are using. Abstract data types may have many attributes, and many behaviours which we are able to define ourselves.

It might be useful to think of the class as, for example, a machine like one which makes security badges for visitors to a company. The machine makes a standard pattern of badge (printed cardboard insert, plastic cover, pin) and defines the required attributes for each one such as the visitor's name, their own employer and the person they are visiting, perhaps even a photo of the visitor. Each badge which the machine makes is an object – a single 'instance ' of the class – and it is each badge which contains the 'state' data for the attributes defined by the class. The class contains the attributes, but it is the objects which actually contain the state data (the person's name, their photograph etc.). Each badge will have a standard behaviour – a standard set of methods defined by the class. Note that these are not different for each object. If the 'class machine' fixes a safety pin onto the back of the badge, then it will have the methods of being put on and taken off etc, and all objects will have exactly the same behaviour, even though their state data is different (Fig. 5.1).

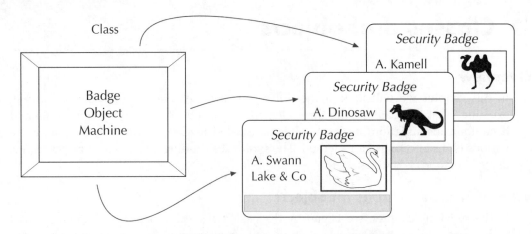

Fig. 5.1: The class acts like an object machine.
This class machine manufactures 'badge' objects.

Each object created by the class is a single 'instance' of that class, and this is why the term 'instantiation' is used in object-oriented terminology. 'Instantiation' means the creation of a single instance of a class – i.e. an object.

Question 5.2	What may be different for all objects in a class, and what remains the same?

All the objects in a class may have different attribute values (state data), but their allowed behaviours are all the same.

State, identity and behaviour

In the previous chapter, we stated that a class is defined by three elements:

1. A unique name
2. Attributes
3. Methods

In contrast, an object is defined by:

1. Identity
2. State
3. Behaviour

In each of these three cases, the property of the class relates in some way to the property of the object (Fig. 5.2). The attributes of the class allow each object to contain state data – one value for each attribute. The methods of the class define the possible behaviours of the object. However, the concept of identity is slightly more complex than the name of the class.

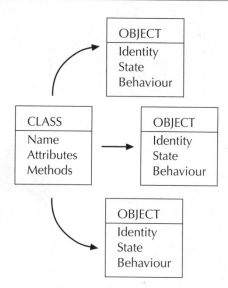

**Fig. 5.2: Classes are identified by a unique name, and embody
attributes and methods. Objects have identity, state and behaviour.**

It is possible for a specific object to be identified by a unique name. In an oilfield control
system for example there might be a fixed and limited number of individual oil pumps,
each one easily identifiable by a unique name, e.g. 'Oil Pump 1', 'Oil Pump 2' etc.
However, this simplicity of identity is not always the case. In some situations, there are
many objects constantly being created and destroyed. If it is raining, what identifies each
raindrop? It would be absurd to suggest that we could name every raindrop, but each
does exist and therefore must have some kind of unique identity. In some cases, the idea
that each object can have a unique name falls down. What in fact differentiates one raindrop from another is simply the space that it occupies at a particular time. The identity of
any object may be ultimately definable only by this space/time relationship (Fig. 5.3). In
object-oriented programs which have to keep track of a large number of objects which
are constantly being instantiated and destroyed, objects will be identified by their
memory locations rather than by unique names. Objects which are predictable are identified, like classes, by unique names, but objects which are unpredictable are identified
by location.

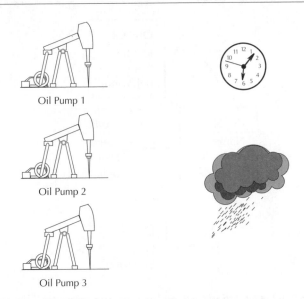

Fig. 5.3: Objects of predictable number and lifetimes (like oil pumps) have unique names. Unpredictable objects (like raindrops) are identified by the space and time they occupy.

It is sometimes possible to differentiate objects by key attributes, in the same way that records in an indexed file or database table can be accessed by some unique data field(s). However, this is not what is meant by object identity, and it is perfectly possible for more than one object to have identical state values for all attributes.

Question 5.3   What is the difference between the name of a class and the identity of an object?

Each class has a single unique name which identifies a particular abstract data type. An object may have a unique name, or a unique data 'key', but its identity may ultimately be defined only by the memory location which it occupies at a particular time.

The key differences between a class and its objects may be summarised as follows:

- Once we have defined a class, it exists all the time a program is running, whereas objects may be created and destroyed at run time.

- For a single class, there may be any number of objects instantiated at any one time (possibly no objects at all).

- A class has a unique name, attributes and methods. An object has identity, state and behaviour.

- A class provides no state values for the object attributes. These can only be given values when applied to specific objects.

Constructors

When we instantiate an object in a program, there are certain processes which must take place. As we noted above, objects must have a unique identity, which is ultimately defined by the space which that object occupies at a particular time. In a program, this means memory space, and instantiation of an object always involves reserving enough memory for the state data of that object. It does not have to reserve memory for the methods since, unlike the attribute values, these are consistent for all objects of the class. Therefore they only need to exist once for the class, not once for every object. The exception to this is very short methods which may be declared 'inline' – inside the body of the class itself. Inline methods are duplicated for every object. This is purely an implementation detail of C++, and does not affect the general principle that methods are an identical set shared between all objects in the class.

The special method which reserves memory for a newly instantiated object is known as the 'constructor'. In addition to the reservation of memory space, the constructor may also be extended to include other processes such as the initialisation of the state data of the object.

Question 5.4   What is the primary role of the constructor?

To reserve memory for a newly instantiated object.

There are three basic kinds of constructor:
1.   the default constructor
2.   user-defined constructors
3.   the copy constructor

The default constructor

The default constructor takes no parameters, and performs no processing other than the reservation of memory. It will always be called by the compiler if no user defined constructor is provided. The default constructor is not referred to by the programmer in the class definition.

User defined constructors

If parameters or initialisation processing are required when an object is created, then the programmer has to define a constructor method explicitly. It is possible to have more than one constructor in a class providing that the different versions are defined by differences in the parameter list. This is known as 'overloading' and gives more flexibility to the ways in which an object may be instantiated (see Chapter 12).

The copy constructor

A copy constructor is a simple concept, since it is really a way of using the assignment (=) operator when creating new objects. It allows us to express things like:

new_object object2 = object1

i.e. the new object is to be equal to the existing object.

The copy constructor allows us to instantiate an object as an exact copy of another in terms of its attribute values – in the example above, the attribute values of 'object2' on instantiation would be copied from those of 'object1'. The only difference between the objects will be their identities since their states and behaviours will be the same until one or other changes state. The default copy constructor can be used on any objects without being explicitly defined, though it is possible to provide a user defined copy constructor if additional processing is required, or if the default behaviour is inappropriate, perhaps because the objects contain pointers. Since the default copy constructor copies pointer addresses rather than the data they reference, we may in some cases have to override this behaviour.

C++ syntax

Instantiating objects

In order to instantiate objects, we need to call on an abstract data type – a 'class' in C++. As we know, each class has a unique name by which it may be identified. For the moment we will also only be creating objects which have unique names. The syntax for creating objects without unique names will be explained in the next chapter. Objects instantiated with unique names are those whose lifetimes and identities are predictable at compile time.

For the examples which follow, we will be using the 'BankAccount' class as described in Chapter 4, so code examples assume the inclusion of our header file 'bankacct.h'.

An object is instantiated in C++ by declaring its type, followed by its name, just like other data types, e.g.

```
int x;                  // an instance of type 'int'
char y;                 // an instance of type 'char'
BankAccount z;          // an instance of type 'BankAccount'
```

When we declare 'x' to be of type integer, it means that we can treat 'x' in the same way as any other integer, and perform integer arithmetic on it. By declaring 'z' to be of type 'BankAccount', we likewise treat z as any other BankAccount, which means it will have the attributes and methods defined by the class.

Creating multiple objects

One of the most important aspects of creating objects of a class is that there can be as many objects of that class instantiated as may be needed. For example, we might create three bank accounts as follows:

```
BankAccount account1;
BankAccount account2;
BankAccount account3;
```

Any of these three objects may now 'receive messages', which means that they can respond to use of their methods.

'Sending messages' by using methods

A class, as we know, is divided into two parts, the 'private' part (which is hidden from the outside, and contains the state values) and the 'public' part (which usually contains the methods). These public methods are the only things which we can use in association with an object of the class. There is no direct access to the private elements.

When an object is identified by a unique name, anything in the public part of the class (usually methods) can be called by putting a period (the 'dot operator') between the name of the object and the method, e.g.:

```
account1.setAccountNumber(100);
```

This calls the 'setAccountNumber' method for the class to which 'account1' belongs (in this case the 'BankAccount' class), and sets the private attribute 'account_number' to 100. Note that the method requires an integer parameter to do this. Calling a method of an object is known as 'sending a message'. In the example above, the message 'setAccountNumber' is sent to the object 'account1'.

The only messages which we can send to an object are those defined as methods in the public part of the class. Nothing in the private part of the class can be accessed via the dot operator (or any other operator). We cannot, for example, do this:

    account1.account_number = 100; // invalid reference to private attribute

This is not allowed, since 'account_number' is private, and the dot operator can only access public elements of the class.

Any instantiated object can be sent messages using the dot operator. In the following example, three account objects are instantiated (note that we can declare them all in one statement if we wish, just like simple data types), have their account numbers set, and then displayed by calling the appropriate methods.

```
#include "bankacct.h"
#include <iostream.h>
void main( )
{
    BankAccount account1, account2, account3;
    account1.setAccountNumber(100);
    account2.setAccountNumber(110);
    account3.setAccountNumber(120);
    cout << "Account Numbers Are:" << endl;
    cout << account1.getAccountNumber( ) << endl;
    cout << account2.getAccountNumber( ) << endl;
    cout << account3.getAccountNumber( ) << endl;
}
```

The output from this program should be:

    Account Numbers Are:
    100
    110
    120

Calling the constructor

We stated previously that whenever an object is instantiated, a method known as the 'constructor' is called to reserve memory for that object. Whether or not we explicitly define it, the constructor is called automatically by the compiler when an instance of an object is created. When for example we write 'BankAccount account1' to instantiate 'account1', we are implicitly calling the constructor.

Limitations of the default constructor

A default constructor is called if no user-defined constructor is provided in the class definition, but it has limited application since it only allocates memory for the object being instantiated. It is not possible to pass any parameters to the default constructor, nor to make it perform or call any other processes. However, it may in practice be appropriate when creating an object to perform some initial processing, such as giving initial state values to some or all of the attributes. We can do this by writing a user defined constructor method, possibly with parameters, replacing the default version. Although initialisation processes do not have to be put into a constructor (a separate method could be written to do this), the advantage is that the constructor does not have to be explicitly called when creating an object, as any other method would have to be.

A user defined constructor

As noted above, if we define our own constructor there is no need to call a separate initialisation function when creating objects – since any object will have a constructor, all initialisation processing can be put into it. It is important to note that when providing our own constructor, we do not have to worry about the reservation of memory for the object. That crucial role of the default constructor is automatically (and invisibly) included even when we define our own.

Coding a constructor

An object constructor in C++ has three important aspects:

1. It takes the same name as the class
2. It may take arguments
3. It cannot return a value

The constructor prototype

Since the name of a constructor is the same as that of the class, then a constructor for the 'BankAccount' class would also be called 'BankAccount'. Its prototype would therefore appear in the class definition (in our header file) as follows:

```
class BankAccount
{
...
public:
    BankAccount();
...
};
```

Note that since the constructor cannot return a value, it has no return type and no type can be stated. This is an important distinction between the constructor and other methods – C++ functions normally require a return type, which defaults to 'int' if none is stated.

Defining the constructor out-of-line

To define a constructor out of line, we use the scope resolution operator as usual to separate the class name and the method name. Of course, for a constructor these names are identical, as the following example (assuming a class called 'Object') demonstrates:

```
Object :: Object( )
{
                // constructor definition
}
```

What then might a user-defined constructor such as this do? Its typical role would be to initialise the state of objects when they are created. In the case of the BankAccount class, a likely initialisation process would be to set the 'current_balance' attribute to zero, since it will otherwise contain a garbage value. (This could cause our 'deposit' and 'withdrawal' methods to produce some strange results.) Of course, we could have a separate method to do this, but it would have to be called explicitly by the programmer. By doing it in the constructor we 'kill two birds with one stone'. Our out-of-line constructor definition (added to the methods in the header file) might be:

```
BankAccount :: BankAccount()
{
    current_balance = 0.00;
}
```

A user defined constructor such as this can therefore perform any processes which are appropriate to the instantiation of an object.

Parameterised constructors

The previous example has no parameters, but it is also possible to pass parameter arguments to a user-defined constructor. This gives us the opportunity to create objects with different initial states dependent on the parameters which are passed when the constructor is called. In the case of a newly created bank account, we might wish to set the initial balance to values other than zero (after all, banks don't usually let you open accounts with no money!). The prototype of a constructor taking such a parameter might be:

```
BankAccount(float start_balance);
```

and it could use the parameter to set the initial value of the current balance as follows:

```
BankAccount::BankAccount(float start_balance)
{
    current_balance = start_balance;
}
```

If we have this constructor declared, then whenever we create an instance of the bank account class, we have to supply a parameter argument – the default constructor which takes no arguments is no longer available to us, having been replaced by our user-defined constructor. A BankAccount object can therefore only be created with a float value provided as an argument, e.g.:

```
BankAccount account1(100.00);
```

This creates a BankAccount object with an initial balance of £100.00.

Default parameter values

What if we want to be able to instantiate objects with a parameter some of the time, but not always? One way in which this can be achieved is by the use of default values for parameter arguments. Any single parameter to a method (or function) can be given a default value in C++, for example we can give 'start_balance' a default value of zero:

```
public:
    BankAccount(float start_balance = 0);
```

This means that if a BankAccount object is created with no parameter argument, then the value of 'start_balance' will default to zero, but if a value is provided then the default will be overridden, as the following code fragment demonstrates:

```
#include <iostream.h>
#include "bankacct.h"
void main()
{
    BankAccount account1;                  // will use default value
    BankAccount account2(100.00);          // will use value provided
    cout << "Balance 1: £" << account1.getCurrentBalance() << endl;
    cout << "Balance 2: £" << account2.getCurrentBalance() << endl;
}
```

The output from this program is:

Balance 1: £0
Balance 2: £100

Functions or methods with more than one parameter can also have default values, provided that no parameters with default values are followed by others without defaults e.g.

aFunction (int x, int y = 10) is okay, but
aFunction (int x = 10, int y) is not

Using the copy constructor

To use the (default) copy constructor, all we need to express is that one newly instantiated object equals another object of the same class. In the following example, BankAccount object 'account4' is instantiated to be equal to 'account1' (i.e. all the attribute values will be taken from those of account1).

BankAccount account4 = account1;

In this line of code, the default constructor being called is the copy constructor – one which copies all the attribute values of an existing object to another object of the same class. Note that since the copy constructor is a different method from the constructor, it is not affected by any parameters we may have added to our user-defined constructor.

A user-defined copy constructor

It is also possible to create your own copy constructor, defined by the fact that it takes a reference to an object of the same class as a function argument, for example:

BankAccount(const BankAccount& copied_account);

might be a prototype for a copy constructor of the account class (other versions might also take additional parameters). You will recall that the '&' (ampersand) character is used to denote 'pass by reference', and the 'const' prefix indicates that the parameter object cannot be modified by the method. Clearly, the copy constructor needs to refer to an existing object of the class in order to copy its attribute values, but why must it be passed by reference rather than by value? This is simply because when we pass a parameter by value, then a copy of it is made when the function is called. What makes a copy of an object? The copy constructor! Therefore passing an object to a copy constructor by value would result in an unresolvable recursive call.

A copy constructor will usually access the attribute values of the parameter object using the dot operator. You will notice that we do not have to access its attributes via selector methods because both objects belong to the same class. Attributes referred to directly are, of course, those belonging to the object being instantiated. Attributes referenced by the dot operator are those being copied from the parameter object. A 'BankAccount' copy constructor definition might look like this:

```
BankAccount::BankAccount(const BankAccount& copied_account)
{
    account_number = copied_account.account_number;
    strcpy(account_holder, copied_account.account_holder);
    current_balance = copied_account.current_balance;
}
```

If we declare a copy constructor, then we must also declare an ordinary constructor, since the compiler will no longer automatically use the default version. In effect, a user-defined copy constructor overrides the default constructor. The reverse is not true however – the default copy constructor is still available even if we define our own constructor.

It is important to note that if a copy constructor is used to instantiate an object, any user-defined constructor will not be called (since the copy constructor replaces the constructor), so any processing which takes place in the ordinary constructor will not be executed. Therefore it may be necessary to duplicate code in both the constructor and the copy constructor. An alternative is to instantiate the object first and then copy its attributes, and which method is more appropriate depends on the programming context.

Summary of key points from this chapter

1. A class is an 'object factory' which can instantiate many objects of that class. Each object encapsulates its own state data.

2. A class has a unique name and defines attributes and methods. An object has identity, state and behaviour.

3. Object identity may be a unique name or simply the space an object occupies at a particular time. It may have a unique data key but this is not the definition of identity.

4. The 'constructor' method creates an object by reserving memory space for it. It may also perform other programmer-defined tasks.

5. The default constructor is not declared but called by the compiler. More than one user-defined constructor may be defined to replace it.

6. The copy constructor instantiates an object as an exact copy of another object of the same class. A user defined copy constructor takes a reference to an object of the class as a parameter.

7. An object may be instantiated by using the name of the class, the name of the object and any required parameters. This calls the appropriate constructor.

8. Object methods may be called using the 'dot operator'.

Exercises

1. Assume that an account object is to be created using the parameterised constructor previously described. This will have to be put into your header file containing the BankAccount class definition.

Instantiate a BankAccount object using a parameter argument, and set its other attributes. Demonstrate the use of the copy constructor by creating another account which has equal attribute values.

2. Using the 'BankAccount' class methods described in Chapter 4, write a program to test these methods as follows:

   a) Create three bank accounts, two with start balances of £0.00, and one with £100.00.

   b) Set the account numbers to 1, 2 and 3 respectively.

   c) Set the names of the account holders.

   d) Credit account 1 with £50.00.

   e) Credit account 2 with £75.00.

   f) Debit account 3 with £75.00.

   g) Display all the account numbers, holders and balances.

3. Create your own 'XYCoordinate' class (to define points on an xy graph), with attributes and methods as appropriate. Define your own constructor taking parameters to set the initial position of a point (or default to 0,0). Instantiate several objects of the class and demonstrate their methods and the use of the default copy constructor.

6 Object lifetimes and dynamic objects

Overview

This chapter investigates object lifetime (persistence) and visibility within a program, and compares external, automatic, static and dynamic objects in terms of these properties. The destructor method is introduced, working in conjunction with the constructor to create and destroy dynamic objects at run-time. The new and delete operators are applied to the creation and destruction of dynamic objects, and the arrow operator is used as the mechanism for sending messages to dynamic objects.

Object persistence and visibility

There are a number of factors which affect the persistence and visibility of an object during the run time of a program. Some objects may exist throughout the running of a program, and may be visible in all modules. Other objects may exist momentarily within the limited scope of a particular method or statement body. Between these two extremes we may have a range of lifetimes and visibility among instantiated objects.

Types of object

There are four types of object (or in fact any other data type) which we may instantiate in a program. The first three are objects with specific names, but the fourth, dynamic objects, cannot be identified in this way:

1. *External (global) Objects*   Persistent (in existence) throughout the lifetime of a program and having 'file scope' – visibility throughout the module source file. May be visible in more than one module, perhaps visible in all modules (global).

2. *Automatic (local) Objects*   Persistent and visible only throughout the (local) scope in which they are created.

3. *Static Objects*   Persistent throughout a program but only visible within their local scope.

4. *Dynamic Objects*   Lifetime may be controlled within a particular scope.

These types of object all serve different purposes, and require different forms of language syntax for their creation, access and destruction. In our examples so far, we have only created objects with specific names (in fact they have all been 'automatic' objects), but we have also discussed the possibility that some objects cannot have unique names, and are identified only by the space which they occupy at a particular time.

In some programs there may be a fixed number of clearly identifiable objects whose existence is predictable in all runs of a program. When objects are predictable enough to be identified at compile time, we are able to give them unique names. Such objects may be either 'external', 'static' or 'automatic' depending on their required persistence and visibility as defined by scope. In contrast, dynamic objects are those which cannot be identified at compile time, either in terms of their number or their identities, and their lifetimes may be controlled independently of scope.

External (global) objects

An external object is one which is persistent and visible throughout a program module – i.e. its scope is an entire module (source file). It may also be made visible in other modules. Objects which fall into the category of 'external' would be ones whose numbers and identities remained constant throughout an application.

For example, if we are monitoring 6 petrol pumps in a garage forecourt simulation program, then there are unlikely to be changes to this setup when the program is running. Even if a pump is out of action it does not cease to exist, it simply changes its state (to 'empty' or 'broken' for example). In this kind of scenario, the objects can have unique names (e.g. pump1, pump2 etc). They also persist for the lifetime of the program. If they are instantiated as software objects when the program starts up, then they will exist in the program until it shuts down, since the physical pumps also persist in reality (Fig. 6.1).

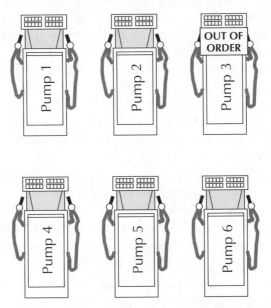

Fig. 6.1: Some objects persist throughout an application. These petrol pumps have predictable lifetimes and identities.

Such objects may be regarded then as 'external' objects – those which persist throughout the program lifetime. External objects are always global for the module in which they are declared, and are often global throughout the system – this means that they are 'visible' throughout all program modules. However, depending on implementation we might have objects which are persistent throughout the lifetime of the program but not global (not visible throughout all modules). This is purely an implementation detail relating to 'linkage' – the way in which the linker resolves the visibility of objects between modules. An object with a name which is local to a module is said to have 'internal linkage', whereas those whose names are visible in multiple modules have 'external linkage'.

Automatic objects

As well as external, global objects, we may also have a number of locally declared 'automatic' objects – objects which exist in a predictable manner for a particular period of time. The key difference between an external and an automatic object is that whereas an automatic object is instantiated within the scope of part of a program module, an external object is instantiated outside of any scope (in C++ scope is defined by braces). 'Automatic' objects are automatically destroyed when they fall out of the scope in which they were instantiated.

For example, we might have a system with some form of object-oriented menu driven user interface, with one of the objects in the system a 'help' menu. Since the help menu only needs to be visible to the user when s/he requires help, it does not need to exist for the whole lifetime of the program, but only needs to be instantiated when required, and can be automatically destroyed when no longer needed. Since there will only ever be one help menu, and the circumstances in which it will be required are constant and predictable, then we can give it a unique name, and confine its existence to a particular 'scope' in the program – the part where the help menu is visible (Fig. 6.2.)

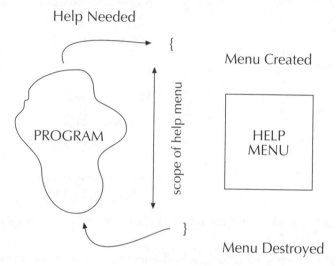

Fig. 6.2: The existence of an automatic object is predictably defined by its scope (delimited in C++ by braces).

The existence of an automatic object is therefore delimited by the scope of the part of the program in which it is instantiated. Depending on where it is instantiated, this may mean that the object is in existence for the whole time the program is running, but not necessarily visible throughout run-time. This is because even if an automatic object persists throughout a program module, it cannot be made visible in other modules in the system.

Static objects

From the examples above, we can see that external objects are persistent and visible throughout the lifetime of a program, whereas automatic objects are only persistent and visible within the scope in which they are declared. There is also the possibility in C++ to explicitly declare a variable or object which has the scope (in terms of visibility) of an automatic object but the lifetime of an external object. In other words, an object like 'help menu' in Fig. 6.2 could be created once and once only (persisting from its creation to the termination of the program), but with its visibility delimited by the scope within which it is declared. This is known as a 'static' object. Why might we wish to create a static object? In general terms, when we wish an object's state to persist even when it is not in scope (and therefore not visible). A example might be the kind of menu which includes different data depending on its state, such as some kind of configuration menu (Fig. 6.3). In this type of menu, the possible options would be different depending on the current configuration, so that the menu might display 'mono screen' as an option while the current configuration is colour, but 'colour screen' if the current state is mono. In cases like this, it is useful if the menu can 'remember' its state from the last time it was in scope.

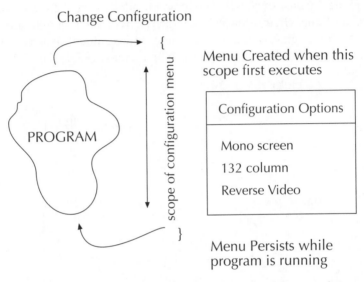

Fig. 6.3: A static object can retain its state even when out of scope.

Question 6.1   What is the difference in lifetime and visibility between external, automatic and static objects?

External objects exist for the lifetime of the program and their visibility is global. Automatic objects exist as long as they remain in scope and are visible only within that scope. Static objects are created and visible within a particular scope, but persist from their point of creation until the end of the program.

Dynamic objects

It may be that objects in a system are not predictable enough to be instantiated as external, static or automatic objects. This is the case when we are unable to predict at compile time:

1. Object Identities
2. Object Quantities
3. Object Lifetimes

For example, if we return to the garage forecourt simulation scenario, it would probably be the case that the vehicles present on the forecourt at any one time need to be represented as objects in the system. These questions need to be addressed:

1. What is the identity of each vehicle?

2. How many vehicles will be on the forecourt at any one time?

3. How long will a particular vehicle be on the forecourt?

Of course, none of these questions can be answered when the program is being written or compiled, only when it is running!

In these circumstances, neither external, automatic nor static objects can be used to represent vehicles, since such objects need to be predictable – they require unique names, are of fixed number and fixed lifetimes. We need to represent unpredictable combinations of vehicles using objects which can be dynamically instantiated and destroyed at run time to represent the vehicles entering and leaving the system.

The way in which such collections of dynamic objects may be managed will be dealt with in a later chapter, but the first step is to investigate how dynamic objects may be created and destroyed.

Question 6.2   In what circumstances are objects with unique names unsuitable for use in a particular program context?

When we cannot predict the identities, numbers and lifetimes of the objects which will be represented at run time, then they cannot be uniquely named (i.e. they cannot be external, static or automatic.) If objects are unpredictable, then they must be represented dynamically.

Creating dynamic objects

When creating dynamic objects, we cannot give them the unique names which are possible with other types of object. This means that we have to have some other way of referencing objects at run time, and in practice this is done with pointers. We have already discussed the use of pointers to memory locations, for example in referencing the address of the first character of a string, and the use of pointers to reference dynamic objects is similar. However, we still need a mechanism to create dynamic objects, and this is through the use of dynamic memory allocation. In C++, a pointer can be directed to an area of dynamically allocated memory at run time in order to reference a newly created object. In this way, the constructor can be called via the pointer.

Destroying dynamic objects – the destructor method

We have already looked at the constructor method, and how it creates a software object by reserving memory for the object's attributes. We also know that, whether or not we define it, a constructor is always called when an object is created – the default constructor is used if the programmer does not supply one to override it (to perform additional processes such as initialising attribute values). An object cannot be instantiated without some form of constructor to reserve memory because the existence of any object depends on it occupying memory space. Indeed, the identity of a dynamic object depends entirely the memory location it occupies at a particular time.

If an object cannot be instantiated without a constructor method, it follows that an object cannot be destroyed without a 'destructor' method. This is a method which allows us to destroy an object, and if we do not define one, a default destructor is called whenever an object is destroyed. Its primary purpose is to free the memory used by the object. Like the constructor, it can be extended by the programmer to perform additional functions if required, though unlike the constructor it cannot take parameters. The destructor executes when the object is destroyed either specifically by the programmer (in the case of dynamic objects), by falling out of scope (automatic objects), or by the program terminating (external and static objects).

Cleanup and 'garbage collection'

As we have noted, the default constructor reserves memory for a new object. The default destructor correspondingly frees the memory used by the object when it has been destroyed. This type of process is known as 'cleanup' – freeing up memory when the data it contains is no longer of use. As we will see, although this is done for us when the destructor is called by automatic objects falling out of scope, if we are handling dynamic objects we have to do our own memory cleanup by explicitly calling the destructor. If a dynamic object falls out of scope before we have called the destructor, then the destructor is not called automatically and no cleanup will take place. This can have serious consequences for memory management in our programs. Some languages have a facility known as 'garbage collection' which is able to trawl though memory disposing of dynamic objects which are no longer being used (i.e. no longer referenced by a pointer), and to recover memory more efficiently than the destructor. However, since C++ has no garbage collection mechanisms the onus is on us to make sure that we do not leave unwanted objects lying around in memory.

Calling the destructor

The destructor, then, is the direct corollary of the constructor, freeing the object's memory space which was reserved by the constructor. The destructor call for an automatic object is implicit – it happens when (and only when) that object falls out of scope. In contrast, the destructor call for a dynamic object must be explicitly stated – it is the programmer's responsibility.

The advantage of explicitly calling the destructor ourselves (rather then letting it be called when an object falls out of scope) is that it gives us the same kind of control over the end of an object's life that we already have over its beginning. When we call an object constructor in a program, we are explicitly defining where we want that object's lifetime to begin. When we put a destructor into a program we are explicitly defining where we want that object's lifetime to end. This does not replace the existing constraints on object lifetimes defined by their scope – an object still cannot extend its life beyond its scope – but it gives us an additional mechanism for control.

Question 6.3   What is the role of the destructor in terms of the 'cleanup' of unwanted objects?

The destructor frees the memory occupied by objects when they are destroyed. For memory 'cleanup' when dynamically created objects are destroyed, the destructor must be called explicitly.

There is however an important difference between the destructor being called implicitly by the compiler and explicitly by the programmer. That is, only objects created dynamically can be destroyed dynamically. Objects created as external, static or automatic objects cannot be destroyed explicitly by the programmer.

C++ syntax

In the previous chapter we looked at the creation of objects with unique names, created within the scope of a function ('main', although objects may be created within any function or method). Before investigating dynamic objects, we should contrast the instantiation of external, static and automatic objects.

The lifetime of named objects

When we create a named object in a program, its lifetime and visibility is controlled only by its scope. Named objects, as we have stated, may be of three types:

1. *Automatic Objects*

   Objects instantiated inside the local scope of a function or other structure with its body defined by braces. They only exist while they are in scope.

2. *External Objects*

   Objects instantiated outside any function body. These have 'file scope' and exist for the lifetime of the program.

3. *Static Objects*

   Objects instantiated inside local scope and having local visibility, but persisting from their declaration to the end of the program.

In all three cases, we only have control over the instantiation of objects, not over their destruction which is controlled automatically by the compiler.

Automatic object declaration

The objects which we instantiated in the previous chapter were automatic objects – declared inside the local scope of a pair of braces. Since braces delimit all block structures in C++ (functions, 'if' statements, loops etc.) then we can declare automatic objects within any of these. The following object is automatic because it is declared inside the body of 'main'. It will be visible anywhere inside 'main', and will persist until 'main' finishes:

```
void main( )
{
    BankAccount account1;
    ...
```

There is in fact a keyword ('auto') which may be used to precede automatic objects, but it serves no useful purpose since this is the default type of any object declared within a local scope.

External object declaration

An external object is declared outside the scope of any braces, for example:

```
BankAccount account1;
void main( )
{
    ...
```

This declaration of objects is all we are able to do outside of scope – we cannot for example call any methods of 'account1' except inside the braces of a function body. Why then might we wish to declare an external object, as opposed to one declared inside a scope? The main reason for doing this would be to make the object visible in other source files which are in the same system, since only externally declared objects can be referenced in other program modules. This is known as 'external linkage'.

External linkage

As noted above, external objects and variables are those declared outside the body of any function (i.e. not enclosed within braces). In a system containing several program modules, such objects may be declared as 'extern' in other modules if their visibility needs to extend beyond the file scope in which they are defined. For example, if the external object 'an_object' (of the class 'Object') is declared in one module, it must also be re-declared in other modules which reference the object, but the compiler has to be made aware that it is in fact the same object being referenced in all modules. This can be achieved with the 'extern' keyword (Fig. 6.4), and is known as 'external linkage' – linking the declaration of an object in the scope of one file with the declaration of the same object in separate files. The object must be declared in one module, and then declared as an 'external' object in all other modules which reference it. In Fig. 6.4, 'an_object' is declared in the source file of 'prog1' (in this case where the 'main' function is also defined), and declared as an external object in 'prog2' and 'prog3', allowing the object to be referenced in those files also.

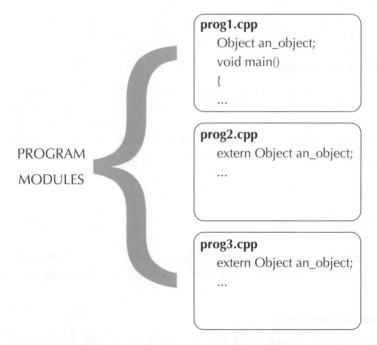

PROGRAM

MODULES

prog1.cpp
Object an_object;
void main()
{
...

prog2.cpp
extern Object an_object;
...

prog3.cpp
extern Object an_object;
...

Fig. 6.4: An external object declared in one module may be made visible in other modules via the 'extern' keyword.

Question 6.4   In what circumstances would we need to use the 'extern' keyword?

The 'extern' keyword is needed if the same object or item of data must be visible in more than one source file. Since it can only be declared once, it must be declared as 'extern' in all other modules.

Static object declaration

A static object is declared, like an automatic object, within a local scope. However, it is only initialised once, regardless of the number of times it falls in and out of scope. In the following function, a static object is contrasted with an automatic object. Both will come into scope when the function is executed, but the automatic object ('account1') will be created and destroyed each time. The static object ('account2') will be instantiated only once (the first time the function executes) and will persist until the end of the program:

```
void aFunction( )
{
    BankAccount account1;
    static BankAccount account2;
    ...
}
```

The advantage of a static object is that because it persists, it can retain its state even when it is not in scope. A static object cannot also be declared 'extern' – i.e. it can only be visible within one module (source file).

Instantiating objects of different types

The following program contrasts the instantiation of external, automatic and static objects (of a simple 'TrafficLight' class) and demonstrates their visibility and lifetimes:

```
/*
    LIGHTS.CPP   Program to demonstrate object scope
                 using a simple TrafficLight class
*/
#include <iostream.h>
// these constants are used to relate integer values to the
// colours of a simple two-colour traffic light
const int RED = 1;
const int GREEN = 2;
// the TrafficLight class definition
class TrafficLight
{
private:
// the integer attribute stores the colour as 1 or 2
    int colour;
public:
    TrafficLight( );
    void changeColour( );
    void showColour( );
};
// the constructor initialises 'colour' to RED (1)
TrafficLight::TrafficLight( )
{
    colour = RED;
}
// the 'changeColour' method changes the colour from RED to GREEN or vice versa
void TrafficLight::changeColour( )
{
    if(colour == RED)
    {
        colour = GREEN;
    }
    else
```

```
    {
        colour = RED;
    }
}
// the 'showColour' method displays the current colour as a text string
void TrafficLight::showColour( )
{
    if(colour == RED)
    {
        cout << "RED" << endl;
    }
    else
    {
        cout << "GREEN" << endl;
    }
}
// this is the declaration of an external object
TrafficLight external_light;
// 'main' demonstrates the scope of the various types of object
void main( )
{
// although the external object is declared outside of any function,
// it can only be sent messages from inside a function or method
    external_light.changeColour( );
    for(int i = 0; i < 2; i++)
    {
// display the loop counter
        cout << "times the loop has executed: " << i << endl;
// an automatic object is declared. It will be instantiated twice,
// each time the loop executes
        TrafficLight automatic_light;
// changeColour will turn the light from red (its initial state) to green
        automatic_light.changeColour( );
// a static object is declared. it will be instantiated
// once, the first time through the loop
        static TrafficLight static_light;
// changeColour will have a different effect each time through the loop,
// because the static object retains its state
        static_light.changeColour( );
// the output will show that the state of the static object has persisted, so
// that the second time through the loop it has changed back from green to red
        cout << "The automatic light is ";
        automatic_light.showColour( );
        cout << "The static light is ";
        static_light.showColour( );
    }
// the external light still retains its state until the end of the program
    cout << "The external light is ";
    external_light.showColour( );
}
```

If we run the program, we can see that the external object may be referenced inside the body of 'main'. We can also see that whilst a new automatic object is created and destroyed each time the loop executes, the static object is only created once, retaining its state as it falls in and out of scope. The output is:

times the loop has executed: 0
The automatic light is GREEN
The static light is GREEN
times the loop has executed: 1
The automatic light is GREEN
The static light is RED
The external light is GREEN

Dynamic object syntax

In this chapter we have discussed objects being dynamically created and destroyed as a program is running. We have previously looked at the syntax for the creation (instantiation) of objects by the constructor method, which reserves memory space for the new object and performs any user-defined initialisation processing (using parameters to the constructor if required).

The additional syntax required for handling dynamic objects falls into three areas:

1. *Creating and destroying dynamic objects* The 'new' and 'delete' operators, object pointers

2. *Calling the methods of dynamic objects* The 'arrow' operator (–>)

3. *Defining a destructor method* The 'tilde' (~) character

Controlling the lifetime of dynamic objects

External and static objects persist as long as the program in which they are declared, and are destroyed when it terminates. An automatic object is defined by its scope, and is destroyed when it passes out of scope. We have no other control over the lifetimes of these objects, which are destroyed by the compiler at the appropriate time. If we are to exercise more control over the lifetime of objects, we need to be able to destroy objects at will, as well as create them. In other words we need to be able to call the 'destructor' method as well as call the constructor.

The syntax which we have used to call the constructor in previous chapters is only applicable to the instantiation of named objects, and a different form of the constructor call has to be used to create unnamed, dynamic objects. We also need to be able to explicitly call the destructor, rather than simply allowing objects to fall out of scope. To handle the dynamic memory allocation of data, including objects, C++ includes the operators 'new' and 'delete'. These operators are used to dynamically call object constructors and destructors respectively via the use of pointers. It is important to note that they are operators, not keywords, so they can be 'overloaded' (given new meanings by the programmer – see Chapter 11).

Creating dynamic objects – the 'new' operator

C++ includes this special memory allocation operator ('new') for use in object constructors, though it may be used to allocate storage for variables of other types as well. The effect of 'new' is to allocate memory via a pointer of the required type. The syntax is based on the creation of a pointer, and then direction of that pointer to an area of memory which will contain an object.

The following example creates a pointer able to reference objects of class 'BankAccount':

```
BankAccount* account_pointer;
```

This pointer is now able to point to an object of the BankAccount class. The pointer can be directed to any 'BankAccount' instantiated using the 'new' operator (this assumes a constructor with no parameters):

```
account_pointer = new BankAccount;
```

Or the creation of the pointer and the constructor call can be put into a single line:

```
BankAccount* account_pointer = new BankAccount;
```

'account_pointer' is not the name of an object, but the name of a pointer to an object. It is able to point to any dynamic object of that class, and may be redirected at run-time to point to various dynamic instances of the BankAccount class. It is important to note that dynamic objects instantiated using 'new' do not have names – they simply occupy a memory space which may be referenced by a pointer. The following example shows the redirection of a object pointers – the assignment operator allows the second pointer to be directed to the same object as the first pointer:

```
#include "bankacct.h"
void main( )
{
// create two pointers of the class
    BankAccount* account_pointer1;
    BankAccount* account_pointer2;
// use one to instantiate a new object of the class
    account_pointer1 = new BankAccount;
// redirect the other pointer to point to the same object
    account_pointer2 = account_pointer1;
// etc...
```

At this point in the program, both pointers now reference the object, and either could be used to send messages to it (i.e. call its methods). Although pointers to dynamic objects may be redirected, it is, however, essential that a dynamic object is being referenced by at least one pointer at any one time, otherwise it will be lost and inaccessible.

Calling the methods of a dynamic object

In order to send a message to a dynamic object (i.e. to call a method), the pointer must be de-referenced before the object's public interface (methods) can be accessed. Therefore, instead of the dot operator, the de-referencing 'arrow' operator must be used for objects instantiated in this way:

```
pointer_name ->methodName( );
```

To contrast the two types of method call, consider the following example, which assumes the use of a non-parameterised constructor and the BankAccount class method 'deposit':

```
#include "bankacct.h"
void main( )
{
// first we create an automatic object...
    BankAccount account_1;
// then, in contrast, a dynamic account object..
    BankAccount* account_2 = new BankAccount;
// account_1 is an object, account_2 is a pointer to an object.
// they would call the same method differently as follows:
    account_1.deposit(100.00);
```

```
        account_2-> deposit(100.00);
    }
```

The following example demonstrates the redirection of pointers by calling the methods of referenced objects using the arrow operator:

```
#include "bankacct.h"
#include <iostream.h>
void main( )
{
// create two pointers of the class
    BankAccount* account_pointer1;
    BankAccount* account_pointer2;
// use one to instantiate a new object of the class
    account_pointer1 = new BankAccount;
    account_pointer1 -> setAccountNumber(20);
// redirect the other pointer to point to the same object
    account_pointer2 = account_pointer1;
// create a new object using the original pointer
    account_pointer1 = new BankAccount;
    account_pointer1 -> setAccountNumber(30);
    cout << "Account number referenced by pointer 1 is: " <<
    account_pointer1 -> getAccountNumber( ) << endl;
    cout << "Account number referenced by pointer 2 is: " << account_pointer2 ->
    getAccountNumber( ) << endl;
}
```

The output from this program is

Account number referenced by pointer 1 is: 30
Account number referenced by pointer 2 is: 20

There are many advantages to the instantiation of objects dynamically using pointers rather than creating them as named objects, such as the ability to destroy them while they are still in scope, and to handle disparate objects in 'container classes' whereby groups of objects can be handled in organised collections such as stacks, queues and lists. It also allows us to implement 'run time polymorphism' (see Chapter 14.) There are also potential problem areas, such as keeping track of which pointers are currently referencing an object, making sure that all objects have at least one pointer referencing them and taking responsibility for 'cleanup' when objects are no longer required.

Question 6.5 When we instantiate dynamic objects using 'new', why is the dot operator replaced by the arrow operator when calling object methods?

The dot operator is used to call the public methods of an object which has a unique name. In contrast, a dynamic object does not have a unique name, but is referenced by a pointer. The arrow operator serves both to 'dereference' the pointer and to call the appropriate method.

Destroying dynamic objects – the 'delete' operator

You may have noticed that in the previous two examples, although we created dynamic objects by calling the constructor with 'new', there was no explicit call to the destructor. If dynamic objects are allowed to fall out of scope in this way then there is no automatic destructor call (and therefore no execution of any code defined in the destructor), and no 'cleanup' of memory. Whilst this does not matter in these specific examples (since the objects only fall out of scope when the program terminates) it would matter very much in larger scale programs.

C++ includes the 'delete' operator to destroy objects which have been instantiated dynamically using 'new' – 'delete' explicitly calls the destructor, which destroys the object currently referenced by the pointer, as follows:

```
delete pointer_name;
```

Note that this destroys the object (by freeing its memory space), not the pointer. The pointer is still available to point to other objects of the class. The following example shows how a single pointer is used to create and then destroy two objects in turn:

```
#include "bankacct.h"
void main( )
{
// create a pointer of the BankAccount class
    BankAccount* account_pointer;
// use it to instantiate a new object of the class
    account_pointer = new BankAccount;
// destroy the object with 'delete'
    delete account_pointer;
// create a new object using the original pointer
    account_pointer = new BankAccount;
// destroy the object
    delete account_pointer;
}
```

Directing pointers to 'NULL'

It is worth noting that a pointer which is not directed to an object may point to any random area of memory, so how can we tell if it is referencing an object or not? This problem can be addressed by directing any pointers which are not currently referencing objects to 'NULL', which is equivalent to the base memory address (address 0). This is a constant declared in (among others) the standard header files 'stddef.h' and 'stdlib.h', and is automatically included in 'iostream.h'. Before referring to NULL in a program therefore we must include one of these files. Pointers of any type can be directed to NULL by using the assignment operator as follows:

```
#include <stddef.h>
void main( )
{
    int* x = NULL;
    char* text_string = NULL;
    BankAccount* account_pointer = NULL;
    // etc...
```

Explicit direction of pointers to NULL is a useful device for checking what a pointer is addressing, because we can use NULL in conditional statements, e.g:

```
if(account_pointer == NULL)
{
    cout << "no object referenced";
}
else
{
    cout << account_pointer -> getAccountHolder( );
}
```

It is good practice always to initialise pointers to NULL when they are declared. Not only does it allow us to check if a pointer is referencing a valid object, but using 'delete' with a pointer which is directed to NULL is guaranteed to be harmless. In contrast, calling 'delete' with an unused pointer referencing some random area of memory is asking for trouble!

Losing objects

As noted previously, if a pointer to an object created with the 'new' operator is allowed to pass out of scope without the 'delete' operator being used, then the destructor will not be called. The object will still exist but be 'lost' – since it has no pointer to reference it, it will be unreachable. In a large program, 'garbage' objects such as this may eventually cause memory management problems. It is up to the programmer to ensure that every object has at least one pointer referencing it any any given time. Of course, a single object may be referenced by many pointers. One potential pitfall to be aware of is that using the same pointer to instantiate many objects is perfectly acceptable, but every time 'new' is used, the pointer is redirected to a new area of memory. It does not automatically destroy any object which the pointer may already be referencing. Unless another pointer is already pointing to that object, it will be lost.

Defining a destructor method

In the above examples, we have been calling the default destructor which, like the default constructor, does not need to be defined by the programmer. Its sole function is to free the memory previously allocated to the deleted object. However, we may extend the destructor to perform other processes if we wish.

Like the constructor, the destructor has certain characteristics which mark it out from other methods.

1. It takes the same name as the class, preceded by the 'tilde' character (~)
2. It cannot take arguments
3. It cannot return a value

For a class called 'Queue' for example, both the constructor and the destructor would also be called 'Queue', but the name of the destructor would be preceded by the tilde, which would also appear in any out of line definition of the destructor method (this example omits all other methods and attributes):

```
class Queue
{
public:
    Queue();        // constructor prototype
    ~Queue();       // destructor prototype
};
// out of line destructor definition
Queue::~Queue
{
                    // body of destructor method...
}
```

It is a useful convention for the destructor (if defined) to follow the constructor (if defined) in the class declaration, followed by the other methods.

As with the constructor, if the default destructor (which frees the memory allocated to an object) is all that is required, there is no need to state it explicitly, but if some processing is required to take place when an object is destroyed, then the destructor has to be specified. Unlike a constructor, a destructor cannot take parameters and cannot therefore be 'overloaded', i.e. there can only ever be one destructor per class. In contrast (as we will see in Chapter 12) there may be more than one constructor for one class. As stated previously, the destructor method is invoked whenever an object is destroyed. This may be done by the compiler (in the case of external, static and automatic objects) or explicitly by the programmer (in the case of dynamic objects).

Destructor calls for different object types

External and static objects are destroyed when a program terminates, automatic objects are destroyed automatically by the compiler when they fall out of scope, and dynamic objects must be explicitly destroyed by the programmer. In the following example, various objects of a class called 'Object' are created and destroyed. Messages are output via the constructor and destructor to show the sequence of object creation and destruction:

```
#include <iostream.h>
#include <string.h>
class Object
{
private:
    char name[20];
public:
    Object(char* name_in);
    ~Object( );
};
Object::Object(char* name_in)
{
    strncpy(name, name_in, 19);
    name[19] = '\0';
    cout << "constructor called for " << name << endl;
}
Object::~Object( )
{
    cout << "destructor called for " << name << endl;
}
// this is the instantiation of an external object
// which will persist for the lifetime of the program
Object external_object("External Object");
void main( )
{
    cout << "Beginning of main" << endl;
    {
// an automatic object is instantiated which will be destroyed
// when it falls out of scope
        Object auto_object("Automatic Object");
// a static object is instantiated which will persist
// for the lifetime of the program
        static Object static_object("Static Object");
    }
// the automatic object will be destroyed here as it falls out of scope
// a dynamic object is instantiated...
```

```
    Object* object_pointer = new Object("Dynamic Object");
// and explicitly destroyed...
    delete object_pointer;
    cout << "End of main" << endl;
}
// the static and external objects will be destroyed here
```

Using braces without an associated control structure is unlikely to find a useful application, but it does serve to demonstrate that braces are the arbiter of the scope of any automatic object.

Running this program gives the following output:

Constructor called for External Object
Beginning of main
Constructor called for Automatic Object
Constructor called for Static Object
Destructor called for Automatic Object
Constructor called for Dynamic Object
Destructor called for Dynamic Object
End of main
Destructor called for Static Object
Destructor called for External Object

Question 6.6   What kind of object requires the destructor to be explicitly called by the 'delete' operator?

Dynamic objects must have their destructors called by the 'delete' operator. In fact, 'delete' cannot be used with any other type of object.

Dynamic object creation and destruction – an example

The following program uses the 'new' and 'delete' operators to dynamically call the constructor and destructor for 'Car' objects, representing them being put in and out of a garage. Points to note are the use of the pointer to dynamically create and destroy the car objects, the direction of the pointer to NULL when not referencing an object which allows us to test whether or not a car is in the garage at a particular time, and the 'cleanup' at the end – destroying any dynamic car object which exists when the program terminates.

The header file defines a simple 'Car' class with a single attribute.

```
/*
    CAR.H      definition of the 'Car' class
*/
#include <string.h>
class Car
{
private:
// the only attribute of a 'Car' is its colour
    char colour[10];
public:
    Car(char* colour_in);
    char* getColour();
};
```

```
// the constructor sets the colour using its parameter
Car::Car(char* colour_in)
{
    strncpy(colour, colour_in, 9);
    colour[9] = '\0';
}
// 'getColour' returns the colour
char* Car::getColour( )
{
    return colour;
}
```

The 'main' function creates and destroys 'Car' objects using a single pointer ('garage'):

```
/*
    CARMAIN.CPP
*/
#include "car.h"
#include <iostream.h>
void main( )
{
// declare and initialise a 'garage' (a pointer of the Car class)
    Car* garage = NULL;
// temporary stores for keyboard input
    int menu_choice = 0;
    char temp_colour[10];
// loop to put cars in and out of the garage
    while(menu_choice != 3)
    {
        cout << "Enter 1 to put car in garage, 2 to remove it, 3 to quit ";
        cin >> menu_choice;
// if user chooses to put a car in, and the garage is empty
        if(menu_choice == 1 && garage == NULL)
        {
            cout << "Enter colour of car ";
            cin >> temp_colour;
// instantiate a new 'Car' object via the pointer
            garage = new Car(temp_colour);
// display the colour of the car to get some run time feedback
            cout << "Colour is " << garage -> getColour( ) << endl;
        }
// if the user chooses to remove a car, and there is a car in the garage
        if(menu_choice == 2 && garage != NULL)
        {
// destroy the current object
            delete garage;
// reset the pointer to NULL
            garage = NULL;
            cout << "Car removed" << endl;
        }
    }
// cleanup! (not really necessary at the end of the program, but demonstrates the syntax)
    if(garage != NULL)
    {
        delete garage;
    }
}
```

Here is an example test run of the program:

> **Enter 1 to put car in garage, 2 to remove it, 3 to quit** 1
> **Enter colour of car** red
> **Colour is red**
> **Enter 1 to put car in garage, 2 to remove it, 3 to quit** 2
> **Car removed**
> **Enter 1 to put car in garage, 2 to remove it, 3 to quit** 1
> **Enter colour of car** blue
> **Colour is blue**
> **Enter 1 to put car in garage, 2 to remove it, 3 to quit** 3

The advantage of the 'new' and 'delete' operators is that the number of objects created during the run of a program need not be defined at compile time. However, to achieve the dynamic creation and destruction of objects we need some way of effectively managing the pointers that will reference the dynamic objects. One way of doing this is to put object pointers into arrays, as in this modified example of the garage program which declares an array of ten 'Car' pointers. Although the general structure of the program is similar to the previous example, we now have a choice of ten garages to put cars in and out of:

```
/*
    GARAGES.CPP   demonstrates how an array of pointers may be used
                  to manage a collection of dynamic objects
*/
#include "car.h"
#include <iostream.h>
void main( )
{
// declare and initialise an array of 'garages' (pointers of the Car class)
    Car* garages[10];
// set all the pointers to NULL. The variable 'i' declared here will be in
// scope for the rest of the program, and is used in all the 'for' loops
    for(int i = 0; i < 10; i++)
    {
        garages[i] = NULL;
    }
// temporary stores for keyboard input
    int menu_choice = 0;
    char temp_colour[10];
    int garage_number;
// loop to put cars in and out of garages
    while(menu_choice != 3)
    {
        cout << "Enter 1 to put car in garage, 2 to remove it, 3 to quit ";
        cin >> menu_choice;
// if user chooses to put a car in
        if(menu_choice == 1)
        {
            cout << "The following garage numbers are empty ";
            for(int i = 0; i < 10; i++)
            {
                if(garages[i] == NULL)
                {
// display 'i + 1' so that the first garage number is 1, not 0
```

```
                            cout << (i + 1) << ", ";
                    }
            }
            cout << endl << "Enter garage number for car to occupy ";
            cin >> garage_number;
// if the user has entered the number of an empty garage
            if(garages[garage_number - 1] == NULL)
            {
                    cout << "Enter colour of car ";
                    cin >> temp_colour;
// instantiate a new 'Car' object via the pointer
                    garages[garage_number - 1] = new Car(temp_colour);
                    cout << "Colour is " << garages[garage_number - 1] -> getColour( ) << endl;
            }
            else
            {
                    cout << "That garage is not empty" << endl;
            }
        }
// if the user chooses to remove a car
        if(menu_choice == 2)
        {
            cout << "The following garage numbers are occupied ";
            for(i = 0; i < 10; i++)
            {
                    if(garages[i] != NULL)
                    {
// display 'i + 1' so that the first garage number is 1, not 0
                            cout << (i + 1) << ", ";
                    }
            }
            cout << endl << "Enter garage number to empty ";
            cin >> garage_number;
// if the user has entered the number of an empty garage
            if(garages[garage_number - 1] != NULL)
            {
                    cout << garages[garage_number - 1] -> getColour( ) << " car removed" << endl;
// destroy the object
                    delete garages[garage_number - 1];
// reset the pointer to NULL
                    garages[garage_number - 1] = NULL;
            }
            else
            {
                    cout << "That garage is unoccupied" << endl;
            }
        }
    }
// cleanup! (not really necessary at the end of the program,
// but demonstrates the syntax)
    for(i = 0; i < 10; i++)
    {
        if(garages[i] != NULL)
        {
            delete garages[i];
        }
    }
}
```

This is an example test run that puts two cars in garages and removes one:

> *Enter 1 to put car in garage, 2 to remove it, 3 to quit 1*
> *The following garage numbers are empty 1, 2, 3, 4, 5, 6, 7, 8, 9, 10*
> *Enter garage number for car to occupy 4*
> *Enter colour of car orange*
> *Colour is orange*
> *Enter 1 to put car in garage, 2 to remove it, 3 to quit 1*
> *The following garage numbers are empty 1, 2, 3, 5, 6, 7, 8, 9, 10*
> *Enter garage number for car to occupy 9*
> *Enter colour of car purple*
> *Colour is purple*
> *Enter 1 to put car in garage, 2 to remove it, 3 to quit 2*
> *The following garage numbers are occupied 4, 9,*
> *Enter garage number to empty 4*
> *orange car removed*
> *Enter 1 to put car in garage, 2 to remove it, 3 to quit 3*

This is acceptable if there is a fixed maximum number of objects which may need to exist in the system. A better (though more complex) way is to use some kind of manually created linked list or tree of objects. The best way (and the usual object-oriented approach) is to use a 'container' object into which all other objects are put, and which provides the facilities for controlling creation, access and destruction of dynamically created objects. Containers come in many forms and are able to contain objects of single classes or mixed classes depending on requirements. The internal workings of a container do not have to be known to the application programmer, who only needs to know the methods which are available for an object of the container class. Whilst the internal implementation (encapsulated into the container class definition) may indeed be a list or a tree of some kind, we do not have to know about the internal implementation in order to use container objects of the class. This frees us from the responsibility of managing complex sets of pointers. Container class libraries are a common element in object-oriented languages since they have such general applications, and C++ is no exception, with the Standard Template Library (STL) providing a number of container types. Some examples of containers will be investigated in Chapter 15.

Summary of key points from this chapter

1. Objects may be external, static, automatic or dynamic. External objects have global visibility in at least one program module, and persist for the lifetime of the program. The lifetime and visibility of automatic objects is delimited by scope. Static objects also have their visibility delimited by scope, but persist from their instantiation to the end of the program.

2. Dynamic objects are needed when object identities, quantities and lifetimes cannot be predicted at compile time.

3. The destructor method is the corollary to the constructor – it frees the memory space of a destroyed object.

4. 'Cleanup' of memory space is not done automatically with dynamic objects – it is the programmer's responsibility to destroy redundant objects explicitly. C++ has no 'garbage collection' mechanisms to relieve us of this task.

5. A destructor (like the constructor) has the same name as its class, but is identified by the tilde (~) character. Destructors cannot take parameters or return values.

6. We can use 'new' and 'delete' to dynamically instantiate and destroy objects at run time.

7. Dynamic objects are instantiated using pointers of the class type.

8. Messages are sent to dynamic objects using the 'arrow' operator (->) which de-references the pointer.

9. Pointers may be redirected to different objects of the class or to NULL.

10. Sets of dynamic objects may be managed using data structures such as arrays, lists, trees etc. or by using 'container classes' provided by software vendors.

Exercises

1. The following code shows a 'BankAccount' object being created as an automatic object, and its methods being called. Rewrite the code so that the object is created with the 'new' operator, and destroyed by the 'delete' operator before it passes out of scope. Use the appropriate operator to call the methods:

```
#include <iostream.h>
#include "bankacct.h"
void main( )
{
    BankAccount an_account;
    an_account.setAccountNumber(100);
    cout << an_account.getAccountNumber( );
}
```

2. Pointers can be redirected to any object of their class. This means that we can use them to sort objects. Write a 'swap' function (similar to that described in Chapter 3) which is able to swap two pointers of the 'BankAccount' class. The simplest way to pass the pointers is by reference, though you could pass them by value and dereference them inside the function using the asterisk dereferencing operator.

3. One simple way of handling dynamic objects is to put them into an array. Declare an array which is able to act as a container for up to 20 'BankAccount' object pointers, and initialise them all to NULL. Remember that NULL is a standard constant which is declared in a number of header files including 'iostream.h'. Any pointer can be directed to NULL: e.g.

    a_pointer = NULL;

4. Using your array of 'BankAccount' pointers, create a program which allows the dynamic creation and destruction of bank accounts. Accounts should be opened and closed at will while the program is running, with unused or closed accounts defined by a NULL pointer.

7 The metaclass

Overview

This chapter discusses the concept of the metaclass, and how it differs from the class. The different roles of class attributes and methods as opposed to object attributes and methods are outlined, also the relationship between constructors/destructors and the metaclass. The term 'metadata' is introduced in the context of class definitions. A further use of the 'static' keyword is introduced as the mechanism for giving metaclass behaviour to the C++ class construct.

The role of the metaclass

It may seem inappropriate to discuss the metaclass in this book, since there is no direct implementation of it in C++. However, the metaclass concept encompasses some important aspects of the role of classes, and therefore provides a useful framework for discussion.

The use of 'meta' as a prefix has a wide range of meanings, including, simply, 'about'. The term 'metaclass' is similar in usage to 'metalanguage' – a language used to describe some other language (i.e. the metalanguage tells us about the language). There are also a number of terms where 'meta' is used to imply some form of abstraction (such as 'metaphysics'). From these interpretations we may conclude that the metaclass tells us about the class, and may be seen as an abstraction of the class in the same way that the class (as an 'abstract data type') is an abstraction of a set of objects.

The metaclass is often described as the 'class of a class', which may seem a rather odd expression, but it can be explained as follows.

The class, as we know, holds the attributes and methods which will apply to objects of the class – it is the class of the objects.

The metaclass holds the attributes and methods which will apply to the class itself – therefore it is the class of the class! (Fig. 7.1)

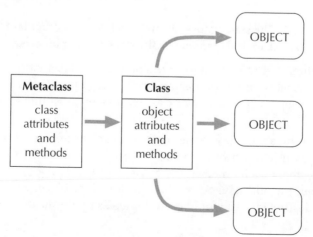

Fig. 7.1: The 'class' is the class (attributes and methods) of the objects. The 'metaclass' is the class of the class.

Every class has one (and only one) metaclass, and the metaclass contains those parts of a class which are not appropriate to be duplicated for every specific object.

The metaclass may seem a rather esoteric concept, but it is basically a repository for those parts of a class which must exist at the run time of a program, whether or not there are objects of the class in existence.

What kinds of things are appropriate to the class, but not to the objects of that class? Let us begin by reviewing the relationship between classes and objects.

Limitations of object attributes and methods

A class (as we have so far investigated it) acts as a kind of blueprint or skeleton for objects of the class. The class does not exist as a specific entity, but is the abstract representation of a user-defined data type. It defines the attributes which all objects in the class will contain to represent their state, and the methods which may be used to send messages to them.

When an object is created, its attributes will have state values, independent of the state values of other objects. For example, if we instantiate 3 'fuel tank' objects, all 3 will have an attribute of 'fuel level', but each object may have a different state value for that attribute (Fig. 7.2).

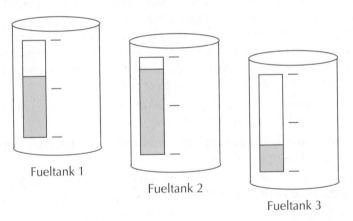

Fueltank 1

Fueltank 2

Fueltank 3

**Fig. 7.2: The state values of 'fuel level' for each 'fuel tank'
object are independent of the state of other objects.**

However, sometimes we may want to have a physical representation of something about a whole class of objects rather than about one object in particular. Suppose we want to know how many objects of a particular class exist at any one time – where do we record this information?

With what we know about classes and objects, we can see that there would be serious drawbacks to having an attribute in each object which stored this total. It would be possible to implement such an attribute, but to avoid each object containing a different total, that attribute would have to be changed for every object each time a new object was created or destroyed, and would be an unnecessary duplication of the same data.

Question 7.1 Where do the attributes defined by a class actually reside when a program is running?

Attribute values exist in objects of the class, whereas the class defines what the state attributes will be for any object. The state values only exist in the objects, and are not accessible directly by the class.

Class attributes

Consider a large system which keeps track of vehicles passing through a controlled traffic system, representing each vehicle as a dynamic object created when that vehicle enters the system and destroyed when it leaves. If we wanted to know at any one time how many vehicles were in the system, then each 'vehicle' object would have to have a constantly updated count of how many vehicles (objects) currently existed, every single time another vehicle entered or left the controlled traffic area. This is clearly an inappropriate approach – details about the whole class should not be the responsibility of specific objects.

What we need therefore is not an attribute duplicated for every object, but a single attribute for the whole class. It is true of course that we could have a simple counting variable outside the class itself, but this would undermine the principles of encapsulation by making the attribute simply a global variable, open to manipulation from outside the class. In order to encompass such attributes inside the class, we are able to make a distinction between 'object attributes' (those which are duplicated for each object) and 'class attributes' (those which exist only once for each class). The terms 'instance variable' and 'class variable' are sometimes used to mean the same thing as 'object attribute' and 'class attribute' respectively.

Given that we want to have class attributes as well as object attributes, but need to keep them encapsulated in the abstract data type, where do we put them? We cannot put them in the class, since, as we know, all attributes defined in the class are properties of individual objects. The answer, as you may have worked out by now, is to put them in the metaclass.

The metaclass, then, is a repository for class attributes which only have one instance, regardless of how many objects of the class exist. In the traffic system referred to above, the metaclass might for example hold an attribute called 'vehicle_count' (Fig. 7.3), which would be incremented each time a vehicle entered the system (and an object was instantiated) and decremented when a vehicle left (and the object was destroyed). Class attributes are in essence any data which tells us about the class as a whole rather than a specific object.

It is important to note that, despite conceptual differences, the class and metaclass are inextricably linked, and that class attributes are just as 'visible' to objects of the class as object attributes are. Indeed, in C++ the metaclass and the class are part of the same structure. However, object attributes belong to individual objects and are not accessible by the class.

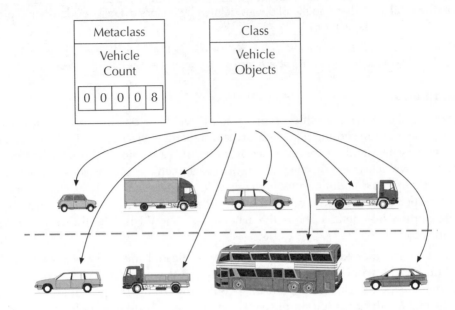

Fig. 7.3: The metaclass contains class attributes which have one instance per class, such as a count of instantiated objects.

Question 7.2   What is the difference between a class attribute (or 'class variable') and an object attribute (or 'instance variable'). Suggest one example of each from a class of 'customer account' objects.

A class attribute exists once for the whole class. An object attribute is duplicated for each object. i.e. for n objects there will be one class attribute but n object attributes. For 'customer account' objects, an example of an object attribute would be 'account balance', whereas 'number of accounts' would be a class attribute.

Class methods

Having established that the metaclass contains class attributes, let us examine the role of 'class methods'. Like class attributes, they also exist in the metaclass, and are as visible to objects as they are to the class.

Consider our example of a class attribute which keeps a count of how many objects exist in a 'live' system at any one time. If we wish to return the current state of this count, we will need some method to do so. It is perfectly acceptable to access class attributes with object methods – as we have stated there is no difference in visibility from an object's point of view between an object attribute and a class attribute. However, what happens if there are no objects instantiated when we want to return the count? If there are no objects currently in existence, then we have no mechanism by which to call the method which returns the count, so we cannot access the class attribute! This is where we need a class method, which is usable by the class directly, whether or not any objects of the class exist. Class methods, like class attributes, reside not in the class but in the metaclass (Fig. 7.4). Class methods may only access class attributes since object attributes can only be accessed by objects.

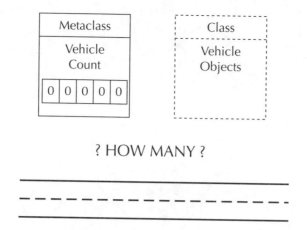

? HOW MANY ?

Fig. 7.4: When no objects of the class exist, class methods (residing in the metaclass) allow access to class attributes.

Another useful role of class methods is simply to group together similar functions that do not operate on specific objects. For example, a 'Date' class would have attributes such as 'day', 'month' and 'year', and a number of methods to manage individual date objects. However, there are also a number of processes related to dates that do not apply to particular date objects. These include functions like converting an integer in the range 1 to 7 to a string containing the day name, or converting a number to the name of the month. It is appropriate to attach such general date functions to a date class by making them class methods.

Question 7.3	The only example used so far of a class attribute is a 'population' counter – i.e. one which counts how many objects of a class there are at any one time. Can you suggest another type of attribute which might suitably reside in the metaclass?

Another common class attribute is one which has common data throughout the class, what we might term a 'class constant', such as a method which returns the name of the class to which objects belong. In a system which has objects of many classes, this is sometimes useful! Since the class name will be consistent for all objects in the class, putting this attribute in the metaclass avoids unnecessary duplication. (This is not the only answer to the question of course!)

Other components of the metaclass

Apart from class attributes and methods relating to them, what else can go in the metaclass? In practice, C++ makes no further distinction between parts of the class and the metaclass, and as we will see, subsumes both class and object attributes and methods into the 'class' body. However, there is a semantic distinction between ordinary methods and those which create and destroy objects – the constructor and the destructor. Both of these methods are said to reside in the metaclass. The reason for this is simply that since objects do not create objects (or where would the first object come from?), then the method which creates them cannot be an object method. Therefore the constructor belongs to the metaclass rather than the class. A similar argument follows for destructors; an object cannot destroy itself, it is destroyed by the permanent instantiation of the class – the metaclass (Fig. 7.5).

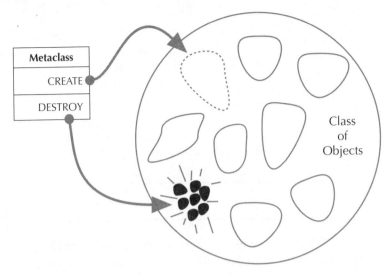

Fig. 7.5: Methods which create and destroy objects (constructors and destructors) are said to reside in the metaclass.

Question 7.4　What resides in the metaclass?

Class attributes, class methods, constructors and destructors.

Much of the above is a semantic distinction which has few practical implications in C++, and the concept of the metaclass is only a significant element in Smalltalk programming. Other object-oriented languages such as Eiffel [Meyer, 1988] have little time for it.

For our purposes, the main thing is to be clear about why some attributes and methods belong to the metaclass (and exist once for the whole class) and others belong to the class (and exist for every object in the class). C++ doesn't have a separate metaclass construct in its syntax, but it does make this important distinction.

Metadata

A similar and semantically related term is 'metadata'. The term applies to any data which describes other data, such as a class definition or perhaps a database table record structure. The term may be applied to real-world data too: 'There are real-world things that describe other real-world things. A part description in a catalog describes manufactured parts. A blueprint describes a house. An engineering drawing describes a system' [Rumbaugh et al, 1991 p.70]. A class, as we know, has a metaclass which describes the data associated with it, and the class in turn describes the data associated with objects. The metaclass, then, is the metadata for the class, which in turn is the metadata for the objects. The term 'meta-object' is therefore sometimes used to refer to the class definition (Fig. 7.6).

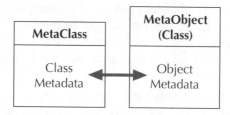

Figure 7.6: The metaclass provides 'metadata' about the class itself. The class in turn provides metadata about objects. It may therefore be seen as a 'metaobject'.

'Metadata' may also be taken to mean generic classes and methods ('templates' in C++) which are able to act on a range of types. This approach, known as 'genericity', will be discussed in Chapter 12.

Question 7.5   In what way can a class definition be seen as an example of 'metadata'?

Metadata is data which describes other data. Since the class describes the data present in objects, it is metadata for objects, or a 'meta-object'.

C++ syntax

The only new syntax needed to implement the metaclass concept in C++ is the 'static' keyword, which we introduced in the previous chapter. Indeed, the usage is similar, since in both contexts it is used to allow data to persist even when the variable or attribute which contains it is not in scope. Since there is no separate metaclass in the syntax, attributes and methods which belong to the metaclass are defined only by this keyword. We will see that class methods can be called not only by objects of the class but by the class itself using the scope resolution operator (::).

Any attribute or method which is appropriate to the metaclass must be preceded by the keyword 'static', so that for example an integer class attribute called 'total_objects' would be defined as follows:

```
static int total_objects;
```

An ordinary class method could be used to return the value of this attribute, but a class method to return it would also be preceded by the 'static' keyword (inline in this example):

```
static int returnTotalObjects()
{
    return total_objects;
}
```

This class method may be called at run time by using the name of the class with the scope resolution operator, as follows:

```
ClassName::returnTotalObjects();
```

However, note that the word 'static' is not used with constructors or destructors, even though they conceptually belong to the metaclass. Since they can only be class methods, there is no appropriate distinction to be made, and 'static' is not a usable prefix.

In the following example, the vehicle monitoring system is used, with the class partially implemented (there are many other possible attributes and methods we might wish to include in a realistic system). The main point of this example is to demonstrate the use of a class attribute ('vehicle_count') and its associated method ('getVehicleCount') to keep track of how many vehicle objects are instantiated at any one time. The constructor increments this count when a vehicle is created, and the destructor decrements it when a vehicle is destroyed.

Note that the 'static' keyword only appears inside the class. When a static method is defined outside the class, 'static' only precedes the prototype, and is not used with the out of line definition.

```
#include <string.h>   // for 'strncpy'
class Vehicle
{
private:
//   we may have a number of object attributes, for example:
     char registration_number[10];
//   this is a class (static) attribute
     static int vehicle_count;
public:
//   the constructor – semantically this is in the metaclass,
//   but it is never preceded by the static keyword since
//   it cannot be an object method
     Vehicle( );
//   The destructor
     ~Vehicle( );
//   object methods...
     void setRegistrationNumber(char* reg_no_in);
     char* getRegistrationNumber( );
//   and a class (static) method
     static int getVehicleCount( );
};
Vehicle::Vehicle( )
{
     vehicle_count++;
}
Vehicle::~Vehicle( )
{
     vehicle_count– –;
}
void Vehicle::setRegistrationNumber(char* reg_no_in)
{
     strncpy(registration_number, reg_no_in, 9);
     registration_number[9] = '\0';
}
char* Vehicle::getRegistrationNumber( )
{
     return registration_number;
}
//   note that the class method definition is not preceded with 'static'
int Vehicle::getVehicleCount( )
{
     return vehicle_count;
}
```

Reserving memory for class (static) attributes

There is something else we have to be aware of with metaclass (static) attributes, and it must be resolved before we can use a class which contains them in a program.

The role of the constructor is primarily to reserve memory for the new object it instantiates, though it may do other processing as well. The class itself does not occupy memory (apart from being part of the executable code) because it contains no data – it only provides the blueprint for the objects which themselves will contain state data. The metaclass therefore, since it is part of the class blueprint, does not automatically reserve any memory for itself, which raises the question, where in memory are class attributes stored?

In fact, the onus is on us to reserve storage for all class attributes in our programs. This must be done after the class has been declared but before the class is used in a program, using the scope resolution operator in a similar style to the linking of object methods to the class. For example, to reserve storage for the class attribute 'vehicle_count' used in the above example, and to initialise it to zero, we would do the following:

```
int Vehicle::vehicle_count = 0;
```

This must be done outside the class body, after the definition of the class itself, so that the compiler is aware of both the class and the attribute. When our programs become larger and we begin to separate class definitions (in header files) from their method definitions (in .CPP files), class attributes should be defined in the method definition file. Note that the keyword 'static' is not used when memory is reserved for a class attribute. If a numeric class attribute is to be initialised to zero, then this need not be stated, since it is the default. We could therefore reserve storage for 'vehicle_count' as follows, and it would initialise to zero:

```
int Vehicle::vehicle_count;
```

Example programs

When we create objects of the 'Vehicle' class, the constructor increments the vehicle count attribute by one. In the following example, the class method is used before any objects are instantiated to display the current number of objects on the screen (using 'cout'). Then an object of the class is instantiated, and the incremented count is displayed twice, once by the object and once by the class. Note that both the object and the class may be used to call a class method but of course it can only be called by an object if an object of the class has been instantiated:

```
#include <iostream.h>
#include "vehicle.h"
void main( )
{
    cout << "Count = " << Vehicle::getVehicleCount( ) << endl;
    Vehicle vehicle1;
    cout << "Count = " << vehicle1.getVehicleCount( ) << endl;
    cout << "Count = " << Vehicle::getVehicleCount( ) << endl;
}
```

The rather unexciting output from this program should be:

```
Count = 0
Count = 1
Count = 1
```

A better demonstration of our vehicle counter would be to create and destroy a number of dynamic objects while the program is running. In this example, dynamically instantiated vehicles are referenced by an array of pointers, which acts like a stack (i.e. the last vehicle created is the next to be destroyed). Although this is not very realistic, it does demonstrate the class attribute being continually updated. In practice, a more flexible data structure such as a linked list might be more appropriate, but the class attribute and method would be utilised in much the same way.

```cpp
#include <iostream.h>
#include "vehicle.h"
void main( )
{
    // create an array of 10 vehicle pointers and variables
    // for user input and array indexing
        Vehicle* vehicles[10];
        int user_input;
        int array_index = 0;
    // loop until user chooses 'quit'
        while(user_input != 3)
        {
            cout << "Enter 1 for arrival, 2 for departure, 3 to quit ";
            cin >> user_input;
    // instantiate a new vehicle, providing the array is not full
            if(user_input == 1 && array_index < 10)
            {
                    vehicles[array_index] = new Vehicle;
                    array_index++;
            }
    // destroy the last vehicle in the array, unless it is empty
            if(user_input == 2 && array_index > 0)
            {
                    array_index– –;
                    delete vehicles[array_index];
            }
    // display the current vehicle count
            cout << "Count = " << Vehicle::getVehicleCount() << endl;
        }
}
```

An example test run follows:

```
Enter 1 for arrival, 2 for departure, 3 to quit 1
Count = 1
Enter 1 for arrival, 2 for departure, 3 to quit 1
Count = 2
Enter 1 for arrival, 2 for departure, 3 to quit 2
Count = 1
Enter 1 for arrival, 2 for departure, 3 to quit 1
Count = 2
Enter 1 for arrival, 2 for departure, 3 to quit 2
Count = 1
Enter 1 for arrival, 2 for departure, 3 to quit 2
Count = 0
Enter 1 for arrival, 2 for departure, 3 to quit 1
Count = 1
```

Enter 1 for arrival, 2 for departure, 3 to quit 2
Count = 0
Enter 1 for arrival, 2 for departure, 3 to quit 3

Class attributes and methods give us a simple and safe way of maintaining information about a class, independent of the existence of any objects of that class. The various aspects of the metaclass demonstrated above (constructors, destructors, class attributes and methods) give us control over, and information about, classes of dynamic objects.

Summary of key concepts from this chapter

1. The metaclass holds class attributes and methods.

2. Metadata is data about other data.

3. Class (static) attributes exist once for the class, regardless of how many objects are instantiated. Object attributes are duplicated for every instance.

4. Class attributes are visible to both class methods and object methods.

5. Class (static) attributes do not automatically have memory space allocated – this has to be done explicitly outside the class.

6. Class methods may be called by both the class (using the scope resolution operator) and objects (using the dot operator).

7. Class methods may be called by the class even when no objects of the class exist.

Exercises

1. Create a class called 'Object', which includes a class method for returning the current number of objects in existence. The attribute which records this should be incremented each time a new object is instantiated. Include a class method which returns the name 'Object' when called. Remember to reserve memory for the class attributes outside the class body, where they may also be initialised.

2. Write a short program to test the 'Object' class. Create several instances of the class and check that the count and the name are being correctly returned.

3. Create a class called 'Banana' which includes a class attribute and method to count banana objects. Suggest some other counters and/or class constants that might usefully be Banana class attributes. Contrast these with suggestions for attributes which would be more appropriately defined for each banana.

4. Add a class attribute and associated class method to the 'BankAccount' class to keep a count of bank account objects.

8 Inheritance and classification hierarchies

Overview

This chapter explores inheritance, and how it allows object types to be organised into classification hierarchies. Examples of generalisation and specialisation of object classes are introduced, and the criteria for defining a class as 'a kind of' some other class. The way in which inheritance allows us to extend the functionality of existing classes is outlined, as is the role of abstract classes in a hierarchy. In C++, the 'protected' keyword is introduced as the mechanism for allowing classes to access inherited attributes, while public derivation is used to allow objects to access inherited methods.

What is inheritance?

Inheritance is one of the most powerful features of object-oriented programming. By organising classes into a 'classification hierarchy', it gives an extra dimension to the encapsulation of abstract data types because it enables classes (and therefore objects) to inherit attributes and methods from other classes. The inheriting class can then add extra attributes and/or methods of its own.

The terminology used for inheritance encompasses a number of terms (see table) which are largely interchangeable:

Derived Class or *Subclass* or *Child Class*	A class which inherits some of its attributes and methods from another class
Base Class or *Superclass* or *Parent Class*	A class from which another class inherits
Ancestor	A class's ancestors are those from which its own superclasses inherit
Descendant	A class's descendants are those which inherit from its subclasses

What then is the purpose of inheritance? Why should we wish to 'inherit' the attributes and methods of one class into another? There are two complementary roles of inheritance in an object-oriented application:

1. *Specialisation:*   Extending the functionality of an existing class
2. *Generalisation:*   Sharing commonality between two or more classes

These two are not by any means mutually exclusive, and we might say that they are 'top down' and 'bottom up' approaches respectively to exactly the same type of structure. In the 'top down' approach we are starting with a base class and deriving from it (specialising it). With the 'bottom up' approach, we start with separate classes and generalise a common base class from them. In practice the two tend to be part of the same iterative process of analysis and design, though the 'top down' specialisation approach is the one more associated with the re-use of existing classes.

The product of inheritance of this kind is known as a 'classification hierarchy' – a relationship between classes whereby one class can be said to be 'a kind of' (AKO) other class. As we traverse the hierarchy from top to bottom, we move from 'generalisation' to 'specialisation' of classes – adding functionality by extending what exists at each level of the hierarchy to create more specialised versions of the class. Fig. 8.1 shows a simple classification hierarchy of buildings. At the root of the hierarchy tree is a generalised 'base' class called 'Building', from which 'Commercial', 'Public' and 'Domestic' buildings inherit.

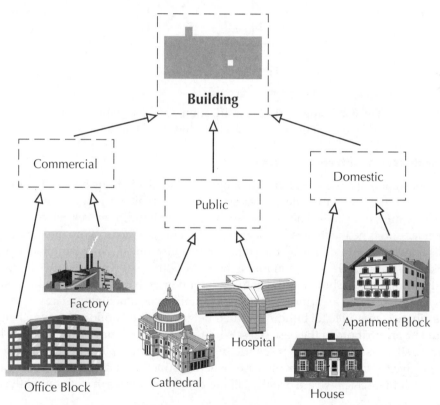

Fig. 8.1: A classification hierarchy of buildings. From top to bottom of the hierarchy we move from generalisation to specialisation.

'Commercial', 'Public' and 'Domestic' buildings are therefore all 'a kind of' building. 'Kinds of' commercial building might be factories, office blocks, hotels etc, 'kinds of' public buildings hospitals, cathedrals, libraries, stations and so on, whilst apartment blocks and houses are 'kinds of' domestic buildings. The use of arrows in this and other diagrams indicates an 'inherits from' relationship (i.e. derived classes point to their base classes), a notation from the Unified Modelling Language (UML).

'a kind of' or 'a part of'?

Each level of a classification hierarchy contains more specific types of class, each one of which must be 'a kind of' the class from which it inherits. It is important to make this distinction between a class which is 'a kind of' other class and one which is 'a part of' another class. For example, we would not make 'apartment' a derived class of 'apartment block', since it does not make sense to say 'an apartment is a kind of apartment block'. An apartment is not 'a kind of' apartment block but 'a part of' it (Fig. 8.2). Such 'part of' types will be discussed in the next chapter.

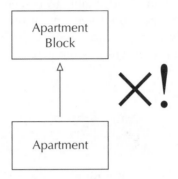

Fig. 8.2: Inappropriate classification – an apartment is not 'a kind of' apartment block, but 'a part of' one.

Different classes or different states?

When designing a class hierarchy, we have to make distinctions between objects which need to be represented by different classes, and those which belong to the same class but may have different states. This means analysing whether differences between objects are dependent on type (such as a house being different to a factory) or state (i.e. the differences may be accounted for by the state of attribute values). For example, we would be unlikely to create a classification hierarchy such as that shown in Fig. 8.3. Here, we can see that 'Building' is shown as the base class for both 'tall building' and 'short building'. This is not, however, an appropriate classification, since it actually relates to the state of an attribute common to all buildings – their height. Since all buildings have a height, this should be an attribute in the base class. While 'tall building' may be said to be 'a kind of' building, it does not in fact represent a distinct type. After all, what specific meanings can we give to 'short' and 'tall'? In cases where distinctions are not clear cut but seem to be on a 'sliding scale', we are usually talking about differences in state rather than differences in behaviour.

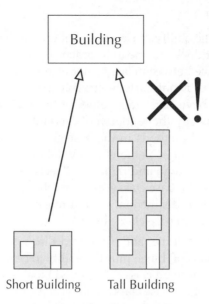

Fig. 8.3: Inappropriate classification. The distinction between tall and short buildings depends on state attribute.

Identifying differences in class

Given the above, how do we make distinctions between objects which differ in class, and those of a single class which simply differ in state? Such decisions sometimes depend on the context rather than any golden rule. For example, if we have a class called 'vehicle', how might we inherit from it into subclasses? Would we make a distinction in terms of separate classes between 'goods vehicle' and 'passenger vehicle', or simply include an attribute called 'load type' which may have 'goods' or 'passenger' as state values? The answer is, it depends on what distinctions there might be between goods and passenger vehicles in the context of the application. If the only distinction between them is their load type, and all other attributes and behaviours will be the same, then only an attribute is required. If, however, 'load type' is a key distinction between types which will lead to different sets of behaviours (perhaps at a border crossing where each type has a separate set of customs checks) then it may be appropriate to make a type distinction between 'goods' and 'passenger' vehicles. Even the short/tall building example would justify different classes if the context (e.g. fire regulations) requires different behaviours.

Question 8.1   Draw a classification hierarchy with the class 'tree' at the bottom. Justify your distinction between types, and suggest attributes which might be inherited by derived classes. Suggest a class which might be 'a part of' one of your classes (and therefore not part of the hierarchy).

An example might have 'tree' being the base class for 'deciduous' and 'evergreen', with perhaps 'fruit bearing' as a further subclass of 'deciduous'. A simple attribute might be 'height'. 'Branch' would be an example of 'a part of' a tree, rather than 'a kind of' tree.

What do objects inherit?

We have talked about the ability of classes to 'inherit' both attributes and methods from 'base classes', but what does this mean in practical terms? The key point is that we are talking about inheritance between classes, not objects. Remember that a class does not contain any state values, it only acts as the 'blueprint' to define what attributes each object in the class will have. The state values of those attributes are contained in individual objects. When we say that a 'derived' class inherits from a 'base' class, it means that all the attributes and methods in the base class are automatically included in the derived class. The derived class is therefore by default identical to a base class, but we can build on it to further extend and refine it. Objects of the derived class do not inherit anything from objects of the base class – as far as objects are concerned there is no hierarchy. This is an important distinction, since it means that derived class objects do not inherit any state values from base class objects.

Fig. 8.4 shows two classes, 'Line' and 'Coloured Line'. Because 'Coloured Line' has all the attributes and methods of 'Line', plus the ability to be drawn in different colours, it is appropriate to make it a derived class – 'Coloured Line' is a kind of 'Line'. Note how the attributes and methods of the base class are inherited – they will automatically be part of the derived class definition. 'Coloured Line' objects can use both their own and inherited methods, i.e. they will understand the messages 'draw' (an inherited method) and 'set colour' (a method specific to their own class). However, when we create objects of the two classes there is no reference between them in terms of attribute values. Objects have their own states, independent of other objects.

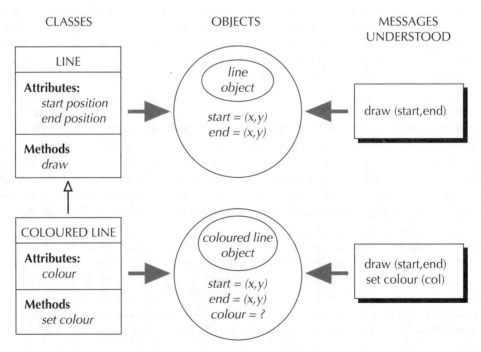

**Fig. 8.4: 'Coloured Line' is a derived class of 'Line'
and inherits its attributes and methods.**

Specialisation – extending functionality

The example above, whereby the functionality of 'Line' is extended to produced a 'Coloured Line' demonstrates a fundamental principle of object-orientation – creating a new class by extending (specialising) one which already exists. Much object-oriented software development centres on the re-use of existing software components (classes). However, the particular class which a programmer requires for a specific application may not be available. What object-orientation offers in such a circumstance is the ability to extend an existing class to meet new requirements, without having to affect the original class in any way. An abstract data type is both closed (in that it has an encapsulated, private part which cannot be affected by external manipulation) and open (in that it allows itself to be used as part of a larger software unit). The 'Line' class is unaffected by being the base class for 'Coloured Line'. The fact that the base class has been inherited from does not affect it nor the ability to create objects from it. We can also derive as many other classes from a single base class as we like, so we might for example have another class called 'Dotted Line' inheriting from 'Line' and adding the ability to draw itself as a row of dots (Fig. 8.5). (What happens if you also want a 'Coloured Dotted Line' class will be discussed in a later chapter on 'multiple inheritance').

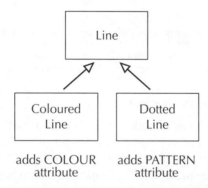

**Fig. 8.5: The 'Coloured Line' and 'Dotted Line' classes
extend the existing functionality of the 'Line' class.**

As another example of extending for re-use, we might take a situation where a programmer needs a class to represent a timing device, perhaps in some kind of automated production control system. Let us assume that s/he already has a class available (maybe s/he wrote it for another program, or maybe it comes from someone else's class library), and maybe this class is called 'Timer'. It no doubt has a number of methods to return the times between various start and stop states. It is just what the programmer needs, except that in the context of the new program, a new unit of time has to be applied. Perhaps the work schedules on the production line are divided into 10 minute intervals which need to be included in the methods of the timer. What can the programmer do? With object-orientation, it is a simple task for the programmer to 'inherit' all the existing functionality of the 'Timer' class into a new derived class (Perhaps 'Extended Timer') and add the extra required functionality (Fig. 8.6)

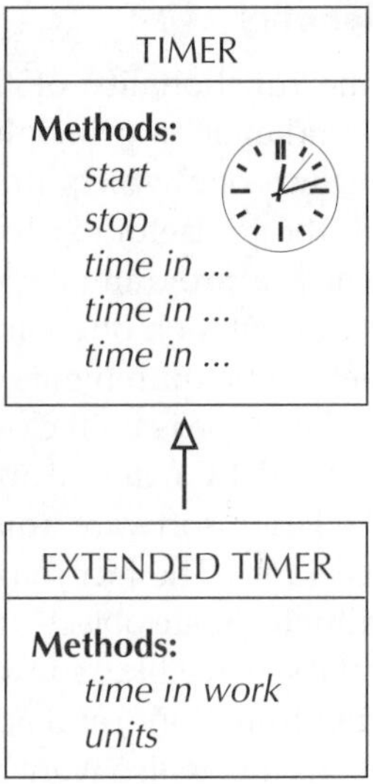

Fig. 8.6: The 'Extended Timer' class extends the functionality of the 'Timer' class.

Question 8.2   In what sense is an existing class both 'open' and 'closed'?

A class is 'open' in the sense that it is easily extensible through the mechanism of inheritance. However it is also 'closed' because inheritance does not compromise the integrity of the existing class.

Generalisation – sharing commonality

When analysing a particular application, we often find that some objects share some of their attributes and associated methods with other objects. This raises the question of the best way to partition a problem into abstract data types. Do we go for many closely defined classes, which may mean the duplication of some shared attributes and methods in different similar classes? Or do we have fewer classes to avoid duplication (putting similar types into one general class) which will mean objects sharing some irrelevant and redundant attributes and methods? To take an illustrative example of real world objects, if we are modelling the animals in a zoo, do we have a separate class for every animal (duplicating attributes such as 'legs' and 'colour') or do we have one giant 'animal' class which contains all possible animal attributes, not all of which would apply to any one animal (only the duck billed platypus has both 'fur' and 'beak' as attributes! – Fig. 8.7 on the following page). Inheritance allows us to resolve such problems because it enables the sharing of common elements between classes without having to repeat their definition for each separate class.

Fig. 8.7: Without inheritance, we face a choice between many overlapping classes or one over-general class.

Abstract classes

We will often find that some of the base classes in our hierarchies do not represent anything concrete enough to instantiate as objects in their own right. Such a class only exists as a 'holder' for the shared (inherited) attributes and methods of derived classes and is known as an 'abstract' class, because it does not represent a concrete type of object. From a previous example, a class such as 'Building' does not in itself represent anything other than a generalisation defining the shared characteristics of other classes. Such classes cannot usefully be used to instantiate objects without the further detail provided by the specialised derived class types. In a large classification hierarchy there may be many 'abstract classes' which represent only parts of objects and are not instantiated in their own right. To ensure that only appropriate classes are instantiated, it is possible when implementing the code to create 'pure' abstract classes which are explicitly declared as abstract and cannot be used to create objects.

In creating an 'animal' hierarchy, we will probably find several levels of abstraction. We might begin with a base class 'animal' which would contain the attributes and methods common to all animals. From this we might derive more specific (but still abstract) classes such as mammals and birds. Such a hierarchy could be very large and complex, but only the specific classes at the bottom of the hierarchy would represent concrete types of animal (Fig. 8.8). Indeed we would probably have to go further than this in practice, since 'pig' for example is really rather abstract – each breed is 'a kind of' pig with breed-specific behaviours.

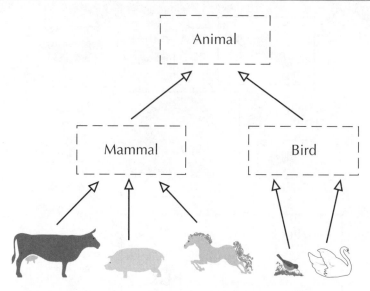

Fig. 8.8: Base classes are frequently 'abstract' – they are not specialised enough to represent objects without further detail.

It is not the case however that a base class is always abstract. For example, in an electronic circuit simulation program we might use the class 'Resistor' as the base class for a number of types of resistor – e.g. those which are affected by heat ('ThermoResistor') and light ('PhotoResistor'). However, the base class still represents an actual component, so it is perfectly reasonable to instantiate objects of type 'Resistor' as well as objects of the classes which inherit from it (Fig. 8.9).

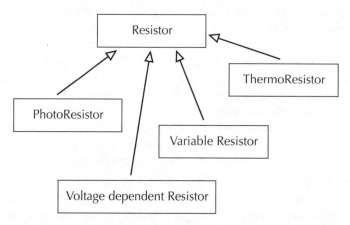

Fig. 8.9: Not all base classes are abstract. 'Resistor' is both a concrete class (able to be instantiated) and a base class for specialisations.

Question 8.3   How can inheritance reduce duplication of attributes and methods in different classes?

Inheritance allows attributes and methods common to two or more classes to be 'pooled' into a separate base class from which other derived classes may inherit. Such a base class may be 'abstract' – not intended for instantiation.

Creating a class hierarchy

As a practical example of sharing common attributes and methods using the generalisation approach to inheritance, we might look at an 'Employee' class appropriate to a company's personnel records. Employee attributes might include details which are applicable to all employees, such as their name and position. However, other attributes might only apply to certain members of staff, such as 'department number' (members of the board may not be in any particular department), or 'salary' (which would not apply to some workers who are hourly paid). Without inheritance we would have to either create completely separate classes for 'Director' and 'Hourly paid worker' (and all other types of employee, duplicating many attributes and methods for each class), or create a large general class of 'employee'. In the latter case we would have to include all possible attributes and methods of any employee in the class, meaning many would not be applicable to particular employee 'objects'. As with our 'animal' scenario, this leads to much redundancy and unnecessary complication.

Using inheritance, we can put all the attributes and methods which apply to all employees into a base class (an abstract 'employee'). We can then inherit from this class to create more specialised classes for various employee categories. These would add their own attributes and methods to those inherited from the employee class.

In this way the basic class can be built on to cater for all types of employee which exist now or may exist in the future. 'Employee' is an example of an 'abstract' class, since it would not be appropriate to instantiate objects from it. To represent the employees that exist in the real world, some further detail must be supplied by derived classes before useable objects can be instantiated.

Depending on the sets of shared attributes and methods identified in the system, a complex multi-level hierarchy might be developed such as that in Fig. 8.10.

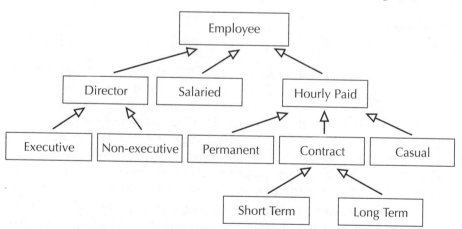

Fig. 8.10: Some classification hierarchies may be complex and multi-level.

Inheritance and object-orientation

Inheritance is a key feature of object-orientation, because it allows us to implement 'polymorphism', itself a mechanism for generalising the processes in our programs to work with disparate sets of objects. In addition to the benefits outlined above, whereby inheritance reduces duplication and allows existing classes to be reused, inheritance allows us to treat all objects in a class hierarchy in the same way. In later chapters we will see how this gives us control over large sets of dynamic objects.

C++ Syntax

Syntax introduced

The following new syntax is introduced to allow inheritance in C++

1. The colon operator (:) to denote inheritance
2. 'public' and 'private' derivation of object methods from a base class
3. The 'protected:' keyword to allow derived classes to access inherited attributes

Inheriting from a base class – the colon operator

We will begin with a very simple class which represents a single integer. The class definition below shows the class ('BaseClass') which has one attribute ('x') and two methods, 'setX' and 'getX'. This class does not on its own include any aspects of inheritance. The two methods are declared in-line as they are very short:

```
class BaseClass
{
private:
    int x;
public:
    void setX(int x_in)
    {
        x = x_in;
    }
    int getX()
    {
        return x;
    }
};
```

The following derived class definition ('DerivedClass', which will represent two integers) demonstrates the syntax used for inheritance. The derived class will inherit the attribute 'x' from the base class and have access to the public methods 'setX' and 'getX'. It also extends the functionality of 'BaseClass' by adding its own attribute ('y') and the methods 'setY' and 'getY'. These are exclusive to the derived class, and cannot be used by objects of the base class. In other words, objects of the base class contain one integer (the 'x' attribute) and its associated methods but objects of the derived class will contain two integers (the 'x' and 'y' attributes) and the methods associated with both.

In order for 'DerivedClass' to inherit from 'BaseClass', the colon operator follows the class name, and then the derivation type and the name of the class from which it inherits:

```
class derived_class_name : public/private base_class_name
```

Derivation – public or private?

The derivation type may be either 'public' or 'private'. Public derivation is the more usual type, and is used for the examples in this book. It allows objects of a derived class access to the public part (usually the methods) of the base class as well as its own class.

Private derivation is less common, and means that a derived class object may only use the methods defined in the derived class, not those inherited from the base class. However, derived class methods may utilise base class methods to implement their own behaviour.

In this example, 'DerivedClass' is derived publicly from 'BaseClass':

```
class DerivedClass : public BaseClass
{
private:
    int y;
public:
    void setY(int y_in)
    {
        y = y_in;
    }

    int getY()
    {
        return y;
    }
};
```

If we use these classes in a program, then we can instantiate objects of both classes. Objects of the base class will have the attributes and methods of the base class only, but derived class objects will have both these and the attributes and methods defined in the derived class, as follows:

```
#include <iostream.h>
void main()
{
// create an instance of each of the classes
    BaseClass base_object;
    DerivedClass derived_object;
// set the x attribute value for the base class object
    base_object.setX(7);
// set both the x and y attribute values for the derived class object
    derived_object.setX(12);
    derived_object.setY(1);
// display the value of the x attribute which both objects have
    cout << "base x = " << base_object.getX() << endl;
    cout << "derived x = " << derived_object.getX() << endl;
// display the value of the y attribute which only the derived class object
// has
    cout << "derived y = " << derived_object.getY() << endl;
}
```

The output from the program looks like this:

```
base x = 7
derived x = 12
derived y = 1
```

Accessing inherited attributes – the 'protected' keyword

The previous program demonstrated that an object of a derived class can use the public methods of a class from which it inherits. It cannot, however, access the private attributes of the base class, and neither can its methods. In other words, although an object of class 'DerivedClass' can use 'BaseClass' methods which access attribute 'x', its own methods cannot refer directly to that attribute. This can cause problems when we need to implement certain methods.

For example, let us assume that we wish to add a method to the derived class which will make the value of the 'x' attribute of an object equal to the value of the 'y' attribute. It might look like this:

```
void DerivedClass::xEqualsY()
{
        x = y;
}
```

This seems simple enough, since any object of the derived class will have both an 'x' attribute and a 'y' attribute. However, we are unable to legally express 'x = y' with our current base class, as 'x' is declared as 'private' and we are only allowed to access the public part of the base class.

To overcome this problem, we can replace the 'private' keyword in the base class with an alternative keyword: 'protected', allowing the derived class direct access to its own attribute 'x'. The 'protected' keyword thus allows derived classes access to attributes inherited from a base class, without making them public.

In the following example, the use of 'protected' attributes in the base class allows us to implement the derived class method 'xEqualsY'. Only the changes to the class definitions and program have been included – other elements would remain unchanged.

```
class BaseClass
{
// note the use of the 'protected' keyword. this allows methods in
// derived classes to refer to their own 'x' attribute by name
protected:
        int x;
...
class DerivedClass : public BaseClass
{
...
        void xEqualsY()
        {
            x = y;
        }
...
```

We can now use this method since it is able to access both the 'y' attribute and the inherited 'x' attribute, and update the 'x' attribute directly. If we add the following lines to our previous program, we can see that this is the case:

```
void main()
{
        ...
        derived_object.xEqualsY();
        cout << "derived x = " << derived_object.getX() << endl;
}
```

Running our revised program, we get the following output, showing the alteration of the 'x' attribute in the derived class object to equal the value of 'y':

```
base x = 7
derived x = 12
derived y = 1
derived x = 1
```

Question 8.4   What advantage do we have when inheriting from a class whose attributes are 'protected' rather than 'private', and what does 'public derivation' mean?

If we inherit from a class whose attributes are 'protected' then we can refer to these inherited attributes in methods of the derived class. Otherwise we only have access to the public part of the class. 'Public derivation' means that objects of the derived class can use public methods of the base class. 'Private derivation' means that only derived class methods can be used by derived class objects, i.e. inherited public methods become private in the derived class.

The 'employee' example

The previous example outlines the syntax required for inheritance, but does not provide very interesting or useful objects. We referred earlier to the use of inheritance in a set of classes representing company employees. In order to code a simplified example based on this scenario we will assume that the following attributes are appropriate to three different types of employee.

Director:	personnel ID, name, shareholding
Salaried Worker:	personnel ID, name, department number, annual salary
Hourly Paid Worker:	personnel ID, name, factory section, hourly rate

Although these attributes are a small subset of the likely data in a real employee records system, they should be enough to demonstrate the application of inheritance. In this case, we can use inheritance to avoid duplicating the shared attributes ('personnel ID', which we will assume to be an integer code number, and 'name') in separate classes by pooling the common attributes into an 'abstract' base class called 'employee'. We can then extend this class by inheriting from it into the three 'concrete' classes which add their own class-specific attributes (Fig. 8.11).

The UML notation used here to indicate inheritance is a rather more formalised version of the arrows seen in earlier figures. A single (outline) arrow head points to the base class, with lines joined to all derived classes. This version of the notation is typically seen in CASE tools. Note that the attribute 'employee count' is underlined to show that it is a class (static) attribute, likewise the 'get employee count' method.

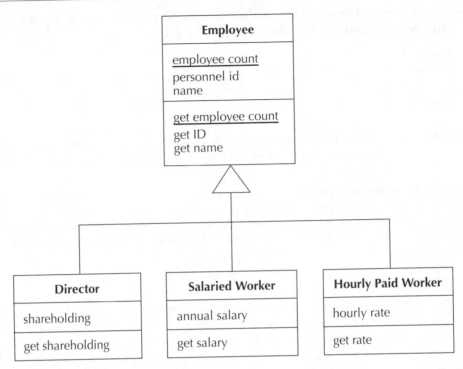

Fig. 8.11: Classification hierarchy for the 'employee' example using UML notation.

The organisation of the source code

In previous code examples we have typically dealt with one, or at most two, simple classes, and for the sake of simplicity we have seen header files containing both class and method definitions. This approach, whilst acceptable for very short examples, does not scale up to larger systems due to the potential for linker errors where header files are included in more than one other file, and can also lead to excessive compilation times. The following example (comprising as it does four classes) demands a more flexible structure. This involves separating the class definitions (in header files) from the definitions of their methods (in separate .CPP files), with the 'main' function in a separate file again. This means that each .CPP file must be separately compiled before the whole program is linked together. You will need to use the facilities of your particular compiler to link the .OBJ files generated by compilation into an executable, but modern development environments have simple tools to do this.

In this example, we still have a single header file, but the method definitions and 'main' appear in separate .CPP files. This is the header file:

```
/*
    EMPLOYEE.H    header file for the 'Employee' class and its derived classes,
                  'Director', 'Salaried' and 'HourlyPaid'
*/
// class 'Employee'
class Employee
{
protected:
    static int employee_count;
```

```
        int personnel_id;
        char name[30];
public:
        Employee();
        static int getEmployeeCount();
        int getID();
        char* getName();
};
// class 'Director', inherits from 'Employee'
class Director : public Employee
{
private:
        int shareholding;
public:
        Director();
        int getShareholding();
};
// class 'Salaried', inherits from 'Employee'
class Salaried : public Employee
{
private:
        float annual_salary;
public:
        Salaried();
        float getSalary();
};
// class 'HourlyPaid', inherits from 'Employee'
class HourlyPaid : public Employee
{
private:
        float hourly_rate;
public:
        HourlyPaid();
        float getRate();
};
// end of EMPLOYEE.H
```

Each of the three classes has a separate file containing the definitions of its methods. These are the methods for the 'Employee' class. Note that the reservation of memory for the class attribute takes place in the .CPP file, not in the header file:

```
/*
        EMPLOYEE.CPP  method definition for the 'Employee' class
*/
#include "employee.h"
#include <iostream.h>
// reserve memory for the class attribute 'employee_count' (defaults to zero)
int Employee::employee_count;
// 'Employee' constructor
Employee::Employee()
{
// increment the employee count
        employee_count++;
// generate a unique id from the employee count
        personnel_id = employee_count;
// get the name from the keyboard
        cout << "Enter employee name ";
        cin >> name;
```

```
}
// class method to return the employee count
int Employee::getEmployeeCount()
{
    return employee_count;
}
// selector method to return the personnel id
int Employee::getID()
{
    return personnel_id;
}
// selector method to return the employee's name
char* Employee::getName()
{
    return name;
}
// end of EMPLOYEE.CPP
```

This is the file containing the definitions of 'Director' methods.

```
/*
        DIRECTOR.CPP   method definitions for the Director class
*/
#include "employee.h"
#include <iostream.h>
// Director constructor
Director::Director()
{
// get the shareholding from the keyboard
    cout << "Enter shareholding for " << name << " ";
    cin >> shareholding;
}
// Director selector method
int Director::getShareholding()
{
    return shareholding;
}
// end of DIRECTOR.CPP
```

The salaried worker file:

```
/*
        SALARIED.CPP    method definitions for the 'Salaried' class
*/
#include "employee.h"
#include <iostream.h>
// Salaried constructor
Salaried::Salaried()
{
// get the annual salary from the keyboard
    cout << "Enter annual salary for " << name << " ";
    cin >> annual_salary;
}
// Salaried selector method
float Salaried::getSalary()
{
    return annual_salary;
}
// end of SALARIED.CPP
```

Finally, this is the file of method definitions for the 'HourlyPaid' class (perhaps it should be the 'Working' class?):

```
/*
     HOURLY.CPP method definitions for HourlyPaid class
*/
#include "employee.h"
#include <iostream.h>
// HourlyPaid constructor
HourlyPaid::HourlyPaid()
{
// get the hourly rate from the keyboard
    cout << "Enter hourly rate for " << name << " ";
    cin >> hourly_rate;
}
// HourlyPaid selector method
float HourlyPaid::getRate()
{
    return hourly_rate;
}
// end of HOURLY.CPP
```

The program in 'main' instantiates objects of the three derived classes to estimate the annual payments to the different categories of employee in dividends, salaries and wages.

```
/*
     EMPMAIN.CPP    Program to demonstrate objects of the derived classes of 'Employee'
*/
#include "employee.h"
#include <iostream.h>
void main()
{
// use constants to size the arrays used to contain employees
    const int DIRECTORS = 2;
    const int SALARIED = 2;
    const int HOURLY_PAID = 4;
// use constants to set a standard dividend and working hours in a year
    const float DIV_PER_SHARE = 3.50;
    const int HOURS_IN_YEAR = 40 * 52;
// create 3 arrays of the different employee types using the constants
// (very small to make the program easy to test). the constructors will be
// called here, asking for keyboard input
    cout << "Directors:" << endl;
    Director directors[DIRECTORS];
    cout << endl << "Salaried workers:" << endl;
    Salaried salaried[SALARIED];
    cout << endl << "Hourly paid workers:" << endl;
    HourlyPaid hourly_paid[HOURLY_PAID];
// 'i' is used as a loop index
    int i;
// initialise temporary stores
    float total_dividend = 0, total_salary = 0, total_wages = 0;
// iterate through the directors array, working out their total dividends
    for(i = 0; i < DIRECTORS; i++)
    {
        cout << "Processing director, ID number " << directors[i].getID() << endl;
        total_dividend += (directors[i].getShareholding() * DIV_PER_SHARE);
    }
```

```
// iterate through the salaried array, working out total salaries
    for(i = 0; i < SALARIED; i++)
    {
        cout << "Processing salaried worker, ID number " << salaried[i].getID() << endl;
        total_salary += salaried[i].getSalary();
    }
// iterate through the hourly paid array, working out total wages
    for(i = 0; i < HOURLY_PAID; i++)
    {
        cout << "Processing hourly paid worker, ID number " << hourly_paid[i].getID() << endl;
        total_wages += (hourly_paid[i].getRate() * HOURS_IN_YEAR);
    }
// display the results
    cout << endl << "Payments due to workforce of " << Employee::getEmployeeCount()
        << " are:" << endl;
    cout << endl << "Total dividends: £" << total_dividend << endl;
    cout << "Total salaries: £" << total_salary << endl;
    cout << "Total wages: £" << total_wages << endl;
}
```

Running the program causes the various constructors to take data from the keyboard before calculating and displaying the results. Notice that each time an object is instantiated, the base class constructor (in 'Employee', which asks for the employee's name) is called first, followed by the constructor for that particular derived class

Directors:
Enter employee name Black
Enter shareholding for Black 500
Enter employee name White
Enter shareholding for White 150
Salaried workers:
Enter employee name Brown
Enter annual salary for Brown 20000
Enter employee name Green
Enter annual salary for Green 15000
Hourly paid workers:
Enter employee name Scarlet
Enter hourly rate for Scarlet 5.00
Enter employee name Magenta
Enter hourly rate for Magenta 7.50
Enter employee name Mysteron
Enter hourly rate for Mysteron 3.50
Enter employee name Indestructible
Enter hourly rate for Indestructible 4.50
Processing director, ID number 1
Processing director, ID number 2
Processing salaried worker, ID number 3
Processing salaried worker, ID number 4
Processing hourly paid worker, ID number 5
Processing hourly paid worker, ID number 6
Processing hourly paid worker, ID number 7
Processing hourly paid worker, ID number 8

Payments due to workforce of 8 are:

Total dividends: £2275
Total salaries: £35000
Total wages: £42640

Inheriting constructors

A derived class will always inherit the constructor of the base class, as well as having its own. The base class constructor is always called first, followed by the derived class, and so on down the tree if there are several levels of inheritance. This is because a constructor reserves memory appropriate to the needs of its class – an inherited constructor reserves memory for inherited attributes. In the example program, the constructor will be called for each object in the array. In each case, the 'Employee' constructor is executed first, followed by the specific constructor for the derived class being instantiated. Note how the name of the employee which is captured by the base class constructor is used in the derived class constructors.

If the base class constructor takes no parameters, then this inheritance of the constructor is implicit, but if it does take parameters, then these must be stated explicitly in each derived class. This is because a derived class constructor looks for a base class constructor with a matching argument list. In the following example, we have a fragment of a 'Customer' class which takes the name of the customer as an argument to the constructor (use of the 'strncpy' function assumes inclusion of the 'string.h' header file.)

```
class Customer
{
private:
    char customer_name[30];
public:
    Customer(char* name_in);
};
Customer :: Customer(char* name_in)
{
    strncpy(customer_name, name_in, 29);
    customer_name[29] = '\0';
}
```

Any constructors of derived classes must also take this parameter. The following example shows the constructor prototype of a derived class called 'AccountCustomer':

```
class AccountCustomer : public Customer
{
private:
    int account_number;
public:
    AccountCustomer(char* name_in);
};
```

The constructor definition must explicitly refer to the names of the base class constructor and the inherited parameter as follows:

```
AccountCustomer::AccountCustomer(char* name_in) : Customer(name_in)
{
        // constructor body
}
```

Note that the 'AccountCustomer' constructor has to re-iterate the inherited constructor parameter ('name_in'), and that the colon operator is used to indicate inheritance (in a similar way to its use in the derived class definition). The type of the parameter (char* in this case) is not used in the base class parameter list, only its name.

Question 8.5   Why might we want to inherit the parameters to a constructor?

Since parameters to a constructor are usually to initialise the object on instantiation, and derived class objects inherit the attributes of base classes, it is reasonable to assume that any initialisation appropriate to a base class object is probably appropriate to a derived class object.

It is also possible to add to the parameter list when defining derived class constructors. If we wished to pass the account number as a parameter to the 'AccountCustomer' constructor, it could be added to the parameter list as follows:

```
// the prototype...
AccountCustomer(int number_in, char* name_in);
// and the constructor definition...
AccountCustomer::AccountCustomer(int number_in, char* name_in): Customer(name_in)
{
    account_number = number_in;
}
```

Instantiated objects of the derived class would use the inherited parameter for the base class constructor, and the additional parameter for their own constructor. Objects of the two classes might be instantiated as follows:

```
void main()
{
    Customer a_customer("Jane");
    AccountCustomer another_customer(1, "John");
    // etc...
}
```

Inheriting destructors

Derived classes also inherit the destructors of base classes, and these are called in the reverse order of the constructors. For example, if class B inherits from class A, and class C inherits from class B. then the sequence of constructor calls for an object of class C would be A, then B, then C. In contrast, its sequence of destructor calls would be C, then B, then A. Since destructors cannot take arguments, explicit inheritance of parameters is not an issue.

Summary of key points from this chapter

1. Inheritance allows classes to inherit attributes and methods from other classes in a classification hierarchy.

2. Inheritance allows specialisation (extending the functionality of an existing class) and generalisation (sharing commonality between two or more classes).

3. Inheritance is appropriate where a class can be said to be 'a kind of' other class.

4. Inheritance allows use to reuse existing classes to create new classes which are appropriate to a particular application – this is specialisation. Inheriting from a class does not affect the integrity of that class – objects of the original class may still be instantiated.

5. Generalisation assists us in removing redundancy and duplication among classes, and gives us a semantic organisation via the classification hierarchy.

6. Some base classes are abstract – they are not specific enough to be instantiated as objects, but act as holders for common attributes and methods of derived classes.

7. In C++, the 'protected' keyword allows the methods of a derived class access to its inherited attributes.

8. Base class constructor methods are automatically called by the constructors of derived classes, but argument lists must be compatible.

9. Destructors are called in the reverse order of constructors.

Exercises

1. Here are two class definitions (attributes only). Using generalisation, put them into an appropriate classification hierarchy so that they both inherit from a common base class.

   Add appropriate methods.

   ```
   class Book                      class Magazine
   {                               {
   private:                        private:
       char title[30];                 char title[30];
       char author[30];                char editor[30];
       char publisher[30];             char publisher[30];
       char ISBN[20];              };
   };
   ```

2. Assuming a need to write a library application, specialise from the 'Book' class to create a 'LibraryBook' class. This needs additional behaviours such as being lent, returned and reserved.

3. In Chapter 5, we added a user-defined constructor to the 'BankAccount' class, with a float parameter to set the initial balance. The constructor prototype looked like this (removing the default value which we also described):

   ```
   BankAccount(float start_balance);
   ```

   This exercise assumes that you have a BankAccount class with this user-defined constructor.

   Create two new classes by inheriting from the existing BankAccount class. They are to be called 'SavingsAccount' and 'ChequeAccount'. Modify the 'BankAccount' class header file to contain the two derived class definitions outlined below.

   SavingsAccount

   Create a derived class of BankAccount called 'SavingsAccount' which adds the attributes of 'withdrawal_notice' (the number of days notice needed before money can be withdrawn) and 'interest_rate'. Methods should be defined to allow the values of these attributes to be returned.

   ChequeAccount

   Create another derived class of BankAccount called 'ChequeAccount' which adds the attribute of 'allowed_overdraft' (how far the account may be overdrawn without incurring a penalty). A method should be included to return its value.

In both cases, the initial values of the additional attributes should be set using parameters to the constructor. Explicitly inherit the ('start_balance') parameter from the base class constructor in the definitions of both of the derived class constructors.

Demonstrate the use of the derived classes as follows:

(a) Instantiate an object of the 'SavingsAccount' class called 'savings_account1'. Using the parameters to the constructor, set the start balance to £100.00, the withdrawal notice to 30 days and the interest rate to 3.5%. Using appropriate methods, set the account number to 1 and the holder to 'Solent University'.

(b) Instantiate an object of the 'ChequeAccount' class called 'cheque_account_1'. Using the parameters to the constructor, set the start balance to £0.00 and the overdraft limit to £500. Using appropriate methods, set the account number to 2 and the holder to 'SIHE'.

(c) Display all the details of both 'savings_account1' and 'cheque_account1'.

9 Associations and aggregations

Overview

This chapter introduces associations (links between objects) and aggregations (objects that are composed wholly or partly of other objects.) Types of aggregation are described and contrasted with inheritance and container classes. Some characteristics of aggregation are explored along with the different forms of C++ syntax required to implement association and aggregation.

Associations

In previous chapters we have seen a number of example programs that show objects of a single class being 'sent messages' (i.e. having their methods called) within a 'main' function. This, however, does not address the issue of how objects communicate with each other.

In any object-oriented system, we would expect to have many objects of different classes sending each other messages as the program runs. In order to do this, we have to provide links between objects which allow them to communicate. At the level of class design, these links are known as 'associations', and come in three main types:

1. a one to one association, where one object of a class has a link to one other object of a class

2. a one to many association, where one object of a class has links with many objects of a particular class

3. a many to many association, where many objects of one class have links with many objects of a particular class.

Associations more frequently occur between objects of different classes, but also occur between different objects of the same class. A 'BankBranch' object for example may have an association with 'BankAccount' objects, but perhaps another association with other 'BankBranch' objects.

Design representation of associations

In most object-oriented design notations, associations are indicated by some kind of line between the classes. In the UML, a simple line indicates a one to one association, with modifiers to indicate other types. Associations should be given a text label to describe the relationship between the objects, and a small arrow head can be added to the label to indicate the direction of the relationship (Fig. 9.1).

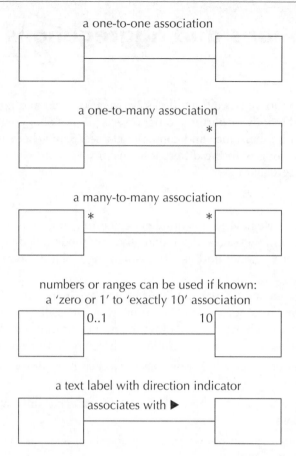

Fig. 9.1: The UML notation for associations

The direction of message passing

When associations are modelled in a design, they are generally assumed to be bidirectional; that is, messages can pass in both directions between the objects. However, it is frequently the case in an implementation that there is no need for a link in both directions. As an analogy, consider a light switch and a light bulb. The switch controls the bulb, but the bulb has no control over the switch. Similarly, we often find cases in software when one object needs to send messages to (and get responses from) another object, but there is never any need for the other object to initiate messages itself. Like the light bulb, it is a 'dumb' object (it never asks any questions, it only obeys orders!) In contrast, a bidirectional link, in this case between objects of the same class, might be two 'Person' objects who marry. One would hope that, unlike the light bulb and switch relationship, messages pass in both directions. Fig. 9.2 shows these relationships in UML notation; a link in one direction can be shown by adding an arrow head to the association line. As well a labels (e.g. 'married to'), associations can have 'role names' (e.g. 'husband' and 'wife') attached to the appropriate ends of the line.

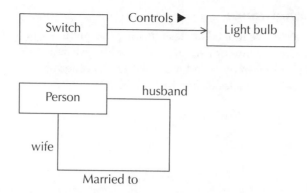

Fig. 9.2: Associations may need to be implemented
in one direction only or in both directions.

Booch uses the term 'actor' for an object that acts upon other objects, 'server' for an object that is only acted upon, and 'agent' for an object that does both [Booch, 1994 p.99]. Many object-oriented systems will have a single actor (or 'controller') object which manages the system interface and forwards messages to various agents and servers.

Associations in applications

The examples above do not have much direct relevance to programming. A more useful approach might be to look at possible associations in a given application, such as a class timetabling system that allows lecturers to be allocated to course modules that are in turn assigned to classrooms. In this application we might find a number of 'one to many' associations (where one object has links with a number of other objects), such as the relationship between a lecturer and the course modules s/he teaches. Assuming there is no double staffing, one lecturer teaches many modules, but each module has only one lecturer. This kind of link would probably be implemented in both directions, so that our timetabling system might allow us to query the lecturer object for its associated modules, but also to query a given module for its associated lecturer object. We might also discover many to many associations like an association between modules and rooms; one module may be taught in many classrooms, and each classroom plays host to many different modules. A one to one association might exist between a lecturer and his/her teaching contract, so that each lecturer has one contract (perhaps detailing their individual teaching, research, consultancy and administration hours) and each contract applies to an individual lecturer. All these associations are shown in Fig. 9.3.

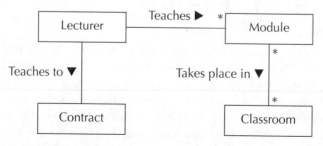

Fig 9.3: The associations in the timetable example.

Aggregation v. inheritance

In the previous chapter we looked at classification hierarchies where classes inherit from other classes in order to share or extend functionality. We saw how objects are classified by their position in a hierarchy as 'a kind of' ('AKO') other object, e.g. an estate car is a kind of car which is in turn a kind of vehicle (Fig. 9.4).

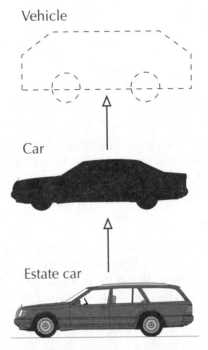

Vehicle

Car

Estate car

Fig. 9.4: In classification hierarchies, each level is a kind of ('AKO') the level above.

Some associations also form hierarchies, but they are very different from inheritance. These special types of association are described by various terms, including the following:

- Aggregation
- Composition
- Part-Whole
- A Part Of (APO)
- Has-a
- Containment

In this type of hierarchy, classes do not inherit from other classes, but are composed of other classes. What this means in practice is that an object of one class may have its representation defined by other objects rather than by the attributes (simple data types and data structures) we have used so far. The enclosing class does not inherit any attributes or methods from these other included classes, so it is not a classification relationship. Rather, it is a relationship (an association) between objects. An object of the enclosing class is composed wholly or partly of objects of other classes. Any object that has this characteristic is known as an 'aggregation'.

Question 9.1   Suggest an example of an 'aggregation' and its component parts.

There are many possible answers here, for example: a computer whose components are screen, keyboard, mouse and processor box, or a flower whose components are stem, leaves, head and petals.

Containment v. containers

A commonly used term for this type of class relationship is 'containment', but there is a semantic difference between this term and the idea of a 'container' which also may contain objects of other classes, but does not depend on them for its representation. Therefore, although they can both be seen as types of aggregation, we should draw an important distinction between containment and containers, as follows:

1. In 'containment', a composition hierarchy defines how an object is composed of other objects in a fixed relationship. The aggregate object cannot exist without its components, which will probably be of a fixed and stable number, or at least will vary within a fixed set of possibilities.

2. A 'container' is an object (of a 'container class') which is able to contain other objects. The existence of the container is independent of whether it actually contains any objects at a particular time, and contained objects will probably be a dynamic and possibly heterogenous collection (i.e. the objects contained may be of many different classes).

Fig. 9.5 contrasts containment and a container using the example of a car. One end of a car (usually the front) comprises the engine compartment (with its integral component, the engine), and the other is storage space for luggage (the boot). The relationship between the car and the engine is one of containment; the engine is an essential component of the car. A car object which does not consist partly of an engine object is not a car, since it is unable to exhibit the behaviour expected of one. In contrast, the integrity of the car as an object is not affected by what is in the boot, which is simply a 'container', existing independently of its contents.

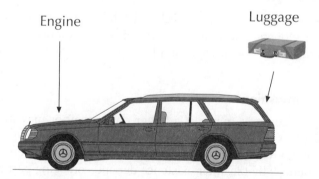

Engine

Luggage

Fig. 9.5: The car and its engine have a containment relationship. In contrast, the boot is a container, existing regardless of what it contains.

It may contain a suitcase, a tool kit, 500 bananas or nothing at all, but this does not affect the car object. Container classes will be discussed in chapter fifteen. In practice, there is a range of possibilities between these two extremes of fixed components and flexible containers where the idea of aggregation may be applied. Indeed, we should also make a distinction between 'aggregation' and 'composition' in the UML, where composition is seen as a stronger form of aggregation. Although it is not necessarily easy to draw the line between them, the examples that follow may help.

Question 9.2 What is the key difference between 'containment' and a 'container'?

'Containment' implies that the aggregate object is made up of components; without the components the object could not exist. 'Containers' exist independently of their contents; they are simply able to contain other objects.

Composition: 'parts explosions'

A common analogy for composition is the 'exploded parts' diagram, or 'parts explosion' commonly used for pieces of machinery. The whole component (a clock for example) is shown in a diagram of 'exploded' parts, so that we see all the different internal discrete objects that compose the whole discrete object. In UML notation, this is represented by a solid diamond on the class of the object that is made up of the components (Fig. 9.6).

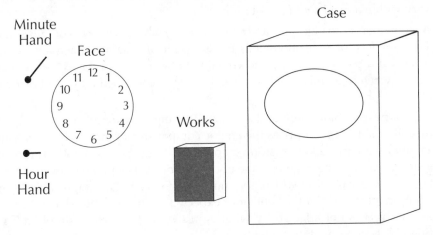

Fig. 9.6: A 'parts explosion' shows the discrete components of an aggregate object.

These compositions of objects may well exist in several layers, so that objects are composed of component objects which themselves are composed of other objects. The 'works' component of the clock, for example, would itself be composed of a collection of smaller parts.

Aggregation or composition?

The objects which comprise parts of a larger object may or may not be 'visible' from outside the object. Composition implies that the internal objects are not seen from outside, whereas aggregated objects may be directly accessed. Some components have a 'lifetime dependency'; that is, their existence depends on being part of the aggregation, while others might have an existence independent of the larger object. Aggregations suggest that objects have some visibility or existence outside the hierarchy, such as a three piece suite where the objects are part of an aggregation, but can also be seen to have a separate existence. The distinction is not that important, but is drawn differently in the UML, with a hollow rather than a filled diamond. Perhaps we can make a distinction in the case of the clock between composition (the components in Fig. 9.6) and aggregation in terms of the clock battery. The battery is a component, but it has a lifetime and visibility independent of the rest of the clock (Fig. 9.7).

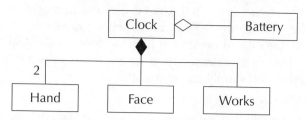

Fig. 9.7 UML notation uses a solid diamond to indicate a composition relationship, but an outline diamond for more flexible aggregations.

Abstraction and aggregation

Aggregation is primarily a relationship between objects, rather than a relationship between classes. When we discussed classification hierarchies, we saw that many of the classes that served as base classes were abstract; they did not represent objects that could usefully be used in a program. In contrast, the elements of a composition hierarchy must be objects at run time in order to create an object of the aggregate class. For example, to make a 'Door' object we must also instantiate objects of classes lock, handle, hinge, letterbox etc, but we do not need to instantiate an object of class 'Vehicle' in order to make a 'Bus'.

Properties of aggregations

Rumbaugh [Rumbaugh et al, 1991 p.37] notes that there are certain properties associated with the objects in an aggregation that make them different from normal associations. Taking a graphics drawing program as an example, we can make certain distinctions (Fig. 9.8):

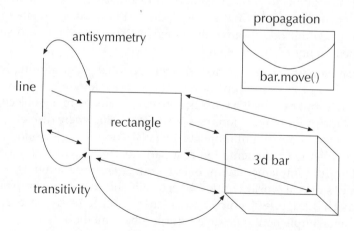

Fig. 9.8: Properties of an aggregation are founded on the relationships between composing objects.

Transitivity   if A is a part of B and B is part of C, then A is part of C e.g. If 'line' is part of 'rectangle', then 'line' is also part of '3D bar'.

Antisymmetry   if A is part of B, then B is not part of A e.g. If 'line' is part of 'rectangle', then 'rectangle' cannot be part of 'line'. This makes the aggregation relationship more 'unequal' than simple associations.

Propagation   The environment of the part is the same as that of the assembly e.g. What happens to the 3D bar affects what happens to the components. If '3D bar' is moved or deleted then so is 'rectangle' and 'line'. Again, this is different to an association where the objects are independent of each other and simply communicate.

Aggregation can be fixed, variable or recursive:

Fixed   The particular numbers and types of the component parts are predefined. e.g. a rectangle is composed of four right angled lines enclosing an area.

Variable   The number of levels of aggregation is fixed, but the number of parts may vary. In a graphical user interface, a 'window' object may consist of components from a given set of possibilities (title bar, control buttons, scroll bars etc) but the ones used are not always the same.

Recursive   The object contains components of its own type, like a Russian doll (each one containing a smaller doll). An object of the 'graphics object' class in a computer aided design program may be composed of other objects of the same class (and so ad infinitum!)

Question 9.3   Is a locomotive a fixed or variable aggregation? What about a train?

A locomotive is an example of a fixed aggregation because it is composed of a fixed set of components. A train is a variable aggregation; it will consist of at least one locomotive and some (zero or more) wagons, but the numbers of these may vary widely.

Partial aggregations

To say that objects are sometimes composed of other objects is clearly the case when looking at concrete examples in the real world, but how does it relate to programming, particularly when our objects are often much less concrete than hardware components such as 'wheel', 'engine', 'mouse' etc?

The most common use of aggregation in object-oriented programming is a partial application, whereby one class uses one or more objects of another class in order to represent its internal state, but may well have other attributes which are not objects. In many cases these are not the pure compositions of a parts explosion, where discrete physical components create a larger object, but more abstract collections of objects and attributes which together provide the implementation of a particular class. Often, the contained objects are artifacts of the implementation, objects which are programming tools rather than representations of real world entities. Booch calls this a 'uses for implementation' relationship [Booch, 1994, p.180] which is to say that one class uses objects of other classes in order to provide implementation details for its object methods.

Delegation

Rumbaugh [1991, p 284] makes the distinction between aggregation and 'delegation' whereby the use of objects as implementation components for other objects may involve using only part of their interface. This means that an object which is used in an aggregation may not be fully utilised by the object that contains it, because only part of its behaviour might be appropriate in a particular context. This is particularly useful in situations where we might otherwise consider using inheritance, but do not want to inherit all the behaviours of a class. We may want to implement some kind of business system including account customers, and have an 'AccountCustomer' class already available. However, it might contain methods which are inappropriate for our new application because our new class is not truly 'a kind of' the existing class, but merely similar. Perhaps the existing class allows a customer to have more than one account number, and we might not want this feature in our system. If we inherit from the existing class then we will have to inherit all the attributes and methods into our new class, including behaviours which are inappropriate. Delegation gives us an alternative approach, namely that we can delegate some of the behaviour of our new class to an object of the existing class without inheriting from it. In this way we use the containment of the object to mask any behaviours we do not wish to use. Our new customer class can contain an object of the 'AccountCustomer' class and use those behaviours which are appropriate to implement its own behaviours.

Question 9.4   In the last chapter, we said that 'private derivation' meant that an object of a derived class could not directly use methods inherited from a base class, but that its own methods could use these inherited methods to provide their own implementation. What do you see as the difference between this and 'delegation' which means that a class uses an object of another class to implement some of its behaviours?

In practice, using a class to implement another class's behaviour or using an object to do the same thing are different means to the same end. However, it is perhaps semantically preferable to use delegation, because private derivation is using inheritance where in fact the derived class is probably not 'a kind of' the base class. This may be the case when we are not using all of the base class's characteristics.

Examples of aggregation

As an example of aggregation of both real world components and implementation constructs, we might wish to create a class to represent objects of a 'superstore' type, in order perhaps to simulate waiting times for customers at the checkouts. We might model the class using a collection of simple data types as attributes, but for a realistic application this might be rather complex. It may be preferable to model certain components of the store as objects, so that we might include 'checkout' objects, 'customer queue' objects etc. In turn some of these objects may be aggregations of other objects – the 'checkout' may comprise a bar code reader, a till and a weighing scale for example.

We may also wish to use other objects as implementation details in order to create appropriate data structures. For example, we might create objects to contain randomly generated sets of groceries so that we can implement 'customer' objects. Whether these are implemented as arrays, stacks, queues etc is not really important. Objects of any of these classes might be instantiated to provide the required behaviour.

We have the flexibility to model some aspects of a class as other objects, and others as simple attributes. A 'Till' object may contain for example another object of class 'ChequePrinter', but perhaps also a simple float attribute to maintain the current level of cash it contains.

Not all aggregations are fixed over time, so that an object which acts as a component part of another object may not always be present. For example, some checkouts may not have a scale present at a particular time. However, to model the two possibilities as separate classes is problematic, because an object cannot change its class. Were we to have two classes of 'Checkout with Scale' and 'Checkout Without Scale', objects created as instances of one class could never belong to the other class. An aggregation is much more flexible than this because it allows a particular checkout to either have a scale or not at any time, and to change this state dynamically. Such variations in composition can be dealt with in the implementation. In C++ we would use a pointer to an object rather than an object itself, so that at any one time we may or may not be referencing a particular component.

Designing classes using aggregation

One of the ways in which aggregation can be useful is in writing classes which contribute towards 'open' object-oriented systems. We have stated before that one of the prospective benefits of object technology is the creation of 'software ICs' [Cox, 1986, p.26] – the software equivalent of reusable 'plug in and go' electronic hardware components. However, one of the practical problems which has frustrated this aim is the difficulty of combining elements from different class libraries with their own classification hierarchies. Inheritance in this context is a rather restrictive device, given the fixed nature of the relationships between classes, and the problem is further compounded by the wide range of potential application environments (operating systems, GUIs etc) requiring hardware-specific implementations. How then can reuse be achieved beyond the confines of one class library or one operating environment? It has been suggested that a 'layered' approach (similar to the ISO/OSI seven layer model for network software) may help to achieve this end [Corbett, 1993 p.14]. This model can be represented by an inverted pyramid (Fig. 9.9), each level of which represents a category of classes. Objects at each level may be constructed from aggregations of objects at lower levels (preferably the level immediately below). One aspect of this is that all the components we use, however simple, are objects, which is a reflection of the Smalltalk philosophy in which everything (even to the level of integers, strings etc) is an object.

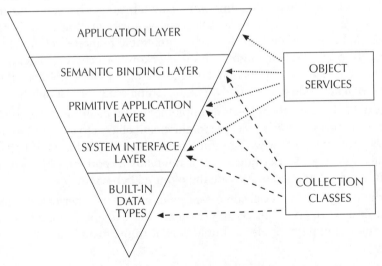

**Fig 9.9: Corbett's 'application class framework',
providing a model for layered aggregation.**

Each layer in the model contains classes at a particular level of detail. The layers suggested by Corbett [1993, p 15] are:

1. Built in data types

   This is the level which needs to be encapsulated, since it is at the machine representation level that data types vary so much between platforms and operating systems.

2. System interface layer (wrapping types into classes).

   The simple data types are encapsulated at this level as classes in order to be 'open'. The environment-specific representation of these standard data types is hidden behind the interface of the objects. These might include such basic components as strings, enumerated types, booleans, numbers and characters. A similar approach is used in Java where the basic data types also have 'wrapper' classes to encapsulate them. For example, as well as an 'int' data type there is an 'Integer' class.

3. The primitive application layer (attributes).

   Objects appropriate in scale to be attributes of classes may be modelled here. Modelling attributes as classes in their own right affords the opportunity to add methods to them rather than the enclosing class having responsibility for all attribute behaviour. Classes at this level might be of the scale of 'name', 'address', 'account number' etc, composed of types defined in the system interface layer.

4. Semantic binding layer (classes).

   At this level is the aggregation of 'attribute' objects into classes appropriate for application sized objects. Objects such as 'customer', 'account' and 'bank' would appear at this level, composed of primitive application layer objects.

5. Application layer (programs).

   At the highest level, we instantiate our large scale objects in the final application.

Question 9.5   How might aggregation assist in making object-oriented programs more portable?

By making larger scale objects aggregations of smaller objects in place of simple data types, the higher level classes should be able to be ported across hardware platforms without encountering problems of low level data representation.

C++ syntax

There are two basic ways in which associations and aggregations are implemented

1. Objects contain objects
2. Objects contain pointers to objects

When writing fixed aggregations, we use the first approach of putting objects inside objects. However, when more flexibility is required for variable aggregations, we use embedded pointers. We also use pointers to implement simple associations.

Implementing fixed aggregations

To implement a fixed aggregation in C++, classes are defined with objects of other classes inside them. To take an example of a real world object, we might define an aircraft as being composed of a number of fundamental components (Fig. 9.10).

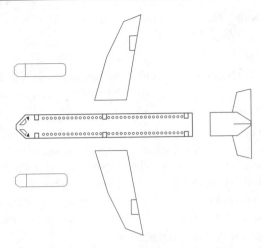

Fig. 9.10: A real world aggregation – an aircraft assembled from discrete components.

The aircraft is at this level of analysis a fixed aggregation, because an aircraft object has a fixed set of discrete components (another simple 'parts explosion'). For large scale assemblies, this is typical of the way in which manufacture is broken down between manufacturing plants, possibly in different countries. The intention is, of course, that the separately manufactured components are compatible with each other, allowing the aggregation to function when they are all assembled. This is a useful analogy for the way that software components should be 'composable' into larger systems via compatible interfaces.

A simplified set of major components might be objects of classes PortWing, Starboard-Wing, Engine, Fuselage and Tailplane. Assuming these classes have been defined elsewhere, a class definition for 'Aircraft' might have a 'private' part as follows:

```
class Aircraft
{
private:
    PortWing port_wing;
    StarboardWing starboard_wing;
    Engine engine1, engine2;
    Fuselage fuselage;
    Tailplane tailplane;
// etc...
};
```

Each of the composing objects would be members of classes defined elsewhere with their own methods. An 'Aircraft' object would be able to call on these methods in defining its own behaviour. For example, an aircraft might have the method 'turnToPort', which would need to alter the elevators and ailerons on both wings and turn the tailplane rudder by calling on their methods (The component behaviours for this method are based on a state table in [Coplien, 1992 p.368]):

```
void Aircraft :: turnToPort();
{
    port_wing.elevatorUp();
    starboard_wing.elevatorUp();
    port_wing.aileronUp();
    starboard_wing.aileronDown();
```

```
        tailplane.rudderLeft();
}
```

Activities of some composing objects will depend on the states of others. This is an example of 'propagation', whereby the environment of the part is the same as that of the assembly. In some cases, the behaviour of component objects is constrained by the state of the aggregation. For example, the aircraft doors may well stay closed when the engines are above idling speed, which we might code something like this (assuming a constant called 'IDLE'):

```
void Aircraft :: openDoors()
{
    if(engine1.getSpeed() > IDLE || engine2.getSpeed() > IDLE)
    {
        // do not open doors!
    }
    else
    {
        fuselage.openDoors();
    }
}
```

In this example, sending the message 'openDoors' to the aircraft will only invoke the Fuselage 'openDoors' method if the engines are not above idling speed. The state of the aircraft therefore 'propagates' to the state of the doors.

Constructing aggregations with parameters

One aspect of instantiating objects that are aggregations is how to call parameterised constructors of any contained objects. When an object is created, any contained objects must be created at the same time, which implies that their constructors must be called. In some cases, none of the composing objects have parameterised constructors, so their instantiation is straightforward. However, if the constructors of contained objects take parameters then we need a syntax that will allow them to be supplied via the constructor of the aggregation. In the following example, a 'Car' object is instantiated containing four 'Wheel' objects and one 'Engine' object. Since both the 'Wheel' and 'Engine' classes in this case require parameters to the constructor, the arguments are passed directly to them via the constructor of the aggregation using the colon operator.

```
#include<iostream.h>
// definition of class 'Wheel'
class Wheel
{
private:
    int diameter;
public:
    Wheel(int diameter_in);
    int getDiameter();
};
Wheel::Wheel(int diameter_in)
{
    diameter = diameter_in;
}
int Wheel::getDiameter()
{
    return diameter;
```

```
}
// definition of class 'Engine' with 'cc' (cubic capacity) attribute
class Engine
{
private:
    int cc;
public:
    Engine(int cc_in);
    int getCC();
};
Engine::Engine(int cc_in)
{
    cc = cc_in;
}
int Engine::getCC()
{
    return cc;
}
// definition of class 'Car'; an aggregation of 4 wheels and an
// engine plus an additional attribute (passengers)
class Car
{
private:
    Wheel nearside_front, offside_front, nearside_rear, offside_rear;
    Engine engine;
    int passengers;
public:
    Car(int diameter_in, int cc_in, int passengers_in);
    void showSelf();
};
// out of line constructor - note the use of the colon operator to allow aggregation
// parameters to be passed directly to the constructors of contained objects
Car::Car(int diameter_in, int cc_in, int passengers_in) :
    nearside_front(diameter_in),
    offside_front(diameter_in),
    nearside_rear(diameter_in),
    offside_rear(diameter_in),
    engine(cc_in)
{
    passengers = passengers_in;
}
// method to display attribute values
void Car::showSelf()
{
// any wheel will do here, since they are all the same size
    cout << "Wheel sizes are all " << nearside_front.getDiameter() << endl;
    cout << "Engine capacity is " << engine.getCC() << endl;
    cout << "Number of Passengers is " << passengers << endl;
}
void main()
{
// instantiate a car object
    Car my_car(24, 500, 2);
// display its components
    my_car.showSelf();
}
```

Output from the program is:

Wheel sizes are all 24
Engine capacity is 500
Number of Passengers is 2

Implementing variable aggregations

In a variable aggregation a component part may not always be present at run time. We can represent this possibility by using a pointer rather than an object inside the class. Looking again at objects from the superstore example, this code fragment shows a pointer of class 'Scale' inside the class definition of 'Checkout' :

```
class Checkout
{
private:
    Scale* the_scale;
    // other components / attributes etc.
public:
    // scale methods
    void addScale();
    void removeScale()
    // etc...
};
```

This pointer could be instantiated to NULL in the 'Checkout' constructor, but then be used to instantiate a dynamic object of class 'Scale' if required:

```
void Checkout::addScale()
{
    the_scale = new Scale;
}
```

Likewise, a scale could be removed...

```
void Checkout::removeScale()
{
// destroy the object
    delete the_scale;
// redirect the pointer to NULL
    the_scale = NULL;
}
```

However, bearing in mind that some objects in an aggregation may have a lifetime independent of the aggregation, it may not be appropriate to create and destroy the Scale object. If it exists elsewhere, then it can simply be referenced by the Checkout class, by passing a 'Scale' pointer to the 'addScale' method:

```
void Checkout::addScale(Scale* scale)
{
    the_scale = scale;
}
```

In this case, removing the scale from the aggregation would simply mean directing the pointer away from it without calling delete:

```
void Checkout::removeScale()
{
    the_scale = NULL;
}
```

Which of these two strategies is appropriate depends entirely on whether the object in an aggregation needs to have a separate existence outside it.

Implementing associations

There is much debate about how associations should be implemented in C++, particularly because they can become very complex. However, these examples aim to show the simplest possible implementations using basic syntax. More sophisticated solutions using class libraries would be more likely in professional systems [Rumbaugh, 1996, McCausland, 1996]. The association examples here will be modelled with a single pointer (for a single association) or with an array of pointers (for a multiple association).

One to one links in one direction

The simplest association to model would be a link in one direction between two objects, so that one object can send messages to another. To demonstrate the syntax, we will implement something resembling the light switch and bulb example, but in this case use a button and a light object. The button will act as a toggle, so that each time it is pressed the light changes state; turns on if it is off and off if it is on. In the 'Button' class, the association is modelled by providing a pointer to a 'Light' object as an attribute. To simplify making classes visible to each other, all the code is in a single file:

```cpp
#include <iostream.h>
// these constants make the code a little more readable
const int OFF = 0;
const int ON = 1;
// the Light class has no knowledge of the Button class. objects of this
// class are what Booch terms 'Agents' (they do not act upon other objects,
// but are acted upon by other objects)
class Light
{
private:
    int light_state;
public:
    Light();
    void changeState();
    void showState();
};
Light::Light()
{
    light_state = OFF;
}
void Light::changeState()
{
    if(light_state == OFF)
    {
        light_state = ON;
    }
    else
    {
        light_state = OFF;
    }
}
void Light::showState()
{
    if(light_state == OFF)
```

```
    {
        cout << "light is off" << endl;
    }
    else
    {
        cout << "light is on" << endl;
    }
}
// the button class is an 'Actor'; it acts upon a Light object. the
// association is implemented with a pointer
class Button
{
private:
    Light* light_bulb;
public:
    Button(Light* bulb);
    void press();
};
// the constructor makes the link between the associated objects
Button::Button(Light* bulb)
{
    light_bulb = bulb;
}
// the press method sends a message to the associated object
void Button::press()
{
    light_bulb -> changeState();
}
void main()
{
// instantiate a light, then use it as a parameter to the constructor
// of the Button object
    Light* Big_Light = new Light;
    Button Light_Button(Big_Light);
// this little menu driven program sends messages to the Button object
// it, in turn, sends messages to the Light object
    int choice = 0;
    while(choice != 2)
    {
// show if the light is on or off
        Big_Light -> showState();
        cout << "Enter 1 to press light button, 2 to quit ";
        cin >> choice;
// pressing the button changes the state of the light
        if(choice == 1)
        {
            Light_Button.press();
        }
    }
    cout << "End of program" << endl;
}
```

A brief interactive run:

light is off
Enter 1 to press light button, 2 to quit 1
light is on
Enter 1 to press light button, 2 to quit 1

light is off
Enter 1 to press light button, 2 to quit 2
End of program

One to one link in two directions

An example of a one to one association which has a bidirectional link, in this case between objects of the same class, might be two 'Person' objects who marry. As indicated earlier, this is a relationship where, unlike the light bulb and switch relationship, messages pass in both directions. In order to model this relationship, both classes must include a reference (via a pointer) to the linked object. Because both objects are members of the same class, they both communicate through their 'partner' pointers. In this case, each object can send and receive messages, but a level of complexity is introduced because we must ensure that both ends of the link are updated together. It is no use one partner getting divorced if the other partner does not know about it!

```
/*
    MARRIAGE.H demonstrates a link between objects of the same class. This would
              appear on a design as an association from a class to itself. Note
              that in this example all modifications to the link (i.e. 'marry' and
              'divorce') must be applied to both objects at the same time.
*/
#include <iostream.h>
#include <string.h>
// a Person has a name and an association with 0 or 1 partners, also
// an object of the Person class
class Person
{
private:
    char name[40];
    Person* partner;
public:
    Person(char* name_in);
    char* getName();
    void marry(Person* spouse);
    void divorce();
    void showPartner();
};
// the constructor sets the name from a parameter, and initialises
// the person as single (i.e. no link to another person object)
Person::Person(char* name_in)
{
    strncpy(name, name_in, 39);
    name[39] = '\0';
    partner = NULL;
}
// getName returns the name
char* Person::getName()
{
    return name;
}
// 'marry' makes the link with another Person object
void Person::marry(Person* spouse)
{
    partner = spouse;
}
```

```
// 'divorce' removes the link by resetting the pointer to NULL
void Person::divorce()
{
    partner = NULL;
}
// if the person has a partner, their name is displayed
void Person::showPartner()
{
    if(partner != NULL)
    {
        cout << name << " is married to " << partner -> getName() << endl;
    }
    else
    {
        cout << name << " is single" << endl;
    }
}
/*
    MARRIAGE.CPP  example program that makes and removes a link
                  between two 'Person' objects. Because this class
                  does not automatically update the association at
                  both ends, messages such as 'marry' and 'divorce'
                  must be sent to both objects.
*/
#include "marriage.h"
void main()
{
// instantiate two 'Person' objects
    Person* fred = new Person("Fred");
    Person* wilma = new Person("Wilma");
// display their partners; they will have defaulted to being single
    fred -> showPartner();
    wilma -> showPartner();
// will you take this pointer to be your lawful wedded object?
    fred -> marry(wilma);
    wilma -> marry(fred);
// I will...
    cout << "But after the ceremony..." << endl;
    fred -> showPartner();
    wilma -> showPartner();
// then after the honeymoon is over...
    fred -> divorce();
    wilma -> divorce();
    cout << "Then again, some time later..." << endl;
    fred -> showPartner();
    wilma -> showPartner();
}
```

A test run shows how the links change when updated specifically at both ends for the shortest marriage in history:

Fred is single
Wilma is single
But after the ceremony...
Fred is married to Wilma
Wilma is married to Fred

Then again, some time later...
Fred is single
Wilma is single

Automatically updating associations with the 'this' pointer

The example above shows that associations can be implemented as links in both directions, but the implementation is rather lacking. It leaves the user of the class responsible for updating both ends of the association. It may be preferable to code a mechanism that automatically updates the other end of a link when we create it in a given object. In general terms, if we have a method that forges a link with another object, then it should also make that link in the other direction by passing itself to a similar method of the other object. How, then, can an object pass itself to another object? In C++ this can be done with a pointer called 'this' which all objects have as part of their structure. All objects can refer to themselves with the 'this' pointer, as the following example program shows. Here, we have two different classes, 'Office' and 'Secretary', with a one to one association between them. In the implementation, making a link between an office and a secretary automatically makes the link in the other direction, from the secretary to the office. Unlike the 'Light' program, the classes appear in separate files. Note how the 'forward declarations' of classes are needed to allow the different files to compile:

```
/*
    OFFICE.H Class definition for the 'Office' class
*/
// because the class needs to be aware that the Secretary class
// exists, this forward declaration allows the code to compile
class Secretary;
class Office
{
private:
    int room_number;
    Secretary* secretary;
public:
    Office(int number);
    int getRoomNumber();
    Secretary* getSecretary();
    void addSecretary(Secretary* sec);
};
/*
    SECRETRY.H Definition of the 'Secretary' class
*/
// because class 'Secretary' needs to be aware of class 'Office'
// we declare its name here as a 'forward declaration'
class Office;
class Secretary
{
private:
    char role[80];
    Office* office;
public:
    Secretary(char* role_in);
    char* getRole();
    void addOffice(Office* room);
    Office* getOffice();
};
```

The method definitions for the two classes are:

```
/*
        OFFICE.CPP   Method definitions for the 'Office' class
*/
#include "office.h"
// because the 'addSecretary' method uses the 'addOffice' method of the
// Secretary class, the forward declaration in the header file is not
// enough. we also need to include the full class definition:
#include "secretry.h"
// the constructor sets the room number
Office::Office(int number)
{
    room_number = number;
}
// selector methods to return office number and secretary
int Office::getRoomNumber()
{
    return room_number;
}
Secretary* Office::getSecretary()
{
    return secretary;
}
// implement the association; add a secretary
void Office::addSecretary(Secretary* sec)
{
// direct the association pointer to the secretary
    secretary = sec;
// pass 'this' object back to the secretary
    secretary -> addOffice(this);
}
/*
        SECRETRY.CPP   method definitions for the 'Secretary' class
*/
#include "secretry.h"
#include <string.h>
// the constructor sets the secretary's role
Secretary::Secretary(char* role_in)
{
    strcpy(role, role_in);
}
// selector methods to return the role and office
char* Secretary::getRole()
{
    return role;
}
Office* Secretary::getOffice()
{
    return office;
}
// implement the association; direct the pointer to an office
void Secretary::addOffice(Office* room)
{
    office = room;
}
```

This short test program simply creates objects of both classes and demonstrates that the association automatically updates at both ends:

```
/*
      OFFICEMN.CPP   Program to demonstrate the automatic
                     updating of both ends of an association
*/
#include "office.h"
#include "secretry.h"
#include <iostream.h>
void main()
{
// instantiate an 'Office' object
      Office* faculty_office = new Office(101);
// instantiate a 'Secretary' object
      Secretary* secretary = new Secretary("faculty secretary");
// add the secretary to the office. the secretary will automatically
// have the office assigned to him/her
      faculty_office -> addSecretary(secretary);
// display the links from both ends of the association
      cout << "The " << secretary -> getRole() << " is in room ";
      cout << secretary -> getOffice() -> getRoomNumber() << endl;
      cout << "Room number " << faculty_office -> getRoomNumber() << " houses the ";
      cout << faculty_office -> getSecretary() -> getRole() << endl;
}
```

The output from the program is:

The faculty secretary is in room 101
Room number 101 houses the faculty secretary

The example demonstrates how an association can be automatically updated, but only works in a single direction (i.e. adding a secretary to an office). The reverse association is not automatic; adding an office to a secretary does not add that secretary to the office. This requires a rather more complex piece of code that will not be investigated here (but you might like to think about it!).

Multiple associations

To implement multiple associations, we should ideally use appropriate classes from a library [Rumbaugh, 1996], but we can also use simple arrays to demonstrate the principle. In previous exercises and examples we have seen arrays of bank accounts, vehicles and employees, but all declared in 'main'. In this example, we model the relationship between a bus company and its buses by encapsulating an array of pointers of class 'Bus' in a class called 'BusCompany'. In this example, the link is implemented in one direction only, so buses do not have a link to the company (but see the exercises at the end of the chapter!).

```
/*
      BUS.H      header file for the 'Bus' class
*/
class Bus
{
private:
      char registration[10];
      int year_of_manufacture;
      char bus_type;
```

```
public:
    Bus(char* reg, int year, char type);
    char* getRegistration();
    char getBusType();
    int getYearOfManufacture();
};
/*
    BUS.CPP  Method implementations for the 'Bus' class
*/
#include <string.h>
#include <iostream.h>
#include "bus.h"
// the constructor sets the attributes from the parameter list
Bus::Bus(char* reg, int year, char type)
{
    strncpy(registration, reg, 9);
    registration[9] = '\0';
    year_of_manufacture = year;
    bus_type = type;
}
// selector methods
char* Bus::getRegistration()
{
    return registration;
}
int Bus::getYearOfManufacture()
{
    return year_of_manufacture;
}
char Bus::getBusType()
{
    return bus_type;
}
/*
    BUSCO.H  header file for the 'BusCompany' class
*/
// the header file for the Bus class is needed because the BusCompany
// refers to it
#include "bus.h"
class BusCompany
{
private:
// an array of 'Bus' pointers to implement the association
// between 'BusCompany' and 'Bus'
    Bus* buses[30];
    char company_name[30];
    int number_of_buses;
public:
    BusCompany(char* name);
    char* getCompanyName();
    int getNumberOfBuses();
    int addBus(Bus*);
    int removeBus(char* search_reg);
    void showFleet();
};
/*
    BUSCO.CPP  Method implementations for 'BusCompany' class
*/
```

```
#include <string.h>        // for 'strncpy' and 'strcmp'
#include <iostream.h>
#include "busco.h"
// constructor
BusCompany::BusCompany(char* name)
{
    strncpy(company_name, name, 29);
    company_name[29] = '\0';
// initialise the pointers in the array to NULL
    for(int i = 0; i < 30; i++)
    {
        buses[i] = NULL;
    }
// start with no buses
    number_of_buses = 0;
}
// selector methods
char* BusCompany::getCompanyName()
{
    return company_name;
}
int BusCompany::getNumberOfBuses()
{
    return number_of_buses;
}
// modifiers
int BusCompany::addBus(Bus* new_bus)
{
// look for an empty slot in the array to add the bus into
    for(int i = 0; i < 30 && buses[i] != NULL; i++)
    {}
// if an empty slot was found, add the bus and return 1 (true)
    if(i < 30)
    {
        buses[i] = new_bus;
        number_of_buses++;
        return 1;
    }
// otherwise, return 0 (false)
    else
    {
        return 0;
    }
}
// this method removes a bus from the fleet if it matches the
// registration number entered at the keyboard. the method returns
// 1 if a match was found, 0 if not. because the conditional
// statements are more deeply nested than in the addBus method,
// a flag is set rather than directly returning 1 or 0
int BusCompany::removeBus(char* search_reg)
{
// the flag is set to a default of 0 (false)
    int found = 0;
// iterate through the array, checking each pointer which is referencing
// a 'Bus' object (i.e. not pointing to NULL)
    for(int i = 0; i < 30; i++)
    {
        if(buses[i] != NULL)
```

```
        {
// the 'strcmp' function (included in string.h) returns 0 if the strings are the same
        if(strcmp(buses[i] -> getRegistration(), search_reg) == 0)
            {
                buses[i] = NULL;
                number_of_buses--;
// set the 'found' flag to 1 (true)
                found = 1;
            }
        }
    }
// the value of 'found' will be zero unless 'strcmp' has successfully
// matched the registration number
    return found;
}
// the 'showFleet' method displays the details of the buses referenced by the
// pointer in the array
void BusCompany::showFleet()
{
// display the company name
    cout << endl << "Current fleet list for " << company_name << " bus company" << endl;
// iterate through the array looking for buses
    for(int i = 0; i < 30; i++)
        {
// if a bus is present, display its details
        if(buses[i] != NULL)
            {
                cout << "Bus registration: " << buses[i] -> getRegistration();
                cout << ", manufactured in " << buses[i] -> getYearOfManufacture();
                if(buses[i] -> getBusType() == 's')
                    {
                        cout << ", a single decker" << endl;
                    }
                else
                    {
                        cout << ", a double decker" << endl;
                    }
            }
        }
}
/*
    BUSMAIN.CPP     Program to test the associated objects
                    Bus and BusCompany
*/
// only the BUSCO.H header file is needed because it already includes BUS.H
#include "busco.h"
#include <iostream.h>
void main()
{
// create some buses. since they will have a life independent of the bus
// company (they may have been previously owned and may be sold on the others)
// the company does not control their lifetimes
    Bus* bus1 = new Bus("P223TYU", 1996, 's');
    Bus* bus2 = new Bus("L989HHG", 1993, 'd');
    Bus* bus3 = new Bus("M543BVC", 1994, 's');
// create a bus company
    BusCompany bus_company("OceaniaBus");
// add two buses. In this example we are ignoring the return value of the method,
```

157

```
// but it will return 0 if there is no room to add a bus
    bus_company.addBus(bus3);
    bus_company.addBus(bus1);
// show the current fleet
    cout << "Two buses have been added to the fleet" << endl;
    bus_company.showFleet();
// remove one bus, getting the search registration from the keyboard
    char search_reg[10];
    cout << "Enter the registration number of the bus to be removed ";
    cin >> search_reg;
    if(bus_company.removeBus(search_reg) == 1)
    {
        cout << "Bus " << search_reg << " removed" << endl;
    }
    else
    {
        cout << "Bus " << search_reg << " not found" << endl;
    }
// add another bus
    bus_company.addBus(bus2);
// show the modified fleet
    cout << "A new bus has been added to the fleet" << endl;;
    bus_company.showFleet();
// display the number of buses in the fleet
    cout << "The " << bus_company.getCompanyName() << " bus company has ";
    cout << bus_company.getNumberOfBuses() << " buses in its fleet" << endl;
}
```

The output from this (not very interactive) test program is:

Two buses have been added to the fleet
Current fleet list for OceaniaBus bus company
Bus registration: M543BVC, manufactured in 1994, a single decker
Bus registration: P223TYU, manufactured in 1996, a single decker
Enter the registration number of the bus to be removed M543BVC
Bus M543BVC removed
A new bus has been added to the fleet
Current fleet list for OceaniaBus bus company
Bus registration: L989HHG, manufactured in 1993, a double decker
Bus registration: P223TYU, manufactured in 1996, a single decker
The OceaniaBus bus company has 2 buses in its fleet

Summary of key points from this chapter

1. A classification hierarchy shows the inheritance relationships between classes. In contrast, a composition hierarchy shows the containment relationships between objects. Associations allow objects to send messages to one another.

2. A composition hierarchy describes an aggregation of objects which together are component parts of another object.

3. Some forms of aggregation are fixed, constant relationships, whilst others are containers for unpredictable sets of objects. Between these two extremes there may be many combinations of aggregate classes.

4. Some aggregations are like 'exploded parts' diagrams – the object is an assembly of a clear set of discrete components.

5. Aggregation involves levels of abstraction, though in a different way to inheritance.

6. Aggregations have certain properties (transitivity, antisymmetry and propagation) and may be of various types (fixed, variable or recursive).

7. Delegation is the use of contained objects to provide some of the behaviours of another class. It is a more flexible approach than inheritance if the new class is not truly 'a kind of' the other class.

8. Aggregation is a flexible approach to associations between objects which are not inheritance. It does not preclude the possibility of objects changing their roles in an aggregation at run time.

9. A 'layered model' approach to aggregation may assist in creating 'open' class libraries, portable between systems.

10. In C++, classes may contain declarations of objects or pointers to objects which may be dynamically referenced. Either or both of these may be used in a single class as appropriate to model associations or aggregations.

Exercises

Aggregation

Here are two class definitions for 'Wheel' and 'Bike'. The 'Bike' class is simply an aggregation of 'Wheels'.

```
class Wheel
{
private:
    int size;
public:
    Wheel(int wheel_size)      { size = wheel_size; }
    int getSize()              { return size; }
};
class Bike
{
private:
    Wheel front_wheel, back_wheel;
public:
    Bike(int wheel_size);
    int getFrontWheelSize() { return front_wheel.getSize(); }
    int getBackWheelSize() { return back_wheel.getSize(); }
};
Bike::Bike(int wheel_size) : front_wheel(wheel_size), back_wheel(wheel_size)
{}
```

1. Create an instance of class 'Bike' and test its methods.

2. Add a 'Rider' class with one attribute (name of rider), a parameterised constructor to set this name when an instance of the class is created, and a method to return the rider's name.

3. Include an object of class 'Rider' in your 'Bike' class, and modify the 'Bike' methods as appropriate so that a bike is able to return the name of its rider. Test these modifications in 'main'.

4. Replace the 'Rider' object with a pointer, so that a bike may or may not have a rider at a particular time. Add 'Bike' methods to add and remove the rider, ensuring that the pointer is referencing NULL when a rider is not present. Add a destructor to ensure that any 'Rider' object being referenced when a bike is destroyed is also deleted. Test these modifications in 'main'.

Association

1. Create classes called 'Telephone' and 'Desk' that have a one to one association. Implement and demonstrate methods to find out the telephone number for a particular desk (e.g. 'help desk', 'reception desk' etc), and the name of the desk that has a given telephone number. You do not have to make the associations automatic in this exercise.

2. Modify the 'Bus' class so that a bus implements a link with its bus company. Modify the 'addBus' method of the 'BusCompany' class so that it updates the association in both directions (so that the link between the bus and the company is automatically made). Replace the example 'main' function with a more interactive program.

An example program

In the preceding chapters we have seen how to create classes and to test their methods using simple 'main' functions, but we have not seen numbers of objects of different classes combining together to create a program of any scale. Now that we have covered the fundamental concepts of encapsulation, inheritance, association and aggregation, we can begin to create something like an object-oriented program. This example is based on a simplified hotel rooming system which uses a number of objects of different classes.

Some object-oriented programs involve a number of objects with devolved responsibilities, collaborating with each other and sharing control. Many other applications however tend to have one 'controller' object which manages the system. This is one such example, where the 'Hotel' object manages all the objects within it in what Booch would call a 'using' relationship – the hotel uses objects of the other classes to implement the system behaviour. Although it is not 'fully object-oriented' (it does not use polymorphism for example, since we have not yet covered it) it should give a flavour of object-oriented programming.

System description

The Solent Hotel has 5 function rooms (numbered 1–5) and 40 bedrooms (6–45). Bedrooms 6–15 are single, and bedrooms 16–45 double. When customers arrive at the hotel, they are booked into the first available room of the required type. Their name is recorded, along with the payee (i.e. who is paying for the room.) This is recorded as 'PRIVATE' if the customer is the payee, or the name of a company or organisation may be entered. The tariffs are £40 for a single bedroom, £55 for a double bedroom and £200 for a function room. There is one set of presentation equipment in the hotel which may be moved between function rooms.

The system enables customers to be booked into any available room, and ensures that a room is made available for further bookings as soon as it is vacated. It also allows the presentation equipment to be moved between rooms.

The system as implemented does not deal with dates, so that bookings, equipment movements and rooms becoming available are purely run time events.

The system produces the following reports on screen:

1. How many rooms (of all types) are currently occupied.
2   The room numbers of bedrooms currently occupied, and the details of the residents.
3. The room numbers of function rooms currently occupied.
4. Which function room currently contains the presentation equipment.
5. What the day's income will be given the state of room occupancy at a specific time.

The class diagram

The UML class diagram shows the classes in the system, their attributes and methods. It also shows the inheritance, association and aggregation relationships between the various objects, and 'multiplicity' (i.e. how many objects are involved in certain relationships). The notation for multiplicity was seen in Chapter 9 (Fig. 9.1). The program comprises objects of classes 'Hotel', 'Customer', 'PresentationEquipment',

'Bedroom' and 'FunctionRoom'. 'Bedroom' and 'FunctionRoom' are derived classes of a base class 'Room'. 'Hotel' is composed of 'Bedrooms' and 'Function Rooms'. 'PresentationEquipment' is aggregated inside 'FunctionRoom' and 'Customer' has an association with 'Room'. Class attributes and methods are underlined.

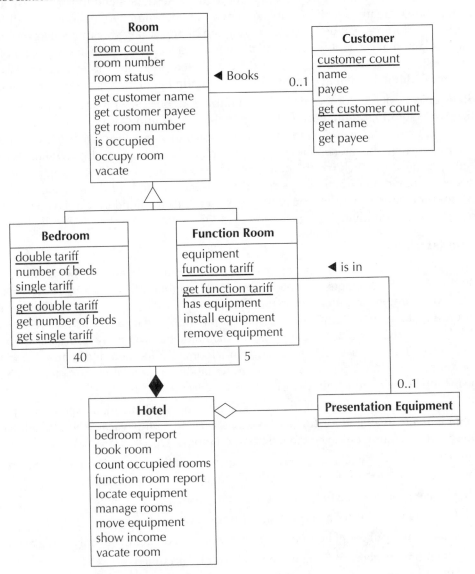

Fig. Ex.1: UML class diagram showing the classes, associations, attributes and methods in the 'Hotel' program.

One thing which does not appear on an object-oriented design is the 'main' function, since it is not an object. While it is not inherently 'wrong' to use main in an object-oriented program, it is perhaps better to try to devolve all responsibilities to objects, leaving main to simply start the ball rolling and instantiate the first object. This is what happens here – main is used to instantiate an object of the 'Hotel' class, which from its constructor calls its own methods and the methods of other contained objects.

Calling methods from within methods

For objects to 'pass messages' to each other, they must be able to call each others' methods, and sometimes also call their own methods. Within the methods of a class, we may call other methods of the same class as if they were normal function calls – that is to say they do not need to be preceded with an object name. In the example, we can see that the Hotel has a method called 'manageRooms' which controls the overall process. This calls a number of other methods of the Hotel class directly. Methods of other objects may be called from within methods as we have already seen them called from main – by preceding the method name with the name of the object (or pointer for a dynamic object). The only proviso is that the object receiving the message must be visible (in scope) when the method is called. In the case of the hotel, all the objects are aggregated within the hotel or other objects which themselves are in the hotel (customers are in rooms which are in turn in the hotel for example), so they are visible to all methods of the hotel, either directly or via some other object.

There are two new aspects of syntax which are introduced in this example. In Chapter 3, we looked at the storage of strings in arrays, but indicated that strings could also be stored using dynamic memory. The syntax for doing this, and also for declaring 'enumerated types,' is outlined below.

Strings using dynamic arrays

In Chapter 3 we discussed the ways in which strings may be represented in C++, using both arrays and pointers of type char. A strategy for strings was suggested which involved storing strings in arrays and manipulating them (for example to pass them to and from functions) using pointers. The problem with arrays of course is that they have to be of an appropriate size, but in many cases we will not know the size of a string until run time. Therefore we generally find ourselves erring on the side of caution and declaring large arrays just in case we need them, when in fact in many cases this is just memory going to waste. A more efficient and flexible way of handling strings is to dynamically allocate an array at run time which is just big enough to hold a particular string and no longer. This can be done using the 'new' operator in a similar way to the dynamic instantiation of an object. This statement dynamically allocates an array of 10 chars for example:

```
// declare a pointer of type char
char* string;
// dynamically allocate an array
string = new char[10];
```

Of course this is only useful if we can size the array not with a literal number but with the size of a given string at run time. To find out the size of a string, we can use a standard C function called 'strlen' which is defined in 'string.h'. The syntax is:

```
size = strlen(char*)
```

'strlen' returns the size of a string in characters, so we can use it to find out the size of a particular string and then dynamically allocate an array of that size, plus one extra character for the terminating '\0'. Then we can copy the original string into the array. In this example, we will assume that an object attribute ('customer_name') has been declared as a char pointer. In a method of the class, the original string is entered at the keyboard using 'cin' into a large array. This is only a temporary variable declared within the scope of the method so its size is not going to cause a problem. Then the size of the string is used to dynamically allocate the attribute, and the string is copied to it from the temporary array:

```
// attribute declared in the class definition
    char* customer_name;
    ...
// in an object method, a temporary array is declared
    ...
    char buffer[80];
    cin >> buffer;
// 'strlen' is used to get the size of the string entered at
// the keyboard
    int string_size = strlen(buffer);
// an array of the appropriate size is instantiated (string
// length + 1) and the string is copied into it
    customer_name = new char[string_size + 1];
    strcpy(customer_name, buffer);
    ...
```

In the example program, a similar process is used for the attributes of 'Customer'

Because the array is dynamically allocated, it must also be explicitly destroyed using 'delete' before falling out of scope (probably in the object destructor). When deleting dynamically allocated arrays, a special version of 'delete' is used:

```
delete [] customer_name;
```

Enumerated types

We often find attributes that only have a fixed set of possible values. A switch for example might only have two possible states, on or off. However, we cannot easily represent such attributes using the simple data types. We might represent a switch in a class using an integer, and use a value of 0 to represent 'off' and 1 to represent 'on', but of course this does not stop the integer from containing other undesirable values, and does not make the code very clear. Consider these two methods of a 'Switch' class:

```
void Switch::turnOn()
{
    switch_state = 1;
}
void Switch::turnOff()
{
    switch_state = 0;
}
```

The 1 and the 0 have a fairly arbitrary relationship with the attribute. We could make it more readable by using constants as follows:

```
const int ON = 1;
const int OFF = 0;
```

This will make the methods a little more readable but we are still using an integer to represent the attribute.

A better way to represent such values is the 'enumerated type'. This is a data type (declared by the keyword 'enum') which allows us to provide a given set of possible values for an attribute which relates to integer values but each value can be given a descriptive name. This is an enumerated type definition for a 'switcher':

```
enum switcher {off, on};
```

The definition of an enumerated type usually appears outside the scope of any class or function.

By default, the states defined in the braces correspond to numbers starting at 0 and incrementing by 1 each time, so that in this case off = 0 and on = 1. We may, if we wish, supply other values, for example to start at 1:

```
enum medal {gold = 1, silver = 2, bronze = 3};
```

Instances of an enumerated type can be declared in a program. This instantiates a switcher called 'switch_state'

```
switcher switch_state;
```

With 'switch_state' as an attribute of the 'Switch' class, our previous methods might be defined as:

```
void Switch::turnOn()
{
    switch_state = on;
}
void Switch::turnOff()
{
    switch_state = off;
}
```

Because it is a data type, an enumerated type can also be used as the return type of a function or used as a parameter.

Enumerated types are used to represent two attributes in the hotel program. In addition, an enumerated type is used to simulate the ANSI standard 'bool' type in the 'hotel.cpp' file. This is declared as:

```
enum bool {false, true};
```

If you have an ANSI standard compiler, then this can be removed from the source code.

The source code

In the preceding chapters we have seen how larger programs are generally decomposed into a number of separate files to make the code more manageable and reduce compilation times. This program consists of nine different files, shown in Fig. Ex2. The arrows indicate 'compilation dependencies' where headers need to be included in order for files to successfully compile.

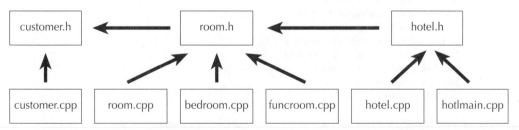

Fig. Ex2: The files in the Hotel program and their compilation dependencies.

Here, then, is the example program source code. Its interface, being portable, is very crude, but this could easily be remedied by adding the various screen handling functions (clear screen, colours, text windows etc.) that are available with most compilers. Since these are not standard, there is no point in trying to include them here.

```
/*
     CUSTOMER.H      header file for the 'Customer' class
                     The 'Customer' class has a class attribute to count customer objects
                     and two object attributes (dynamically allocated strings) passed
                     to the constructor.
*/
class Customer
{
    static int customer_count;
    char* name;
    char* payee;
public:
// parameterised constructor
    Customer(char* customer_name, char* payee_name);
// destructor
    ~Customer();
// selector methods
    char* getName();
    char* getPayee();
// class selector method
    static int getCustomerCount();
};
********************************************************************************
/*
     CUSTOMER.CPP definitions of 'Customer' class methods
*/
#include "customer.h"
#include <string.h>
// reserve storage for the class attribute
int Customer::customer_count;
// the constructor gets the details from the keyboard
Customer::Customer(char* customer_name, char* payee_name)
{
// the name and the payee are dynamically allocated using the
// 'new' operator. The 'strlen' function is used to find their size,
// before a dynamic arrays are created and the strings copied to them
    int string_size;
// find size of customer name
    string_size = strlen(customer_name);
// allocate the necessary size of dynamic array (add an extra character for the '\0')
    name = new char[string_size + 1];
// copy the name into the attribute
    strcpy(name, customer_name);
// allocate and copy the payee name using a similar process
    string_size = strlen(payee_name);
    payee = new char[string_size + 1];
    strcpy(payee, payee_name);
// add to the customer count
    customer_count++;
}
// the destructor decrements the customer count and frees the memory
// occupied by the name and payee strings
Customer::~Customer()
{
    customer_count--;
    delete[] name;
    delete[] payee;
}
```

```
// simple selector methods
char* Customer::getName()
{
    return name;
}
char* Customer::getPayee()
{
    return payee;
}
// class (static) selector method
int Customer::getCustomerCount()
{
    return customer_count;
}
```

****

```
/*
    ROOM.H   Header file for 'Room' class
*/
```

// we include the 'Customer' class header here so that the Room class
// can declare a pointer of that class as a member
```
#include "customer.h"
```
// 'PresentationEquipment' has no definition, but objects can be instantiated,
// even though there are no methods to call
```
class PresentationEquipment
{};
```
// an enumerated type is defined to represent room occupancy. a room will
// be either vacant or occupied
```
enum status {vacant, occupied};
```
// 'Room' is an abstract base class. It contains a pointer of class 'Customer'
// to model the association between the two classes. the link is in one direction only
```
class Room
{
protected:
    status room_status;
    static int room_count;
    int room_number;
    Customer* customer;
public:
// constructor
    Room();
// modifier methods
    void occupyRoom(char* customer_name, char* payee_name);
    void vacate();
// selector methods
    int getRoomNumber();
    char* getCustomerName();
    char* getCustomerPayee();
    status isOccupied();
};
```
// Bedroom is a derived class of 'Room'
```
class Bedroom : public Room
{
private:
    static float single_tariff;
    static float double_tariff;
    int number_of_beds;
public:
// constructor
```

```
        Bedroom();
// selector method
    int getNumberOfBeds();
// class selector methods
    static float getSingleTariff();
    static float getDoubleTariff();
};
// another enumerated type is defined to record the presence or
// absence of the presentation equipment
enum present_status {absent, present};
// 'FunctionRoom' is derived from 'Room'
class FunctionRoom: public Room
{
private:
    present_status equipment;
    PresentationEquipment* presentation_equipment;
    static float function_tariff;
public:
// constructor
    FunctionRoom();
// modifier methods
    void installPresentationEquipment(PresentationEquipment*);
    void removePresentationEquipment();
// selector methods
    static float getFunctionTariff();
    present_status hasEquipment();
};
//************************************************************************************
/*
    ROOM.CPP        Method definitions for the 'Room' class
*/
#include "room.h"
#include <stdlib.h>   // for NULL
// reserve memory for the class attribute 'room_count'
int Room::room_count;
// the constructor generates the room number from the static counter,
// initialises the 'Customer' pointer to NULL and sets the status
// to vacant
Room::Room()
{
    room_count++;
    room_number = room_count;
    customer = NULL;
    room_status = vacant;
}
// when a room is occupied, a 'Customer' object is dynamically instantiated,
// passing the name and payee parameters form this method to the constructor.
// the room status is set to occupied
void Room::occupyRoom(char* customer_name, char* payee_name)
{
    customer = new Customer(customer_name, payee_name);
    room_status = occupied;
}
// when a room is vacated, the object is destroyed, and the pointer returned to NULL
void Room::vacate()
{
    delete customer;
    customer = NULL;
```

```
    room_status = vacant;
}
// simple selector methods
int Room::getRoomNumber()
{
    return room_number;
}
// these methods return data via another method of the contained object
char* Room::getCustomerName()
{
    return customer -> getName();
}
char* Room::getCustomerPayee()
{
    return customer -> getPayee();
}
// this method uses the enumerated type as its return value
status Room::isOccupied()
{
    return room_status;
}
*******************************************************************************
/*
    BEDROOM.CPP   Method definitions for the 'Bedroom' class
*/
#include "room.h"
// reserve memory for the tariffs
float Bedroom::single_tariff = 40.00;
float Bedroom::double_tariff = 55.00;
// the constructor initialises the number of beds according to the room number
Bedroom::Bedroom()
{
    if(room_count > 5 && room_count < 15)
    {
        number_of_beds = 1;
    }
    else
    {
        number_of_beds = 2;
    }
}
// object selector method
int Bedroom::getNumberOfBeds()
{
    return number_of_beds;
}
// class (static) selector methods
float Bedroom::getSingleTariff()
{
    return single_tariff;
}
float Bedroom::getDoubleTariff()
{
    return double_tariff;
}
*******************************************************************************
/*
    FUNCROOM.CPP Method definitions for the 'FunctionRoom' class
```

```
*/
#include "room.h"
#include <stdlib.h>   // for NULL
// reserve memory for the tariff class attribute
float FunctionRoom::function_tariff = 200.00;
// the constructor initialises the room as empty of equipment
FunctionRoom::FunctionRoom()
{
    presentation_equipment = NULL;
    equipment = absent;
}
// this method directs the internal pointer to the address of an object
// passed as a parameter
void FunctionRoom :: installPresentationEquipment(PresentationEquipment* pointer)
{
    presentation_equipment = pointer;
    equipment = present;
}
// since the lecture equipment is moved but still exists, the object
// is not deleted - the pointer is simply redirected
void FunctionRoom :: removePresentationEquipment()
{
    presentation_equipment = NULL;
    equipment = absent;
}
// selector methods
float FunctionRoom::getFunctionTariff()
{
    return function_tariff;
}
present_status FunctionRoom::hasEquipment()
{
    return equipment;
}
*************************************************************************************
/*
    HOTEL.H   declaration of the 'Hotel' class
*/
#include "room.h"
// the 'Hotel' class is an aggregation of rooms of the two types,
// and also contains an object of the 'PresentationEquipment' class.
// it acts as the interface object to the system, via its 'manageRooms'
// method. all input and output resides in the 'Hotel' class, which means
// that the interface could be easily changed without the underlying classes
// being affected
class Hotel
{
private:
// the hotel is a 'composition' aggregation of 5 function rooms and 40 bedrooms
    FunctionRoom function_room[5];
    Bedroom bedroom[40];
// it also aggregates a set of presentation equipment, though this is not
// as fixed as a composition relationship
    PresentationEquipment lecture_set;
public:
// constructor
    Hotel();
// modifier methods
```

```
        void manageRooms();
        void bookRoom();
        void vacateRoom();
        void moveEquipment();
// selector methods
        void locateEquipment();
        void countOccupiedRooms();
        void bedroomReport();
        void functionRoomReport();
        void showIncome();
};
```

```
/*
    HOTEL.CPP   Method definitions for the 'Hotel' class
*/
#include "hotel.h"
#include <iostream.h>
// if your compiler does not support the standard 'bool' type,
// then this enumerated type easily simulates it. remove this line
// if your compiler does recognise 'bool':
enum bool {false, true};
// the hotel constructor installs the presentation equipment in
// function room 1, and then starts the main controlling method
Hotel::Hotel()
{
// pass the address of the presentation equipment object to the
// first function room
    function_room[0].installPresentationEquipment(&lecture_set);
// start the main menu in the 'manageRooms' method
    manageRooms();
}
// 'manageRooms' contains an iterating menu to provide the
// user interface to the system. It calls other methods of 'Hotel'.
void Hotel::manageRooms()
{
    int menu_choice = 0;
    do
    {
        cout << "Hotel Rooming System" << endl;
        cout << "1. Book Room" << endl;
        cout << "2. Vacate Room" << endl;
        cout << "3. Count of Occupied Rooms" << endl;
        cout << "4. Bedrooms Report" << endl;
        cout << "5. Function Rooms Report" << endl;
        cout << "6. Equipment Location" << endl;
        cout << "7. Move Equipment" << endl;
        cout << "8. Projected Income For Today" << endl;
        cout << "9. Quit" << endl;
        cout << "Enter choice ";
        cin >> menu_choice;
        switch(menu_choice)
        {
// each case calls another method of the 'Hotel' class
            case 1 : bookRoom(); break;
            case 2 : vacateRoom(); break;
            case 3 : countOccupiedRooms(); break;
            case 4 : bedroomReport(); break;
            case 5 : functionRoomReport(); break;
```

```
                case 6 : locateEquipment(); break;
                case 7 : moveEquipment(); break;
                case 8 : showIncome();
        }
    } while(menu_choice != 9);
}
// 'bookRoom' scans through the appropriate array to book a customer into the
// first available (lowest numbered) room
void Hotel::bookRoom()
{
// local variables for user input
    int room_type;
    int beds_required;
    char customer_name[80];
    char payee_name[80];
// local control variables
    bool room_available = false;
    int counter;
// get the required room type
    cout << "Enter room type (1 for bed, 2 for function) ";
    cin >> room_type;
// if a bedroom is required...
    if(room_type == 1)
    {
        cout << "Enter number of beds required (1 or 2) ";
        cin >> beds_required;
// if a single bedroom needed, check rooms indexed 0 to 9...
        if(beds_required == 1)
        {
            counter = 0;
            while(bedroom[counter].isOccupied() && counter < 10)
            {
                counter++;
            }
// if we found an empty room before counting through all ten, change the
// value of 'room_available'
            if(counter < 10)
            {
                room_available = true;
            }
        }
// if a double bedroom needed for Mr. & Mrs. Smith, check rooms indexed 10 to 39...
        else
        {
            counter = 10;
            while(bedroom[counter].isOccupied() && counter < 40)
            {
                counter++;
            }
// if we found an empty room before counting through to forty, change the
// value of 'room_available'
            if(counter < 40)
            {
                room_available = true;
            }
        }
// if the appropriate types of bedroom are all full
        if(room_available == false)
```

```
        {
            cout << "No bedrooms available" << endl;
        }
// if a room is available, book it
        else
        {
// enter the customer name
            cout << "Enter name of customer booking bedroom ";
            cin >> customer_name;
// enter the payee name
            cout << "Enter name of payee (company name or \"PRIVATE\") ";
            cin >> payee_name;
            cout << customer_name << " is booked into bedroom " << (counter + 6) << endl;
// occupy the room
            bedroom[counter--].occupyRoom(customer_name, payee_name);
        }
    }
// if a function room is required
    else
    {
        counter = 0;
        while(function_room[counter].isOccupied() && counter < 5)
        {
            counter++;
        }
        if(counter >= 5)
        {
            cout << "No function rooms available" << endl;
        }
        else
        {
// enter the customer name
            cout << "Enter name of customer booking function room ";
            cin >> customer_name;
// enter the payee name
            cout << "Enter name of payee (company name or \"PRIVATE\") ";
            cin >> payee_name;
// occupy the room
            cout << customer_name << " is booked into function room " << (counter + 1)
                << endl;
            function_room[counter].occupyRoom(customer_name, payee_name);
        }
    }
}
// 'vacateRoom' allows a customer to leave, and makes the room available
void Hotel::vacateRoom()
{
// local variables
    int room_number;
    bool was_occupied = false;
// display the numbers of occupied function rooms
    cout << "Occupied function rooms are:" << endl;
    for(int i = 0; i < 5; i++)
    {
        if(function_room[i].isOccupied())
        {
            cout << (i + 1) << " ";
        }
```

```cpp
    }
    cout << endl;
// display the numbers of occupied bedrooms
    cout << "Occupied bedrooms are:" << endl;
    for(i = 0; i < 40; i++)
    {
        if(bedroom[i].isOccupied())
        {
            cout << (i + 6) << " ";
        }
    }
    cout << endl;
// ask the user which room to vacate
    cout << "Enter number of room to vacate ";
    cin >> room_number;
// if the room is an occupied function room, vacate it
    if(room_number >=1 && room_number <=5)
    {
        if(function_room[room_number-1].isOccupied())
        {
            function_room[room_number-1].vacate();
            was_occupied = true;
        }
    }
// if the room is an occupied bedroom, vacate it
    else
    {
        if(bedroom[room_number-6].isOccupied())
        {
            bedroom[room_number-6].vacate();
            was_occupied = true;
        }
    }
// check to see if a room was actually occupied and vacated, and display
// an appropriate message
    if(was_occupied == true)
    {
        cout << "Room number " << room_number << " vacated" << endl;
    }
    else
    {
        cout << "Room " << room_number << " was not occupied" << endl;
    }
}
// 'moveEquipment' reallocates the equipment to another function room
void Hotel::moveEquipment()
{
    int current_location;
// display the current room location of the equipment
    for(int i = 0; i < 5; i++)
    {
        if(function_room[i].hasEquipment())
        {
            cout << "Presentation equipment is in room " << (i+1) << endl;
            current_location = i;
        }
    }
// get the new room number
```

```cpp
    int room_number;
    cout << "Which room do you wish to move it to? ";
    cin >> room_number;
// if a valid room number, move the equipment
    if(room_number >= 1 && room_number <= 5)
    {
        function_room[room_number - 1].installPresentationEquipment(&lecture_set);
        function_room[current_location].removePresentationEquipment();
        cout << "Equipment moved to room " << room_number << endl;
    }
// if not a valid room number, leave the equipment where it is and display
// a message
    else
    {
        cout << "Invalid function room number" << endl;
    }
}
// 'locateEquipment' displays the number of the function room containing the
// presentation equipment
void Hotel::locateEquipment()
{
    for(int i = 0; i < 5; i++)
    {
        if(function_room[i].hasEquipment())
        {
            cout << "Presentation equipment is in room " << (i+1) << endl;
        }
    }
}
// 'countOccupiedRooms' uses the class method 'getCustomerCount' to
// display the number of customers in the hotel
void Hotel::countOccupiedRooms()
{
    cout << "Number of rooms currently occupied is " << Customer::getCustomerCount()
        << endl;
}
// 'bedroomReport' displays the room numbers, occupants and payees of
// occupied bedrooms
void Hotel::bedroomReport()
{
    for(int i = 0; i < 40; i++)
    {
// if this room is occupied, display its details
        if(bedroom[i].isOccupied())
        {
            cout << "Room number " << bedroom[i].getRoomNumber() << " is occupied by ";
            cout<< bedroom[i].getCustomerName() << ", with Payee "
                << bedroom[i].getCustomerPayee() << endl;
        }
    }
}
// 'functionRoomReport' displays the room numbers of occupied function rooms
void Hotel::functionRoomReport()
{
    cout << "The following function rooms are occupied: ";
    for(int i = 0; i < 5; i++)
    {
        if(function_room[i].isOccupied())
```

```
            {
                cout << function_room[i].getRoomNumber() << ", ";
            }
        }
        cout << endl;
    }
// 'showIncome' scans through the rooms, adding the income from an
// occupied room to the total
void Hotel::showIncome()
{
// local variables
    float total_income = 0;
    float tariff;
// add the income from occupied function rooms to the total
    for(int i = 0; i < 5; i++)
    {
        if(function_room[i].isOccupied())
        {
            total_income += FunctionRoom::getFunctionTariff();
        }
    }
// add the income from occupied bedrooms to the total, applying the
// different tariffs for single and double rooms
    for(i = 0; i < 40; i++)
    {
        if(bedroom[i].isOccupied())
        {
            tariff = bedroom[i].getNumberOfBeds();
            if(tariff == 1)
            {
                total_income += Bedroom::getSingleTariff();
            }
            else
            {
                total_income += Bedroom::getDoubleTariff();
            }
        }
    }
// display the result
    cout << "the total projected day\'s income is: £" << total_income << endl;
}
*****************************************************************************
/*
    HOTLMAIN.CPP   The 'main' function that creates the Hotel object
*/
#include "hotel.h"
// in 'main', an object of the 'Hotel' class is instantiated. its constructor does the rest.
void main()
{
    Hotel solent_hotel;
}
```

10 Introduction to polymorphism

Overview

In this chapter, the various types of polymorphism are introduced and classified and 'ad hoc' and 'universal' polymorphism are compared. Coercion and casting are demonstrated using C++ syntax.

The meaning of 'polymorphism'

The word 'polymorphism' is derived from a Greek word ('polumorphos') with two roots:

Polus (many) + Morphe (shape/form) = Polumorphos

It therefore means 'many-shaped' or 'having many forms'. The English word 'polymorphe' dates from the 19th century and was originally applied to different animal forms arising in the same species, or different types of crystal in the same chemical compound. When applied to object-oriented programming, it is used to mean different forms of data being handled by the same type of process. This is achieved by various forms of 'overloading'; allowing operators and functions to behave differently in different contexts. We may contrast this with the term 'monomorphic' which is sometimes used to refer to non object-oriented languages, and simply means 'having a single form'; functions and operators have fixed and single meanings. However, languages tend not to be entirely monomorphic, since operators are usually given the polymorphic ability to work with more than one data type (see 'coercion' later in this chapter). Just to make things more confusing, there are many different forms of polymorphism! However, the underlying philosophy of polymorphism is that it ultimately makes programs easier to express, because it reduces the number of different names we need to use for processes which are similar but not identical.

When used in the context of object-oriented programming, polymorphism means that it is possible to 'overload' (use to mean more than one thing) the symbols that we use in a program, so that the same symbol can have different meanings in different contexts. What do we mean by 'symbol'? In fact it encompasses two fundamental components of our program source code:

1. operators
2. function (method) names

Since both may be overloaded to give polymorphic behaviour, we have both 'operator overloading' and 'function overloading', and both of these have more than one aspect. In essence, however, it means that the same symbol or function name can be used to apply to different processes. In this chapter, we will introduce the various types of polymorphism and attempt to categorise them into types applicable to the available facilities in C++. Following chapters will cover in detail the overloading of operators and methods.

Many types of polymorphism

Although there are many types of polymorphism they all have a common aspect, which is the ability to generalise the messages that we send to objects. We can apply a generic name to a collection of methods implemented differently by different classes, and objects of those classes will respond in class-specific ways to the same message. This 'message' will be in practice the calling of a method associated with an object or the use of an operator with objects as operands.

As a general example of polymorphic responses to a single message, we might ask the same question of a number of people of different religious faiths. The question we ask (i.e. the message we send) is the following:

'What year is it?'

If you ask this question of, for example, a Christian, a Muslim and a Jew, you may well get three different answers, because their calendars started counting at different points in history. No doubt there are many variations on calendars in the world, giving many different answers to the same question depending on the cultural 'class' of the person answering. Something similar happens when a method is called in an object-oriented program. That method may have the same name in different classes, but the response of objects in each class may well be different. The important point is that we do not need a different message to send to every different type of object in our system. A single message is enough; each object is capable of supplying its own response, defined by the class to which the object belongs. Polymorphism devolves responsibility for interpreting a message down to the level of the object.

In a program we might define a method called 'Print' in a number of classes, but each version of 'Print' would be specifically tailored to the class of the object being printed. An object of class 'Cheque' will respond to the message 'Print' in one way, an object of class 'Report' in another, a 'Photograph' object in yet another (Fig. 10.1). We do not have to define methods with entirely different names such as 'PrintCheque', 'PrintReport' and 'PrintPhotograph' which would make our programs much less flexible. Because the objects themselves take responsibility for their different responses to the same message, we are free to send generic messages to any set of objects with similar but class specific behaviours.

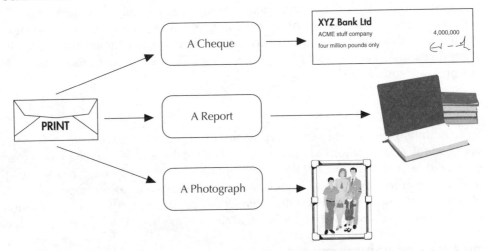

Fig. 10.1: Polymorphism means that different objects can respond to the same message in different, class-specific ways.

Question 10.1   What makes a method 'polymorphic'?

Methods are polymorphic when they are implemented differently for different types of object.

Categorising polymorphic techniques

Since there are a number of types of polymorphism it may be useful to classify some key terms and their relationships. Cardelli and Wegner produced a 'taxonomy' (classification) of polymorphic techniques [Blair et al, 1991 p.81] which is primarily divided into 'ad hoc' and 'universal' types (Fig. 10.2), and provides a basis for an important general distinction.

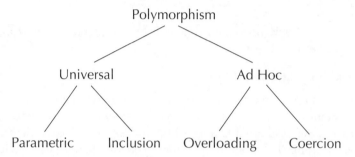

Fig. 10.2: Cardelli and Wegner's taxonomy of polymorphic techniques.

Put simply, this is that 'ad hoc' polymorphism is applicable in both traditional and object-oriented programming environments, whereas 'universal' polymorphism only applies to object-oriented systems. As the figure indicates, there are further subdivisions of these types, 'ad hoc' polymorphism covering 'overloading' (which means specifically overloading a function name by different sets of parameters) and 'coercion' (the temporary conversion from one data type to another). 'Universal' polymorphism divides into 'parametric' (using different parameter lists to create different instances of a single method or class) and 'inclusion' (overloading methods in a classification hierarchy). However, it will be necessary to expand on these terms in order to apply the various forms in C++.

What follows is an attempt to summarise the various types of polymorphism that may be implemented in C++.

Ad hoc polymorphism

'Ad hoc' is a Latin phrase which (roughly translated) means 'for this purpose only'. In other words, we use it to describe forms of overloading when they are applied in specific rather than generalised contexts. Strictly speaking, the term 'ad hoc polymorphism' only applies to what is known as 'coercion' (described later in this chapter) and the overloading of function names by their parameter lists, what we might call 'parametric overloading' (though it is usually referred to simply as 'overloading'). One reason for grouping these together under the 'ad hoc' heading is that they are applicable both to procedural and object-oriented programming.

Universal polymorphism

Whereas ad hoc polymorphism is characterised by the fact that it only works on a fixed set of types, universal polymorphism can be applied to a general set of types which do not need to be specifically defined. There are two ways of doing this; one is to use 'parametric polymorphism' (implemented with templates and described in Chapter 12). The other is to use inclusion polymorphism (implemented with a classification hierarchy and described in Chapters 13 and 14).

Question 10.2 What differentiates 'ad hoc' and 'universal' polymorphism?

Ad hoc polymorphism is applied 'for this purpose only'; i.e. can be applied to a given function without reference to any other. In contrast, universal polymorphism is applied generally to many types of object.

The various types of polymorphism that will be discussed in detail in the following chapters are summarised below.

Operator overloading (Chapter 11)

Although there is some semantic similarity between coercion and operator overloading, there are important distinctions between them. Coercion only translates from one type into another to allow assignments and arithmetic to take place. Operator overloading provides new meanings for existing operators to enable them to work with user defined types. Overloaded operators are generally inherited by derived classes.

Parametric overloading and genericity (Chapter 12)

We can apply polymorphism via parameters in two ways – parametric overloading (separate methods defined for each parameter set) or genericity (single methods and classes able to handle parameters of different types).

parametric overloading

This gives us the ability to define a number of methods with the same name in a single class, differentiated by their parameter lists. A useful context is the overloading of a constructor to give alternative ways of creating an object of a particular class.

genericity

'Genericity' or 'parametric polymorphism' refers to the creation of methods which are generic; applicable to a range of objects. Whereas a method name overloaded by parameters will execute different implementations of the method depending on the type(s) of parameter(s) it is passed, a generic method will execute the same implementation but be able to accept a range of types as parameters. This is particularly useful when implementing container classes (to build objects which contain other objects). In C++, genericity is achieved by the use of templates (only introduced in version 2 of the language and fully implemented in version 3). The power of templates allows us to build whole generic classes, so that the creation of objects can depend on the types of parameters provided to the constructor.

Method polymorphism (Chapter 13)

This means using the same name for methods in different classes in a classification hierarchy. As we know, a method defined in a base class is inherited by all derived classes, which may or may not override that method definition. This may mean that a single method definition can be applied to all classes in the hierarchy, or that some or all of the classes define their own version of that method, either expanding or replacing the method which has been inherited.

Run time polymorphism (Chapter 14)

This is method polymorphism or operator overloading where the type(s) of objects using the methods or operators are not known until run time. In this case the compiler has to use 'dynamic binding' to work out which version of the method/operator definition to call. Messages in the source code are sent to a 'static' identifier (a base class), and the messages are received at run time by a 'dynamic' identifier (a derived class). When we are using dynamic objects in a system, we frequently need to bind them to their methods at run time.

Question 10.3   Why is genericity a form of universal polymorphism, while overloading is 'ad hoc'?

Genericity means that a single function or class can be used with all types, and the key characteristic of universal polymorphism is that it applies to all types, not just specifically chosen ones. In contrast, overloading is done for one function or method at a time, regardless of any other functions in the system.

C++ syntax

While most of the syntax of polymorphism will be dealt with in the detailed chapters which follow, it is useful to look at how automatic coercion works and also the syntax for 'casting', the explicit coercion from one data type to another. Although this has only limited application, there are occasions when it can prove useful.

Coercion

The arithmetical operators with which we are familiar in all programming languages exhibit a form of polymorphism known as 'coercion'. While coercion itself is not an object-oriented concept, it serves as a useful introduction to the idea of symbols (in this case arithmetic operators) performing similar operations on different data types.

In C++, if we write something like:

```
int x = 4 + 5;
```

we are using the addition (+) operator in a way which the compiler recognises – the context of adding two integers.

Likewise if we write:

```
float y = 5.9 + 4.55
```

then the compiler uses the '+' operator to add two floats. Any of the built-in numeric types can be added in this way. In this sense the operators are already overloaded (can be used in more than one context) because there is a single operator for 'ints', 'floats', 'longs' etc, not a separate operator for each data type. Clearly life would be well nigh impossible if this were not the case, since we would also need a different operator for all possible combinations of different numeric data types, e.g. adding a 'float' to an 'int', or a 'long' to a 'double'! When such operations happen in most programming languages, implicit conversions take place so that we can perform arithmetic on mixed data types. For example, if we perform the following arithmetic in C++:

```
int x = 10;
float y = 7.5;
double z = x * y;
```

the compiler converts the 'lower' data types in an expression into the same type as the 'higher' one ('lower' and 'higher' relate to the size of data storage). In this case, there will be a conversion of 'x' (an integer) into a float, and a conversion of the result of 'x * y' (both floats) into a double. These conversions are invisible to the programmer.

Casting

The fixed conversions between types provided by coercion can be extended explicitly if required. Explicitly converting one data type to another is known as 'casting' and is also common in non object-oriented languages.

Casting is necessary when the temporary results generated in the course of evaluating an arithmetic expression can cause overflow errors or loss of precision.

Question 10.4 What is the difference between 'coercion' and 'casting'?

Coercion is something the compiler does by default. Casting is something we must do explicitly. Both, however, temporarily convert the data type of a variable.

There are two very similar ways in which we can explicitly change the data type of a variable for the purposes of a temporary calculation. The first is the casting syntax which is also used in C:

(data-type) variable

In this example, variable 'x' is temporarily converted to a float:

(float) x

The other syntax is only available in C++, and achieves exactly the same result but puts the brackets around the variable name, not the type:

data-type (variable)

so our conversion above would appear as

float (x)

In the examples which follow, the latter C++ syntax will be used. However, in certain rather obscure cases this form of casting will not work, and the alternative C syntax is required.

The following program takes two integers from the keyboard and calculates the mean average. As it stands there are some potential problems with it which the use of casts can alleviate:

```
#include <iostream.h>
void main( )
```

```
    {
        int x, y, mean;
        cout << "Enter 2 integers:" << endl;
        cin >> x;
        cin >> y;
        mean = (x + y) / 2;
        cout << "Mean average is: " << mean << endl;
    }
```

First of all, let's run the program:

Enter 2 integers:

3

3

Mean average is 3

This seems ok, but what happens if the numbers we add are somewhat larger? Potentially, the intermediate value of 'x + y' which is calculated before the division may be larger than the maximum storage capacity of an integer data type. In the following example, 'x' and 'y' are given values whose sum will be greater than the maximum storage of a 2 byte integer

Enter 2 integers:

32000

32000

Mean average is -768

The result here is clearly nonsense, because the intermediate result has been truncated. In such circumstances, we can cast the integers used in the expression into larger data types so that the intermediate value is never too large for the available storage. In the revised version of the program, 'x' is cast to a long integer. This also has the effect of causing the compiler to automatically coerce 'y' to a temporary long, because it always converts the operands of an expression to the type of the 'highest' variable (i.e. the one with the largest storage).

```
    #include <iostream.h>
    void main( )
    {
        int x, y, mean;
        cout << "Enter 2 integers:" << endl;
        cin >> x;
        cin >> y;
        mean = (long(x) + y) / 2;
        cout << "Mean average is: " << mean << endl;
    }
```

Running the program again with the previous data gives us a correct result:

Enter 2 integers:

32000

32000

Mean average is 32000

While we have used casting to deal with the problem of over-large intermediate results in an expression, there is another potential flaw in our program which casting can solve. This is the fact that the mean average of two integers is not necessarily an integer. In fact it will more often than not have a decimal fraction. Leaving aside the cast to 'long' for the moment, we might therefore modify the original program as follows, so that the result of the expression (i.e. 'mean') is a float rather than an integer:

```
include <iostream.h>
void main( )
{
    int x, y;
    float mean;
    cout << "Enter 2 integers:" << endl;
    cin >> x;
    cin >> y;
    mean = (x + y) / 2;
    cout << "Mean average is: " << mean << endl;
}
```

This may look like a solution, but in fact it does not fully solve the problem. If we run the program as it stands, we still fail to get a decimal part in the result:

Enter 2 integers:

3

2

Mean average is 2

Why does this happen? It happens because although the result of the expression is stored in a float variable, the operands on the right hand side of the expression are integers, so there is no automatic conversion to a higher type. Again, casting is a useful tool. In this case, we can cast the two integers to temporary floats. This allows us to have a fractional part in the result, and achieves the extra storage required for large intermediate results, since the storage of a float is greater than the storage of an integer.

The final version of our program now looks like this:

```
include <iostream.h>
void main( )
{
    int x, y;
    float mean;
    cout << "Enter 2 integers:" << endl;
    cin >> x;
    cin >> y;
    mean = (float(x) + y) / 2;
    cout << "Mean average is: " << mean << endl;
}
```

Now we can run the program with large numbers and/or numbers which produce fractional results:

Enter 2 integers:

3

2

Mean average is 2.5

Casting is a useful tool to have when writing arithmetic expressions in C++, because in certain circumstances it means the difference between an accurate result and nonsense. We should always be aware that the temporary values which are being stored when an expression is being evaluated may cause overflow errors or loss of accuracy. In these cases, casting can usually solve the problem.

Summary of key points from this chapter

1. Polymorphism means 'having many forms'. In an object-oriented program, methods and operators can have many forms by being 'overloaded' in various ways.

2. Polymorphism passes the responsibility for responding to a message to the object. The same message evokes class-specific responses in different objects.

3. Cardelli and Wegner classified polymorphic techniques into 'ad hoc' and 'universal' types. Ad hoc techniques (overloading and coercion) are not unique to object-oriented languages, but universal techniques are.

4. In object-oriented systems, we can classify those types of polymorphism that relate to methods and operators together, because they exhibit similar characteristics, including the ability to be dynamically bound at run time.

5. Genericity (parametric polymorphism) is a powerful tool allowing us to create generic functions, methods and classes.

6. Coercion is an automatic activity of the compiler, converting data types to 'higher' types in expressions.

7. In C++, we can explicitly cast data types into new (temporary) types in order to maintain accuracy in arithmetic expressions.

Exercises

1. When displaying 'char' variables in a 'cout' statement, the character, not the ASCII value is displayed. In contrast, an integer variable displays a number. Write a program that counts from 92 to 122, displaying each number and its ASCII character by casting from type 'int' to type 'char'.

11 Operator overloading

Overview

In this chapter, the applications and syntax of operator overloading are explained. Syntax examples show how relational, arithmetic and assignment operators can be overloaded.

Operator overloading

Operator overloading means making the compiler's built in operator symbols work with classes defined by the programmer. Operators such as the arithmetic and relational operators have certain fixed meanings, applicable to all the built in data types such as int and float, but we can also make these operator symbols work with our own classes. This is made possible in some object-oriented languages by overloading the meaning of an operator, so that its behaviour can be polymorphic; implemented differently for different classes. This is a similar idea to that of coercion, which allows a single operator to be used with a range of types.

To perform operations on classes similar to those available for the built in data types, we need to explicitly overload the chosen operators so they can be applied to objects of a specific class. For example, if we want to use the addition operator (+) with objects, the compiler will have to interpret statements like:

object3 = object1 + object2

It can only do this if we code the mechanism ourselves. In effect, the '+' operator (and also the '=' operator) will have to be overloaded to become a method of the class (i.e. one which objects of the class can use.) By overloading operators in this way we can give all the classes in a system a common interface, allowing us to perform similar operations on a range of different objects (Fig. 11.1).

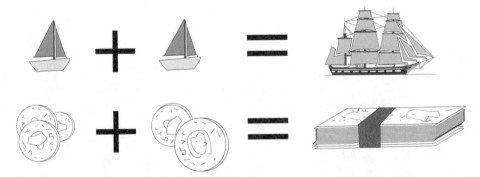

Fig. 11.1: Operator overloading allows the same set of operators
to be used with objects of many different classes.

Question 11.1 What kinds of objects might benefit from being able to use overloaded operators such as the arithmetic operators?

Objects whose state is defined by numeric data may find overloaded operators useful. Another example is strings; a 'String' class might usefully overload the '+' operator for concatenation (appending one string to another).

Overloading and the assignment operator

One operator that is already overloaded to work with objects as well as simple data types is the assignment ('=') operator. We have already used this in the context of the default copy constructor in Chapter 5. Remember that we can instantiate an object by making that object's attribute values equal to those of another object that already exists. The syntax, you may recall, is to use the assignment operator:

```
class_name object2 = object1;
```

This means that 'object2' is instantiated with the same state as 'object1'. In fact we are not restricted to using the assignment operator in a copy constructor; it has the default behaviour of making one object's attributes equal to those of another object. We are able to state:

```
object2 = object1;
```

and all corresponding attributes will be copied from 'object1' to 'object2'. Although the compiler provides this default behaviour, we may alternatively override this with our own overloaded version of the assignment operator. This is needed where pointers are involved (for example pointers to strings of characters); there may be pointers inside the object that by default will simply have the address they reference copied to the other object, rather than the actual data. In such cases, we may well wish to override this default behaviour of redirecting pointers, and replace it with a mechanism that copies the actual data from one object to another. As a general rule of thumb, if we have had to implement a copy constructor to deal with pointers, then we need to do the same for the assignment operator (and vice versa).

Overloading operators for a class

Assignment is a fundamental operation on all classes and types, which is why a default implementation is provided. However, no default behaviour is provided for other operators when used with classes, so we need to specifically overload operators for objects that we want to use in arithmetic or relational expressions.

Suppose we have written a class that represents a set of student grades, and create a separate object of this type in a program for each student. Perhaps the objects have just two attributes like this:

Student Grade
maths grade
english grade

Each subject grade attribute might be an integer representing a percentage grade. No doubt there would be various methods associated with the class, but what overloaded operators might be useful? Operations we might want to perform on 'StudentGrade' objects could include (among others) looking for the highest grade, sorting into order and finding the average.

To find the highest grade, and also for sorting, an overloaded '>' (greater than) operator would be useful. How about the average student grade? We would need to add all the student totals together and then divide by the number of students. We might do this by returning the various values from each object and processing them outside the objects, but this would be a bit clumsy and not a very object-oriented approach. How much better it would be if we could say something like:

    grade_total = student1 + student2;

and thereby get a total of grades from 'student1' and 'student2' stored in 'grade_total' (i.e. add two student grade objects together). Explicit (user-defined) operator overloading is about this kind of process, where appropriate operator functions can be applied to new data types as well as those which are an inherent part of the language.

Question 11.2   Which operator would we overload to find out if two student grades are the same?

We would overload the '==' operator.

The semantics of overloaded operators

In the example above we are using the addition operator to add two objects together, which is what we would expect it to do. In practice, an operator can be overloaded to mean something totally different from what we might expect, so that it is possible for instance to overload the '+' operator so that it would subtract one object from another! Clearly, although this is possible it results in highly obscure and unreadable code. Operator overloading must be done in the spirit of the what is being overloaded. The '+' operator for example should only be overloaded to add objects together (though 'adding' can reasonably include concatenation; adding one string of characters to the end of another).

Inheritance of overloaded operators

Like other methods, operators overloaded in one class are inherited by derived classes. The exception to this is the assignment ('=') operator which, because it has a default behaviour for all objects, can only be explicitly overridden for individual classes and not automatically for their descendants. The user-defined behaviour of any other operator may be inherited by descendant classes, but may well need to be overridden anyway since operators tend to work on the whole object rather than just one or two attributes. Our addition operator in the 'StudentGrade' example uses all the given attributes, and if there were more subject grades then these would also be part of the process. Therefore, any changes to the attribute set of classes deriving from 'StudentGrade' would require changes to the behaviour of the addition operator.

Let us assume that the 'StudentGrade' class described above represents one set of students who are studying two subjects, but that it also serves as a base class for a class called 'ExtendedGrade'. This class is used to represent students who are studying a wider range of subjects than just English and Maths. For example, they may have a set of five subjects, inheriting two from the base class (Fig. 11.2 shows this inheritance using UML notation.)

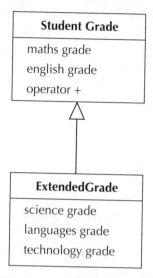

Fig. 11.2: 'ExtendedGrade' objects will inherit the overloaded '+' operator from 'StudentGrade' but it will not have an appropriate functionality.

'ExtendedGrade' will inherit the overloaded '+' operator from 'StudentGrade', but this will not be appropriate for adding together objects of the derived class. Although it will work with two 'ExtendedGrade' objects, it can only return as a result an object of the 'StudentGrade' class, i.e. it can only generate totals for the Maths and English grades. 'ExtendedGrade', then, will need its own overloaded operator.

In general terms, although overloaded operators (other than '=') are inherited by derived classes, it is often necessary to redefine their behaviour for all classes in a hierarchy.

Question 11.3   Why are inherited overloaded operators often not very useful in the derived class?

Because operators tend to address the object as a whole rather than a subset of its attributes, their semantics are more class specific than other methods. Therefore an inherited overloaded operator may not be appropriate to a derived class object.

C++ Syntax

The syntax required for overloading operators in C++ is:

1. The 'operator' keyword;

2. Any of the 40 operators that can be overloaded, listed in Stroustrup [1995, p.592]. These operators are also listed at the end of this chapter.

Although there are a large number of operators that may be overloaded, we are most likely to find overloading useful for the arithmetic and relational operators described in Chapter 3.

The default assignment operator

Since the assignment operator has a default behaviour, we do not necessarily need to overload it. In the following example, one object of the 'Point' class is made to equal another object of the same class:

```
/*
    POINT.H    definition of 'Point' class
*/
class Point
{
private:
    int x, y;
public:
    void setXY(int x_in, int y_in);
    int getX();
    int getY();
};
// the 'setXY' method sets the values of both co-ordinates
void Point::setXY(int x_in, int y_in)
{
    x = x_in;
    y = y_in;
}
// selector methods to get the values of 'x' and 'y'
int Point::getX()
{
    return x;
}
int Point::getY()
{
    return y;
}
```

This program tests the behaviour of the default assignment operator

```
#include "point.h"
void main()
{
// instantiate two 'Point' objects
    Point point1, point2;
// set the position of point1 to 100,100
    point1.setXY(100, 100);
// use the default behaviour of the '=' operator to give 'point2' the same coordinates
    point2 = point1;
// retrieve and display the coordinates of the points
    cout << "The position of point 1 is " << point1.getX() << "," << point1.getY() << endl;
    cout << "The position of point 2 is " << point2.getX() << "," << point2.getY() << endl;
}
```

Output from the program shows the position of the second point is the same as that of the first:

The position of point 1 is 100,100
The position of point 2 is 100,100

This use of the default behaviour of the assignment operator is perfectly adequate in many cases, but we must be aware of two aspects of using the operator with pointers:

1. Pointers to dynamic objects
2. Objects with pointers inside them

Pointers to dynamic objects:

As we saw in Chapter 6, if the assignment operator is used with dynamic objects then it simply redirects the pointer on the left. For example, if 'point1' and 'point2' were pointers referencing dynamic objects, then the following line of code would simply redirect 'point2' to the address of 'point1':

```
point2 = point1;
```

This means that if 'point1' is destroyed, then 'point2' is no longer referencing a valid object. To ensure that the assignment actually copies the second object to the first, we can dereference the pointers:

```
*point2 = *point1;
```

This dereferencing technique can be used for any operator used with dynamic objects. However, this is *only* safe if all the pointers involved are currently referencing objects, otherwise memory will be corrupted.

Objects with pointers inside them:

Similar problems can arise when pointers are used inside objects. Again, the copying object only copies the addresses, not the data from the original object, with similar potential for disaster if the original object disappears. In this case, the solution is to provide our own overloaded assignment operator. The syntax for doing this is described later in this chapter.

Question 11.4   What is wrong with this code fragment?

```
Point* xy1;
Point* xy2 = new Point(0,0);
*xy1 = *xy2;
```

We should not assign the value of the object referenced by xy2 to the dereferenced pointer xy1, because xy1 is not pointing to an object. Therefore we are copying an object to unassigned memory.

Syntax for operator overloading

The syntax for overloading an operator is as follows, using the keyword 'operator':

return_type operator symbol (parameter list...)

The return type for relational operators is a boolean value (the ANSI standard states that all relational operators return type 'bool'), which may be true or false, typically represented by 1 or 0 respectively (Fig. 11.3).

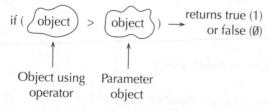

Fig. 11.3: Relational operators return true or false.

Arithmetic operators return an object of the appropriate class (Fig. 11.4), generally the same class as the other objects in the expression.

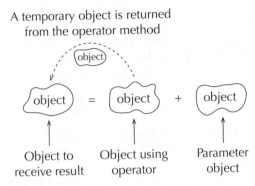

Fig. 11.4: Arithmetic operators return an object of the appropriate class.

In either case, the parameter list generally consists of an object of the class, passed by reference rather than by value to avoid making an unnecessary copy. The 'const' prefix is therefore frequently used to indicate that, although the object has been passed by reference, it should not be modified by the method. For a class called 'Object', we might expect to see methods such as:

- 'less than' (a relational operator): **int operator < (const Object& object);**
- 'minus' (an arithmetic operator): **Object operator - (const Object& object);**

Overloading relational operators

The easiest operators to overload are the relational operators (described in Chapter 3), because their return value only has to represent true or false, which (as indicated above) we can represent with 1 and 0 respectively.

For this example, we will overload the equality operator (==) for the 'Point' class so we can compare two points and see if they are equal. The method will return an integer and take another object of the 'Point' class as a parameter, i.e.

int operator == (const Point& point);

Remember that the parameter object is passed by reference simply to avoid making an unnecessary copy. The implementation of the method will return 1 if the attribute values of one object match the attribute values of the other, otherwise it will return zero.

This is how the class declaration appears after adding the overloaded operator:

```
class Point
{
private:
    int x, y;
public:
    void setXY(int x_in, int y_in);
    int getX();
    int getY();
    int operator == (const Point& point);
};
```

This is the definition of the overloaded '==' operator. It compares both attributes with the parameter object's attributes, returning true or false as appropriate. This implementation returns an integer with the value 1 (true) or 0 (false), but the 'bool' data type can be used instead if available:

```
int Point::operator == (const Point& point)
{
    if(x == point.getX() && y == point.getY())
    {
        return 1;
    }
    else
    {
        return 0;
    }
}
```

This example program shows the equality operator being used with Point objects:

```
#include "point.h"
#include <iostream.h>
void main()
{
// instantiate two 'Point' objects
    Point point1, point2;
// set the positions of the objects to be identical
    point1.setXY(100, 100);
    point2.setXY(100, 100);
// compare the points with the overloaded operator
    if(point1 == point2)
    {
        cout << "Point " << point1.getX() << ", " << point1.getY();
        cout << " and point " << point2.getX() << ", " << point2.getY();
        cout << " are the same" << endl;
    }
}
```

The output from this program is:

Point 100, 100 and point 100, 100 are the same

Overloading operators for the 'StudentGrade' class

For the next example, we will overload an operator for the StudentGrade class described earlier in this chapter. The class (before adding any operators) might look something like this:

```
class StudentGrade
{
private:
    int maths_grade;
    int english_grade;
public:
// constructor
    StudentGrade();
// selector methods
    int getMathsGrade();
    int getEnglishGrade();
// modifier methods
    void setMathsGrade(int grade_in);
    void setEnglishGrade(int grade_in);
};
```

```
// the constructor initialises the grades to eliminate any 'rogue' values
StudentGrade::StudentGrade()
{
    maths_grade = 0;
    english_grade = 0;
}
// selectors
int StudentGrade::getMathsGrade()
{
    return maths_grade;
}
int StudentGrade::getEnglishGrade()
{
    return english_grade;
}
// modifiers
void StudentGrade::setMathsGrade(int grade_in)
{
    maths_grade = grade_in;
}
void StudentGrade::setEnglishGrade(int grade_in)
{
    english_grade = grade_in;
}
```

If we wanted to add two student grade objects together without an overloaded operator, we would have to do something like the following (assuming we have two objects called 'student1' and 'student2' containing grades, and a third object called 'grade_total' which is to contain the overall grade):

```
#include "studgrad.h"
void main( )
{
    StudentGrade grade_total, student1, student2;
// some code would be necessary here to put the various
// grades into the student grade objects
    int temp_maths, temp_english;
    temp_maths = student1.getMathsGrade() + student2.getMathsGrade();
    grade_total.setMathsGrade(temp_maths);
// and so on for the English grade...
}
```

Clearly this is rather clumsy and inflexible. What we want to be able to do (as we noted earlier in the chapter) is something much simpler like:

```
grade_total = student1 + student2;
```

but the compiler won't recognise the data type 'StudentGrade' (which all student grade objects are instances of) as being one of its built in types which can be added. Therefore we will have to overload the '+' operator so that it can be used with objects of this class.

The relational operators return a single value representing true or false, but the arithmetic operators must return an object. For example, the addition operator must return an object which contains the result of the addition. If we were to add together two 'StudentGrade' objects, then we would be evaluating expressions like:

```
grade3 = grade1 + grade2;
```

The addition of 'grade1' and 'grade2' returns an object, the value of which is assigned to 'grade3' (using either the default or a user defined assignment operator).

To add two StudentGrade objects together, then, we could include the following proto-type in the class declaration:

StudentGrade operator + (const StudentGrade& grade_in);

Because the addition operator returns a result, the return type is an object of the class containing the appropriate totals, in this case of course a 'StudentGrade' object. This is followed by the keyword 'operator' and the '+' symbol, because it is the '+' operator we want to overload. The parameter is also an object of the class (passed by reference), which is added to the object calling the method. When we say:

grade_total = student1 + student2;

it is 'student1' which calls the operator method, with 'student2' as it's argument and 'grade_total' as its return value. All of the C++ arithmetic operators can be overloaded in this way.

When the overloaded operator is called, we will add the Maths grades of the two objects together, and also the English grades. In order do this we must access the attributes of the object which is calling the method, and the attributes of the parameter object. Because the overloaded operator is an object method, we are able to access the private attributes of the parameter object directly using the dot operator. The attribute 'maths_grade' of the parameter object can therefore be referred to as:

grade_in.maths_grade

Since the operator has to return an object of the class as the result of the addition, we have to create a temporary object in the body of the method. This object exists long enough to pass the result of the operator to the receiving object. In the following example, a temporary object of the StudentGrade class called 'temp_student' is instanti-ated. As soon as the result of the method has been returned, this object will fall out of scope and be destroyed.

If the method body is defined outside the class, it will appear as follows. Note the syntax of return type, class name, scope resolution operator, 'operator' keyword, overloaded symbol and parameter list. The implementation of the method takes advantage of the fact that both the parameter object and the returned object are members of the same class as the one using the method, so their attributes can be directly accessed using the dot operator. An alternative implementation could simply use methods to get and set the various values being calculated.

```
StudentGrade StudentGrade::operator + (const StudentGrade& grade_in)
{
// create a temporary object of the class to hold the calculated values
    StudentGrade temp_student;
// add the attributes of the two objects, storing the results
// in the attributes of the temporary object
    temp_student.maths_grade = maths_grade + grade_in.maths_grade;
    temp_student.english_grade = english_grade + grade_in.english_grade;
// return the temporary object as the result of the method
    return temp_student;
}
```

The following program shows how the overloaded '+' operator can be used with objects of the StudentGrade type. Note that, unlike the other StudentGrade objects, 'grade_total' does not have its initial values set by calling methods. The same is true of the temporary object instantiated in the implementation of the operator + method. This is why the initialisation of values in the constructor is important, because we may otherwise be adding a grade to an existing 'garbage value' which happens to be in that attribute by default.

```
#include <iostream.h>
#include "studgrad.h"
void main()
{
// create three objects of class StudentGrade
    StudentGrade student1, student2, grade_total;
// give the first two initial values
    student1.setMathsGrade(50);
    student1.setEnglishGrade(65);
    student2.setMathsGrade(43);
    student2.setEnglishGrade(49);
// use the '+' operator to add two objects together, putting the result
// in the third object
    grade_total = student1 + student2;
// display the result
    cout << "Total Maths " << grade_total.getMathsGrade() << endl;
    cout << "Total English " << grade_total.getEnglishGrade() << endl;
}
```

The output from this program would be:

Total Maths 93

Total English 114

To make this into a more realistic example, we could use an array of 'StudentGrade' objects to make them more easily processed, and produce an average grade for each subject. In this example, a constant is used to size the array. Instead of using literals in the code we will also enter the grades at the keyboard:

```
#include <iostream.h>
#include "studgrad.h"
void main()
{
// use a constant for the number of students. only 2 in this
// example to keep the test run short!
    const int MAXSTUDENTS = 2;
// create an array of student grade objects
    StudentGrade students[MAXSTUDENTS];
// create a separate grade total object
    StudentGrade grade_total;
// temporary store for grades entered from the keyboard
    int temp_grade;
// loop to enter grades for all students - 'i + 1' is used in the output
// simply to avoid starting at 'student 0'
    for(int i = 0; i < MAXSTUDENTS; i++)
    {
        cout << "Enter Maths grade for student " << i + 1 << " ";
        cin >> temp_grade;
        students[i].setMathsGrade(temp_grade);
```

```
        cout << "Enter English grade for student " << i + 1 << " ";
        cin >> temp_grade;
        students[i].setEnglishGrade(temp_grade);
    }
// iterate through the array, using the overloaded '+' operator to
// add all the student grades together. note that we cannot use
// the '+=' shorthand with the objects since it has not been explicitly
// overloaded for use with this class
    for(i = 0; i < MAXSTUDENTS; i++)
    {
        grade_total = grade_total + students[i];
    }
// display the results. note that the averages may include decimal fractions
// so they are declared as floats, and the operands are also
// cast to floats from integers
    float average_maths, average_english;
    average_maths = float(grade_total.getMathsGrade())/MAXSTUDENTS;
    average_english = float(grade_total.getEnglishGrade())/MAXSTUDENTS;
    cout << endl << "Average grades are:" << endl;
    cout << "Maths: " << average_maths << endl;
    cout << "English: " << average_english << endl;
}
```

The actual output of this program will, of course, depend on the values entered. In the following test run, data entered at the keyboard is shown in italics:

Enter maths grade for student 1 45
Enter english grade for student 1 32
Enter maths grade for student 2 75
Enter english grade for student 2 81
Average grades are
Maths: 60
English: 56.5

Overloading the assignment operator

Earlier in this chapter we looked at the default assignment operator, and indicated that it is sometimes necessary to provide our own implementation of this operator if an object contains pointers. The following example ('NamedPoint') modifies our earlier 'Point' class so that it includes a pointer of type char used to reference a dynamic array. This array will hold a string of characters representing the name of the point. This class includes a copy constructor as well as the overloaded assignment operator because they are generally similar; both copy data from one object to another. The class definition is:

```
class NamedPoint
{
private:
    int x, y;
    char* name;
public:
    NamedPoint(char* name_in);
    NamedPoint(const NamedPoint& n);
    ~NamedPoint();
    void setXY(int x_in, int y_in);
    void getXY(int& x_out, int& y_out);
    char* getName();
```

```
NamedPoint& operator = (const NamedPoint& in);
void show();
};
```

Notice that a destructor is also required to clean up memory when the object is destroyed.

Let us look at the important methods of the class, including the assignment operator:

The constructor:

The constructor allocates enough dynamic memory to hold the name of the object by finding the length of the parameter string (using the 'strlen' function) and adding 1 to it for the terminating '\0'. Then the memory is reserved using the 'new' operator and the parameter string is copied (using 'strcpy') into the attribute.

```
NamedPoint::NamedPoint(char* name_in)
{
    x = 0;
    y = 0;
    name = new char[strlen(name_in)+1];
    strcpy(name, name_in);
}
```

The copy constructor:

The copy constructor is very similar to the constructor in that it must also reserve memory for the name of the object. The difference is that the parameter is not a string but an object, from which the location and name are copied.

```
NamedPoint::NamedPoint(const NamedPoint& n)
{
    x = n.x;
    y = n.y;
    name = new char[strlen(n.name)+1];
    strcpy(name, n.name);
}
```

The destructor:

The destructor frees up the memory used by the name by calling the array version of the 'delete' operator.

```
NamedPoint::~NamedPoint()
{
    delete [] name;
}
```

The assignment operator:

The assignment operator is almost identical to the copy constructor, except that it frees up the memory occupied by the previous name before reallocating memory for the new name. You will also notice that it has a return value (an object of the NamedPoint class) though you might expect the method to be 'void'. A void method would certainly allow you to make one object equal to another, because the object that calls the method simply copies its own attribute values from a parameter object, just like the copy constructor. Why, then do we return a value? in fact it is only necessary in order to be consistent with the behaviour of the assignment operator on built in data types, which can be 'chained' together. For example, the following syntax is valid in C++:

```
int x, y, z;
x = 10;
z = y = x;
```

This declares three integers, gives a value to one of them and then makes the other two equal to it in a single statement. This implies that an object using the assignment operator must always return a copy of itself that may then be used by another assignment operator (Fig. 11.5).

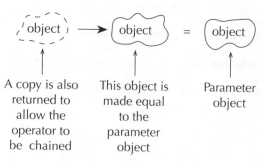

| A copy is also returned to allow the operator to be chained | This object is made equal to the parameter object | Parameter object |

Fig. 11.5: The assignment operator changes the object but also returns a copy to allow operators to be chained together.

How, then, does an object return a copy of itself from a method? The answer is to use the 'this' pointer, first introduced in Chapter 9. Remember that the 'this' pointer is effectively an attribute of the class that always references the current object. We may return 'this' to provide a copy of the object to another assignment operator. In order for an overloaded assignment operator to work properly in all contexts, it must return a reference to an object of the class, so the 'this' pointer is de-referenced in the implementation of the method:

```
NamedPoint& NamedPoint::operator = (const NamedPoint& in)
{
// copy the other object's position
    x = in.x;
    y = in.y;
// clear the old name from memory
    delete [] name;
// copy the other object's name
    name = new char[strlen(in.name)+1];
    strcpy(name, in.name);
// return the de-reference of 'this' object to allow the operator to be chained
    return *this;
}
```

The 'show' method simply displays the state of the object

```
void NamedPoint::show()
{
    cout << name << " X: " << x << " Y: " << y << endl;
}
```

This example program tests the constructor, copy constructor and assignment operator:

```
#include "npoint.h"
void main()
{
// construct and display two 'NamedPoint' objects
    NamedPoint point1("origin"), point2("destination");
    point1.setXY(0,0);
    point2.setXY(100,150);
    cout << "Details of point 1: " << endl;
    point1.show();
    cout << "Details of point 2: " << endl;
    point2.show();
// demonstrate the copy constructor by creating a third object
    NamedPoint point3 = point1;
    cout << "Details of point 3 after copy constructor from point 1: " << endl;
    point3.show();
// demonstrate the assignment operator by changing the third object
    point3 = point2;
    cout << "Details of point 3 after assignment to point 2: " << endl;
    point3.show();
}
```

The output from this program is:

Details of point 1:
origin X: 0 Y: 0
Details of point 2:
destination X: 100 Y: 150
Details of point 3 after copy constructor from point 1:
origin X: 0 Y: 0
Details of point 3 after assignment to point 2:
destination X: 100 Y: 150

A class that has methods including a default constructor, a copy constructor, a destructor and an assignment operator can safely be used in most of the contexts in which ordinary data types are used, including being assigned, declared and used as 'pass by value' parameters to methods and functions. Because these methods are so important, they are all supplied as defaults to user defined classes. However, as we have seen, we sometimes need to provide our own implementations of these methods where more complex classes containing pointers are created. The provision of these methods gives the class what Coplien calls 'orthodox canonical class form' [Coplien, 1992 p.38], which is a complicated way of saying that all your classes should have these methods. You should consider for each of your classes whether the default implementations are acceptable or whether you need to 'roll your own'.

Using operator overloading

There are many aspects to the overloading of operators in C++, far too many to be covered in this chapter. The primary reason for overloading operators is so that objects of different classes can be manipulated in standard ways, for example to be used as parameters to generic functions. This application is one which we will investigate in the next chapter.

Operators that may be overloaded

The following table of operators that may be overloaded comes from Stroustrup [1995, p.592]. Most of these you will probably never want to overload! Many are beyond the scope of this book and only necessary for specialist applications.

- Dynamic memory management:

    new   **delete**

- Arithmetic and assignment operators:

+	-	*	/	%
+=	-=	*=	/=	%=
++	--	=		

- Bitwise operators (including bitwise assignment and shifting):

^	&	|	~			
^=	&=	|=	<<	>>	>>=	<<=

- relational operators:

<	>	==	!=	<=	>=

- logical operators

!	&&	||

- de-referencing operators

    ->*   ->

- comma operator   ,
- function call operator   ()
- subscripting operator   []

For more detail, see Stroustrup [1995, Chapter 7 pp.225–254 and pp.592–594]

Summary of key points from this chapter

1. Operators may be overloaded to work with user defined data types (objects). This is an extension of the idea of coercion, which allows a single operator to be applied to a range of data types.

2. The assignment operator has a default behaviour when applied to objects, copying the attribute values from one object to another. This behaviour may need to be overridden where objects contain pointers.

3. Operators such as the addition operator may be overloaded to work with objects. It is important, however, that the normal meanings of operators are not distorted (for example subtracting with the addition operator). Operators should be overloaded in the spirit of their normal usage.

4. Operators are inherited by derived classes in a similar way to other methods. However, this is not the case with the assignment operator; derived classes do not inherit overloaded assignment operators.

5. The syntax for overloading operators involves the 'operator' keyword and one of the 40 available operators which the programmer is allowed to overload.

6. Relational operators return 'true' or 'false', arithmetic operators return an object containing the result of the expression and assignment operators return a copy of 'this' object to allow the operator to be chained.

Exercises

1. Write an overloaded addition (+) operator for the 'Point' class that adds the coordinates of one object to the coordinates of another. Write a program to test the operator.

2. Overload the '>' (greater than) operator so that it can be used with 'StudentGrade' objects. In other words, the following expression should be valid:

```
if(student1 > student2)
{
    ...
}
```

The overloaded operator method should compare the total grade score (i.e. Maths and English grades added together) and return one if the comparison is true, zero if it is false. If your compiler supports it, use 'bool' as the return type.

3. Create an array of five 'StudentGrade' objects and sort them using the overloaded '>' operator.

4. Implement an 'ExtendedGrade' class as outlined in this chapter, and provide a new version of the overloaded '+' operator for it.

5. A popular candidate for making into a class is the 'String', to encapsulate the rather complex handling of arrays we have seen so far to handle text based attributes. Using the 'NamedPoint' class as the starting point, remove the integer attributes and associated methods to leave only the string element (the pointer to 'char' and the methods associated with it). Then add overloaded relational operators and an addition operator that will concatenate two strings (i.e. add one string to the end of another).

12 Polymorphism by parameter

Overview

In this chapter, the use of parameters to give polymorphic behaviour to functions and object methods is discussed. This covers two general types of polymorphism; overloading and genericity (or parametric polymorphism). The use of C++ templates in creating truly generic functions is explained.

Using parameters for polymorphism

In Chapter 10, two different approaches to the overloading of methods by parameters were introduced:

1. *Overloading*

   'ad hoc' overloading of a method name by differences in parameters – each version of the method requires a different implementation.

2. *Parametric Polymorphism*

   Genericity of a function, method or class able to handle different parameter types. All data types are handled by a single implementation.

Parametric overloading

Ad hoc overloading of functions by differences in their parameter lists is a facility available in non object-oriented code, since it can be applied to any function, whether that function is an object method (i.e. declared as part of a class) or not. Because we are first and foremost interested in the object-oriented approach, our discussion will ultimately focus on the ability to overload methods by their parameters within a single class. However, we will begin by examining how to overload a simple function independent of class definitions.

Overloading a function using parameter lists is a simple concept. It means that we can give the same name to more than one function providing they have different sets of parameters. The following functions would be different because the parameter types are different; one takes a float parameter and one takes an int parameter. Even though both functions have the same name, the compiler recognises them as having different implementations:

```
aFunction(float value_in)
aFunction(int value_in)
```

The compiler can also tell apart functions that have different numbers of parameters, as in this example:

```
anotherFunction(int value1)
anotherFunction(int value1, int value2)
```

Overloading as 'ad hoc' polymorphism

This kind of polymorphism is classified as 'ad hoc' because each version of an overloaded function requires a specific implementation. Fig. 12.1 shows a possible set of functions in a traditionally structured program. Each function processes an array of integer data types only, returning different types of average.

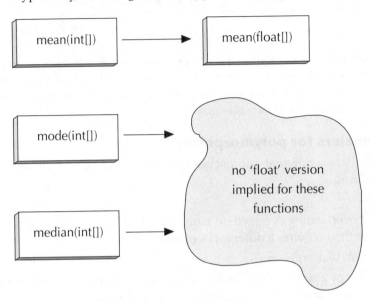

Fig. 12.1: Overloading by parameter. Since it is an 'ad hoc' method, it is used 'for this purpose only'

If we overload one of these functions to deal with float values as well as integers, this has no effect on any of the other functions. The overloaded function ('mean' in Fig. 12.1) now has multiple forms (it is polymorphic) but its polymorphism is 'for this purpose only'; it has no effect on any of the other functions. They do not inherit the ability to handle float parameters, nor are they obliged to follow suit by supplying their own versions of the 'float' function.

The compiler can deduce which version of the function to call by the type of the parameter argument passed when the function is called. If 'mean' is called with an integer array parameter, then the integer version of the function will be executed, but if a float array parameter is provided, then the float version will be called.

A particular function or method name may be overloaded many times, and for each different set of parameters, a different definition of the named function is implemented (Fig. 12.2).

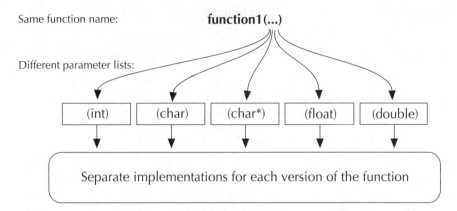

Fig. 12.2: An overloaded function has a different
implementation for each parameter list.

You may have noticed that no return types have been suggested for these examples. This is because functions cannot be overloaded by return type, only by parameter.

In an object-oriented system, we can use this facility to define more than one method with the same name in a single class. This is particularly useful for example in overloading the constructor, so that we can create new objects with different sets of arguments.

Question 12.1   What might be the advantage of being able to overload the constructor?

Having an overloaded constructor gives us different ways of creating objects, allowing us to give certain default behaviours to a given constructor and override other behaviours with parameters. Since we can overload the constructor as many times as we like, this is a more flexible mechanism than simply giving default parameter values to a single version of the constructor.

Parametric polymorphism (genericity)

The primary application of parametric polymorphism, also termed 'genericity', is in object-oriented systems, since it is a means of handling all data types, including user defined types, in a generic way. Such methods are therefore applicable to a range of objects. There is an important distinction to be made between functions which are simply overloaded by their parameters, and truly generic functions. We have discussed the possibility of having an overloaded function name which will execute different implementations of the function depending on the type(s) of parameter(s) it is passed. In contrast, however, a generic method will execute the same implementation but be able to accept a range of types as parameters. Fig. 12.3 illustrates that a generic function has a single implementation, but is able to handle a range of data types.

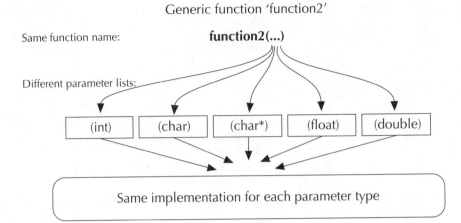

Fig. 12.3: A generic function has a single implementation for all data types.

In C++, genericity is achieved by the use of templates. A template will operate on any data type for which the internal implementation is appropriate. For example, a template function which compares two objects using the '>' operator and returns the higher will operate on any data type for which the '>' symbol is applicable. Since, through operator overloading, we can explicitly overload the '>' operator to work with objects of any classes we wish, templates can be a very useful tool in object-oriented systems.

What then are the differences in practice between overloading by parameter list, and genericity? In simple terms it comes down to this:

- We often need to perform a similar process on different data types
- The data type(s) being processed are passed to a method as parameters
- With parametric overloading, each type of parameter will cause the compiler to use a different (type specific) method
- With genericity, a single generic function is able to process all data types, including those defined by the programmer (i.e. objects) – all data types are handled by one (type generic) method
- Genericity allows us to create generic classes, as well as simply using generic functions as methods

Question 12.2 In what way can genericity be seen as a more productive technique than overloading?

Because overloading requires a different implementation to be provided for all possible parameter types, it is not easily extensible to handle new types. In contrast, a generic function only has one implementation which may be used for all parameter types, even those which may not be defined yet. This means that genericity provides a much greater degree of reusability than overloading.

Generic functions

Genericity is a more powerful tool than parametric overloading for object-oriented systems because it does not have to anticipate the type of data parameters which may be supplied at run time. Therefore it is able to handle dynamic objects of disparate types. However, this approach only works if we are able to process all data types in a particular way, which means we have to have a common interface for all objects used as parameters. Fig. 12.4 illustrates the working of a generic method ('ISEQUAL?') which compares two objects and returns 'TRUE' if they are equal.

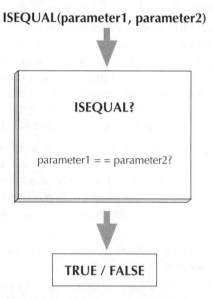

ISEQUAL(parameter1, parameter2)

ISEQUAL?

parameter1 = = parameter2?

TRUE / FALSE

Fig. 12.4: The generic 'ISEQUAL' function is able to process any pair of parameters able to respond to the '==' operator.

With a generic function like this, the parameters can be of any type. However, they must be able to be processed by the function, which in this case means they must be able to use the '==' operator. The clear implication here is that all objects which are liable to be used by this function must have an overloaded version of the '==' operator.

This need for all arguments to a generic function to be able to respond to operators holds true for object methods as well. Consider another generic function ('GREATER_OF') which displays the greater of two parameters (Fig. 12.5). The definition of what constitutes 'greater than' (i.e. the response to the '>' operator) will be defined by the type of the parameters actually passed – this is not the responsibility of the function.

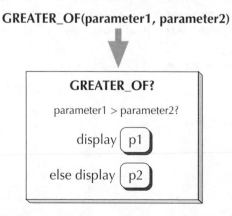

GREATER_OF(parameter1, parameter2)

GREATER_OF?

parameter1 > parameter2?

display p1

else display p2

Fig. 12.5: The 'GREATER_OF' function displays the greater of two parameters using the '>' operator and calling a display method.

In a case like this, the generic function can only work if all objects passed to it have not only an overloaded '>' operator but also a method able to respond to a 'display' message. Of course these may be inherited from base classes, and not necessarily specifically defined for each type.

If we do not have a generic function applicable to all classes, then it will be necessary to have different implementations of a function for each data type in the system – i.e. use parametric overloading to cater for all possible parameter types. The problem with this approach is that not only does a separate function have to be defined for each data type when the program is written, but if any new types are added later then new functions have to be written for each one. With a generic function, new types can be easily accommodated provided they have the appropriate overloaded operators, and/or methods.

Simple parameter overloading however does have uses which do not overlap with generic functions. For example, it can be used to provide several similar methods in a single class which in effect give the user options about whether or not to pass parameters to those methods. This can be particularly useful in overloading the constructor – objects can be created with various sets of parameters depending on the context.

Question 12.3 What potential problems do we need to be aware of when attempting to write a generic function?

Because the same function definition will be used with all data types, we have to make sure that all our code is completely generic so that any parameter types passed to it can be effectively handled. When creating class definitions which may be used with generic functions, it is essential that we are aware of any constraints which the function implementation has in terms of demanding, for example, that objects can respond to certain operators.

C++ syntax

First, we will examine how simple parametric overloading is applied to non object-oriented functions. The 'absolute value' of a number is the number without a sign. For example, the absolute value of –45 is 45. Our first example describes an overloaded 'absoluteValue' function, with versions for integer and float parameters. Before demonstrating the overloading of this function, let us first consider the kind of problem which overloading addresses.

In this example program, there is a function called 'absoluteValue' which takes an integer parameter as a reference (i.e. it changes the value of the variable passed to it directly). It is called in 'main' by both an integer and a float.

```
#include <iostream.h>
void absoluteValue(int& value_in)
{
    if(value_in < 0)
    {
        value_in = –value_in;
    }
}
void main()
{
    int x = –5;
    float y = –5.5;
    absoluteValue(x);
    absoluteValue(y);
```

```
        cout << "Absolute value of x is " << x << endl;
        cout << "Absolute value of y is " << y << endl;
}
```

The following output shows what happens when the program is run:

Absolute value of x is 5

Absolute value of y is –5.5

Clearly, the function has successfully returned the absolute value of the integer, but not the float. Why is this? In fact the program only runs at all because the compiler tries to compensate for the use of an inappropriate parameter by coercing the integer argument parameter into a float (your compiler will probably give you a warning about this when it type checks the source code). As we have previously discussed, coercion is always a temporary type conversion using a copy of the data. In this case, we wanted to use 'pass by reference' in the function, but the compiler could only provide a copy (i.e. the parameter is passed by value). Therefore the original data was not processed and 'y' remained negative.

In this example, the 'absoluteValue' function is overloaded – two versions are provided, one for integer parameters and one for floats:

```
void absoluteValue(int& value_in)
{
    if(value_in < 0)
    {
        value_in = –value_in;
    }
}
void absoluteValue(float& value_in)
{
    if(value_in < 0)
    {
        value_in = –value_in;
    }
}
```

Although the bodies of the functions are identical, they process different data types. If we run the same program again, we will find that both 'x' and 'y' are successfully converted to their absolute values:

Absolute value of x is 5

Absolute value of y is 5.5

This time, the call to 'absoluteValue(x)' still uses the int version, but the call to 'absoluteValue(y)' calls the float version, successfully passing by reference.

In-class overloading – overloading the constructor

We can use this ability to overload a function name (by differences in parameter lists) inside our classes by overloading methods. This example shows how we might overload the constructor of the BankAccount class to allow objects to be created with different sets of parameters.

This modified class definition shows a set of prototypes for overloading the constructor:

```
class BankAccount
{
private:                        // or 'protected:', if generalised
```

```
    int account_number;
    char account_holder[20];
    float current_balance;
public:
// four overloaded constructors with different parameter lists
    BankAccount();
    BankAccount(float start_balance);
    BankAccount(char* holder_in);
    BankAccount(float start_balance, char* holder_in);
// other methods as before...
};
```

Each of the four versions of the constructor must now be defined. In each case, the 'current-balance' and 'account_holder' attributes are initialised, either from parameter arguments or by values assigned inside the constructor body.

The first version takes no parameters, so may be called as if it were the default constructor, However, it does initialise the two attributes:

```
BankAccount::BankAccount()
{
    current_balance = 0.00;
    strcpy(account_holder, "UNDEFINED");
}
```

The second version takes a parameter to set the start balance:

```
BankAccount::BankAccount(float start_balance)
{
    current_balance = start_balance;
    strcpy(account_holder, "UNDEFINED");
}
```

The third version takes a parameter to set the name of the account holder:

```
BankAccount::BankAccount(char* holder_in)
{
    current_balance = 0.00;
    strncpy(account_holder, holder_in, 19);
    account_holder[19] = '\0';
}
```

The final version sets both attributes using parameter arguments:

```
BankAccount::BankAccount(float start_balance, char* holder_in)
{
    current_balance = start_balance;
    strncpy(account_holder, holder_in, 19);
    account_holder[19] = '\0';
}
```

In the following program, the four different constructors are called by using different parameter lists. Note how the parameterised objects in this example are declared in an array. You may remember that we declared and initialised some simple arrays in Chapter 3 by separating the initial values by commas. With some compilers we can also do this when initialising an array of objects, but brackets must be used around the argument list for each object, even if the list is empty. Alternatively we could create an array of pointers and instantiate dynamic objects:

```
#include "bankacct.h"
#include <iostream.h>
```

```
void main()
{
// declare an array of four BankAccount objects with their
// parameters calling the various different constructors
    BankAccount account[4] = {
        BankAccount(),
        BankAccount(100.00),
        BankAccount("Mr. Poor"),
        BankAccount(1000.00, "Ms. Rich")
    };
// display the attribute values of the accounts
    cout << "Balances and holders of the accounts are:" << endl;
    for(int i = 0; i < 4; i++)
    {
        cout << "Balance = £" << account[i].getCurrentBalance();
        cout << ", Account holder is " << account[i].getAccountHolder() << endl;
    }
}
```

The output from this program is:

Balances and holders of the accounts are:

Balance = £0, Account holder is UNDEFINED

Balance = £100, Account holder is UNDEFINED

Balance = £0, Account holder is Mr. Poor

Balance = £1000, Account holder is Ms. Rich

Template functions

Templates are a very powerful tool which we will investigate in more detail when looking at the implementation of container classes. However, the following is a very simple example of a template function which is able to process parameters of all data types which can respond to the '>' operator.

The syntax for creating a template function is:

template<class *type_name*> *return_type function_name (parameter_list...)*

'template' is a C++ keyword, and the name of the generic class name must be enclosed in pointed brackets (<...>). The class type name can be anything, but most examples use 'T', a convention we will follow here. It acts as an alias for any data type actually passed to the function (whether that data type is int, char, bank account, banana or whatever).

This example is a template definition for an 'isGreater' function which returns 'true' or 'false' depending on whether the first parameter is greater than the second. An enumerated type is used to simulate the ANSI bool type.

```
/*
    TGREATER.H      definition of template
                    'isGreater' function
*/
enum bool {false,true} // remove this if your compiler has a bool type
template<class T> bool isGreater(T x, T y)
{
    bool is_greater;
    if(x > y)
    {
        is_greater = true;
```

```
    }
    else
    {
        is_greater = false;
    }
    return is_greater;
}
```

The following program tests the template function using integers. Note that the function call itself is no different to normal function calls.

```
#include "tgreater.h"
#include <iostream.h>
void main()
{
    int x, y;
    bool z;
    cout << "Enter two integers" << endl;
    cin >> x;
    cin >> y;
    z = isGreater(x,y);
    if(z == true)
    {
        cout << "the first integer is greater than the second" << endl;
    }
    else
    {
        cout << "the first integer is less than or equal to the second" << endl;
    }
}
```

Example output from two program runs:

Enter two integers
3
6
the first integer is less than or equal to the second

Enter two integers
8
2
the first integer is greater than the second

The point about this type of function is that we can send it pairs of parameter arguments of any type, even objects of our own user-defined classes. As well as sending it a pair of integers, for example, we could sent it two objects of the 'StudentGrade' class, as described in Chapter 11. You may recall that one of the exercises for that chapter was to overload the '>' operator so that 'StudentGrade' objects could respond to it. The following program uses the template function with objects of this class:

```
#include "studgrad.h"    // modified header
#include "tgreater.h"
#include <iostream.h>
void main()
{
// create two StudentGrade objects
    StudentGrade student1;
```

```
        StudentGrade student2;
        // local variables
        bool true_or_false;
        int temp_grade;
        // get the grades from the keyboard
        cout << "Enter Maths grade for first student ";
        cin >> temp_grade;
        student1.setMathsGrade(temp_grade);
        cout << "Enter English grade for first student ";
        cin >> temp_grade;
        student1.setEnglishGrade(temp_grade);
        cout << "Enter Maths grade for second student ";
        cin >> temp_grade;
        student2.setMathsGrade(temp_grade);
        cout << "Enter English grade for second student ";
        cin >> temp_grade;
        student2.setEnglishGrade(temp_grade);
        true_or_false = isgreater(student1, student2)
        // call the template function and display the result
        if(true_or_false == true)
        {
            cout << "The first student has higher grades" << endl;
        }
        else
        {
            cout << "The first student\'s grades are not higher" << endl;
        }
    }
```

An example test run of this program follows:

Enter Maths grade for first student 67
Enter English grade for first student 56
Enter Maths grade for second student 43
Enter English grade for second student 40
The first student has higher grades

Summary of key points from this chapter

1. Parameters can be used to provide polymorphic behaviour by using two different techniques – overloading and genericity (parametric polymorphism).

2. With overloading, a different implementation of a given function is provided to deal with each different parameter type.

3. Object methods (such as the constructor) may be overloaded with different parameter lists.

4. With genericity, a single function or method implementation is used with all parameter types.

5. Generic functions require that all parameter types passed to them are able to respond to the internal processes of the function such as the use of arithmetic or relational operators. This means that objects passed as parameters to generic functions may need to have overloaded operator methods.

6. Genericity is provided in C++ by 'template' functions.

Exercises

1. Overload a function called 'getMax' by providing two implementations. The first should take as its parameter an array of integers, and return the highest integer in the array. The second should take an array of chars as a parameter, and return the highest value which corresponds to a letter in the ASCII table. If no letters are found in the array, the function should return 0. Assume a size of 10 for both arrays. Test both functions in 'main'.

2. Using a template, write a generic 'isGreatest' function that returns the largest element in an array. The function will need two parameters: an array (of type 'T') and an integer to pass the size of the array. Test the function with both simple data types and objects that have the necessary '>' operator (e.g. 'StudentGrade' or your 'string' class from the Chapter 11 exercises).

3. Using a template, write a generic 'meanAverage' function that returns the average of an array (of type 'T'). Write the function so that it will work for the built in data types. What difficulties do we face in applying a function like this to objects such as 'StudentGrade'?

13 Method polymorphism

Overview

In this chapter we will investigate polymorphic object methods in a classification hierarchy. The static binding of overloaded methods to their appropriate classes at compile time is discussed, and the syntax for calling inherited methods within overriding methods is outlined.

Function name overloading

In a monomorphic language, there is always a one to one relationship between a function name and its implementation. A function such as 'print' for example, would have one and only one possible definition. In an object-oriented system, (where functions are replaced by object methods) the relationship may be one to many – there may be many different implementations of a 'print' method (Fig. 13.1). The name of the method becomes a more abstract concept, covering a range of different implementations appropriate to different classes of objects. There may be as many different implementations of this 'print' method as there are classes in the hierarchy, or perhaps more if there is also 'in-class' polymorphism using overloading.

Monomorphic Function – 1 to 1 Relationship

Polymorphic Methods – 1 to Many Relationship

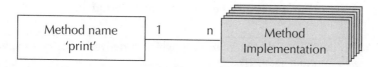

Fig. 13.1: A monomorphic function has only one possible implementation. A polymorphic method has many.

Overloading method names

When discussing classification hierarchies, we looked at how the methods of a base class are inherited by derived classes. For example, a method called 'print' defined in the base class may be called by any object of any derived class. However, this is a rather restrictive facility if we can only use the inherited method. Looking again at our 'Timer' class which was used as a base class for 'ExtendedTimer', it might usefully have a method called 'display' to show some data on the screen. Our derived class 'ExtendedTimer' would inherit this method, but it would not necessarily be adequate – how for example are we to display state data for attributes unique to the derived class which the base class method is not aware of? We could of course define an entirely separate method with a different name to display data from ExtendedTimer objects, but this is not a very satisfactory solution. In fact, object-orientation allows us to override any inherited method by defining a derived class method with the same name. We also have the facility, if required, to call any inherited methods within this new method so that the functionality of the existing implementation can be re-used and extended. We could therefore either create a 'display' method for the ExtendedTimer which completely replaces the inherited method, or alternatively one that calls the inherited method and then adds some extra functionality of its own (Fig. 13.2).

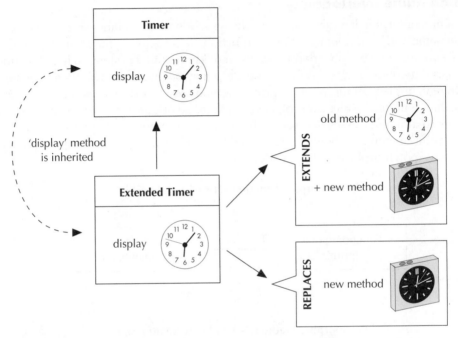

Fig. 13.2: An inherited method may be used without modification, but it may also be extended or overridden.

Question 13.1 What are the three ways in which a derived class can implement a polymorphic method?

A derived class can implement a polymorphic method by inheriting it unchanged, by replacing it with a different implementation or by extending it, adding to the existing implementation.

Static binding

When we have 'inheritance polymorphism' of this kind, with identically named methods in different classes, the compiler has to resolve which method is being called by a particular object, and 'bind' the appropriate method to that object. This is done by identifying the class to which that object belongs, a similar process to that which identifies the classes of objects used with an overloaded operator. In both cases, there may be more than one interpretation of the operator or method depending on the class of objects with which it is being used. When this process takes place at compile time it is called 'static binding' (also known as 'early binding'). When we create external, static or automatic objects in a program, they all have unique identifiers which have a similar role to simple variable names – the object's name is associated with a particular area of data storage. Whenever an object is created, it's identifier is associated with the name of the class to which it belongs.

For example, if we have a class called 'FuelPump' and we instantiate an object of that class, that object will have a unique name, such as 'fuel_pump1', and any methods called can be traced to that object's class. In the following code fragment, a FuelPump object ('fuel_pump1') is instantiated and a method ('turnOn') is called:

```
...
FuelPump fuel_pump1;
fuel_pump1.turnOn();
...
```

Clearly, the 'turnOn' method being called must be that of the FuelPump class, since the source code states that this is the class of fuel_pump1. If the method is overloaded by other classes, then the same clarity of binding applies. Let us assume that there is another class called 'WaterPump' which also has a method called 'turnOn'. Our code fragment might include objects of both classes:

```
...
FuelPump fuel_pump1;
WaterPump water_pump1;
fuel_pump1.turnOn();
water_pump1.turnOn();
...
```

The compiler is able to identify the classes to which the two objects belong, and 'bind' their respective (overloaded) methods to them. This is what we mean by static binding, whereby the classes to which objects belong (and therefore the methods that need to be bound to them) may be identified at compile time. All types of object, including dynamic objects, are statically bound by default. However, we do have the option with dynamic objects of implementing 'dynamic binding'. This will be discussed in the next chapter.

Question 13.2   When does static/early binding of methods take place, and what does it bind together?

Static binding takes place at compile time. It binds together the class of an object and a method call to that object to identify which implementation of a (possibly polymorphic) method to use.

Overloaded methods in a classification hierarchy

In the previous example, we looked at two different 'pump' classes which used an overloaded name for different implementations of a 'turnOn' method. It might be reasonable to assume that, in addition to the behaviours of being turned on and off, there are some other common aspects of water and fuel pumps which might usefully be generalised into a common base class. This would probably be an abstract class – one which does not contain enough detail to instantiate objects in its own right, but allows specialised types of 'pump' to inherit shared characteristics from it. Fig. 13.3 indicates that both 'FuelPump' and 'WaterPump' inherit from a common ancestor, an immediate base class called 'Pump' (Using UML notation for inheritance).

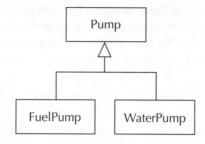

Fig. 13.3: 'Pump' is an abstract base class of 'FuelPump' and 'WaterPump'.

Abstract methods

Our discussion here becomes rather hypothetical, but it may be that the 'turnOn' methods of fuel and water pumps are (for whatever technical reason) very different. Therefore the definitions of the two methods have nothing in common. However, for reasons of design the 'Pump' class should have a 'turnOn' method. This is because it is not good practice to have overloaded method names in separate parts of a class hierarchy which do not have a common root, since the methods are then applied in an 'ad hoc' way with no reference to each other. Whilst this may not seem to be an issue at this stage, it will become clear when we deal with dynamically bound objects why there should be this consistency of method names in a classification hierarchy. The question then arises, what is the implementation of the 'turnOn' method in the 'Pump' class if it is not used for common elements of the two other methods? In fact, the method does nothing functional at all – it exists as a 'placeholder' for the name of the method so that all derived classes may implement their own versions of 'turnOn' (Fig. 13.4). It is, to all intents and purposes, an 'abstract' method – one which has no implementation. Such methods are an important design artifact, so just because a method does nothing, it does not mean it should not be declared! Abstract methods are common components of an abstract class.

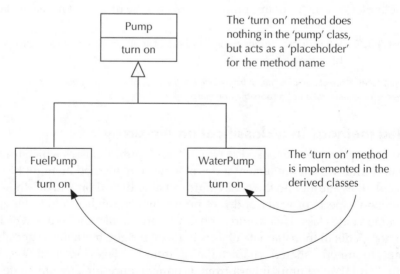

The 'turn on' method does nothing in the 'pump' class, but acts as a 'placeholder' for the method name

The 'turn on' method is implemented in the derived classes

**Fig. 13.4: The 'turn on' method in the 'Pump' class
is an abstract method with no implementation.**

Question 13.3   What is an abstract method, and what is its role in a classification hierarchy?
An abstract method has no implementation. It exists so that its name can be inherited by derived classes. This creates a consistent interface across all the classes in a hierarchy (inclusion polymorphism).

C++ syntax

Polymorphic methods are easy to implement in C++. We simply duplicate the inherited method name in a derived class to override the existing implementation. We need to do this because sometimes we inherit inappropriate or abstract methods.

Overriding inherited methods

You may remember from Chapter 8 a class called 'ExampleClass' which represented a single integer, and another class ('DerivedClass') which inherited from it and added a second integer attribute. A slightly modified version of these two classes follows. Note that the key difference is that the 'cout' statements which output the attribute values are contained in the methods, whereas they previously appeared in 'main' – the 'get' methods which appeared in the previous incarnation of this example have been replaced by 'show' methods:

```
#include<iostream.h>
// the base class
Class BaseClass
{
protected:
    int x;
public:
    void setX(int x_in);
    void showX();
};
void BaseClass::setX(int x_in);
{
    x = x_in:
}
void BaseClass::showX();
{
    cout << "base x = " << x << endl;
}
// the derived class
Class DerivedClass : public BaseClass
{
private:
    int y;
public:
    void setY(int y_in);
    void showY();
};
void DerivedClass::setY(int y_in)
{
    y = y_in;
}
void DerivedClass::showY()
{
    cout << "Derived y = " << y << endl;
}
```

As we know, objects of 'DerivedClass' will have access to the public methods of 'Base-Class', but inherited methods are not always appropriate to derived class objects. Consider the base class method 'showX'. Whether it is used for objects of either the base or derived class, it will always display 'base x =' before the attribute value, even when the derived class is using the method! In this program, objects of both the base and derived classes are instantiated and given values for their 'x' attributes. Then the 'showX' method is called for both objects:

```
void main()
{
// create an instance of each of the classes
    BaseClass base_object;
    DerivedClass derived_object;
// set the x value for the base class object
    base_object.setX(7);
// set the x value for the derived class object
    derived_object.setX(12);
// display the x value for the both objects
    base_object.showX();
    derived_object.showX();
}
```

The output from the program looks like this:

base x = 7

base x = 12

The correct values are returned, but the messages don't make sense. Although the derived class has its own attribute 'x' which can be set via the inherited method 'setX' without problems, when it uses the inherited method 'showX', the base class implementation, which includes a class-specific message, is called, which reads rather strangely.

To overcome this problem, we can use the power of polymorphism to define a new 'showX' method for the derived class which will override the inherited version. Only the changes to the class definition have been included – other elements would remain unchanged.

```
Class DerivedClass
{
    ...
public:
    void showX();
    ...
};
void DerivedClass::showX()
{
    cout << "derived x = " << x << endl;
}
```

By redefining a 'showX' method in the derived class (which will override the inherited version), 'showX' becomes a polymorphic method – the same method name is used in more than one class.

If we run our program again, then we get a rather more satisfactory output, as follows:

base x = 7
derived x = 12

This time the (different) methods return appropriate text as well as the correct values. Since C++ supports polymorphism, whereby different methods may have the same name, the compiler decides which one to use depending on the class of the object which calls it. This means that both the base and derived classes can have methods called 'showX', with the appropriate version 'bound' by the compiler, which identifies the classes of the objects. In the program, the message 'showX' is sent to objects of both the base and derived classes, and they respond in different, class-specific ways. Note that we did not have to alter the code of the program although the internal implementation details of 'DerivedClass' had been altered. This demonstrates one of the key strengths of object-orientation – as long as the interfaces of our classes remain consistent, we are free to alter their implementation, including changing which polymorphic method is being called by a particular statement.

With the first version of our 'DerivedClass', the following line called the 'showX' method of the base class:

```
...
derived_object.showX();
...
```

After we had re-written the class definition, the same line called the 'showX' method of the derived class.

Defining abstract methods

In the previous example, we were overriding an existing method inherited from the base class. In both example program runs, the compiler was able to 'bind' a useable method to the object calling it, even when the specific method was not defined in the class to which the object belonged. This is because if the method being invoked is not found in the class of a particular object, then the compiler will look for a method of the same name in the superclass(es) from which it derives. It will check in the immediate parent class first, and if necessary continue searching up the hierarchy until either a method is found or there are no more superclasses, in which case the compiler will flag an error. However, if the method is 'abstract' in the base class, then there will not be any implementation of that method inherited.

An abstract method exists purely for the purpose of being overridden by methods in derived classes, so in contrast to other methods which may be used throughout a class's descendants, abstract methods must be overridden by all inheriting classes to provide a useful behaviour. What then can we put into the implementation of an abstract method if all the functionality is devolved to derived class versions of the method? As we will see in the next chapter, it is possible to declare 'pure' abstract methods, but only in specific circumstances. A practical alternative approach therefore is simply to leave the body of the method empty as follows:

```
class Pump
{
    ...
public:
    void turnOn() {}
    ...
};
```

This means that objects of class 'Pump' have a 'turnOn' method, even though it has no functionality. In circumstances where we do not have any appropriate behaviour for a base class method, this will at least compile without problem.

Extending inherited methods

In the 'DerivedClass' example, we applied polymorphism to override (replace) an inherited method definition. We may also if we wish simply extend the definition of an inherited method by calling it in a derived class method and adding extra implementation details.

The class definition which follows shows a simple class ('ASCIIChar') which represents a single ASCII character as an object. It has one attribute ('character') and two methods, 'getChar' and 'showChar'. (The attribute is 'protected' to allow it to be accessed by the methods of derived classes).

The 'getChar' method takes an integer parameter, and stores any value which corresponds to a letter in the ASCII table. Otherwise it defaults to store a space. The 'showChar' method displays the appropriate ASCII character on screen by using 'cout', which automatically converts char data types to their appropriate characters.

```
/*
    ASCICHAR.H          definition of ASCIIChar class
*/
#include <iostream.h>   // for cin and cout
class ASCIIChar
{
protected:
    char character;
public:
    void getChar(int char_number);
    void showChar();
};
void ASCIIChar::getChar(int char_number)
{
    // these ranges are the ASCII codes for upper and lower case letters
    if((char_number >= 65 && char_number <= 90)
    || (char_number >= 97 && char_number <= 122))
    {
        character = char_number;
    }
    else
    {
        character = 32;
    }
}
void ASCIIChar::showChar()
{
    // if 'char_number' is not in a letter range, store a space
    cout << "Character is " << character << endl;
}
```

A very simple program using an object of this class follows:

```
#include "ascichar.h"
void main()
{
    ASCIIChar a_char;
    a_char.getChar(97);
    // 97 is the ASCII code for 'a'
```

```
    a_char.showChar();
}
```

Running this program will display the single character 'a'.

Extending the 'getChar' method in a derived class

For this example, we will be specialising the ASCIIChar class. The derived class is going to be called 'UpperCaseChar' since it has the more specific role of converting any stored letters into upper case. As it stands at present, the 'getChar' method (which will be inherited by the derived class) checks if the parameter argument represents a valid character code. If it does, then the 'character' attribute is set to that value. Otherwise the attribute is set to the value 32 (space).

To make this method store only upper case characters, we could simply replace it entirely, but we still need to filter out inappropriate characters, so it seems foolish to abandon it entirely. Fortunately, C++ provides us with the syntax to extend it by including its functionality in a derived class method. This is done using the scope resolution operator (::) to call the inherited method as follows:

```
    classname :: methodname(parameter_list...)
```

The reason for including the class name is that the call otherwise appears recursive – calling 'getChar' inside a method called 'getChar' will recursively and endlessly call itself unless a different class name is provided.

In the 'getChar' method for the derived class, we will first call the existing base class 'getChar' method. Then we will add the case conversion routine. Note how the scope resolution operator is used for the call to the base class method:

```
/*
        UPPRCASE.H      definition of
                        UpperCaseChar class
*/
#include "ascichar.h"
class UpperCaseChar : public ASCIIChar
{
public:
    void getChar(int char_in);
};
void UpperCaseChar::getChar(int char_in)
{
// the base class method is called
    ASCIIChar :: getChar(char_in);
    // if 'character' is not a space, it is a letter
    if(character != 32)
    {
        // 97 to 122 are lower case letters
        if(character >= 97)
        {
            // the upper and lower case ranges are 32 apart in the table
            character -= 32;
        }
    }
}
```

The following program tests objects of the two classes:

```
#include "upprcase.h"
void main()
    // create objects
    ASCIIChar either_case;
    UpperCaseChar upper_case;
    // pass both of them the value 97 (ASCII 'a')
    either_case.getChar(97);
    upper_case.getChar(97);
    // show the attribute value
    either_case.showChar();
    upper_case.showChar();
}
```

The output is as follows:

Character is a

Character is A

A Practical Example

The previous examples demonstrate the key elements of the syntax, but do not perform particularly realistic functions. A slightly more useful example might be a class which models desktop computers in a university inventory system. Such a system might record, for example, the type, current configuration and location of all the PCs owned by the university. Let us assume that the existing 'Computer' class has the following attributes and methods:

Computer
make
model
mouse
hard drive size
CD ROM speed
location
show details
change details

Rather than having separate methods to return or update the state values of individual attributes, there is a single method which shows all details and another which allows some to be updated. There will also be a constructor which will set the initial values of all attributes. To keep the example simple, the attributes are either character strings or numeric values representing various states; the 'mouse' attribute for example might contain 0 for no mouse, 2 for a 2 button mouse and 3 for a 3 button mouse. Clearly a larger set of possible values would be appropriate in a realistic system. The class definition is:

```
/*
    COMPUTER.H    definition of the 'Computer' class
*/
class Computer
{
protected:
```

```
    char make[20];
    char model[20];
    int mouse;
    float hard_drive_size;
    int cdrom_speed;
    char location[20];
public:
    Computer();
    void showDetails();
    void changeDetails();
};
```

'showDetails' here is a simple screen display of state attributes, while 'changeDetails' allows appropriate attributes to be updated via a simple screen interface. It would not be appropriate to alter the 'make' and 'model' attributes after instantiation, but aspects of the machine configuration or location might need to be updated. The constructor initialises all attributes from keyboard input, and in this example takes advantage of the 'changeDetails' method to avoid duplication of code. The method definitions might look something like this (very crude for simplicity's sake):

```
/*
        COMPUTER.CPP method definitions for the 'Computer' class
*/
#include "computer.h"
#include <iostream.h>
// the constructor acquires 'lifetime' attributes from the keyboard
// (attributes that will not change for the lifetime of the machine)
// as well as those that may be changed
Computer::Computer()
{
    cout << "Enter make of computer ";
    cin >> make;
    cout << "Enter model ";
    cin >> model;
// this is a bit of a short cut to avoid code repetition
    changeDetails();
}
// the 'showDetails' method displays all the attribute values
void Computer::showDetails()
{
    cout << endl << "CURRENT MACHINE DETAILS" << endl;
    cout << "Make: " << make << endl;
    cout << "Model: " << model << endl;
    if(!mouse)
    {
        cout << "no mouse attached" << endl;
    }
    else
    {
        cout << "A " << mouse << " button mouse is attached" << endl;
    }
    cout << "Hard drive is " << hard_drive_size << " Mb" << endl;
    if(!cdrom_speed)
    {
        cout << "No CD-ROM" << endl;
    }
    else
```

```
        {
            cout << "With " << cdrom_speed << " speed CD-ROM" << endl;
        }
        cout << "Currently located in room: " << location << endl;
}
// the 'changeDetails' method only changes the state of attributes
// that are not set for the lifetime of the machine. to keep the code
// short and simple it requires input of all attributes, which is
// rather clumsy. a menu driven interface would be better
void Computer :: changeDetails()
{
    cout << endl << "UPDATING MACHINE DETAILS" << endl;
    cout << "Enter number of mouse buttons (or 0 for no mouse): ";
    cin >> mouse;
    cout << "Enter size of hard drive (in Gb): ";
    cin >> hard_drive_size;
    cout << "Enter speed of CD-ROM (or 0 for no CD-ROM): ";
    cin >> cdrom_speed;
    cout << "Enter room number of new location: ";
    cin >> location;
}
```

To demonstrate the class, the following program instantiates a 'Computer' object, shows its initial details, changes them (rather laboriously!), then displays the amended data.

```
/*
        COMPMAIN.CPP  test program for 'Computer' class
*/
#include "computer.h"
void main()
{
// instantiate a 'Computer' object
    Computer computer1;
// display the details set by the constructor
    computer1.showDetails();
// change some attributes
    computer1.changeDetails();
// display the modified details
    computer1.showDetails();
}
```

A sample test run output follows:

Enter make of computer Ratpaq
Enter model P180
UPDATING MACHINE DETAILS
Enter number of mouse buttons (or 0 for no mouse): 0
Enter size of hard drive (in Gb): 1.2
Enter speed of CD-ROM (or 0 for no CD-ROM): 8
Enter room number of new location: 101
CURRENT MACHINE DETAILS
Make: Ratpaq
Model: P180
no mouse attached
Hard drive is 1.2 Mb
With 8 speed CD-ROM
Currently located in room: 101

UPDATING MACHINE DETAILS
Enter number of mouse buttons (or 0 for no mouse): 3
Enter size of hard drive (in Gb): 2
Enter speed of CD-ROM (or 0 for no CD-ROM): 12
Enter room number of new location: 102
CURRENT MACHINE DETAILS
Make: Ratpaq
Model: P180
A 3 button mouse is attached
Hard drive is 2 Mb
With 12 speed CD-ROM
Currently located in room: 102

Specialising the 'Computer' class

If we assume that the class described above is used in an existing application, then it will be suitable for creating objects applicable to all computers in the system. However, what happens if we acquire new machines which have additional characteristics not catered for in our current system? For example, what if we need to connect a number of machines to the Internet, and we wish to incorporate into the system the details of these machines, such as the type of web browser that is available, and the IP address? Such details would not be appropriate to machines not connected, so we would not want to change the existing class, indeed we may not have access to the implementation details of the class in order to do so.

To specialise from the existing 'Computer' class we could inherit its existing functionality into a new class, and then add the new attributes and extend the methods. The following class ('WebComputer') inherits from 'Computer' and re-declares the two methods so that new (polymorphic) versions can be defined.

```
class WebComputer : public Computer
{
private:
    char browser[20];
    char ip_address[20];
public:
    WebComputer();
    void showDetails();
    void changeDetails();
};
```

In a case such as this, the existing methods can be extended by including them in the methods of the derived class. In both cases, all the existing functionality is applicable to objects of the 'WebComputer' class, but additional implementation detail is necessary.

Summary of key points from this chapter

1. Polymorphism allows us to have many versions of a method, each implementation defined in a different class.

2. The ability to redefine a method name in a derived class allows us to tailor inherited methods for use with a derived class object. Inappropriate inherited methods may be overridden or extended by the derived class.

3. The compiler uses 'static binding' to identify the particular version of a polymorphic method when it is called. It is able to identify the class of an object at compile time by the constructor call.

4. If a method in a base class is completely overridden by derived class methods, then that method may have no implementation and is therefore abstract. Abstract classes (which are not specialised enough to instantiate objects in their own right) often have abstract methods.

5. In C++ we can override an inherited method by defining another method with the same name in a derived class. In the derived class method we may also call the base class method and extend its existing functionality.

Exercises

1. Implement the 'Pump' hierarchy in Fig. 13.4. The 'turnOn' methods should display appropriate messages in the derived classes, such as 'pumping water' and 'pumping fuel'. Test the methods in 'main'.

2. Implement the constructor and the two methods declared for WebComputer by extending the inherited versions. Use the appropriate syntax to call the inherited methods within the derived class methods. Test you WebComputer class. What is the side effect of the call to 'changeDetails' in the base class constructor?

14 Run-time polymorphism

Overview

This chapter is about polymorphism in the context of dynamic objects, and how dynamic (late) binding is used to resolve the calling of methods from a hierarchy of dynamic objects. In C++, the uses of virtual methods and base class pointers to ensure dynamic binding are explained, and the syntax for creating pure virtual functions for abstract methods is demonstrated.

Predictable and unpredictable objects

In Chapter 5 we compared two general types of object; those which have predictable identities, quantities and lifetimes and those which are unpredictable in terms of these properties. We illustrated this distinction by making a comparison between oil pumps and raindrops – oil pumps are easily counted and named, but raindrops are not. We are able to predict the persistence of objects such as oil pumps, but cannot predict the persistence of an individual raindrop. Since the identity of a raindrop depends entirely on the space which it occupies at a particular time, this can only be identified at 'rain-time'. In a program, some objects are identifiable at compile time, whereas others can only be identified at run time. In addition, there are occasions when we cannot even predict the class of an object until run time. When dynamic objects have unpredictable classes, we can send them messages using run time polymorphism.

Sending messages to objects of unpredictable classes

When we know the class of an object, then we know how it will respond to a particular message. Even if we do not know which object of a class might receive that message at run time, we still know which method is being called since all objects of a class share the same 'pool' of methods. All raindrops have the same response to the message 'fall' for example.

However, we may have a situation where we are sending a message to an unpredictable collection of objects. If we send the message 'fall' to a number of unpredictable objects of different classes, then we are unable to predict which behaviours will actually result. If the sky contains a number of objects receiving the message 'fall', then we may find a range of responses to that messages depending on the classes of those objects (Fig. 14.1). Raindrops, snowflakes and various other objects in the airspace fall in rather different ways (though like all truly polymorphic behaviours, they are semantically similar).

Fig. 14.1: Unpredictable objects may have a range of responses to a single message such as 'fall'.

Binding polymorphic methods

We discussed in the previous chapter the application of method polymorphism to a class hierarchy, ('inheritance polymorphism') whereby a method name can be overloaded within the hierarchy. It is possible for a method name to be duplicated for every separate class, and for the compiler to 'bind' the appropriate method to the object which is calling it. However, the ability of the compiler to statically bind a particular method at compile time depends on the class of an object being known when the program is being compiled. This ability to predict the class of an object is always the case when dealing with external, static or automatic objects, since they have unique identifiers in the source code. The compiler is able to identify the class of any object of these types by the call to the constructor, since this always refers to the class name. In a previous example we referred to a class called 'FuelPump' and the instantiation of an object of that class with a unique name, ('fuel_pump1'), In an example code fragment, a FuelPump object was instantiated and a method ('turnOn') called:

```
...
FuelPump fuel_pump1;
fuel_pump1.turnOn( );
...
```

Clearly, the 'turnOn( )' method being called must be that of the FuelPump class, since the source code states that this is the class of 'fuel_pump1'. If the method is overloaded by other classes, then the same clarity of binding applies. In the previous chapter, the Water-Pump class also has a 'turnOn' method, but it is clear from the source code which method is being called by each object, because their classes are clearly identifiable from the constructor calls.

```
...
FuelPump fuel_pump1;
WaterPump water_pump1;
fuel_pump1.turnOn( );
water_pump1.turnOn( );
...
```

Even if we use pointers to dynamic objects, then in the examples we have seen so far the class of the object is predictable at compile time. A dynamic raindrop for example is clearly a member of the 'RainDrop' class, and therefore uses whatever methods are defined for that class:

```
...
RainDrop* rain_drop = new RainDrop;
rain_drop -> fall();
rain_drop -> hitGround();
delete rain_drop;
...
```

If we were to rewrite the FuelPump/WaterPump example using dynamic objects, then the two methods can still be statically bound at compile time:

```
...
FuelPump* fuel_pump1 = new FuelPump;
WaterPump* water_pump1 = new WaterPump;
fuel_pump1 -> turnOn();
water_pump1 -> turnOn();
...
```

It is clear from the above examples that objects of all types can have their methods statically bound. In what circumstances, then, can we not predict the class of a dynamic object until run time?

Dynamic binding

When the class of an object cannot be identified at compile time, static (or 'early') binding of methods (and overloaded operators) cannot take place. The identification of which polymorphic methods are being called by the object must then be deferred until run time – this is known as 'dynamic binding' (or 'late binding'). How is it possible, then, to create objects whose classes cannot be identified until run time? In C++, this is possible through the use of base class pointers (static identifiers) to reference dynamic objects of derived classes. To illustrate this, let us return to the abstract base class 'Pump' which we introduced in the previous chapter (Fig. 14.2).

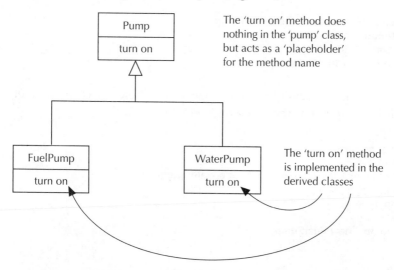

Fig. 14.2: The abstract 'Pump' class, introduced in Chapter 13.

Question 14.1 When do we need to resort to 'dynamic' (or 'late') binding as opposed to 'static' (or 'early') binding?

When the class of an object cannot be identified at compile time, then the methods of its class cannot be bound until run time.

The role of the abstract base class

The base class in this hierarchy represents the common characteristics of both fuel and water pumps, but is not specialised enough to represent an object in its own right. We also suggested that the 'turnOn' method in the base class was purely abstract, acting simply as a placeholder for the name of the method. What, then, is the purpose of an abstract class with abstract methods? In essence, a base class such as 'Pump' is the mechanism which allows us to implement dynamic binding. Messages may be passed via a pointer of the base class to objects of other derived classes at run time. In other words, all we know at compile time is that some kind of 'Pump' object will be instantiated, but we will not know until run time whether that object will be a 'FuelPump' or a 'WaterPump'. The unspecified 'Pump' object will however need to receive messages at run time, so the base class pointer must be able to reference the polymorphic method name. If 'Pump' did not have a 'turnOn' method, then it would be unable to receive that message on behalf of instantiated 'WaterPump' or 'FuelPump' objects at run time.

Base class pointers to derived class objects

All the dynamic objects we have instantiated so far have been referenced by pointers of their own class. However, we do not have to use pointers which belong to the same class as the objects which they reference – as we indicated above, it is also possible to reference objects of any derived or descendant class via a pointer of a base class. To illustrate this, we can return to the code fragment showing the 'turnOn' method being called for dynamic objects of the classes derived from 'Pump'. In the original version, the 'FuelPump' and 'WaterPump' objects are referenced specifically by pointers of their own classes.

```
...
FuelPump* fuel_pump1 = new FuelPump;
WaterPump* water_pump1 = new WaterPump;
fuel_pump1 -> turnOn();
water_pump1 -> turnOn();
...
```

It is, however, equally possible to reference both of these objects by pointers of the base class. This is illustrated by the following code fragment:

```
...
Pump* a_pump;
int pump_type;
cout << "Enter 1 for a fuel pump, 2 for a water pump ";
cin >> pump_type;
if(pump_type == 1)
{
    a_pump = new FuelPump;
}
else
{
```

```
        a_pump = new WaterPump;
    }
    a_pump -> turnOn( );
    ...
```

In this case, a pointer of the base class is being used to reference an object which at run time may belong to either of the derived classes. The 'turnOn' method is also called via this base class pointer, but the message 'turnOn' in fact has more than one possible interpretation depending on the class of the object receiving it. We therefore have an interesting problem – if 'a_pump' is a pointer of the 'Pump' class, then statically binding its 'turnOn' method (i.e. 'turnOn' as defined in the 'Pump' class) will not give us the desired behaviour, because the base class method has no implementation. In cases such as this, we can call the correct method at run time by not binding it at compile time. We can instruct the compiler to wait until the method call is executed at run time before attempting to bind the appropriate method. At that point, the class of the object will be known because the constructor will have been executed. The deferring of binding until the class of an object is known at run time is known as 'dynamic binding', and allows us to implement run time polymorphism.

Question 14.2   What method names must be declared in the base class if the methods of derived classes are to be dynamically bound at run time?

A derived class method can only be bound at run time if the base class pointer is able to respond to that method name (this is because of the type checking which ensures that a method has to exist in the class which calls it). Therefore all methods of any derived class must be declared in the base class if dynamic binding is to take place.

C++ syntax

To implement run time polymorphism in C++, we use the keyword 'virtual' to denote those methods which may be dynamically bound at run time.

For the following examples, we will use objects of classes derived from an abstract base class called 'FlyingMachine' (Fig. 14.3)

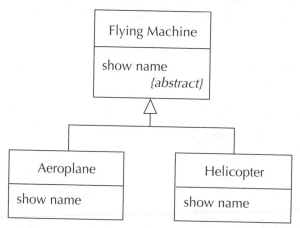

Fig. 14.3: 'FlyingMachine' is an abstract base class for 'Aeroplane' and 'Helicopter'.

'FlyingMachine' acts as the base class for two derived classes, 'Aeroplane' and 'Helicopter'. For the purposes of this example, the classes have no attributes, but each one has a single 'showName' method which allows it to display its name on the screen.

The classes may be defined as follows:

```
#include <iostream.h>
class FlyingMachine
{
public:
    void showName( );
};
class Helicopter : public FlyingMachine
{
public:
    void showName( );
};
class Aeroplane : public FlyingMachine
{
public:
    void showName( );
};
void FlyingMachine::showName( )
{
    cout << "Flying Machine" << endl;
}
void Helicopter::showName( )
{
    cout << "Helicopter" << endl;
}
void Aeroplane::showName( )
{
    cout << "Aeroplane" << endl;
}
```

As our class definitions currently stand, we are able to instantiate dynamic objects of all three classes in various ways. The objects may be instantiated using pointers of their own classes, so that, for example, we could use a pointer of class 'Helicopter' to create helicopter objects, and a pointer of class 'Aeroplane' to create aeroplane objects. However, we may also create objects of either of these classes using a pointer ('flyer') of the base class ('FlyingMachine') as illustrated in Fig. 14.4.

FlyingMachine* flyer;

flyer = new Helicopter;

flyer = new Aeroplane;

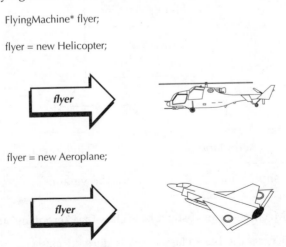

Fig. 14.4: a pointer of the base class is able to reference, instantiate and destroy objects of any derived class.

The following program shows this being done:

```
#include "flying.h"
void main( )
{
    FlyingMachine* flyer;
    flyer = new Helicopter;
    flyer -> showName( );
    delete flyer;
    flyer = new Aeroplane;
    flyer -> showName( );
    delete flyer;
}
```

In this program, objects of the derived classes are successfully instantiated and destroyed via a pointer of the base class. However, the output from the program is this:

Flying Machine
Flying Machine

Although we have created objects of the derived classes, the message returned from the objects is from the method of the base class. Why does this happen? It is because the compiler has statically bound the 'showName' method at compile time, when the identity of the objects is not known. Therefore the compiler binds the method which belongs to the class of the pointer, which is not necessarily the same as the class of the object at run time. After all, a FlyingMachine pointer could point to any of a range of objects at run time from any derived class. (Fig. 14.5) This is totally unpredictable when the compiler is statically binding object methods, so it can only bind the base class method.

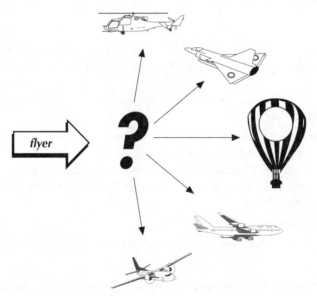

Fig. 14.5: A pointer may reference objects of many classes at run time, but the compiler cannot predict which they will be at compile time.

The 'virtual' keyword

By default, the compiler will always statically bind a method to the class of the pointer. However, we can force the compiler not to bind the method at compile time, but to allow dynamic binding of the object method at run time when the identity of the object being referenced is known. The mechanism for achieving this is simple – it is the 'virtual' keyword.

Whenever a method is declared as 'virtual', then the compiler will not statically bind it at compile time – it will be dynamically bound at run time. In this version of the class declarations, the 'showName' method has been declared to be 'virtual' in all three classes. In fact, as long as the base class method is declared 'virtual', then all the other polymorphic versions of the method will automatically be virtual too.

```
class FlyingMachine
{
public:
    virtual void showName( );
};
class Helicopter : public FlyingMachine
{
public:
    virtual void showName( );
};
class Aeroplane : public FlyingMachine
{
public:
    virtual void showName( );
};
```

If we run the previous program again, the output demonstrates that the appropriate methods are bound to the objects at run time:

Helicopter

Aeroplane

The first call to 'showName' via the 'FlyingMachine' pointer ('flyer') has bound the method of the 'Helicopter' class, but the second has bound the method of the 'Aeroplane' class.

The virtual destructor

There is another aspect to dynamic binding which is important, namely the behaviour of the destructor. The constructor, although it uses a pointer of the base class, explicitly instantiates an object of a named derived class, reserving memory appropriate for an object of that class. The constructor call for the 'Helicopter' object for example clearly states the class of the object:

```
flyer = new Helicopter;
```

However, the (default) destructor being used in the example is called as follows:

```
delete flyer;
```

What size of object does this destroy? in fact it only deletes that part of the object which has been derived from the base class, not those parts which have been constructed from derived classes, because the destructor will, by default, have been statically bound to the class of the pointer. To ensure that the whole object is destroyed, the destructor too must be dynamically bound, meaning that we have to declare a virtual destructor for each class in the hierarchy, even if that destructor has no extra functionality.

A virtual destructor for each class should therefore be added as follows:

```
class FlyingMachine
{
public:
    virtual ~FlyingMachine( ) {}
    virtual void showName( );
};
class Helicopter : public FlyingMachine
{
public:
    virtual ~Helicopter( ) {}
    virtual void showName( );
};
class Aeroplane : public FlyingMachine
{
public:
    virtual ~Aeroplane( ) {}
    virtual void showName( );
};
```

Since in this case the destructors have no bodies, they are declared in line as empty braces.

Question 14.3 What does the 'virtual' keyword instruct the compiler to do?

The 'virtual' keyword instructs the compiler to defer the binding of a polymorphic method call to a particular implementation until run time.

Declaring abstract methods as 'pure virtual functions'

In the last chapter, we looked at abstract methods which have no implementation. This is often the case when the methods of derived classes are dynamically bound, and the implementations of the method are defined in derived classes. Abstract methods may be declared to be 'pure virtual functions' in C++ – any virtual function (i.e. one which is dynamically bound) can be made abstract by the following syntax:

```
virtual method_name( ) = 0;
```

This means that no implementation is provided for the method in this class, and has two implications:

1. The method cannot be invoked by objects of derived classes unless an overriding implementation is specifically provided.
2. No objects of the class containing the abstract method may be instantiated.

If we take our 'Pump' class as an example, the 'turnOn' method would be declared as a pure virtual function as follows:

```
class Pump
{
    ...
public:
    virtual void turnOn( ) = 0;
    ...
};
```

Any class which contains one or more methods declared in this way automatically becomes an abstract class, regardless of whether or not other methods have specific implementations.

Pure virtual functions in the 'FlyingMachine' class

Our example 'FlyingMachine' class is clearly an abstract class, since it is not specialised enough to instantiate objects in its own right. Once we have made its 'showName' method virtual, that can become an abstract method. We might therefore make it a pure virtual function:

```
class FlyingMachine
{
public:
    virtual void showName( ) = 0;
};
```

Although this method has no implementation, its role is to allow the polymorphic methods of derived classes to be dynamically bound. Like 'turnOn' in the 'Pump' class, it exists purely as a means of passing messages to unpredictable objects at run time. If 'FlyingMachine' did not have this virtual 'showName' method, then the expression 'flyer -> showName( )' could not be compiled, since it would attempt to call a method which did not exist in the class of the pointer. It is essential that any methods which are to be dynamically bound are declared in the base class used for the pointer.

A larger example

The program which follows uses the classes 'FlyingMachine', 'Helicopter' and 'Aeroplane' to show the arrivals and departures at an airfield. The airfield is also an object which contains the various aircraft, with hangars modelled by an array of base class pointers (Fig. 14.6).

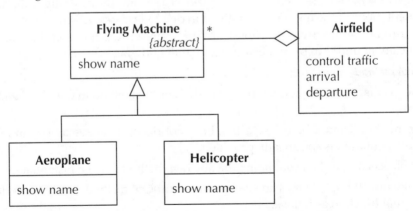

**Fig. 14.6: 'Airfield' is an aggregation of 'FlyingMachine' objects
(aggregation shown here in UML notation using the diamond symbol).**

These are the classes and method definitions:

```
#include <iostream.h>
class FlyingMachine
{
public:
```

```
        virtual ~FlyingMachine() {}
        virtual void showName() = 0;
};
class Helicopter : public FlyingMachine
{
public:
// note that the keyword 'virtual' need not be used before the derived
// class methods. any method which overrides a virtual method in a
// base class is virtual by default
        ~Helicopter() {}
        void showName();
};
class Aeroplane : public FlyingMachine
{
public:
        ~Aeroplane() {}
        void showName();
};
void Helicopter::showName()
{
        cout << "Helicopter";
}
void Aeroplane::showName()
{
        cout << "Aeroplane";
}
// the airfield class allows flying machines to arrive and depart,
// storing them in hangars
class Airfield
{
private:
        FlyingMachine* flyer;
        FlyingMachine* hangar[10];
public:
        Airfield();
        ~Airfield();
        void controlTraffic();
        void arrival();
        void departure();
};
// the constructor initialises pointers in the hangar array to NULL
// it then calls the controlTraffic method
Airfield::Airfield()
{
        for(int i = 0; i < 10; i++)
        {
            hangar[i] = NULL;
        }
        controlTraffic();
}
// the destructor does any necessary cleanup
Airfield::~Airfield()
{
        for(int i = 0; i < 10; i++)
        {
            if(hangar[i] != NULL)
            {
                delete hangar[i];
```

```
            }
        }
        if(flyer != NULL)
        {
            delete flyer;
        }
    }
}
// controlTraffic provides a user interface. The menu allows the user
// to select arrival, departure or quit
void Airfield::controlTraffic( )
{
    int machine_type;
    int option = 0;
    do
    {
        cout << "Enter 1 for arrival, 2 for departure, 3 to quit "
        cin >> option;
        if(option == 1)
        {
            cout << "Enter 1 for Helicopter, 2 for Aeroplane ";
            cin >> machine_type;
// the switch statement instantiates an object of the chosen type
// or directs the pointer to NULL if the choice is invalid
            switch(machine_type)
            {
                case 1: flyer = new Helicopter; break;
                case 2: flyer = new Aeroplane; break;
                default: flyer = NULL;
            }
            if(flyer != NULL)
            {
                arrival( );
            }
        }
        if(option == 2)
        {
            departure( );
        }
    } while(option != 3);
}
// arrival assigns the flying machine to the next available hangar
void Airfield::arrival( )
{
    int i = 0, found = 0;
    do
    {
        if(hangar[i] == NULL)
        {
            hangar[i] = flyer;
            flyer -> showName( );
            cout << " assigned to hangar " << i << endl;
            found = 1;
        }
        i++;
    } while(found == 0 && i < 10);
    if(found == 0)
    {
        cout << "No more hangars" << endl;
```

```
        }
    }
    // departure deletes the object in the chosen hangar
    void Airfield::departure()
    {
        int found = 0;
    // display all the occupied hangars
        for(int i = 0; i < 10; i++)
        {
            if(hangar[i] != NULL)
            {
                hangar[i] -> showName();
                cout << " in hangar " << i << endl;
                found = 1;
            }
        }
        if(found == 0)
        {
            cout << "All hangars empty" << endl;
        }
        else
        {
    // select which machine is to depart
            int choice;
            cout << "Enter hangar number to empty ";
            cin >> choice;
            if(hangar[choice] != NULL && choice >=0 && choice <10)
            {
                delete hangar[choice];
                hangar[choice] = NULL;
            }
            else
            {
                cout << "Invalid entry" << endl;
            }
        }
    }
    // main simply calls the constructor of an airfield object. all other
    // processing is done by object methods
    void main()
    {
        Airfield airstrip1;
    }
```

A sample test run follows. Notice how dynamic objects of both derived types are referenced by the array of base class pointers which represents the hangars. Each object is also able to respond to the 'showName' method with its own name because the method has been dynamically bound:

Enter 1 for arrival, 2 for departure, 3 to quit 1
Enter 1 for Helicopter, 2 for Aeroplane 2
Aeroplane assigned to hangar 0
Enter 1 for arrival, 2 for departure, 3 to quit 1
Enter 1 for Helicopter, 2 for Aeroplane 1
Helicopter assigned to hangar 1
Enter 1 for arrival, 2 for departure, 3 to quit 1

Enter 1 for Helicopter, 2 for Aeroplane 2
Aeroplane assigned to hangar 2
Enter 1 for arrival, 2 for departure, 3 to quit 2
Aeroplane in hangar 0
Helicopter in hangar 1
Aeroplane in hangar 2
Enter hangar number to empty 1
Enter 1 for arrival, 2 for departure, 3 to quit 2
Aeroplane in hangar 0
Aeroplane in hangar 2
Enter hangar number to empty 0
Enter 1 for arrival, 2 for departure, 3 to quit 3

Summary of key points from this chapter

1. When the classes of objects are unpredictable, then their behaviours will also be unpredictable.

2. Objects whose classes can be identified at compile time have their methods statically bound. Those whose classes cannot be predicted must be dynamically bound at run time.

3. A pointer of the base class can be used to instantiate, reference and destroy objects of any derived classes.

4. In order for methods to be dynamically bound, they must be declared 'virtual'. This includes the destructor (though not the constructor). Abstract object methods may be declared as 'pure virtual functions' in C++ using the '= 0' syntax.

5. A class with one or more pure virtual functions cannot be instantiated – i.e. it is a pure abstract class.

6. For a method to be dynamically bound to objects of derived classes in a hierarchy, it must be a member of the base class, whether or not the base class method is abstract.

Exercises

1. Rewrite your 'Pump' classes from Chapter 13, exercise 1, so that the 'turnOn' method is abstract in the base class and can be dynamically bound. Test your classes with the code from pages 232–3.

2. A toy manufacturer makes cuddly toys of four types in three sizes. Some toys are teddy bears and others are bunny rabbits. Teddy bears are dressed as either engine drivers or gardeners, while bunnies are dressed as clowns or bank managers. Teddies make a growling noise and go 'pad pad pad' when they walk, whereas bunnies make a thumping noise and move along going 'bounce, bounce, bounce'. All toys can make a moving along noise, say what job they do and tell you their size by making a noise the appropriate number of times. For example, when asked for its size a size one clown will say 'thump', but a size three gardener will say 'grrr, grrr, grrr'.

   Model the classes as described above in a hierarchy, the highest level of which should be the base class 'CuddlyToy'. There should be an intermediate level of classes 'Teddy' and 'Bunny', and at the lowest level classes of 'EngineDriver', 'Gardener', 'Clown' and 'BankManager'.

Instantiate objects of these classes dynamically using base class pointers, setting the size of the toys via a parameter to their constructors. Remember to pass the 'size' parameter to the base class when coding the derived class constructors (see pages 129–130). Demonstrate that the toys can move along, tell us what size they are and say what job they do using dynamically bound, virtual methods.

3. In a given academic year, students register as either full time or part time. Full time students pay a flat fee for a complete year's course, but the fee for part time students is based on how many units they choose to take, multiplied by the unit fee. Write a 'Student' base class with a 'name' attribute and an enumerated type to indicate whether or not a student has paid their fees. The class should have a 'payFees' method and an abstract 'getFeesDue' method. Add derived classes for full time and part time students, implementing polymorphic 'getFeesDue' methods in these classes.

Provide 'get' and 'set' methods in the base class for the student's name, and a constructor that ensures that fees are initially recorded as unpaid. Use the derived class constructors to set the course fee (in the case of full time students) or the unit fee and the number of units (in the case of part time students).

Test your classes with a program that creates a group of students (using an array of 'Student' pointers to dynamically instantiate derived class objects) and displays the fees due from each student. Ensure that your 'payFees' method is tested.

15 Container classes

Part 1 Container types, data structures and simple containers

Overview

This part discusses container classes and describes the various types of container that may be required for different types of object collection. The containers available in the standard library are discussed, and C++ syntax examples show how simple container classes may be implemented by encapsulating arrays or linked lists of objects.

Containers as a form of aggregation

In Chapter 9 we introduced the idea of aggregation, which includes a number of object relationships. These may be of three general types:

1. fixed aggregations:

    an object is composed of a fixed set of component objects.

2. variable aggregations:

    an object is composed of a variable set of component objects.

3. containers:

    An object exists in its own right, but is able to contain other objects.

You may remember that Fig. 9.5 used a car to illustrate the difference between 'containment' (fixed or variable aggregations where objects are components of other objects) and 'containers' (where one object holds collections of other objects). The engine compartment of a car has a containment relationship with the engine, which is an essential component of the enclosing object. In contrast, the boot exists regardless of its contents, but is able to contain various collections of other objects. You may also recall that one of the characteristics of a container is that it can persist even if it contains nothing.

What is a container?

There are containers all around us, and without them life would be very difficult, since containers allow us to collect and organise numbers of other objects. Fig. 15.1 shows a few containers of various types.

Fig. 15.1: Some examples of containers that can hold collections of other objects.

A bus, for example, contains passengers, a coal truck contains coal, an envelope may contain a letter and a diskette may contain data files, perhaps with directories providing another level of aggregation. Just from these examples, we can see that there are differences in the characteristics of different containers. Some containers have limitations on the type of objects they may contain, so that a coal truck might only ever contain coal, whereas an envelope may contain a wide range of items provided they are of a suitable size and weight (letters, photographs, cheques etc.) Some containers have limited mechanisms for adding and removing objects; people must enter a bus through a door in a particular sequence, which may be dictated by ticket numbers, whereas coal is loaded in a rather more informal manner! The organisation of objects within the container may vary too. For example, the organisation of files on a diskette must be very strict for us to be able to add files, remove them and access the data on the disk, while a pile of groceries in a shopping trolley has no particular order or control over access. Another aspect of containers is constraints on the number of objects they can hold. For some containers the maximum number of objects is fixed; buses have a fixed passenger capacity and diskettes have a fixed size of data storage. In contrast, a bin liner always has enough available expansion for just one more soggy tea bag!

Question 15.1 What characteristics of a container can be identified for a CD case?

A CD case contains objects of a single class in a particular sequence and has a fixed maximum storage capacity. It allows random access to the objects (CDs) in the container.

Containers in software

In this chapter, we will look at some containers that may be implemented in software. These range from the simplest types, such as containers for a fixed number of objects of a single class, to more complex structures that may contain dynamic collections of objects of many classes.

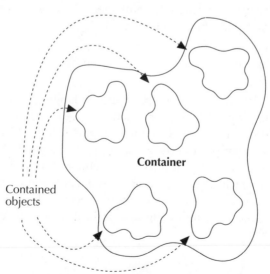

Contained objects

Container

Fig. 15.2: A container is an object of a container class. It contains other objects.

A container in an object-oriented program is usually instantiated as an object of a container class. A container class object encapsulates inside it the mechanism for containing other objects, and providing the necessary behaviour for adding, removing and accessing the objects it contains (Fig. 15.2). Incidentally, the use of a 'cloud' to represent an object, found in a number of illustrations in this chapter, is adapted from the design notation of Grady Booch [Booch, 1994].

Like all classes, a container class gives us the opportunity for reuse, so that container objects (being fairly generic in nature) can be usefully instantiated in many programs. This frees us from having to recreate complex data structures in every program requiring the management of a collection of objects.

We have already used simple containers in some of our example programs. In Chapter 6, we used both a single pointer and an array of pointers to represent 'garages', in a sense modelling a real life container. In Chapter 14 we used an array of 'FlyingMachine' pointers to contain aircraft of various derived classes. In this case the array modelled a set of hangars; again reflecting a real life container. In fact an array is a very useful way of containing collections of objects, since it is simple to manage and allows direct access to its elements. However, it also has certain characteristics that may not always be appropriate. For example, it is always of a fixed size and the data is indexed in a fixed sequence. Although we have used data structures to contain other objects, we have not so far modelled the containers themselves as objects. This may be done by encapsulating the data structures inside the definitions of container classes.

Container types

There are many different types of container, and container class libraries provided with most object-oriented languages have a range of container classes with various behaviours and internal implementations. In the past, C++ compilers from different vendors had different libraries, some based on inheritance and some based on genericity. The standard C++ library uses genericity to implement the classes, a technique that will be described in the second part of this chapter.

If a library class is available, it is usually better to re-use it. We can, however, build our own container classes quite simply, which can be a useful exercise in understanding how containers work.

Although container class libraries can vary between languages and compilers, they will all provide a similar set of classes to the standard C++ library. Typically we will find general data structures such as vectors (arrays) and lists (with their implementations encapsulated behind a simple interface), along with classes providing specific access protocols (e.g. how objects can be put into and removed from the collection). Template based libraries usually include two general types of container class; the underlying data structures such as arrays and lists, and the more specialised types that are built on them such as stacks and queues. The following table indicates the main container classes in the standard C++ library.

Container	Ordering	Random access?	Indexable?
vector	by index	yes	yes
list	by insertion	yes	no
stack	by insertion	no	no
queue	by insertion	no	no
priority queue	by size	no	no
deque	by index and insertion	yes	yes
set	sorted	yes	no
multiset	sorted	yes	no
map	by sorted key	yes	yes, by data type
multimap	by sorted key	yes	yes, by data type

Container classes like these are abstract concepts that are implemented using traditional data structures such as arrays and lists. Once they are encapsulated into classes, however, we do not have to be aware of their implementation details. There is also a lot of overlap between the different containers in the table because some definitions are purely to do with structure, but others constrain access methods. The stack for example, which has strict access rules, may be built on either a vector or a deque, both of which have very open access.

Ordered and unordered collections

An ordered collection is a very general type of container which could be modelled using a range of internal implementations. Since it is ordered, there simply has to be some mechanism for referencing objects in the container in the required order, usually the order in which the objects were originally added, but sometimes by other criteria such as sorting by key or size. It is worth bearing in mind that certain operations are possible on ordered collections that are not possible on unordered collections; we can access the first or last elements for example, operations that would clearly not apply to unordered collections. All the containers in the standard library have some kind of ordering, even where the type of container does not necessarily demand it.

If an ordered collection is sorted, then we have to ensure that any objects put into the collection are in fact sortable, perhaps by being able to respond to an overloaded '>' or '<' operator.

Direct and indirect containers

A direct container contains the actual objects, whereas an indirect container simply holds pointers to the objects. Indirect containers are the more useful type because they allow us to use polymorphism to manage different types of object in the same container. A single object may also be referenced by more than one indirect container (i.e. it can be in more than one container at the same time).

Question 15.2 What must underlie the public interface of any container object?

In order for a container to work, some kind of data structure that implements its behaviour must lie behind its interface. Typically, some kind of vector or list may be used.

The vector:

The terms 'vector' and 'array' are often used synonymously because a vector is simply an array that has only one dimension. An array, in contrast, can have multiple rows and columns but all the examples in this book have only one dimension. Since we have already used the array to contain objects in previous examples, it seems a good place to start. However, we have not so far seen the encapsulation of an array into a class.

Arrays have many advantages; being instances of a data structure built in to the compiler they are easily declared, easily indexed (by an integer subscript) and relatively easy to handle in a program. Since the indexing is done independently of the contained objects duplicate objects can be contained. The only major drawback of the array is that it must be of a fixed size. As we know, an array can only be declared with a given size and cannot be dynamically resized once declared. It can of course be dynamically allocated at run time, but once it has been created its size is fixed. The only way of resizing an array at run time is to create a new array of the required size and then copy into it all the data from the original array.

In an object-oriented system, arrays are often modelled as classes rather than simply used as data structures. This encapsulates the mechanisms which directly manipulate the array behind a simpler object interface. The vector class allows us to create objects that behave like arrays, but can also dynamically resize themselves and have integral bounds checking to ensure that we do not use elements which have not been properly allocated.

The list:

After the vector, the list is the most fundamental data structure. Unlike an array, it does not have to be declared with a fixed size, because it is only ever as large as the collection of objects it contains. Because a list is maintained by chaining the objects sequentially together there is fast access to the first and last elements but accessing objects elsewhere in the list can be inefficient, unlike the indexed vector.

The stack:

The stack is a classic data structure that in the standard library is based on either a vector or a deque. What defines a stack is not so much its internal structure but its access methods. A stack is a 'LIFO' ('Last In First Out') structure, which means that objects are put into a stack object in order, and only retrievable from it in reverse order (Fig. 15.3). Standard operations for a stack are 'push' (add an item to the top of the stack) and 'pop' (remove the item on the top of the stack.)

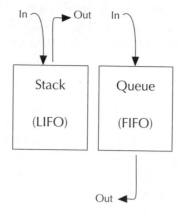

Fig. 15.3: A stack is a 'Last In First Out' structure. In contrast, a queue is a 'First In First Out' structure.

The queue:

Like the stack, the queue is one of the most well known structures (also illustrated in Fig. 15.3). Its implementation in the library is either based on a list or a deque. In contrast to the stack, its access method is 'FIFO' ('First In First Out').

The deque:

The double ended queue, usually known as a deque (pronounced ('deck') is a cross between a queue and a stack because we can add and retrieve objects at both ends (Fig. 15.4). The implementation of the deque in the standard library also allows random access to the elements in the container, which is not the case in the usual definition of a deque.

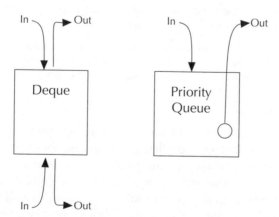

Fig. 15.4: A deque has characteristics of both a stack and a queue in that objects can be added and retrieved at either end. A priority queue puts the largest object to the head of the queue.

The priority queue:

The priority queue allows objects to be prioritised, so that it is a collection ordered by priority rather than by insertion sequence or sorting. The first object out of the queue is not necessarily the first one added, but the one that has the highest priority. In the standard library this is the 'largest' element (Fig. 15.4), which assumes that the contained objects can respond to the appropriate operator. Its implementation is based on either a vector or a deque.

The set:

The key aspect of a set is that there can be no duplicates in it. One way of defining a set is to say that it will discard duplicate additions (without regarding this as an error), so that one might be used for example to collect the uniquely occurring words in a document. Rumbaugh suggests that the set is the best way to implement a multiple unordered association. Although the general concept of a set does not imply ordering of the objects, the standard C++ implementation does in fact order the objects by sorting.

The multiset:

A multiset (sometimes known as a 'bag') is a fairly general type of container, because it has a very open access mechanism. Although it is based on a set, it allows duplicates.

The map:

A map (sometimes known as a 'dictionary', a 'table' or an 'associative array') provides a way of accessing objects by using other objects as the key. For example, we might use a map to create an interview appointment system, with time objects used as keys to objects representing interviewees.

The multimap:

Like the map, the multimap is based on a table of keys and values. It differs, however, in allowing duplicate keys to be contained.

Question 15.3 What type of container would be appropriate to model a 'stack' of aircraft waiting to land at an airport?

A 'stack' of aircraft is not actually a stack! In general terms it is a ordered collection that does not contain duplicates. It is in practice a queue (the first aircraft in is the first one out), but has some aspects of a priority queue, in that if necessary certain aircraft can 'queue jump', perhaps if they are short of fuel.

The use of containers

The primary value of containers in an object-oriented program is that they give us control over collections of objects, particularly dynamic objects that are unpredictable in terms of their persistence. When we want to model objects in a varying collection at run time, we need a simple mechanism for creating, accessing and destroying them without having to explicitly deal with the programming algorithms that allow dynamic objects to be handled. A container class takes responsibility for managing our collections of objects, and all we have to do is to use the methods provided for the container. A typical container might have the kind of methods shown below, allowing us to add objects to the container, find a particular object and remove an object. It is also useful to know if the container is empty or not, and be able to empty ('flush') the container. This type of container class interface is fairly generic; all kinds of object collections can undergo these operations.

Container
add object
find object
flush
is empty?
remove object

Iterators

We have talked about different types of object method in previous chapters; selector methods (to tell us about the state of objects), modifier methods (that let us change the state of objects) constructors and destructors (to create and destroy objects). With container classes, we also need what are known as 'iterator' methods, that allow us to iterate through the contents of a container in order to access the objects inside it. Many iterator methods rely on all the contained objects being able to respond polymorphically to the same messages. For example, we might have a container of graphics objects that are to be displayed on the screen using a 'draw' method. An iterator method could address all the objects in the container in turn, sending the necessary message (Fig. 15.5).

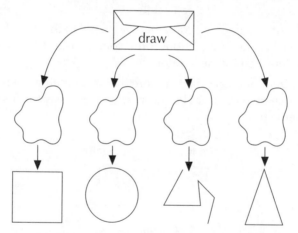

Fig. 15.5: an iterator method will reference the objects in the container. In this case, a collection of graphics objects are all sent the message 'draw'.

Other iterators might destroy all the objects in a container, or scan all the objects looking for a particular one.

Iterator objects

One problem with adding iterator methods to a container class is that they are often not intrinsic behaviours of the container itself, but application specific requirements. Take a method called 'view objects' for example, that displays some information from the objects on the screen. This is not really a fundamental operation of a container, but something that we may wish to do to the objects in that container. The builder of the original container cannot anticipate in advance how the objects need to be viewed. Many other operations might be necessary on a particular collection of objects, and it would be impossible (and unreasonable) to attempt to build all these in as methods of the container class.

To overcome this problem, there are two possible solutions. One is to use what are known as 'callback' functions, where the container class has methods that are given the address of user defined functions that process objects passed to them. That way, all the container class method has to do is to send each object in turn to the external function.

The second solution (as used in the standard library) is to have separate iterator objects that can be associated with a particular container and have the necessary methods to iterate through the container and access its elements. The programmer is then able to write application specific methods to process the objects returned by the iterator. The methods of iterator classes are very simple, typically the four described by [Gamma et al, p.257]:

'first' moves to the first item in the container and 'next' to the next item. 'is done' tells us when we have finished iterating through the container and 'current item' returns the object currently referenced by the iterator.

One advantage of iterator objects is that more that one iterator can be used with a single container. In Fig. 15.6, two iterator objects are shown accessing different parts of a single container at the same time.

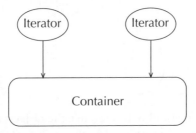

Fig. 15.6: More than one iterator object can be used with a single container object.

C++ Syntax

There are many ways of implementing containers in C++, so the examples which follow serve only as an introduction to the design and implementation of container classes. You may also wish to explore the standard library or any vendor-specific container class libraries which you may have access to.

The simplest container is, of course, the array, and we have seen the array used to contain objects in several example programs. What we have not done is to encapsulate these arrays into container classes; only the simple data structure has been used. The example which follows contrasts the use of an array as a container in its own right with an array-based container object. In the previous chapter, we modelled a set of aircraft hangars as an array of pointers of class 'FlyingMachine':

```
FlyingMachine* hangar[10];
```

This meant that every time it was necessary to interface with the hangars (to put an aircraft in, report on hangar status or take an aircraft out) the array elements had to be directly addressed. Take this code fragment for example, which shows the contents of the hangars:

```
for(int i = 0; i < 10; i++)
{
    if(hangar[i] != NULL)
    {
        hangar[i] -> showName();
        cout << " in hangar " << i << endl;
        found = 1;
    }
}
if(found == 0)
{
    cout << "All hangars empty" << endl;
}
```

Because the array is a data structure rather than a class, we have no encapsulation of its functionality behind a simple interface. If, however, we were to model the hangars as a container object, then we could hide this kind of implementation inside object methods. We might have a method called 'showContents' to perform this behaviour:

```
hangars.showContents();
```

Being able to call this type of method certainly makes the program easier to follow, because the implementation detail need not concern us. We can still model the hangars using the same array and the same algorithms as we used in the program in Chapter 14, but we can encapsulate them inside a class which might look something like this:

```
class Hangar
{
private:
    FlyingMachine* machines[10];
    int aircraft_count;
public:
    Hangar();
    ~Hangar();
    void showContents();
    void aircraftIn(FlyingMachine* machine_in);
    FlyingMachine* aircraftOut();
    int aircraftCount();
    int hangarsEmpty();
};
```

By encapsulating the manipulation of the array behind the object interface, the rest of the program becomes much simpler. It also allows us to pass other responsibilities to the object such as keeping a count of how many aircraft are present. By modelling what was previously a simple data structure as a real world object, we can get a clearer idea of where responsibilities lie and in which classes methods should reside.

If the airport object includes an aggregated object of class 'Hangar' (with all its encapsulated behaviour), the control tower is then able to interrogate the interface of the hangar container for the required behaviours, for example:

```
cout << hangars.aircraftCount() << " aircraft in hangars" << endl;
```

Although we still have to provide the implementation for the methods of 'Hangar', the separation of these methods from other classes makes the system more modular and flexible.

Generic containers

You may have noticed that the public interface of the 'Hangar' class bears a close resemblance to the generic methods that appeared earlier on our 'Container' class diagram. This might lead us to question whether we really need to re-implement an application specific container such as 'Hanger' (that will be of no use in any other application) or whether we can use a more generic implementation that can be used in other programs. To model the hangers we need an ordered, indexed container; perhaps we should build ourselves a 'vector' class or, better still, use an existing class in a library. We can still have a 'Hangar' class for application specific behaviour, but instead of encapsulating a simple array data structure, it would be better to base most of its operations on a 'vector' object aggregated inside the class. The advantages of this approach over using a simple data structure would include automatic bounds checking, dynamic resizing and predefined iterators.

Linked lists of objects

As we have stated, an array is not the most flexible mechanism for implementing containers because resizing arrays can be complex and inefficient. A better approach in cases where the numbers of objects fluctuate widely is the linked list, which allows the size of the container to vary automatically as objects are added and removed. This is because it does not store objects in a fixed physical sequence (though the objects in a list still have a logical sequence.) A list is implemented using pointers; one pointer (the head pointer) references the first object in the list (in our example this will always be the most recently added,) and then each object points to the next one in the list. Fig. 15.7 shows the structure of a simple list of objects. In this case, it is a singly linked list, which means that each object can only point to one other object (the next in the list, or NULL if there are no more objects).

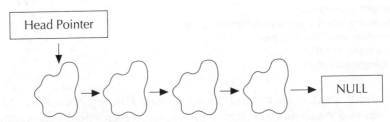

Fig. 15.7: A singly linked list of objects requires a head pointer to reference the object at the head of the list. The remaining objects then reference each other sequentially.

A doubly linked list is where each object has two pointers to reference the objects on either side of it, and two pointers (the 'head' and 'tail' pointers) are used to reference the two ends of the list (Fig. 15.8). This makes certain operations such as deletions easier to accomplish.

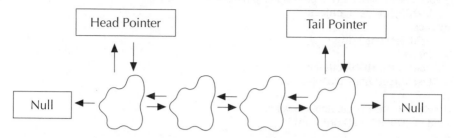

Fig. 15.8: A doubly linked list can be traversed in both directions, since each object points to both its neighbours, and both ends of the list are referenced by pointers.

The next example program demonstrates the creation of a singly linked list of objects of a single class. This is what is known as an 'intrusive' list because the objects themselves have to point to each other, and therefore must contain a pointer of their own class. At this stage, we are not modelling a container class, simply demonstrating the implementation mechanisms for putting objects into lists. The program itself simply instantiates five objects and adds them to the list in turn, iterating through the list at the end to display their attribute values.

Iterating through a list of objects

In order to iterate through a linked list of objects, each object must be accessed via the object which is pointing to it, starting with the head pointer and terminating when a NULL pointer is reached. The following code fragment from 'main' shows how this is done:

```
for(temp = head_pointer; temp != NULL; temp = temp -> getPreviousObject())
{
    temp -> showX();
}
```

'temp' is a pointer of the class which scans through the list of objects, starting with the head pointer ('temp = head_pointer'). The 'while' condition is 'temp != NULL', so that the loop will continue as long as there is a valid pointer in the current object. At the end of each loop, 'temp' is redirected to the object referenced by the current object's pointer ('temp = temp -> getPreviousObject()')

Example program – a linked list of objects

The header file contains the definition of a simple 'ListObject' class (and methods) that can be used to build an intrusive linked list.

```
/*
    LISTOBJ.H    This class is able to create an intrusive linked list.
                 Objects are referenced by pointers contained in other objects.
*/
#include <iostream.h>
class ListObject
{
private:
```

```
// the only attribute is a single integer
    int x;
// each object will contain a pointer to the next object in the list
    ListObject* next_object;
public:
    void setX(int x_in);
    int getX();
    void setNextObject(ListObject* next);
    ListObject* getNextObject();
};
// 'setX' sets the integer attribute value
void ListObject::setX(int x_in)
{
    x = x_in;
}
// 'getX' returns the attribute
int ListObject::getX()
{
    return x;
}
// 'setNextObject' directs the pointer to the next object in the list
void ListObject::setNextObject(ListObject* next)
{
    next_object = next;
}
// 'getNextObject' tells us which is the next object in the list
ListObject* ListObject::getNextObject()
{
    return next_object;
}
```

This example program builds a list of five objects of the 'ListObject' class and then iterates through it:

```
/*
    LISTOBJ.CPP This program creates a linked list of objects
*/
#include "listobj.h"
void main()
{
// declare 'head_pointer' of type ListObject which initially points to NULL
// when the program runs, 'head_pointer' will always point to the most recently
// added object in the list
    ListObject* head_pointer= NULL;
// another pointer, 'temp' is declared to instantiate objects
// before they are added to the list
    ListObject* temp;
// 5 objects are created using a 'for' loop
    for(int i = 1; i <= 5; i++)
    {
        temp = new ListObject;
// the pointer in the object is set to whatever 'head_pointer' is
// currently pointing at
        temp -> setNextObject(head_pointer);
// the object is given an attribute value (just to prove it works!)
        temp -> setX(i);
// before 'temp' is used again, 'head_pointer' is re-directed to point
// at the last created object
```

```
            head_pointer = temp;
    }
// at this point, 'head_pointer' is pointing to the fifth object that
// was created. The first four can only be located by the pointers
// inside other objects. the following iteration reads back through the
// linked list of pointers until it reaches the last object pointer
// (which is NULL)
    for(temp = head_pointer; temp != NULL; temp = temp -> getNextObject())
    {
        cout << "Value of object is " << temp -> getX() << endl;
    }
}
```

The output from this program will be the attribute values of the five objects, seen in reverse order of instantiation as the pointer scans from the last object in the list back to the first as follows:

Value of object is = 5
Value of object is = 4
Value of object is = 3
Value of object is = 2
Value of object is = 1

Creating a container class

A container encapsulates its implementation behind its object methods. To build a container class we need to hide the data structures used to manage the collection of objects. It is also preferable if being in a container does not impinge more than necessary on the contained objects. In the previous example we used an intrusive list, which meant that each object had to be responsible for pointing to the next object in the list. We can improve on this approach by creating a non-intrusive list, in which another type of object (a 'link' object) encapsulated inside the container takes over the responsibility for maintaining the integrity of the pointers that make up the list. Fig. 15.9 shows how a non-intrusive list is organised; the objects themselves do not contain pointers to other objects, but are all referenced by objects of a 'link' class. It is these links which point to each other, and the head pointer always references the last link in the list, not the last contained object.

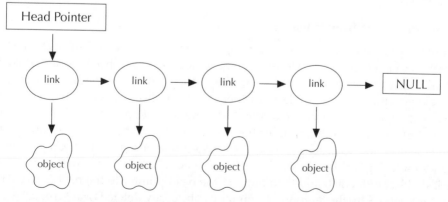

Fig. 15.9: A non-intrusive list. 'Link' objects take over the responsibility of organising the list from the objects in the container.

There are three classes used in the container class example program:

1. Date – The class of the objects that are to be put into the container. Unlike the 'ListObject' example, this class does not contain any implementation code for building the linked list.

2. Link – The class of the links which implement the list used inside the container. Each link contains two pointers, one to point to the next link in the list, and another to reference an object of the 'Date' class.

3. Container – The container class, which is able to contain objects of class 'Date' and manage them using 'Link' objects.

Adding a new object to a container

Since containers generally use pointers to reference the contained objects, adding a new object means passing a pointer to the container via a method. We can do this by instantiating an object outside the container and then passing it as a parameter to a suitable method. This example (similar to the example program in the next listing) assumes a container called 'date_list' with a method called 'addObject' that takes as a parameter a pointer of the class 'Date'. We might add a new object like this:

```
Date* temp;
temp = new Date;
date_list.addObject(temp);
```

This creates an object that can be referenced both inside the container and outside. It might even be referenced by more than one container. However, it may be unnecessary to have the object visible outside the container, if the container has ownership of the object (i.e. if the object has no need to exist except inside the container). In such cases, a more appropriate way to instantiate the object is to use 'new' inside the argument list of the method itself, as follows:

```
date_list.addObject(new Date);
```

This will create the object as part of the method call, and remove the need for another pointer outside the container. In the example program, this is how new 'Date' objects are added to the list based container. In the example, the Date constructor takes data from the keyboard as a shortcut, but in a more realistic system we might pass parameters to the constructor.

Removing an object from a list

A container that only allows us to add objects is rather limited, so our container also has a method to remove objects. Unfortunately, removing objects from a singly linked list is not very easy. If we simply destroy the object, then any object that it references will be lost, along with any other objects further down the list. Therefore the removal of an object requires some redirection of pointers. One way of approaching it is to handle the removal of the object at the head of the list differently to the removal of objects further along the list. This is because removing the object referenced by the head pointer is relatively simple. Fig. 15.10 indicates how this is done. The first step is to direct a pointer to the last object in the list, and then redirect the head pointer to the next object. Then the object referenced by the temporary pointer can be easily deleted or returned.

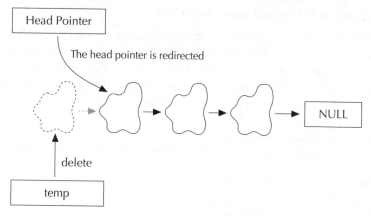

Fig. 15.10: Removing the object at the head of the list involves redirecting
the head pointer and referencing the object using a temporary pointer.

Although the figure shows an object being deleted, the same technique applies for the
deletion of links in a non-intrusive list. The link in such a list always needs to be deleted
to recover memory. However, the object may not be removed. Containers sometimes
have 'ownership' of the objects they contain, which means that they can destroy objects
removed from the container. However, in other cases the container does not own the
objects and simply returns them once they are removed. We need to be aware that sometimes both link and object are destroyed, but sometimes only the link is destroyed.

Removing objects embedded somewhere in the middle of a list is more complex. This is
because once we have located the object to be removed, we also need to identify the
previous object and redirect its pointer past the removed object. Therefore we need to
iterate through the list using two pointers (Fig. 15.11), one to find the unwanted object,
and the other to redirect the pointer of the previous object.

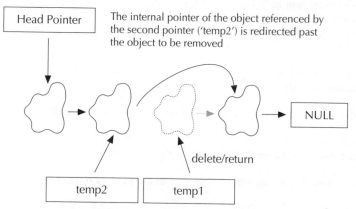

Fig. 15.11: Removing an object from the middle of a singly
linked list can be done using two pointers.

We can see from the code that this is not very easy to express in C++. A doubly linked list
provides an easier means of removing an object, because that object references the
objects on either side of it. This means that both the adjacent objects' pointers can be
accessed and redirected. Of course the trade off is that it is a little harder to implement a
doubly linked list in the first place.

Example program: a list-based container class

This example program shows how a container class may be implemented based on a non-intrusive singly linked list. The example is based on a container of 'Date' objects using the very simple class shown here. The state of the objects is set using keyboard input in the constructor. There is also a method to display the object, and an overloaded equality operator (==) that is used to locate a given date in the container:

```
/*
      DATE.H    the definition of the 'Date' class
                the 'Date' class has three integer attributes to represent day, month and year
*/
class Date
{
private:
    int day;
    int month;
    int year;
public:
    Date();
    void showDate();
    int operator == (const Date& date);
};
/*
      DATE.CPP the method definitions for the 'Date' class
*/
#include "date.h"
#include <iostream.h>
// the 'Date' constructor gets its values from the keyboard
Date::Date()
{
    cout << "Enter day ";
    cin >> day;
    cout << "Enter month ";
    cin >> month;
    cout << "Enter year ";
    cin >> year;
}
// 'showDate' displays the date
void Date::showDate()
{
    cout << "Date is: " << day << "/" << month << "/" << year << endl;
}
// the equality operator
int Date::operator == (const Date& date)
{
    if(day == date.day && month == date.month && year == date.year)
    {
        return 1;
    }
    else
    {
        return 0;
    }
}
```

This is the 'Link' class, which only exists as part of the implementation of the container. Its only behaviours are to direct pointers to other 'Link' objects and to 'Date' objects in order to link the list together:

```
/*
    LINK.H The class definition for the 'Link' class
*/
#include "date.h"
// the 'Link' class allows us to create a non-intrusive list, because it takes
// over responsibility for pointing to both an object and the next link in
// the list
class Link
{
// pointers to the next link in the list and an object of the 'Date' class
    Link* next_link;
    Date* current_object;
public:
    Link();
    void setNextLink(Link* previous);
    Link* getNextLink();
    void setCurrentObject(Date* current);
    Date* getCurrentObject();
};
/*
    LINK.CPP  The method definitions for the 'Link' class
*/
#include <stdlib.h> // for NULL
#include "link.h"
// the constructor initialises the pointers safely to NULL
Link::Link()
{
    next_link = NULL;
    current_object = NULL;
}
// 'setNextLink' directs the link pointer to the next link in the list
void Link::setNextLink(Link* next)
{
    next_link = next;
}
// 'getNextLink' returns a pointer to the next link in the list
Link* Link::getNextLink()
{
    return next_link;
}
// 'setCurrentObject' directs the object pointer to a 'Date'
void Link::setCurrentObject(Date* current)
{
    current_object = current;
}
// 'getCurrentObject' returns a pointer to the referenced date
Date* Link::getCurrentObject()
{
    return current_object;
}
```

The 'List' class is the container. As part of its implementation it contains a 'Link' object as the head pointer.

```
/*
    LIST.H The class definition of the 'List' class
*/
// the 'List' class uses link objects to control the list objects it
// contains
#include "link.h"
class List
{
private:
// the head pointer is to a 'Link' that will itself reference a 'Date'
    Link* head_pointer;
public:
    List();
    void addObject(Date* object_in);
    void showContents();
    Date* removeObject(Date* look_for);
};
/*
    LIST.CPP   The class definition of the 'List' class
               The 'List' class uses link objects to control the objects it
               contains
*/
#include <iostream.h>
#include "list.h"
// the constructor initialises the head pointer to NULL
List::List()
{
    head_pointer = NULL;
}
// 'addObject' adds a new object to the list
void List::addObject(Date* object_in)
{
// declare a new Link to reference the added object
    Link* temp_link = new Link;
// the 'next_link' pointer in the new link object is set to whatever
// the head pointer is currently pointing at.
    temp_link -> setNextLink(head_pointer);
// its 'Date' pointer is directed to the newly added object.
    temp_link -> setCurrentObject(object_in);
// 'head_pointer' is re-directed to point at the last created link object
    head_pointer = temp_link;
}
// a simple iterator that shows the contents of the container
void List::showContents()
{
    for(Link* temp_link = head_pointer; temp_link != NULL;
        temp_link = temp_link -> getNextLink())
    {
        temp_link -> getCurrentObject() -> showDate();
    }
}
// removing an item from a singly linked list is a messy business...
// like many containers, this one identifies an object using its overloaded
// equality operator (==)
Date* List::removeObject(Date* look_for)
{
// declare a local pointer to return the found object
    Date* date_found;
```

```
// set a flag so we can check if a match was found
    int found = 0;
// first of all, is there anything in the container? If not, abort the
// search
    if(head_pointer == NULL)
    {
        found = 0;
    }
// if there is, try to match the parameter object with one in the container
    else
    {
// declare a local 'Link' pointer to iterate through the array
        Link* temp_link;
// see if it is the last object which is to be removed. The overloaded
// equality operator is used to locate the object. The parameter date
// and the pointer returned from the container both have to be de-referenced
// in order to compare the objects
        if(*(head_pointer -> getCurrentObject()) == *look_for)
        {
// direct the temporary pointer to the first Link
            temp_link = head_pointer;
// move the head pointer along the list, past the object to be removed
            head_pointer = head_pointer -> getNextLink();
// point the local Date pointer to the found object
            date_found = temp_link -> getCurrentObject();
// delete the Link object that is no longer required
            delete temp_link;
// set the flag to indicate a successful search
            found = 1;
        }
// if the first object is not the one we want, we had better look through
// the list. we need a second pointer to follow along one link behind
// this is used to bypass the object being removed
        else
        {
// direct the second pointer at the (already checked) head pointer
            Link* temp2 = head_pointer;
// start iterating from the second link onwards
            for(temp_link = head_pointer -> getNextLink();
                temp_link != NULL;
                temp_link = temp_link -> getNextLink())
            {
// if a match is found
                if(*(temp_link -> getCurrentObject()) == *look_for)
                {
// direct the previous link to the one after the found object
                    temp2 -> setNextLink(temp_link -> getNextLink());
// point the local Date pointer to the found object
                    date_found = temp_link -> getCurrentObject();
// remove the unwanted link
                    delete temp_link;
// move the iterating pointer past the deleted link
                    temp_link = temp2;
// set the flag to indicate a successful find operation
                    found = 1;
                }
                else
                {
```

```
// if the current object was not matched, move the trailing pointer along
// before the end of the 'for' loop
                        temp2 = temp_link;
                }
            }
        }
    }
// return a pointer to the found object, which may be NULL if no match was found
    if(!found)
    {
        return NULL;
    }
    else
    {
        return date_found;
    }
}
```

The test program ('LISTMAIN.CPP') test the methods of the 'List' class by adding, displaying and removing 'Date' objects

```
/*
    LISTMAIN.CPP    Program to test the 'List' class
*/
#include "list.h"
#include <iostream.h>
// 'main' simply demonstrates the methods 'addObject', 'showContents'
// and 'removeObject'
void main()
{
// create a 'List' object
    List date_list;
// local variable for menu choice
    int choice;
// iterate until choice is 4 (exit)
    do
    {
        cout << "Enter 1 to add, 2 to show all, 3 to remove, 4 to exit ";
        cin >> choice;
        switch(choice)
        {
// add a new date object (the constructor will take data from the keyboard)
            case 1 : date_list.addObject(new Date); break;
// display the dates in the list
            case 2 : date_list.showContents(); break;
// remove a given date from the list
            case 3 : cout << "Enter details of object to remove" << endl;
                    Date* temp = new Date;
// 'returned' will either be NULL or the same date as 'temp', depending on
// the return value of 'removeObject'
                        Date* returned = date_list.removeObject(temp);
                        if(returned)
                        {
// display and then destroy the date returned
                            cout << "The following date has been removed: ";
                            returned -> showDate();
                            delete returned;
                        }
```

```
                            else
                            {
                                cout << "no match found" << endl;
                            }
                } // end of 'switch'
            } while(choice != 4);
    }
```

A sample test run:

Enter 1 to add, 2 to show all, 3 to remove, 4 to exit 1
Enter day 6
Enter month 6
Enter year 1944
Enter 1 to add, 2 to show all, 3 to remove, 4 to exit 1
Enter day 31
Enter month 12
Enter year 1999
Enter 1 to add, 2 to show all, 3 to remove, 4 to exit 1
Enter day 11
Enter month 11
Enter year 1918
Enter 1 to add, 2 to show all, 3 to remove, 4 to exit 2
11/11/1918
31/12/1999
6/6/1944
Enter 1 to add, 2 to show all, 3 to remove, 4 to exit 3
Enter details of object to remove
Enter day 2
Enter month 2
Enter year 22
no match found
Enter 1 to add, 2 to show all, 3 to remove, 4 to exit 3
Enter details of object to remove
Enter day 31
Enter month 12
Enter year 1999
The following date has been removed: 31/12/1999
Enter 1 to add, 2 to show all, 3 to remove, 4 to exit 2
11/11/1918
6/6/1944
Enter 1 to add, 2 to show all, 3 to remove, 4 to exit 4

Summary of key points from this part

1. A container is a type of aggregation.
2. Containers vary in characteristics such as the ability to contain objects of different types, whether they are of fixed size, and what methods of access they allow.
3. Containers in software give us control over collections of dynamic objects.

4. Container classes provide us with objects of various types, such as vectors, lists, stacks and queues.

5. Containers have iterators to allow various forms of access to the contained objects. Although these can be implemented as methods of the container, they may alternatively be external functions or separate objects.

6. Encapsulating collections of objects inside containers simplifies the interface between the objects and the data structures that are used to contain them.

7. Vectors (arrays) are a useful general mechanism for containing objects, but lists are more flexible since they are not of a fixed size.

8. A list may be singly or doubly linked. An intrusive list requires objects to take responsibility for referencing each other. A non-intrusive list uses link objects to manage the contained objects.

Exercises

1. One of the in-text questions referred to a CD cabinet as an example of a container. Define a simple 'CD' class (maybe with attributes such as 'artist' and 'title') that is able to instantiate CD objects. How could we declare and initialise an array able to store 50 pointers of this class? Why would we want to declare an array of pointers rather than an array of objects?

2. Create a container class called 'CDCabinet' by encapsulating an array inside it. Provide methods to add a CD to the first available position, remove a CD from a given position, and report the positions, artists and titles of all CDs in the cabinet. Write a program to test your container.

Part 2 Heterogenous containers and template classes

Overview

This part of the chapter follows on from the previous discussion of container classes and the data structures that may be used to implement them. It shows how a heterogenous collection of objects with polymorphic methods may be managed in a container. A generic approach to containers using template classes is demonstrated.

A container for heterogenous objects

The container class described previously was able to contain objects of the 'Date' class. It could also, of course, contain objects of any other class derived from 'Date' because, as we know, a base class pointer can be used to instantiate, reference and destroy objects of any derived class.

In the following example we will create a queue of vehicles that may be either cars or lorries (Fig. 15.12).

Fig. 15.12: a queue of vehicles may contain vehicles of different types.

A queue such as this might be used for example in a simulation of a toll booth on a bridge or motorway to estimate waiting times with different traffic flows. The container ('TrafficQueue') is implemented here using an array for simplicity, though other data structures could easily be used.

If we are going to use a base class pointer in a container to reference different objects at run time, then we must make sure that all the objects put into the container have a consistent interface, with methods that can be dynamically bound. In the example program, the 'showDetails' method is defined separately in all three classes and made 'virtual' for dynamic binding. Note that the destructor must also be made virtual so that it too can be dynamically bound.

Fig. 15.13 shows the relationship between the container object ('Traffic Queue') and the contained vehicles. Note that 'Traffic Queue' is an aggregation of 'Vehicle' objects, so all messages sent by the container must be appropriate to vehicles. These messages are then dynamically bound to the specific instances of 'Car' and 'Lorry' objects that exist in the container at run time. In fact the only message sent by the container is 'showDetails', which therefore appears in all three classes in the hierarchy. The static methods are not called by the container, but their return values are dictated by the constructors and destructors of the dynamic objects. The destructors of the classes in the hierarchy are therefore virtual, so that different destructors will execute for different classes of dynamic object.

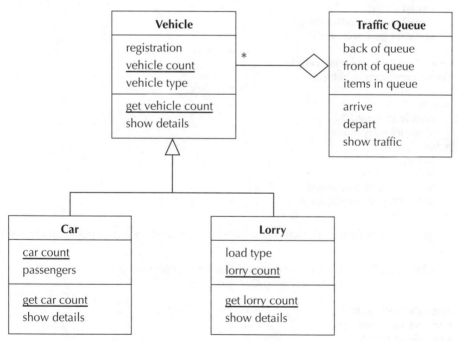

Fig. 15.13: UML diagram showing the relationships between the 'Traffic Queue' container and the contained 'Vehicle' objects.

Example program: a queue of dynamically bound vehicles

The objects in the queue will be derived classes of 'Vehicle'. Given their close relationship and limited methods, they are all defined in the same header file.

```
/*
        VEHICLE.H    The class definition for the 'Vehicle' class and
                     its descendants; 'Car' and 'Lorry'
*/
// 'Vehicle' is an abstract base class for cars and lorries
class Vehicle
{
protected:
    char registration[10];
    char vehicle_type[10];
    static int vehicle_count;
public:
    Vehicle();
    virtual ~Vehicle();
    virtual void showDetails();
    static int getVehicleCount();
};
// class 'Car' inherits from 'Vehicle'
class Car : public Vehicle
{
private:
    int passengers;
    static int car_count;
public:
    Car();
    virtual ~Car();
    virtual void showDetails();
    static int getCarCount();
};
//class 'Lorry' inherits from 'Vehicle'
class Lorry : public Vehicle
{
private:
    char load_type[20];
    static int lorry_count;
public:
    Lorry();
    virtual ~Lorry();
    virtual void showDetails();
    static int getLorryCount();
};
```

The implementations for 'Vehicle', 'Car' and 'Lorry' methods all appear in the same file:

```
/*
        VEHICLE.CPP    The method definitions for the 'Vehicle' class and
                       its descendants; 'Car' and 'Lorry'
*/
#include "vehicle.h"
#include <iostream.h>
#include <string.h>
// reserve memory for the static (class) attribute
int Vehicle::vehicle_count;
// the 'Vehicle' constructor increments the vehicle count and gets the
// registration number from the keyboard
Vehicle::Vehicle()
{
    vehicle_count++;
```

```
        cout << "Enter registration number ";
// because the registration has embedded spaces, 'cin' must be used
// with 'get' methods rather than the overloaded '>>' operator. these are
// described in detail in Chapter 17
        char temp;
        cin.get(temp);
        cin.get(registration, 10);
}
// the virtual destructor decrements the vehicle count. It will automatically
// be called by the dynamically bound destructors of the derived types
Vehicle::~Vehicle()
{
        vehicle_count--;
}
// the base class version of this method shows the two inherited attributes
void Vehicle::showDetails()
{
        cout << "Vehicle is a " << vehicle_type;
        cout << ", registration is " << registration;
}
// the class (static) method that returns the vehicle count
int Vehicle::getVehicleCount()
{
        return vehicle_count;
}
/*
        Method definitions for the 'Car' class
*/
// reserve memory for the class attribute 'car_count'
int Car::car_count;
// the 'Car' constructor
Car::Car()
{
        strcpy(vehicle_type, "Car");
        cout << "Enter number of passengers ";
        cin >> passengers;
        car_count++;
}
// the virtual destructor decrements the car count
Car::~Car()
{
        car_count--;
}
// this version of the virtual method calls the base class version
// as part of its implementation
void Car::showDetails()
{
        Vehicle::showDetails();
        cout << ", with " << passengers << " passengers" << endl;
}
// the class (static) method that returns the car count
int Car::getCarCount()
{
        return car_count;
}
/*
        Method definitions for the 'Lorry' class
*/
```

```
// reserve memory for the class attribute 'lorry_count'
int Lorry::lorry_count;
// the 'Lorry' constructor
Lorry::Lorry()
{
    strcpy(vehicle_type, "Lorry");
    cout << "Enter load type ";
    char temp;
    cin.get(temp);
    cin.get(load_type, 20);
    lorry_count++;
}
// the destructor decrements the lorry count
Lorry::~Lorry()
{
    lorry_count--;
}
// this version also calls the base class version
void Lorry::showDetails()
{
    Vehicle::showDetails();
    cout << ", carrying " << load_type << endl;
}
// the class (static) method that returns the lorry count
int Lorry::getLorryCount()
{
    return lorry_count;
}
```

The 'TrafficQueue' class provides the basic functionality of a queue, but is specifically implemented for objects of the Vehicle class (and its descendants):

```
/*
    TRAFFICQ.H  The class definition for the 'TrafficQueue' class
*/
#include "vehicle.h"
// the container class is sized by a constant, but could easily
// be dynamically allocated if required using a pointer and 'new'
const int SIZE = 4;
class TrafficQueue
{
private:
    Vehicle* queue[SIZE];
    int head_pointer;
    int tail_pointer;
    int items_in_queue;
public:
    TrafficQueue();
    ~TrafficQueue();
    int arrive(Vehicle* arrival);
    Vehicle* depart();
    void showTraffic();
};
/*
    TRAFFICQ.CPP   The method definition for the 'TrafficQueue' class
*/
#include "trafficq.h"
#include <stdlib.h>
```

```
// the constructor initialises all the vehicle pointers to NULL
// it also initialises the array indexes and the counter to 0
TrafficQueue::TrafficQueue()
{
    for(int i = 0; i < SIZE; i++)
    {
        queue[i] = NULL;
    }
    head_pointer = 0;
    tail_pointer = 0;
    items_in_queue = 0;
}
// the destructor is purely for cleanup
TrafficQueue::~TrafficQueue()
{
    for(int i = 0; i < SIZE; i++)
    {
        delete queue[i];
    }
}
// 'arrive' takes a parameter object and places it in the queue.
// if there is no space, the parameter object is deleted
int TrafficQueue::arrive(Vehicle* arrival)
{
// local flag variable to return the success or failure of the operation
    int added;
// if there is no room in the queue set the flag to 0 (false) and delete the
// parameter object
    if(items_in_queue == SIZE)
    {
        added = 0;
// this is not always an ideal approach; you may not want the object destroyed
        delete arrival;
    }
// if the queue has room, add the new vehicle at the back of the queue
    else
    {
        queue[tail_pointer] = arrival;
        tail_pointer++;
// if the end of the array has been reached, start again at
// the beginning
        if(tail_pointer == SIZE)
        {
            tail_pointer = 0;
        }
        items_in_queue++;
// since the vehicle has been successfully added, set the flag to 1 (true)
        added = 1;
    }
// return the flag
    return added;
}
// 'depart' takes the next vehicle from the queue, returns it
// and resets the pointer to NULL.
Vehicle* TrafficQueue::depart()
{
// local pointer to return the first object
    Vehicle* next_vehicle;
```

```
// if the queue is empty, set the pointer to NULL
    if(items_in_queue == 0)
    {
        next_vehicle = NULL;
    }
    else
    {
// remove the first vehicle from the queue
        next_vehicle = queue[head_pointer];
        queue[head_pointer] = NULL;
// move the head pointer along to the next vehicle
        head_pointer++;
// if we are at the end of the array, start again at the beginning
        if(head_pointer == SIZE)
        {
            head_pointer = 0;
        }
// decrement the counter
        items_in_queue--;
    }
    return next_vehicle;
}
// this is a simple iterator that displays the contents of the queue
// starting at the head pointer
void TrafficQueue::showTraffic()
{
// start at the head, and keep going until we reach the end of the
// array or there are no more vehicles
    for(int i = head_pointer; i < SIZE && queue[i] != NULL; i++)
    {
        if(queue[i] != NULL)
        {
            queue[i] -> showDetails();
        }
    }
// if we reached the end of the array, then there may be more vehicles
// before the head pointer, so start at element 0, and keep going until
// we reach the tail pointer
    if(i == SIZE)
    {
        for(i = 0; i < tail_pointer; i++)
        {
            if(queue[i] != NULL)
            {
                queue[i] -> showDetails();
            }
        }
    }
}
```

The test program creates a traffic queue, modelling vehicles arriving and departing on a 'first in first out' basis:

```
#include "trafficq.h"
#include <iostream.h>
void main()
{
// create a traffic queue object
```

```
    TrafficQueue toll_queue;
// local variables for menu choice and testing success of 'add' operations
    int menu_choice = 0;
    int add_ok = 0;
// local pointer used to retrieve vehicles from the queue
    Vehicle* a_vehicle;
// iterate until menu choice is 5 (quit)
    do
    {
// display current totals and menu
        cout << endl << "Vehicles in the queue: " << Vehicle::getVehicleCount() << endl;
        cout << "Total cars: " << Car::getCarCount() << endl;
        cout << "Total Lorries: " << Lorry::getLorryCount() << endl;
        cout << "1. Add car to queue" << endl;
        cout << "2. Add lorry to queue" << endl;
        cout << "3. Get next vehicle" << endl;
        cout << "4. Show traffic queue" << endl;
        cout << "5. Quit" << endl;
        cin >> menu_choice;
        switch(menu_choice)
        {
// add a car, using the return value to check for success or failure
            case 1:    add_ok = toll_queue.arrive(new Car);
                       if(!add_ok)
                       {
                           cout << "No room in the queue for this car!" << endl;
                       }
                       break;
// add a lorry
            case 2:    add_ok = toll_queue.arrive(new Lorry);
                       if(!add_ok)
                       {
                           cout << "No room in the queue for this lorry!" << endl;
                       }
                       break;
// remove the first vehicle in the queue
            case 3:
// return the vehicle from the queue to the local pointer
                       a_vehicle = toll_queue.depart();
// if a vehicle has been returned, display it (then delete it)
                       if(a_vehicle != NULL)
                       {
                           a_vehicle -> showDetails();
                           delete a_vehicle;
                       }
// if no vehicle is returned
                       else
                       {
                           cout << "There are no vehicles in the queue" << endl;
                       }
                       break;
// show the traffic in the queue
            case 4:    toll_queue.showTraffic();
                       break;
        }
    }
    while(menu_choice != 5);
}
```

This example test run shows the different types of vehicle arriving in and departing from the traffic queue:

Vehicles in the queue: 0
Total cars: 0
Total Lorries: 0
1. Add car to queue
2. Add lorry to queue
3. Get next vehicle
4. Show traffic queue
5. Quit
1
Enter registration number A 123 XYZ
Enter number of passengers 4
Vehicles in the queue: 1
Total cars: 1
Total Lorries: 0
1. Add car to queue
2. Add lorry to queue
3. Get next vehicle
4. Show traffic queue
5. Quit
2
Enter registration number Z 666 XXX
Enter load type Beer barrels
Vehicles in the queue: 2
Total cars: 1
Total Lorries: 1
1. Add car to queue
2. Add lorry to queue
3. Get next vehicle
4. Show traffic queue
5. Quit
2
Enter registration number G 84 ORW
Enter load type Rats
Vehicles in the queue: 3
Total cars: 1
Total Lorries: 2
1. Add car to queue
2. Add lorry to queue
3. Get next vehicle
4. Show traffic queue
5. Quit
4
Vehicle is a Car, registration is A 123 XYZ, with 4 passengers
Vehicle is a Lorry, registration is Z 666 XXX, carrying Beer barrels
Vehicle is a Lorry, registration is G 84 ORW, carrying Rats

Vehicles in the queue: 3
Total cars: 1
Total Lorries: 2
1. Add car to queue
2. Add lorry to queue
3. Get next vehicle
4. Show traffic queue
5. Quit
3
Vehicle is a Car, registration is A 123 XYZ, with 4 passengers
Vehicles in the queue: 2
Total cars: 0
Total Lorries: 2
1. Add car to queue
2. Add lorry to queue
3. Get next vehicle
4. Show traffic queue
5. Quit
3
Vehicle is a Lorry, registration is Z 666 XXX, carrying Beer barrels
Vehicles in the queue: 1
Total cars: 0
Total Lorries: 1
1. Add car to queue
2. Add lorry to queue
3. Get next vehicle
4. Show traffic queue
5. Quit
5

Container classes using templates

The problem with the previous list and queue examples is that they are implemented specifically for a particular class of object. A list of dates can only contain 'Date' objects and a queue of vehicles can only contain 'Vehicle' objects.

There are two ways to tackle this problem. One is to insist that all objects that are to be put into containers inherit from a common base class, typically 'Object', that provides a standard polymorphic interface. All descendent classes must then implement the same methods in order to be managed by the containers. The problem with this is that 'Object' will not have the interface methods of application specific classes, so a lot of casting is required to convert from class 'Object' to the classes in an application.

The second option, and the one used to implement the containers in the standard C++ library, is to use template classes (genericity). In Chapter 12, we introduced the template as a way of creating generic functions in C++. A generic function is, you may remember, one which is able to process parameter arguments of different types with a single implementation.

It is also possible to create generic classes, which may be instantiated by parameters of different types. Typically, classes instantiated in this way are container classes, with the class of the objects to be contained represented by a generic type name (typically 'T', as for the generic function example, but can be anything). The syntax for a container class is as follows:

```
template <class type_name> class name
{
    // class definition
```

The use of the 'template' and 'class' keywords has been seen before in the definition of generic template functions, likewise the pointed brackets around the type name.

If we wanted to create a generic stack class, then, we might declare the class like this:

```
template <class T> class Stack
{
    // etc.
};
```

The 'Stack' class can then be used to instantiate stack objects, but the type of object that a given stack may contain is not predetermined by the class definition.

Whenever we wish to refer to the data type or class of the elements which are to be contained on the stack, the alias 'T' is used (again we have seen this use of the alias for the class type in Chapter 12). A generic pointer for example would be:

```
T* a_pointer;
```

When a template stack object is instantiated, this may be a pointer to any data type or class.

Methods of a template class

Since we will probably wish to define a number of methods for the container class, we also need to know the syntax for defining a method of a template class out of line. This takes the following rather convoluted form:

```
template <class type_name> return_type class_name <type_name> :: method_name
(parameter_list...)
```

It looks a little simpler in practice. If we assume that our stack class has a 'push' method ('push' being the standard term for putting something on the stack, 'pop' for removing it) then the declarator (the first line) looks like this:

```
template <class T> void Stack<T> :: push(T* object_in)
{
    // method definition
};
```

Instantiating a template class object

Since an object of a template class is instantiated according to some other data type being provided, the constructor call is a little different to that normally used. The data type which is referred to as 'T' in the class definition must be given after the name of the class, using the familiar pointed brackets:

```
class_name <data_type> object_name(parameter_list...)
```

For a 'Stack' object instantiated to contain a maximum of 20 integers (in our example the stack size will be provided as a parameter to the constructor), the constructor call would be:

```
Stack <int> a_stack(20);
```

Instantiating a dynamic template object

Of course, we can also create dynamic objects of a template class, in which case the rather laborious syntax format is:

*class_name <data_type> *pointer_name = new class_name <data_type> (parameter_list...)*

Like the out-of-line method definition, it looks a bit less confusing in practice. This example instantiates a dynamic 'Stack' object of ten characters (chars):

```
Stack <char> *a_stack = new Stack <char> (10);
```

As in previous examples, the pointer may be declared separately to the constructor:

```
// declare the pointer
Stack <char> *a_stack;
// instantiate the object
a_stack = new Stack <char> (10);
```

Once we have instantiated 'a_stack' we can treat it like any other dynamic object, calling its methods with the arrow operator, and calling its destructor when required:

e.g.   **a_stack -> push('a');**

       ...

       delete a_stack;

A template stack

What follows is the definition of a template 'Stack' class, including a constructor which dynamically sizes the internal array using the 'new' operator. This leads to a bit of interesting syntax in the object attributes. Note that if we were to create a fixed size array of pointers (with five elements in this example) it would be done like this:

```
T* stack_array[5];
```

However, to be able to dynamically size the array, we have to use a pointer, so it becomes a pointer to a dynamic array of pointers! Hence the double asterisk.

```
T** stack_array;
```

This may look confusing, but hopefully makes some sense in the context of this line from the constructor:

```
stack_array = new T*[size];
```

Here we can see that one of the pointers has been used to create the dynamic array using the 'size' parameter.

Because of the way template classes work, their method definitions must appear in the header file along with the class definition.

```
/*
    TSTACK.H    The definition of a template stack class.
                This class can instantiate stack objects able to
                contain objects of any type or class provided at run time.
                Template classes must include their method definitions
                in the header file, not in a separate .CPP file
*/
#include <stdlib.h>   // for NULL
template <class T> class Stack
{
```

```
private:
    int max_stack;          // integer to store size of array
    int next_position;      // integer for array index
    T** stack_array;        // pointer to array of pointers!
public:
    Stack(int size);
    ~Stack();
    int push(T* object_in);
    T* top();
    T* pop();
};
// the template stack constructor uses 'new' to dynamically allocate the array
// and initialises its pointers to NULL
template <class T> Stack<T>::Stack(int size)
{
    max_stack = size;
    next_position = 0;
// dynamically allocate an array of pointers of type T
    stack_array = new T*[size];
// initialise the pointers to NULL
    for(int i = 0; i < size; i++)
    {
        stack_array[i] = NULL;
    }
}
// the destructor does some memory cleanup. it is not essential to
// check if there are remaining objects, since it does no harm to 'delete' a NULL pointer
template <class T> Stack<T>::~Stack()
{
    for(int i = 0; i < max_stack; i++)
    {
        delete stack_array[i];
    }
    delete stack_array;
}
// the 'push' method adds an object to the top of the stack. It returns
// an integer to signal the success or failure of the operation
template <class T> int Stack<T>::push(T* object_in)
{
// if the stack is full, the object cannot be added,
// and the method returns 0 (false)
    if(next_position == max_stack)
    {
        return 0;
    }
// otherwise, add it to the top of the stack and return 1 (true)
    else
    {
        stack_array[next_position] = object_in;
        next_position++;
        return 1;
    }
}
// the 'top' method returns the most recently added object
// from the top of the stack without removing it
template <class T> T* Stack<T>::top()
{
    T* temp;
```

```
// if there are no objects on the stack, then NULL is returned
    if (next_position == 0)
    {
        temp = NULL;
    }
// otherwise, the object on top of the stack is returned
    else
    {
        temp = stack_array[next_position - 1];
    }
    return temp;
}
// the 'pop' method returns and removes the most recently added object
// from the top of the stack
template <class T> T* Stack<T>::pop()
{
    T* temp;
// if there are no objects on the stack, then NULL is returned
    if (next_position == 0)
    {
        temp = NULL;
    }
// otherwise, the object on top of the stack is returned
    else
    {
        next_position --;
        temp = stack_array[next_position];
        stack_array[next_position] = NULL;
    }
    return temp;
}
```

An example stack program

Now we have created a template stack class, we can create stack objects to contain any data type or class. A stack is useful in any context where we want to be able to retrace our steps, for example in a hypertext browser where we may want to step back through previously seen pages. The example program does something similar (if very simplified). It mimics the structure of an adventure game where the player progresses from one scene to another, but is also able go back to the previous scene. Here is a simple 'Scene' class that contains a description of the scene:

```
/*
    SCENE.H  a class that represents a scene in a (very!) simple adventure game
*/
#include <string.h>
class Scene
{
private:
    char description[30];
public:
    Scene(char* description_in);
    char* getDescription();
};
// the constructor gets a description of the scene from its parameter
Scene::Scene(char* description_in)
{
```

```
        strncpy(description, description_in, 29);
        description[29] = '\0';
    }
// 'getDescription' returns the description of the scene
char* Scene::getDescription()
{
    return description;
}
```

Clearly, this is not going to be a very exciting adventure game, since nothing actually happens in the scenes, but at least it gives a feel for the stack structure. The test program allows the user to progress back and forth through a number of scenes.

```
/*
    TSTACKMN.CPP  Program to test the template 'Stack' class
*/
#include "tstack.h"
#include "scene.h"
#include <iostream.h>
// main instantiates a stack of 'Scene' objects, but any data type
// or class could be used to instantiate template stack objects
void main()
{
    int stack_size, choice, pushed;
    Scene* temp;
// instantiate a 'Stack' object with dynamically allocated size
    cout << "Enter size of stack required ";
    cin >> stack_size;
    Stack <Scene> a_stack(stack_size);
    cout << "You are at the beginning. Careful with that axe." << endl;
    do
    {
        cout << "Enter: \t 1 to go to a new scene" << endl;
        cout << "\t 2 to go back" << endl;
        cout << "\t 3 to find out where you are" << endl;
        cout << "\t 4 to exit" << endl;
        cin >> choice;
        switch(choice)
        {
// add a new 'Scene' to the stack
            case 1 : char buffer[80];
                cout << "What is the description of this scene? ";
                cin >> buffer;
                temp = new Scene(buffer);
                pushed = a_stack.push(temp);
                if(!pushed)
                {
                    cout << "No more room for scenes" << endl;
                    delete temp;
                }
                else
                {
                    cout << "You are now in the " << temp -> getDescription() << endl;
                }
                break;
// remove the scene at the top of the stack
            case 2 : temp = a_stack.pop();
// if an object has been popped from the stack, display its description
```

```
                    if(temp != NULL)
                    {
                         cout << "You have returned from the " << temp -> getDescription()
                         << endl;
// since the object has been removed from the stack and we have no further
// use for it, it is destroyed
                         delete temp;
                    }
                    else
                    {
                         cout << "You are at the beginning. Careful with that axe." << endl;
                    }
                    break;
               case 3 : temp = a_stack.top();
                    if(temp != NULL)
                    {
                         cout << "You are currently in the " << temp -> getDescription() <<
                         endl;
                    }
                    else
                    {
                         cout << "You are at the beginning. Careful with that axe." << endl;
                    }
                    break;
          }
     }
     while(choice != 4);
}
```

A thrilling test run follows:

Enter size of stack required 4
You are at the beginning. Careful with that axe.
Enter: 1 to go to a new scene
*   2 to go back*
*   3 to find out where you are*
*   4 to exit*
1
What is the description of this scene? castle
You are now in the castle
Enter: 1 to go to a new scene
*   2 to go back*
*   3 to find out where you are*
*   4 to exit*
1
What is the description of this scene? forest
You are now in the forest
Enter: 1 to go to a new scene
*   2 to go back*
*   3 to find out where you are*
*   4 to exit*
3
You are currently in the forest
Enter: 1 to go to a new scene

> *2 to go back*
> *3 to find out where you are*
> *4 to exit*
>> *1*
>
> *What is the description of this scene? valley*
> *You are now in the valley*
> *Enter: 1 to go to a new scene*
> *2 to go back*
> *3 to find out where you are*
> *4 to exit*
>> *2*
>
> *You have returned from the valley*
> *Enter: 1 to go to a new scene*
> *2 to go back*
> *3 to find out where you are*
> *4 to exit*
>> *2*
>
> *You have returned from the forest*
> *Enter: to go to a new scene*
> *2 to go back*
> *3 to find out where you are*
> *4 to exit*
>> *2*
>
> *You have returned from the castle*
> *Enter: 1 to go to a new scene*
> *2 to go back*
> *3 to find out where you are*
> *4 to exit*
>> *2*
>
> *You are at the beginning. Careful with that axe.*
> *Enter: 1 to go to a new scene*
> *2 to go back*
> *3 to find out where you are*
> *4 to exit*
>> *4*

Genericity of containers

It is useful to consider how generic a container class may be. In this chapter we have created a class called 'List' whose methods are not particularly generic (for example it sends messages directly to 'Date' objects) and may only contain objects of a given class or its derivatives. Our queue class, though demonstrating polymorphic objects, was also constrained to managing only a small set of classes.

In contrast, we created a generic stack able to contain objects of any class. However, the methods it could apply to any given object are of course limited; the more generic a container, the harder it is to anticipate its contents and therefore the less it can do to what it contains. With containers, as with many other aspects of classes, we are often compromising between reusability and functionality. A clear example of this is that our earlier

'List' and 'TrafficQueue' containers had built in iterators to display their contents, which demanded some knowledge of the methods of the objects. A container class library based on polymorphism (with a base class 'Object' as a standard ancestor) could include standard output methods for derived classes to implement, but could not anticipate all types of iterator that users might need. Template classes typically have more general iterators that are able to return each object from the container in turn but do not attempt to send them any messages. That aspect is left to the application programmer.

However generic a container class may be, it will still require some effort on behalf of the programmer to ensure that his/her own classes can be successfully contained by it. Typically, at least one method or overloaded operator will have to be provided to allow objects to be retrieved from the container.

Summary of key points for this part

1. Containers may contain heterogenous collections of objects of different classes. All contained objects must, however, be of classes with a single ancestor. In polymorphic class libraries this base class is usually called 'Object'.

2. When building a container for objects in a classification hierarchy, the container sends messages via the base class, so all methods must be virtual (polymorphic), and all objects must have a common interface.

3. Generic container classes can be constructed using templates, allowing container objects to be instantiated for different types of contained object.

Exercises

1. Write a program to test the template stack class using any data type or object class.

2. One container class which is often used is an 'Array' or 'Vector' class. Encapsulating an array inside a class allows us to simplify its interface and enhance its functionality. A good example of this is the fact that C++ has no bounds checking on arrays. By building an 'Array' class, we can add bounds checking into the internal implementation of the class.

    (a) Write an 'IntegerArray' class that allows integer array objects to be instantiated. It should have suitable methods such as 'add', 'remove' and 'flush' (use your own judgement in deciding what other methods may be appropriate).

    (b) Write a generic 'Array' class by re-implementing 'IntegerArray' as a template class.

3. Our 'List' class is currently only able to contain objects of the class 'Date'. What modifications would it have to undergo in order to be generic (able to contain objects of any class?) Bear in mind that the 'Link' objects currently have pointers to the 'Date' class, and that the container sends some class-specific messages to the contained objects. Rewrite the 'List' and 'Link' classes to make them useable with any data type. Test your code by making a list of dynamically allocated arrays of type 'char'.

16 Multiple inheritance

Overview

In this chapter we look at multiple inheritance, which allows a class to inherit from more than one base class. Uses of this facility are outlined, and potential conflicts between inherited elements are discussed. The role of virtual base classes and scope resolution in resolving ambiguity are demonstrated. Circumstances where multiple inheritance is necessary are contrasted with those where other strategies can achieve similar results. The role of mixins is explained, also the use of interface classes to successfully inherit from more than one class hierarchy. C++ syntax for multiple inheritance, resolving ambiguity and multiply inheriting from classes with polymorphic methods is demonstrated.

Single and multiple inheritance

When we discussed inheritance in Chapter 8, we stated that it is based on 'a kind of' relationships, so that class A may only inherit from class B if it can be said that A is 'a kind of' B. An oak, for example, is 'a kind of' tree, so we could say that 'oak' inherits from 'tree'. This is known as 'single inheritance', where a class inherits from a single base class (though one base class may have many derived classes). Sometimes, however, single inheritance may not be enough to truly describe 'a kind of' relationships which exist between classes. Fig. 16.1 shows two classes, 'tree' and 'flowering plant'. It also shows a 'flowering tree', which is both 'a kind of' tree and 'a kind of' flowering plant. We might therefore make a case for saying that a flowering tree should inherit from both tree and flowering plant, since it will have the characteristics of both. This is 'multiple inheritance' where the derived class inherits from more than one base class.

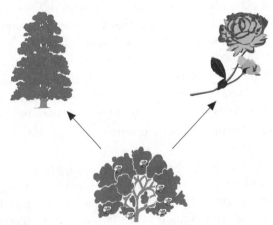

Fig. 16.1: Multiple inheritance: A flowering tree is both
'a kind of' tree and 'a kind of' flowering plant.

Multiple inheritance does not often prove necessary in an object-oriented system, and not all object-oriented languages support it. However, it may be very useful in certain circumstances.

284

As Booch states:

> 'we find multiple inheritance to be like a parachute: you don't always need it, but when you do, you're really happy to have it on hand.' [Booch, 1994, p.124]

Multiple inheritance in software

In the real world, because of the complexity of nature, it is easy to find objects which are, at least to some extent, similar in form and behaviour to more than one other type of object. In software, however, the issues have to be more specifically analysed to see if multiple inheritance truly applies to a situation, or if it causes more problems than it solves. In a classification hierarchy, we have seen how a derived class may inherit the attributes and methods of a single base class. The inherited methods may then be used, extended or overridden by the derived class. This form of inheritance (single inheritance) is frequently all that is required, but occasionally we may want to 'multiply inherit' attributes and methods from more than one other class. (Fig. 16.2)

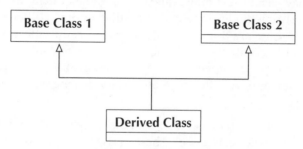

Fig. 16.2: Multiple inheritance – a derived class inherits from more than one base class.

Multiple inheritance has the advantage of allowing us to mix information from more than one source, and extends the potential circumstances where we can reuse existing classes. However, the disadvantages can be that complexity is increased, and conflicts can arise between inherited attributes and methods. A class which inherits from more than one other class is sometimes called a 'join' class, because it joins together two other classes, frequently from the same hierarchy. This means that the classes from which we inherit may well themselves have inherited from a single base class (Fig. 16.3) so we are rejoining branches of a hierarchy tree.

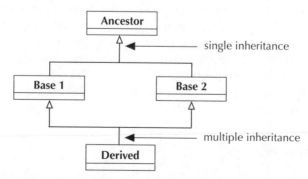

Fig. 16.3: Complexity can be increased by multiple inheritance if multiple base classes have common ancestors.

Question 16.1   What is the difference between single and multiple inheritance?

Single inheritance means that a class can inherit from no more than one other class. With multiple inheritance, a class can have two or more base classes.

Ambiguity in multiple inheritance

In some cases, multiple inheritance is a straightforward amalgamation of two (or more) different classes into a single class. The new class is therefore composed of other classes so that the whole (of the multiply inheriting class) is the sum of its parts (the multiple base classes). This simplicity of structure (similar to aggregation) is not always present, because there may be elements of the inherited base classes which overlap in some way. This may be because the base classes have polymorphic methods. A derived class cannot inherit more than one method with the same name without the programmer providing some clarification of which implementation of the method is being used in a particular context. There may also be a common ancestor in the hierarchy tree, which means that the same attribute or method is inherited more than once via different paths. Because of these possibilities, there are a number of circumstances in which multiple inheritance can cause ambiguity. It is necessary for the programmer to deal with these in the implementation of the classes, using whatever means are available in a particular language, and different languages have different strategies for dealing with these ambiguities.

Specifically, ambiguity can arise when:

1. A derived class inherits two methods with the same name but different implementations from its multiple base classes. These may or may not be semantically different.

2. A derived class overrides a multiply defined inherited method, but calls a base class method as part of its implementation.

3. A derived class accesses an attribute or method inherited from a single ancestor by multiple base classes.

Some examples will suffice to outline the potential problems, using the simple hierarchies shown in Figs 16.2 and 16.3, with the classes 'Ancestor', 'Base 1', 'Base 2' and 'Derived'.

Multiple inheritance of a method name

The first possible ambiguity occurs when a class inherits two different methods with the same name from two base classes (Fig. 16.4). If the derived class simply overrides the name with a different implementation, then there is no ambiguity. However, one of the existing methods may be the one we want to use with objects of the derived class. In this case, a derived class object is unable to use that method name directly, since it is not clear to the compiler which implementation is required. Therefore it is necessary for the derived class to specifically call one or more of the available base class implementations in an overriding method.

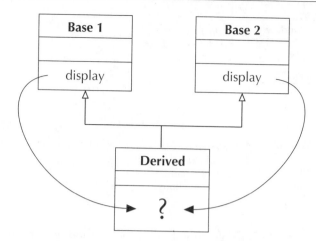

Fig. 16.4: Multiple inheritance can cause ambiguity if a derived class inherits two identically named methods from different base classes.

Interface classes

A further complication arises if methods which share a name are inherited from separate hierarchies. We may find that such methods are semantically unrelated, but both are required to be dynamically bound by the derived class. Since dynamic binding requires a consistent name for a method throughout the hierarchy, how can we have two versions of one polymorphic method? We might rename one method, but what if it comes from a hierarchy which we cannot change – perhaps a library of classes from some third party which does not allow us access to change the source code?

Stroustrup gives an example of a games program which includes the classes 'Window' and 'Cowboy' [Stroustrup 1991, pp 457–459], which we may assume to be in separate hierarchies. Both of these classes have a 'draw' method, but the 'Window' class draws a window and the 'Cowboy' class draws a gun. If we inherit both of these classes into a 'CowboyWindow' class, we want to be able to respond to 'draw' messages sent via the 'Window' hierarchy, but also to 'draw' messages sent via the 'Cowboy' hierarchy. Stroustrup demonstrates how we can overcome this problem by overriding the two 'draw' methods in 'interface classes', effectively creating an extra level of inheritance. The role of the interface classes is to override the inherited 'draw' method so that a 'draw' message sent at run time is renamed, calling a different virtual method in the derived class.

In this example, the interface class 'WWindow' overrides the 'draw' method of the 'Window' class with a method called 'windowDraw', and the other interface class 'CCowboy' overrides the 'draw' method of 'Cowboy' with 'cowboyDraw'. 'CowboyWindow' inherits 'draw' from the two interface classes, which themselves call the virtual methods defined in 'CowboyWindow' (Fig. 16.5). What this means is that 'CowboyWindow will respond to 'draw' messages sent via the 'Window' hierarchy with its 'windowDraw' methods, but 'draw' messages sent via the 'Cowboy' hierarchy will invoke the 'cowboyDraw' method.

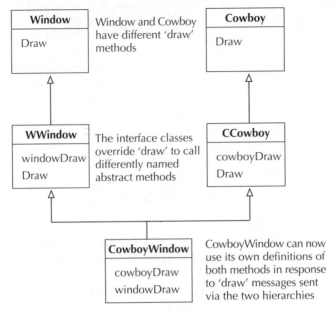

Fig. 16.5: 'Interface classes' may be used to resolve method
name clashes in multiple inheritance hierarchies.

Such problems as these tend to arise in programs which relate to games or operating systems, so fortunately we do not encounter them too often.

Extending a multiply inherited method

The second form of ambiguity arises when we wish to override a method name which occurs in more than one of the base classes, but we want to extend one of the inherited methods to provide our implementation (Fig. 16.6). In this case we will have to specify which of the available methods is being used as part of the derived class method. In terms of syntax, this is very similar to using an inherited method to implement the derived class method – the specific implementation required must be stated.

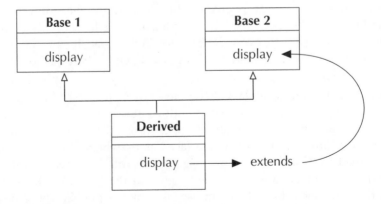

Fig. 16.6: An overriding method which extends an inherited method will
have to specify which version is being used for implementation.

Multiple inheritance of the same attribute or method

The third form of ambiguity is where an attribute or method is inherited from a single ancestor via more than one inheritance path (Fig. 16.7). In this example, the 'Derived' class multiply inherits two instances of the attribute 'value', which is again problematic for the compiler. It may be that two versions of the same attribute are required in the derived class, in which case any inherited methods which reference the attribute must be handled carefully to ensure the correct version of the attribute is being used in a particular context. Alternatively, it may be the case that we do not want to inherit two versions of the same attribute, so we need a strategy to ensure that there is only one instance of it in the derived class. Object-oriented languages must resolve such ambiguities so that attributes and methods inherited in this way are correctly managed by the derived class.

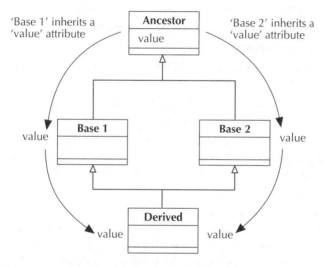

'Derived' inherits two 'value' attributes!

Fig. 16.7: Languages must resolve ambiguity caused by the same attribute being inherited more than once.

Question 16.2   In general terms, what may cause ambiguity in multiple inheritance?

Ambiguity can arise in multiple inheritance when the same attribute or method name is inherited more than once.

Using multiple inheritance

As an example of multiple inheritance, we might take a thermostat – a device which keeps a system at a constant temperature. Thermostats are simple devices, but have two underlying elements:

1.   A temperature gauge.

2.   A switch.

A thermostat connected to a central heating system, for example, will turn the system on and off depending on the temperature.

Were we to model a thermostat in an object-oriented program, we would be looking for appropriate ways to provide these two discrete but connected behaviours. It may be that both of these sets of behaviours are available in existing classes which model temperature gauges and switches A thermostat is therefore both 'a kind of' temperature gauge and 'a kind of' switch, and we might justifiably use inheritance to model these relationships.

For the sake of this example, we will assume that the classes 'Temperature Gauge' and 'Switch' have the following characteristics:

Temperature gauge
Current temperature
Get temperature

Switch
Status
Turn on
Turn off

We have some options on how to model the 'Thermostat' class:

1. Create the class from scratch.

2. Use aggregation – include objects of the temperature gauge and switch classes as components of the thermostat.

3. Use multiple inheritance so that the thermostat can inherit the attributes and methods of both temperature gauge and switch.

Clearly the first option will lead to duplication of existing class functionality and is therefore losing the benefits of inheritance. This also may have other implications for control of the system, since control of a set of objects is often implemented via their membership of a single class hierarchy.

The second option (aggregation) is a possibility, and the choice between this and multiple inheritance in some cases is a matter for the programmer. If the object being modelled is clearly composed of discrete components, but may not really be 'a kind of' either of them then perhaps aggregation is a better reflection of reality, particularly if the new device requires a lot of extra functionality not provided by any of its base classes. If, however, the behaviour of a class may be largely defined in terms of behaviours provided by existing classes then multiple inheritance may be preferable. Again, we should be aware that an aggregate 'Thermostat' will not be in the same hierarchy as either of its components.

One possible advantage for the programmer of the third option, multiple inheritance, is that it gives the methods of the derived class direct access to the inherited attributes. Fig. 16.8 shows 'Thermostat' as a derived class of both 'Temperature Gauge' and 'Switch'. In this case, any methods defined for 'Thermostat' will have direct access to protected attributes of the base classes, which would not be the case with aggregation. The main advantage, however, is that objects of the multiply derived class may be referenced by pointers of any of its base classes.

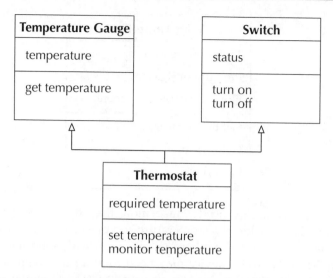

Fig. 16.8: A 'Thermostat' modelled using multiple inheritance
from 'Temperature Gauge' and 'Switch' classes.

Alternatives to multiple inheritance

For an alternative approach, let us visualise some kind of industrial system which includes valves which have to be monitored for the temperature, pressure and flow of water through each valve. A computer model is to be built to capture data from the physical system and allow central control of the system components. Every valve in the system will have associated with it a physical device which will be represented by an 'object' in the system.

The device we need to model has to be able to monitor the temperature, flow and pressure of the water and adjust the valve settings appropriately. It therefore has the characteristics of both a temperature gauge and a pressure and flow gauge, but also has the functionality of a valve controller.

Let us assume that we already have classes which are able to represent two discrete objects:

1. A temperature gauge
2. A pressure and flow gauge.

Both of these objects are passive (they only capture data, they do not have any control mechanisms), and their methods simple return attribute states.

A 'Valve Controller' might therefore inherit from both 'Temperature Gauge' and 'Pressure/Flow Gauge', giving it perhaps the following inherited attributes and methods:

Valve controller
Temperature in °c
Pressure in Kg/cm^2
Flow in metres per second
Get temperature
Get pressure
Get flow

However, the valve controller needs much more than this, since it will be an active device, using the data provided by temperature and pressure/flow gauges to control the valve. There may be a number of other methods to provide information in the light of this data. Our ValveController device may need to add other methods such as 'valve position' (with possible state values of 'open' or 'closed') and methods which controlled the valve according to various relationships between temperature, pressure and flow.

In fact the ValveController is not really 'a kind of' temperature gauge or 'a kind of' pressure/flow gauge, but a much more complex device which simply uses objects of these other classes in its implementation – what Booch calls a 'using relationship'. Although multiple inheritance achieves part of the required result, it probably does not offer anything which could not equally (or better) be achieved by alternative approaches. We might use aggregation (making temperature gauge and pressure/flow gauge objects components of the valve controller) or simply allow the valve controller to send messages to objects of these other classes and receive the appropriate information.

When to use multiple inheritance

Given that we may use sometimes have a choice between multiple inheritance and alternative strategies such as aggregation or association, when is multiple inheritance preferable? The answer to this question depends on a number of factors:

1. What are the semantics of the objects – is our new object 'a kind of' more than one other object, or rather are those other objects 'a part of' our new object, or simply other discrete objects which communicate with it?
2. Will aggregation or association be simpler to implement?
3. If we use multiple inheritance, what ambiguities have to be overcome?
4. Is it necessary that our new object is a derived class?

Booch advises:

> 'Our rule of thumb is that if an abstraction is greater than the sum of its component parts, then using relationships are more appropriate. If an abstraction is a kind of some other abstraction, or if it is exactly equal to the sum of its components, then inheritance is a better approach'   [Booch, 1991, p.116].

One of the key questions we need to address is whether the new object has to be a derived class in order to be effectively managed in the program. As we know, object management mechanisms such as containers require a consistent interface for all the objects they send messages to. This consistent interface is provided in the implementation by pointers of a common base class. Therefore it is essential that any new classes inherit the ability to be referenced by a base class pointer and respond to the messages common to the objects in the hierarchy. This can only be done via inheritance.

Question 16.3 What single factor might cause us to choose multiple inheritance over aggregation as a way of representing an object?

The key advantage multiple inheritance has over aggregation is that it allows objects of the derived class to be dynamically bound in the same hierarchy/hierarchies as its base classes. Incidentally, it is also necessary where virtual methods must be overridden by derived classes – an aggregation cannot do this.

Combining inheritance and aggregation

One possible alternative approach to multiple inheritance is to use single inheritance, so that we inherit from one base class, and aggregate an object of the other class. This decision may well rest on semantics – rather than an object being 'a kind of' multiple base classes, perhaps it is more 'a kind of' one base class but has some characteristics of other objects which may be provided by aggregation or association. It may also be the only pragmatic choice if our implementation language does not support multiple inheritance, though it will limit the potential for the object to respond to messages sent via a class hierarchy. In fact there are a number of 'workarounds' which may be used as alternatives to multiple inheritance [Rumbaugh et al, 1991, pp.67–69]. Languages such as Java (which does not support multiple inheritance) allow 'interfaces' to be described, that are not inherited but may be multiply implemented, giving a similar effect to multiple inheritance.

Mixins

One problem with multiple inheritance is that combining together complete base classes may well involve the inheritance of much that is unwanted. One variation on inheritance is the 'mixin' class – an abstract class which is not intended for the instantiation of objects, but is used purely as a base class for multiple inheritance. A mixin class provides added functionality for existing classes through an abstract set of behaviours that can be applied to more concrete objects. An analogy might be the set of 'extras' applied to higher specification cars across a range of models. The 'executive' mixin might comprise electric sunroof, expensive stereo, sophisticated alarm etc. which can be added to any model type in a range of vehicles. An 'executive' object is never made – it only makes sense as a class when 'mixed in' with an object of an appropriate vehicle class.

For a programming example, we might model a range of electronic components as classes in some kind of circuit simulator, but these may need to be modelled in terms not only of their normal functionality but also of the heat which they generate in operation and any thermal feedback which may result. These characteristics may be represented in a 'mixin' class which can be multiply inherited by all component objects. An example from Booch suggests mixin classes for 'flowers' and 'fruits' to provide the general behaviours of these two types of plant. These classes may then be multiply inherited by specific plants in conjunction with other base classes [Booch, 1994 p.63]. The behaviour of a mixin is generally clearly defined and orthogonal to the class with which it is being combined, so is unlikely to be the cause of any ambiguity.

C++ syntax

The syntax for declaring multiple inheritance in C++ is simple, and dealing with potential ambiguities is also relatively straightforward, though there are a number of subtleties to the syntax in specific contexts (See [Stump, 1993] and [Stroustrup, 1991 pp.201–211] for further discussion). Since there are no default mechanisms for dealing with ambiguous multiple inheritance, the compiler requires us to explicitly resolve it.

Elements of the syntax are:

1. A list of base classes after the colon 'inheritance' operator.
2. The 'virtual' keyword, which may be used to ensure that ancestor classes are only inherited once.

In order for one class to inherit from more than one base class, the class must be declared as follows:

class classname : public base1, public base2

This means that the class will inherit from both 'base1' and 'base2'. Note the comma separator between classes in the base class list.

To return to our 'Thermostat' class, if it was to inherit from the 'TemperatureGauge' and 'Switch' classes, the class definitions might look like this:

```
// the temperature gauge class:
class TemperatureGauge
{
private:
    float temperature;
public:
    float getTemperature( );
};
// the 'Switch' class. remember that 'switch' (with a small 's')
// is a C++ keyword, so the capital 'S' is very important!
enum status{on, off};
class Switch
{
private:
    status switch_status;
public:
    void turnOn( );
    void turnOff( );
};
// 'Thermostat' inherits from both classes
class Thermostat : public TemperatureGauge, public Switch
{
private:
    float required_temperature;
public:
    void setRequiredTemperature(float temp);
    void monitorTemperature( );
};
```

To demonstrate the syntax of multiple inheritance, and explore the resolution of some ambiguities, we will return to a revised version of our 'BankAccount' class. In this version, 'BankAccount' serves as a base class for two derived classes, 'SavingsAccount' and 'ChequeAccount'. These in turn are multiple base classes for the 'InterestChequeAccount' class (Fig. 16.9).

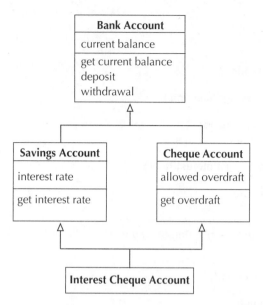

Fig. 16.9: 'InterestChequeAccount' multiply inherits
from 'SavingsAccount' and 'ChequeAccount'.

The class and method definitions are as follows:

```cpp
#include <iostream.h>
// a simplified 'BankAccount' is the base class
class BankAccount
{
private:
    float current_balance;
public:
    BankAccount();
    float getCurrentBalance();
    void deposit(float amount);
    void withdrawal(float amount);
};
BankAccount::BankAccount()
{
    current_balance = 0.00;
}
float BankAccount::getCurrentBalance()
{
    return current_balance;
}
void BankAccount::deposit(float amount)
{
    current_balance = current_balance + amount;
}
void BankAccount::withdrawal(float amount)
{
    current_balance = current_balance - amount;
}
// 'SavingsAccount' inherits from 'BankAccount'
class SavingsAccount : public BankAccount
{
```

```
private:
    float interest_rate;
public:
    SavingsAccount( );
    float getInterestRate( );
};
SavingsAccount::SavingsAccount( )
{
    cout << "Enter interest rate ";
    cin >> interest_rate;
}
float SavingsAccount::getInterestRate( )
{
    return interest_rate;
}
// 'ChequeAccount' inherits from 'BankAccount'
class ChequeAccount : public BankAccount
{
private:
    float allowed_overdraft;
public:
    ChequeAccount( );
    void setOverdraft(float overdraft_in);
    float getOverdraft( );
};
ChequeAccount::ChequeAccount()
{
    cout << "Enter allowed overdraft ";
    cin >> allowed_overdraft;
}
void ChequeAccount::setOverdraft(float overdraft_in)
{
    allowed_overdraft = overdraft_in;
}
float ChequeAccount::getOverdraft( )
{
    return allowed_overdraft;
}
// 'InterestChequeAccount' inherits from both derived classes.
// It has no attributes or methods of its own, but has all the
// attributes and methods of both 'SavingsAccount' and 'ChequeAccount'
class InterestChequeAccount : public SavingsAccount, public ChequeAccount
{
};
```

The following program demonstrates the instantiation of objects of the classes 'SavingsAccount', 'ChequeAccount' and 'InterestChequeAccount'. In this case. there is no ambiguity because we are not attempting to call any methods inherited twice from 'BankAccount' (such as 'deposit'):

```
#include "bankacct.h"    // header as defined above
void main( )
{
    SavingsAccount savings;
    cout << "This is a savings account,  interest rate is: ";
    cout << savings.getInterestRate( ) << "%" << endl;
    ChequeAccount cheque;
```

```
        cout << "This is a cheque account,  allowed overdraft is: £";
        cout << cheque.getOverdraft( ) << endl;
        InterestChequeAccount combined;
        cout << "This is an interest paying cheque account:" << endl;
        cout << "Interest rate: " << combined.getInterestRate( )<<"%" <<endl;
        cout << "Overdraft limit: £" << combined.getOverdraft( ) << endl;
    }
```

Example output from this program:

> *Enter interest rate 6*
>
> *This is a savings account interest rate is: 6%*
>
> *Enter allowed overdraft 500*
>
> *This is a cheque account, allowed overdraft is: £500*
>
> *Enter interest rate 3*
>
> *Enter allowed overdraft 1000*
>
> *This is an interest paying cheque account:*
>
> *Interest rate: 3%*
>
> *Overdraft limit: £1000*

Virtual base classes and scope resolution

In order to deal with the potential ambiguities of the inheritance tree described above, there are some simple syntax strategies. Ambiguity will arise if we attempt to call methods of the multiple base class 'BankAccount' with objects of the 'InterestChequeAccount' class – in effect, each object will have inherited two versions of the same method. A similar problem arises if we attempt to define any methods for the 'InterestChequeAccount' class which do not simply replace inherited versions. If they call on method names which are inherited from both 'SavingsAccount' and 'ChequeAccount', then there must be some resolution of which version is being called. Finally, if a method of 'InterestChequeAccount' needs to refer to attributes declared in 'BankAccount' then they will also (as the classes currently stand) be inherited twice and therefore cause ambiguity – in this context we cannot have two current balances for a single account, so we have to ensure that only one version of the attribute is inherited. Fig. 16.10 shows a modified class hierarchy which demonstrates how some of these difficulties might arise.

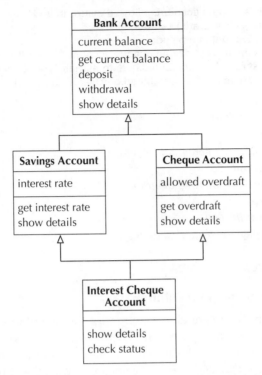

Fig. 16.10: A modified 'BankAccount' class hierarchy with inherent ambiguity.

In the modified hierarchy, a method called 'show details' appears in all four classes. As before, the attributes and methods of the 'BankAccount' class will be inherited via two paths into 'InterestChequeAccount'. In the following class and method definitions, a number of syntax strategies are applied. These are as follows:

1. Use of 'virtual' base classes to avoid multiple inheritance of the same attribute or method. This is indicated on classes inheriting from 'BankAccount' as follows:

   class SavingsAccount : virtual public BankAccount

   ...

   class ChequeAccount : virtual public BankAccount

   ...

   This ensures that any further classes inheriting from these classes will only inherit one 'BankAccount', not two. As well as allowing an 'InterestChequeAccount' object to call methods defined for the 'BankAccount' class, it also allows 'InterestChequeAccount' methods to refer to attributes inherited from 'BankAccount', as in the 'checkStatus' method defined in the example, which refers to the 'current_balance' attribute.

2. Use of the scope resolution operator to identify which polymorphic inherited method is being called. 'InterestChequeAccount' has three versions of the 'showDetails' method, so any call to one of these must be explicit, using the scope resolution operator. Here, the 'showDetails' method for the 'SavingsAccount' class is explicitly called in the derived class version of the method.

   void InterestChequeAccount::showDetails( )

   {

```
        SavingsAccount::showDetails( );
        ...
```

The modified classes and methods are as follows:

```
#include <iostream.h>
class BankAccount
{
protected:
    float current_balance;
public:
    BankAccount( );
    float getCurrentBalance( );
    void deposit(float amount);
    void withdrawal(float amount);
    void showDetails( );
};
BankAccount::BankAccount( )
{
    current_balance = 0.00;
}
float BankAccount::getCurrentBalance( )
{
    return current_balance;
}
void BankAccount::deposit(float amount)
{
    current_balance = current_balance + amount;
}
void BankAccount::withdrawal(float amount)
{
    current_balance = current_balance – amount;
}
void BankAccount::showDetails( )
{
    cout << "Current Balance is: £" << current_balance << endl;
}
// to avoid further derived classes inheriting the same attributes and
// methods more than once from 'BankAccount', it is declared as a
// 'virtual' base class
class SavingsAccount : virtual public BankAccount
{
protected:
    float interest_rate;
public:
    SavingsAccount( );
    float getInterestRate( );
    void showDetails( );
};
SavingsAccount::SavingsAccount( )
{
    cout << "Enter interest rate ";
    cin >> interest_rate;
}
float SavingsAccount::getInterestRate( )
{
    return interest_rate;
}
```

```
    void SavingsAccount::showDetails( )
    {
        BankAccount::showDetails( );
        cout << "Interest rate is: " << interest_rate << "%" << endl;
    }
// 'ChequeAccount' also inherits from 'BankAccount' as a virtual base class
class ChequeAccount : virtual public BankAccount
{
protected:
    float allowed_overdraft;
public:
    ChequeAccount( );
    void setOverdraft(float overdraft_in);
    float getOverdraft( );
    void showDetails( );
};
ChequeAccount::ChequeAccount( )
{
    cout << "Enter allowed overdraft ";
    cin >> allowed_overdraft;
}
void ChequeAccount::setOverdraft(float overdraft_in)
{
    allowed_overdraft = overdraft_in;
}
float ChequeAccount::getOverdraft( )
{
    return allowed_overdraft;
}
void ChequeAccount::showDetails( )
{
    BankAccount::showDetails( );
    cout << "Allowed overdraft is: £" << allowed_overdraft << endl;
}
class InterestChequeAccount : public SavingsAccount, public ChequeAccount
{
public:
    void checkStatus( );
    void showDetails( );
};
// 'InterestChequeAccount' is able to refer to the multiply inherited method
// names by using the class name and scope resolution operator. Note that we could call both
// base class methods, but this would mean that
// 'BankAccount::showDetails' would be called twice, once for each of the
// inherited methods
void InterestChequeAccount::showDetails( )
{
    SavingsAccount::showDetails( );
    cout << "Allowed overdraft is: £" << allowed_overdraft << endl;
}
// this method is able to access 'current_balance' without ambiguity
// because only one instance of this attribute has been inherited due to
// 'BankAccount' being a virtual base class
void InterestChequeAccount::checkStatus( )
{
    if(current_balance > 0)
    {
```

```
        cout << "Pay interest" << endl;
    }
    else
    {
        cout << "Send a large bill" << endl;
    }
}
```

The following program shows that ambiguities have been overcome. 'showDetails' may be successfully called by all three objects, and the base class method 'deposit' is called without ambiguity by the 'InterestChequeAccount' object, which also calls its 'check-Status' methods (accessing the base class attribute 'current_balance').

```
#include "bankacc2.h"   // assumes the modified header file
void main( )
{
    cout << "This is a savings account" << endl;
    SavingsAccount savings;
    savings.deposit(350.00);
    savings.showDetails( );
    cout << "This is a cheque account" << endl;
    ChequeAccount cheque;
    cheque.deposit(50.00);
    cheque.showDetails( );
    cout << "This is an interest paying cheque account:" << endl;
    InterestChequeAccount combined;
    combined.deposit(25.00);
    combined.showDetails( );
    combined.checkStatus( );
}
```

This program generates the following output:

This is a savings account
Enter interest rate 6.5
Current Balance is: £350
Interest rate is: 6.5%
This is a cheque account
Enter allowed overdraft 1000
Current Balance is: £50
Allowed overdraft is: £1000
This is an interest paying cheque account:
Enter interest rate 3
Enter allowed overdraft 500
Current Balance is: £25
Interest rate is: 3%
Allowed overdraft is: £500
Pay interest

Multiple inheritance of a single attribute

When looking at the bank account hierarchy, we had to ensure that the 'current_balance' attribute was only inherited into the 'InterestChequeAccount' class once, although it was inherited via two paths in the hierarchy. Clearly, in this case it was not permissible to have two attributes representing the balance of a single account, and we resolved this by making 'BankAccount' a virtual base class. There are some circumstances, however, when the multiple inheritance of a single attribute is not only acceptable but desirable. To demonstrate, we will use a simplified example which is based on types of railway locomotive. In some parts of the country, there is a mixture of power sources for locomotives, for example some track is electrified and some is not. To allow trains to travel on different track types, some locomotives have more than one type of motor. An electrodiesel for example has an electric motor for travelling over electrified track, and a diesel motor for non-electrified track. In the following class outlines, an 'ElectroDiesel' inherits two 'power_rating' attributes, one from a 'DieselLocomotive' base class and another from an 'ElectricLocomotive' base class. Both of these classes inherit a 'power_rating' attribute from the base class 'Locomotive'. Which of these attributes is being referenced in 'main' by the base class 'setPowerRating' method is defined by the scope resolution operator. This is a rather clumsy syntax, so we might alternatively provide a method in the 'ElectroDiesel' class to set the values of the 'power_rating' attributes. The key point is that the derived class is able to reference both its attributes, resolving ambiguity by qualifying each reference to an attribute by a base class name and the scope resolution operator.

For example:

ElectricLocomotive::power_rating

This is the attribute inherited via the 'ElectricLocomotive' class. In contrast, the identically named attribute inherited from the 'DieselLocomotive' class is referenced as:

DieselLocomotive::power_rating

The following class definitions and 'main' demonstrate this syntax:

```
#include <iostream.h>
// the base class provides the 'power_rating' attribute and a method to set it
class Locomotive
{
protected:
    float power_rating;
public:
    void setPowerRating(float power_in);
};
void Locomotive::setPowerRating(float power_in)
{
    power_rating = power_in;
}
// the two derived classes both inherit the attribute and method
class DieselLocomotive : public Locomotive
{};

class ElectricLocomotive : public Locomotive
{};
// the 'ElectroDiesel' inherits a 'power_rating' attribute from both base
// classes
class ElectroDiesel : public DieselLocomotive, public ElectricLocomotive
{
public:
    void showPower();
};
// the 'showPower' method uses the scope resolution operator to reference
// the inherited attributes, one inherited from 'ElectricLocomotive', the other
```

```
// from 'DieselLocomotive'
    void ElectroDiesel::showPower( )
    {
        cout << "Electric motor power: "
            << ElectricLocomotive::power_rating << endl;
        cout << "Diesel motor power: "
            << DieselLocomotive::power_rating << endl;
    }

    void main( )
    {
// an object of the 'ElectroDiesel' class which has two motors
        ElectroDiesel locomotive;
// the scope resolution operator allows us to call the inherited
// 'setPowerRating' method for specific derived classes, and therefore set
// the two 'power_rating' attributes
        locomotive.ElectricLocomotive::setPowerRating(10000);
        locomotive.DieselLocomotive::setPowerRating(5000);
// the 'showPower' method displays the two motor ratings
        locomotive.showPower( );
    }
```

The output from the program is simply the values of the two 'power_rating' attributes:

Electric motor power: 10000
Diesel motor power: 5000

Multiple inheritance and polymorphic methods

Although we have overcome the potential ambiguities in multiple inheritance by the use of virtual base classes and the scope resolution operator, there is one other aspect which may be important, namely the maintenance of a consistent interface between different objects in a single hierarchy. As we have discussed before, if a collection of dynamic objects of different classes is to be managed successfully, they must have a consistent interface, provided by the methods of the base class. This is because dynamic objects may be referenced by base class pointers at run time, but the pointers must be able to handle messages for objects of all derived classes. In the 'InterestChequeAccount' example, 'checkStatus' is not a method of the base class, so we could not successfully instantiate objects of different bank account types using the base class pointer.

The following 'main' indicates the problem:

```
#include "bankacc2.h"
void main( )
{
    BankAccount* pointer;
    pointer = new InterestChequeAccount;
    pointer -> withdrawal(50);
// the next line cannot compile; not a method of 'BankAccount'
    pointer -> checkStatus( );
}
```

This of course is not a problem confined to multiple inheritance – single inheritance hierarchies have exactly the same behaviour. However, we may find that the necessity for a consistent interface among different classes provides us with certain opportunities in multiple inheritance, namely the ability to create classes which are blends of other classes, rather than combinations of them. Take the following hierarchy, which shows staff members being either lecturers or administrators, but with the possibility that a 'secondment' member of staff is a combination of both (Fig. 16.11)

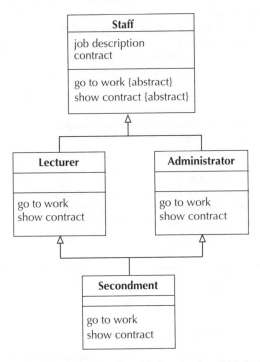

Fig. 16.11: 'Secondment' is a mix of 'Lecturer' and 'Administrator' rather than being the sum of two discrete elements.

In this case, 'secondment' is a lecturer (i.e. someone employed on a lecturing contract) who is working in administration. Therefore a 'secondment' object uses the 'show contract' method of the lecturer class, but the 'go to work' method of the 'Administrator' class. The important point is that all classes have exactly the same interface, so they may be successfully referenced by a pointer of the 'Staff' class, which contains the abstract (virtual) methods for the interface of all classes in the hierarchy.

A definition of these classes follows:

```
#include <iostream.h>
// 'Staff' is the base class, with all attributes and abstract methods
class Staff
{
private:
    char job_description[30];
public:
    virtual void goToWork( ) = 0;
    virtual void showContract( ) = 0;
};
// 'Lecturer' inherits from 'Staff' (single inheritance from virtual base class)
class Lecturer : public virtual Staff
{
public:
    virtual void goToWork( );
    virtual void showContract( );
};
```

```
// 'Lecturer' methods override the abstract methods in the base class
void Lecturer::goToWork( )
{
    cout << "Staff job description: Lecturer" << endl;
}
void Lecturer::showContract( )
{
    cout << "Staff member on lecturing contract" << endl;
}
// 'Administrator' inherits from 'Staff' (single inheritance from virtual base
// class)
class Administrator : public virtual Staff
{
public:
    virtual void goToWork( );
    virtual void showContract( );
};
// 'Administrator' methods override the abstract methods in the base class
void Administrator::goToWork( )
{
    cout << "Staff job description: Administrator" << endl;
}
void Administrator::showContract( )
{
    cout << "Staff member on administration contract" << endl;
}
// 'Secondment' inherits from both 'Lecturer' and 'Administrator'
// (multiple inheritance)
class Secondment : public Administrator, public Lecturer
{
public:
    virtual void goToWork( );
    virtual void showContract( );
};
// 'Secondment' methods are a combination of inherited methods
void Secondment::goToWork( )
{
    Administrator::goToWork( );
}
void Secondment::showContract( )
{
    Lecturer::showContract( );
}
```

Our main function demonstrates that we can reference objects of all derived classes in the hierarchy with a base class pointer, and that the behaviour of 'secondment' is a blend, rather than an amalgamation, of its own base classes.

```
void main( )
{
    Staff* staff_member[3];
    staff_member[0] = new Lecturer;
    staff_member[1] = new Administrator;
    staff_member[2] = new Secondment;
    for(int i = 0; i < 3; i++)
    {
        cout << endl << "Staff member details:" << endl;
        staff_member[i] -> goToWork( );
```

```
            staff_member[i] -> showContract( );
    }
}
```

The output from this program is:

Staff member details:
Staff job description: Lecturer
Staff member on lecturing contract

Staff member details:
Staff job description: Administrator
Staff member on administration contract

Staff member details:
Staff job description: Administrator
Staff member on lecturing contract

Coding an interface class

Although a rather specialised application, the interface class example mentioned earlier has some points of syntax worth exploring. In essence, the interface classes exist purely to rename a message being sent down the hierarchy tree, so that a 'draw' message received by the 'CowboyWindow' class is resolved either by 'WWindow' or 'CCowboy', depending on which hierarchy initiated the message. Each of these interface classes then renames the method before, in effect, passing it back to 'CowboyWindow' for interpretation.

```
#include <iostream.h>
// class 'Window' and class 'Cowboy' are not in the same hierarchy.
// however, they both have 'draw' methods, and these are semantically
// unrelated.
class Window
{
public:
    virtual void draw( );
};
void Window::draw( )
{
    cout << "Draw Window" << endl;
}
class Cowboy
{
public:
    virtual void draw( );
};
void Cowboy::draw( )
{
    cout << "BANG!" << endl;
}
// the interface classes override both versions of 'draw'
// to call virtual methods defined in 'CowboyWindow'
class CCowboy : public Cowboy
{
public:
    virtual void cowboyDraw( ) = 0;
    virtual void draw( );
```

```
};
void CCowboy::draw( )
{
    cowboyDraw( );
}
class WWindow : public Window
{
public:
    virtual void windowDraw( ) = 0;
    virtual void draw( );
};
void WWindow::draw( )
{
    windowDraw( );
}
// class 'CowboyWindow' does not redefine 'draw', so it relies
// on its base classes for implementation. These then call
// 'cowboyDraw' or 'windowDraw' depending on the class of the
// pointer which sends the 'draw' message
class CowboyWindow : public CCowboy, public WWindow
{
public:
    virtual void cowboyDraw( );
    virtual void windowDraw( );
};
void CowboyWindow::cowboyDraw( )
{
    cout << "Yippeeyiyay" << endl;
}
void CowboyWindow::windowDraw( )
{
    cout << "Cowboy Window" << endl;
}
```
```
// main shows the same message ('draw') being passed to
// 'CowboyWindow' objects via base class pointers in different hierarchies.
// although the message is the same, the objects are able to respond
// differently
    void main( )
    {
        Window* w_pointer = new CowboyWindow;
        w_pointer -> draw( );
        Cowboy* c_pointer = new CowboyWindow;
        c_pointer -> draw( );
    }
```

When the program runs, our 'CowboyWindow' responds with the following:

Cowboy Window
Yippeeyiyay

Multiple inheritance with parameterised constructors

Finally, we sometimes inherit from multiple classes with parameterised constructors. If this is the case, then the parameter list of the derived class constructor must be followed by the parameter lists of the base classes, separated by a comma. This is a similar syntax to the multiple inheritance syntax used with the declaration of the class itself:

```
DerivedClass::DerivedClass(...) : base1(...) , base2(...) etc...
```

By way of example, the following class definitions show 'SalariedCommission' (a sales person who receives both salary and commission) inheriting from 'Salaried' and 'Commission'. Both base classes have parameterised constructors which are inherited by the derived class.

```cpp
#include <iostream.h>
class Salaried
{
private:
    float salary;
public:
    Salaried(float start_salary);
    float getSalary( );
};
Salaried :: Salaried(float start_salary)
{
    salary = start_salary;
}
float Salaried::getSalary( )
{
    return salary;
}
class Commission
{
private:
    float commission_rate;
public:
    Commission(float start_commission);
    float getCommission(float sales);
};
Commission::Commission(float start_commission)
{
    commission_rate = start_commission;
}
float Commission::getCommission(float sales)
{
    return (commission_rate * sales) / 100;
}
// the 'SalariedCommission' constructor explicitly inherits the parameter
// lists of both base classes
class SalariedCommission : public Salaried, public Commission
{
public:
    SalariedCommission(float start_salary, float start_commission);
};

SalariedCommission::SalariedCommission(float start_salary, float start_commission)
: Salaried(start_salary), Commission(start_commission)
{}
// 'main' creates an object of the derived class and tests its constructor
// and inherited methods
void main( )
{
    SalariedCommission sales_person(15000.00, 10.00);
    cout << "Salary is: £" << sales_person.getSalary( ) << endl;
    cout << "Commission is: £ "
        << sales_person.getCommission(100000.00);
}
```

Output is:

> **Salary is: £15000**
> **Commission is: £10000**

Summary of key points from this chapter

1. Multiple inheritance applies where a class is 'a kind of' more than one base class.

2. A class which multiply inherits has all the attributes and methods of all its base classes.

3. Ambiguity may arise when using multiple inheritance for a number of reasons. Ambiguity means that an identically named attribute or method is inherited from more than one source.

4. Sometimes the same method may be inherited via more than one pathway from a single ancestor. The scope resolution operator may be used to resolve these ambiguities. In other cases, different methods with the same name may be inherited via separate hierarchies. This problem can be resolved using interface classes.

5. The same attribute may be inherited twice from a single ancestor, and this may be desirable. If it is not, then the ancestor can be made a virtual base class.

6. Alternative strategies to multiple inheritance include aggregation, association ('using' relationships), interface classes and single inheritance combined with aggregation. However, these do not allow the same opportunities for dynamic binding that are possible with multiple inheritance.

7. A class which multiply inherits may be the sum of its parts (if the multiple base classes are entirely separate) or may be a mix of existing classes (if they are in the same hierarchy).

Exercises

1. Earlier in the chapter, we looked at a 'Thermostat' class which multiply inherited from 'TemperatureGauge' and 'Switch'. Expanding on the class definitions provided, write implementations for the two 'Thermostat' methods 'setRequiredTemperature' and 'monitorTemperature'. The thermostat should turn on when the temperature falls below the required temperature. You will need to modify your classes to provide some kind of nominal temperature to represent the reading of the temperature gauge (which you will not actually have!)

2. Re-model the 'Thermostat' as an aggregation of its component parts and compare the syntax.

3. Add another derived class to the 'Staff' hierarchy so that an administrative employee can be seconded to do lecturing work.

17 Persistent objects, streams and files

Overview

This chapter discusses object persistence, and how objects can be made to persist beyond the lifetime of a single program run time, so that they may become common to multiple applications. The characteristics of object-oriented databases as a means for creating and maintaining persistent objects are discussed. Although C++ has no standard mechanisms for implementing persistent objects, the syntax for streams and files is outlined in the context of providing persistent attribute data for objects.

Object persistence

In Chapter 6, we discussed the persistence of objects within a program. The lifetime of an object can vary from a momentary existence inside the body of a function or method, to persistence for the life of the program. However, in all cases we have only looked at objects which exist at run time. None of our previously instantiated objects have been able to persist after the program has finished running, but in practice there are three levels at which objects may persist:

1. Objects persisting during a run of a program.
2. Objects persisting between runs of a single program.
3. Objects persisting between different programs.

Objects which only exist while a program is running are known as 'transient objects' – they have no existence independent of a single program run time. Those whose lifetimes extend beyond the boundaries of a single program run are known as 'persistent objects'.

Storing objects

In order for an object to be persistent, it must be stored on disk in some form. The problem with objects is that they do not fit easily with the traditional formats of stored data. As we have previously discussed, traditional approaches to programming separate processes and data, so that data is easily stored independently of any associated processes. This is not the case with objects, because objects have two aspects:

1. The data associated with attributes.
2. The processes associated with methods.

An object's attributes are unique to that object, and therefore may be stored as a set of data similar to a record in a traditional file. However, the methods are part of the class, shared by all other objects of the class, and these are not so easily stored. If an object is to retain its integrity, both its state and its class need to be stored on disk – not just its state alone. We therefore have two ways of approaching the implementation of persistent objects:

1. Store attribute data independently of methods. This means shifting from an object-oriented approach to a more traditional file based approach when storing object data, and back again when re-loading it.
2. Use an object-oriented database.

Question 17.1 What is a 'transient object'?

A transient object is one whose lifetime does not extend beyond a single program run. Unlike a persistent object, therefore, it does not need to be stored on disk.

Storing objects in traditional files

It is not possible to store all aspects of an object when using traditional types of file organisation, but it is possible to maintain 'pseudo-persistent objects' by storing attribute data in files. While a program is running, objects can write their state data out to disk as a record or series of records, and then this data can be reloaded later during another run of the program. Semantically, we do not really have a persistent object, because only the state of the object has been stored. As we know, an object comprises three parts – state, identity and behaviour. The state can be saved, and the behaviour can to an extent be maintained (albeit separately) by the class definition, but the identity of an object is rather different. In fact, when we rebuild an object from state data stored in a file, we are recreating another object with the same state as the original, rather than maintaining the existence of the original object. However, for most practical purposes this kind of data storage is adequate, though it puts the onus on the programmer to ensure that objects retain their integrity when their classes are represented in source code and their states are saved elsewhere in data files.

Object-oriented databases

> 'In object-oriented databases, not only does the state of an object persist, but its class must also transcend any individual program, so every program interprets this saved state in the same way.' [Booch, 1994, p.76]

Object-oriented databases allow us to store both the class and state of an object between programs. They take the responsibility for maintaining the links between stored object behaviour and state away from the programmer, and manage objects outside of programs with their public and private elements intact. They also simplify the whole process of rendering objects persistent by performing such tasks invisibly.

As well as recognising that persistence has to do with time (i.e. a persistent object can exist beyond the program which created it) we should be aware that it also has to do with space (the location of the object may vary between processors, and even change its representation in the process).

Aspects of object-oriented databases

Object-oriented databases have developed to address two rather distinct needs:

1. Providing databases which can be used to generate applications in their own right.
2. Providing persistent objects for applications generated in other programming languages.

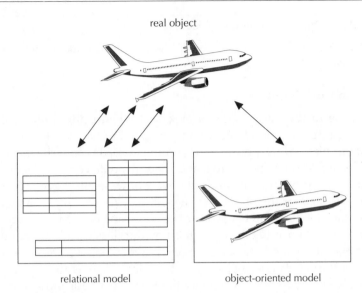

real object

relational model   object-oriented model

Fig. 17.1: Object-oriented databases store objects 'whole' not as disassembled data elements.

Between these two extremes lie a number of variations and a range of definitions as to what might constitute an object-oriented database. The most important characteristic of an object-oriented database is that it is able to store objects 'whole', rather than disassembling them into constituent data sets (Fig. 17.1).

In terms of the way in which these databases work, there are two general types; those which have taken an evolutionary path, extending traditional relational databases to handle objects, and those which are fully object-oriented from the ground up.

There is no single model for object-oriented databases, so the interpretation of what constitutes an Object Database Management System (ODBMS) is dependent on a particular vendor's approach. There are a number of general comparisons which can be made between various database models [Chaudhri, 1993]. In one respect there are a range of data models (e.g. non-first normal form, object-oriented language, functional and semantic models), and also a range of architectures. These include object managers (simple object filing systems), extended database systems (with built in query languages), database programming languages (i.e. extensions to existing languages) and relational object shells (relational databases with object-oriented interfaces).

There are many issues involved in the debate about the value of object-oriented databases (compared to hierarchical, network or relational databases) and the ways in which they may be implemented, but from our point of view their role is simple – storing the objects we create in programs. If we do not have an object-oriented database at our disposal, then storing and retrieving objects is that much harder.

Question 17.2   What are the advantages of storing objects in an object-oriented database as opposed to using traditional file structures?

Because an object-oriented database stores object 'whole' rather than simply storing attribute data, it makes it much easier to handle the objects in different programming contexts. Although it is possible to give the impression of a persistent object by storing its attributes in a traditional file, it is harder to maintain that object's integrity between different programs.

C++ syntax

Unfortunately, C++ does not have any standard facilities for the persistence of objects. In fact it has no I/O syntax at all – all the I/O we have used in the example programs has been via the classes, objects, operators and methods defined in 'iostream.h'.

Streams

A stream is a general term for a data flow, which may be to and from a file, or to and from screen and keyboard, or to and from other 'sinks' and 'sources' of data. An object-oriented stream library contains a number of classes, each of which is appropriate to a different kind of stream. In C++, the 'ifstream' class for example provides us with appropriate methods for managing input disk files.

The 'iostream.h' stream library defined by Stroustrup [1995, pp.325 – 359] is given as a simple basis for the larger stream libraries provided by compiler vendors. As such it is fairly limited, but does provide enough for the storage and retrieval of object attribute data. The library is intended to be used both with simple data types and user defined (object) types. It is also based on the idea of streams being redirectable, so the syntax which we have used to accept keyboard input and produce screen output is easily applicable, (with some modifications) to file I/O. All stream classes are in a classification hierarchy based on the 'ios' class, and provide all the objects, operators and methods needed for console I/O and file handling.

Stream operators and methods

The operators and methods defined by Stroustrup for use with stream objects are as follows:

Output: **<<**   (insertion operator)
          put(char)

Input: **>>**   (extraction operator)
          get(char&)
          get(char*, int, char)

These may be used to handle various types of data such as single characters, numeric data types, strings, strings with embedded spaces and object attribute data.

Stream output

In previous examples, we have seen many statements like the following:

```
cout << "Hello";
```

but where does this syntax come from? In fact, 'cout' is an object of the 'ostream' class (as defined in iostream.h) and '<<' is an overloaded operator of that class able to handle a range of data types. We can further overload this operator to output our own data types. Alternatively, the 'put' method puts a single character into the output stream.

Stream input

Like 'cout', 'cin' is an object, but in this case it is an object of the 'istream' class which relates to the input stream. As you might expect, '>>' is an overloaded operator of the istream class. Again, we can overload this operator to allow the input of objects of user defined types (classes).

When using the input stream, remember that the 'cin' object using the '>>' operator treats whitespace as a delimiter, so that more than one item can be input in a single statement provided they are separated by white space:

```
int x, y, z;
cin >> x >> y >> z;
```

This will read a sequence of three whitespace-separated integers. This is (as we have discovered) a bit limiting, since we sometimes want to input text which includes embedded spaces. In such cases we can use the 'get' method of the 'istream' class. 'get' comes in two versions:

1. The first version of 'get' can be used to get a single 'char'

    prototype: **istream& get(char& c);**

    example: **char char_in;**
                  cin.get(char_in);

2. The second version of 'get' can be used to get a string which may contain spaces. The default terminating character is the newline ('\n') but this can be overridden by another terminating character to accept multi-line input if required:

    prototype: **istream& get(char* p, int n, char = '\n')**

    example: **char buffer[80];**
                  cin.get(buffer, 80);

When the second version of 'get' is used to read a string of characters from the input stream, it always leaves the terminating character ('\n' by default) at the next stream position. This can lead to problems when we next want to read a character or string, because the '\n' (or other terminator) will automatically terminate the next attempt to read from the stream. Therefore we need to read past this terminating character with a single char 'get' before reading in the next set of data. This program demonstrates how *cin.get(char*, int, char = '\n')* allows input of data with embedded spaces, but leaves the terminating character in the stream. The character is then read in and its ASCII value displayed (the ASCII value of '\n' is 10).

```
#include <iostream.h>
void main()
{
// declare a char array to get the characters into
    char buffer[80];
// get a string of characters from the keyboard
    cout << "Type in a string with embedded spaces ";
    cin.get(buffer, 80);
// extract the terminating character from the stream into 'temp'
    char temp;
    cin.get(temp);
// display the text (note the \" to display speech marks)
    cout << "The text entered is \"" << buffer << '\"' << endl;
// display the ASCII value of the character (cast to int so it is not
// used as a newline on the screen). the ASCII value of '\n' is 10
    cout << "The ASCII value of the character left in the stream is " << (int)temp << endl;
}
```

This is a test run:

> *Type in a string with embedded spaces* I am a stream
> *The text entered is "I am a stream"*

The ASCII value of the character left in the stream is 10

Checking data types

Since we often want to do something with input data such as analyse its type for processing or error detection, it is useful to be able to identify the data type of a character. This can be done by standard functions available in a standard C header file called 'ctype.h'. The most useful are:

Function	Returns TRUE (1) for:
int isalpha(char)	$a - z$ or $A - Z$
int isdigit(char)	$0 - 9$
int isspace(char)	space, tab ('\t'), carriage return ('\r'), newline ('\n') or formfeed ('\f')
int isascii(char)	In the ASCII table (i.e. $>= 0$ and $<= 127$)

This simple program shows how we might use the 'isdigit' function to wait for a character in the range $0 - 9$:

```
#include <iostream.h>
#include <ctype.h>
void main()
{
    char x;
    do
    {
        cout << "Enter a single digit in the range 0–9 ";
        cin >> x;
    } while(!isdigit(x));
}
```

The 'ios' class

Both 'ostream' and 'istream' are derived classes of the 'ios' class. This class provides us with some useful methods, including these:

Method	Purpose
int width(int)	Sets a field width – minimum only (will not truncate)
char fill(char)	Sets a fill character
int precision(int)	Sets the precision of floating point numbers
long set(long)	Sets the format of a field

The following program demonstrates how some of these can be used to format data, in this case the output format of a float variable. Note that for each 'cout' statement, all of these formats need to be reset:

```
#include <iostream.h>
void main()
{
    float x = 12.36;
    cout << x << endl;
```

```
// set the field width to 10. the data will right justify by default
    cout.width(10);
    cout << x << endl;
// keep the wide field and change the fill character
    cout.width(10);
    cout.fill('_');
    cout << x << endl;
// left justify the data in the wide, filled field
    cout.width(10);
    cout.fill('_');
    cout.setf(ios::left);
    cout << x << endl;
// set the floating point precision to one decimal place
// (will round up)
    cout.precision(1);
    cout << x << endl;
}
```

The output from this program is:

```
12.36
        12.36
_____12.36
12.36_____
12.4
```

Manipulators

One problem with the 'ios' format specifiers is that each formatting statement has to be made separately from all the others. This means that there is no logical connection between the separate operations. As an alternative approach, we can use 'manipulators' to put the formatting statements directly into the input or output operations. Manipulators are defined in a file called 'iomanip.h', and they have a similar role to the ios format specifiers. Although their functions do not exactly match with the formatting methods of the ios class, many are similar, as the following table shows:

Manipulator	Purpose
setw(int)	Sets a field width – minimum only (will not truncate)
setfill(char)	Sets a fill character
setprecision(int)	Sets the precision of floating point numbers
setiosflags(long)	Calls an ios formatting method

The following program produces exactly the same output as our previous example which used ios flags, but this time uses the manipulators:

```
#include <iostream.h>
#include <iomanip.h>
void main()
{
    float x = 12.36;
    cout << x << endl;
    cout << setw(10) << x << endl;
    cout << setw(10) << setfill('_') << x << endl;
    cout << setw(10) << setfill('_') << setiosflags(ios::left) << x << endl;
```

```
        cout << setprecision(1) << x << endl;
}
```

As the example program indicates, manipulators can be inserted directly into the input or output statements, making the code easier to follow.

Overloading 'istream' and 'ostream' operators

In order to handle the input and output of objects, we need to be able to treat them in the same way as other data types. In previous examples we have seen the use of the '>>' and '<<' symbols to input and output data respectively. As we know, these are in fact operators of the 'istream' and 'ostream' classes, overloaded to handle the various built in data types of C++. Like other operators, they can be further overloaded, and we can do this explicitly to allow them to handle user defined types (classes). We looked at the syntax for overloading operators in Chapter 11, and you may remember that the 'operator' keyword is used, follow by the operator to be overloaded.

In general terms, to overload the insertion operator ('<<') the method prototype would be:

```
    ostream& operator << (ostream&, class_type&);
```

where 'class_type' is a parameter of some user-defined class, passed by reference. The method returns a reference to an 'ostream' object, and also takes one as a parameter. The extraction operator ('>>') can be similarly overloaded with references to 'istream' objects:

```
    istream& operator >> (istream&, class_type&);
```

The stream objects need to be returned from the overloaded operators because this allows them to be chained together, e.g.

```
    cout << "Hello" << name;
```

The following program shows how objects of class 'Person' can be handled by these overloaded operators:

```
/*
    PERSON.H class and method definitions for "person"
*/
#include <iostream.h>
#include <string.h>
class Person
{
private:
    char name[20];
    int age;
public:
    char* getName();
    int getAge();
    void setName(char* name_in);
    void setAge(int age_in);
};
char* Person::getName()
{
    return name;
}
int Person::getAge()
{
```

```
        return age;
    }
    void Person::setName(char* name_in)
    {
        strncpy(name, name_in, 19);
        name[19] = '\0';
    }
    void Person::setAge(int age_in)
    {
        age = age_in;
    }
    // the '>>' operator is overloaded to handle the input of 'Person' objects
    istream& operator >> (istream& in, Person& person)
    {
        char temp_name[20];
        int temp_age;
        cout << "Enter name: ";
    // note that 'get' is used to handle embedded spaces
        in.get(temp_name, 19);
        cout << "Enter age: ";
        in >> temp_age;
    // the object passed by reference has its attributes set
        person.setName(temp_name);
        person.setAge(temp_age);
        return in;
    }
    // the '<<' operator is overloaded to handle the output of 'Person' objects
    ostream& operator << (ostream& out, Person& person)
    {
        return out << "Name: " << person.getName() << endl
        << "Age: " << person.getAge() << endl;
    }
    // in main, a 'Person' is input and output using 'cin' and 'cout'
    /*
        PERSON.CPP
    */
    #include "person.h"
    void main()
    {
        Person a_person;
        cin >> a_person;
        cout << a_person;
    }
```

Running the program simply allows us to input a name and age, which are then displayed back on the screen:

Enter name: *Rip Van Winkle*
Enter age: *100*
Name: Rip Van Winkle
Age: 100

As we will see, this overloading of input and output operators can be used equally effectively when writing and reading object attributes to and from files.

Files

Much of the stream I/O syntax which we have used for previous examples may be used for file handling, but the classes may in some cases not be defined in 'iostream.h' but in another header file (e.g. 'fstream.h' or similar).

The most important classes for file handling in the stream class hierarchy are:

ifstream	(input files)
ofstream	(output files)
fstream	(files for both input and output)

To open a file for output (writing), then, we instantiate an object of the 'ofstream' class. Similarly, a file is opened for input (reading) with an object of the 'ifstream' class. In order to open a file, an object of the appropriate stream class must be instantiated, and associated with a disk file name. These activities may be done in a single statement or separately, by creating the object first and then assigning it to a filename.

Opening files

The two forms of the syntax for opening files are as follows:

Syntax version 1

This version instantiates the object and opens the file in one statement:

> **stream_type object_name (filename, opening_mode);**

For example, we could open an output file as follows, with an ofstream object called 'outfile' and a file called 'test.dat':

> **ofstream outfile("test.dat");**

We do not have to state the opening mode, since it has default values. The default value for an object of the 'ofstream' class is for the file to be opened for output (writing).

Syntax version 2

This version instantiates the object in one statement, and uses the 'open' method to open the file:

> **stream_type object_name;**
> **object_name.open(filename, opening_mode);**

In this example, an object of the 'ifstream' class called 'infile' is instantiated, and then used to open a file called 'test2.dat':

> **ifstream infile;**
> **infile.open("test2.dat");**

Again, the default opening mode is used, which for an 'ifstream' object is for input (reading).

The opening mode is defined by an integer value, but is usually specified via an enumerated type in the 'ios' class which allows us to name the opening modes using the scope resolution operator. The possible opening modes are as follows (as defined by Stroustrup, but may vary between compilers):

Opening mode flag	Effect
ios::in	open for input (default for ifstream)
ios::out	open for output (default for ofstream)
ios::ate	open and seek end of file
ios::app	append all output
ios::trunc	destroys contents of existing file by truncating it to position 0
ios::nocreate	open fails if the file does not exist
ios::noreplace	open fails if the file exists

For example, let us suppose that we want to open a file for output, but ensure that all new output is appended to the end of any existing data in the file. In this case, we would want to open the file to append as follows (using the same object and file name used in the previous 'ofstream' example):

```
ofstream outfile("test2.dat", ios::app);
```

We may find that we need to specify more than one opening mode. This can be achieved by combining modes using the ' | ' character. This example shows how an output file can be opened to truncate the file but for the open to fail if the file does not already exist:

```
ofstream outfile("test2.dat", ios::trunc | ios::nocreate);
```

Another useful method for use with files is 'close': e.g.

```
outfile.close();
```

However, this is only necessary if the file object does not fall out of scope at the point where it must be closed. Otherwise the file object destructor will close the file automatically.

'ostream' file methods

Two of the methods inherited from the 'ostream' class allow us to manipulate the file pointer of an output file. The methods are:

```
ostream& seekp(streampos);
streampos tellp();
```

where 'streampos' represents the character position in a file. 'seekp' moves the file pointer to the given position, whereas 'tellp' returns the current position.

'istream' file methods

With an input stream, we can look at the stream position referenced by the file pointer. The 'peek' method returns the next character to be read without actually reading it:

```
int peek();
```

These two methods are the corollary to 'seekp' and 'tellp' in the ostream class, because they move and report the position of the file pointer respectively:

```
istream& seekg(streampos);
streampos tellg();
```

This program demonstrates some aspects of 'fstream' objects. First, it opens an 'fstream' file object for both input and output, and then writes three characters to the file. Because 'fstream' inherits from 'iostream', it is able to use the insertion and extraction operators in much the same way as 'cin' and 'cout', but the data streams to and from files rather than screen and keyboard. Here, the insertion operator ('<<') is used to write to the file. Then file stream methods are used to position the file pointer ('seekg'), look at the next character ('peek') and read it from the file ('get'):

```
/*
    SEEK&TEL.CPP   Program to demonstrate what 'seekg', 'tellg' and 'peek' are for
*/
#include <fstream.h>
void main()
{
// create an fstream object for both writing and reading
    fstream file("file.dat", ios::in | ios::out);
// send three characters to the file using the insertion operator
    file << 'a';
    file << 'b';
    file << 'c';
// move the input file pointer to position 2
    file.seekg(2);
// display the current position of the file pointer
    cout << "Position of input file pointer is " << file.tellg() << endl;
// look at the next character in the file (position 3) with the 'peek'
// method. since it returns an integer, the ASCII value is displayed
    cout << "ASCII value of next character in the file is " << file.peek() << endl;
// use 'peek' again, this time casting to type 'char' to see the letter
// note that using 'peek' has not moved the file pointer
    cout << "Next character in the file is " << char(file.peek()) << endl;
// retrieve the next character in the file and display it
    char char_in;
    file.get(char_in);
    cout << "Character read from file is " << char_in << endl;
}
```

The output from this program is:

```
Position of input file pointer is 2
ASCII value of next character in the file is 99
Next character in the file is c
Character read from file is c
```

Objects of the 'fstream' class

Objects of the 'fstream' class inherit from the 'iostream' class. 'iostream' multiply inherits from both istream and ostream (Fig. 17.2), so an 'fstream' object has all the methods of both istream and ostream objects.

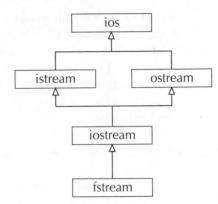

Fig. 17.2: In the 'iostream' class hierarchy, 'iostream' multiply inherits from both 'istream' and 'ostream'. 'iostream' is the base class for 'fstream'. Some compiler implementations may vary.

An 'fstream' object has separate file pointer positions for reading and writing, so we may, for example, use both 'seekp' and 'seekg' with an fstream file. It can also be opened in a range of ways, so we often need to specify more than one opening mode. This file for example is opened for both input and output:

fstream in_and_out("iofile.dat", ios::in I ios::out);

There is no default for 'fstream' objects, so a mode must be defined.

Detecting the end of file

When handling input files, it is essential that we are able to detect the end of file. This may be done with method of the ios class called 'eof' which returns 1 (true) when the end of file is detected:

```
while(!infile.eof())
{
    //...
}
```

File handling with character i/o and file pointers

The following program demonstrates an 'fstream' file being used for character I/O. It indicates how the file pointer may be used, and how single characters may be written to and read from files. Although objects are written and read in a rather different way, manipulating a character at a time is a useful and flexible way of handling data. In this case, a string is written to file, and then the file is modified before the data is read back in and displayed. Be aware, however, that not all compiler's stream libraries behave in exactly the same way.

```
#include <fstream.h>
#include <string.h>
void main()
{
// declare a string of characters in an array
    char string[] = "File handling advice don\'t hold it by the sharp end";
// open a file for I/O
    fstream iofile("File.txt", ios::trunc I ios::in I ios::out);
// this loop counts through the individual characters in the array,
```

```
// until the last character. the size of the string is worked out
// by the 'strlen' function defined in 'string.h'
    for(int i = 0; i <= strlen(string); i++)
    {
// write out one character at a time using 'put'
        iofile.put(string[i]);
    }
// move the file pointer using 'seekp'
    iofile.seekp(21);
// show the current position using 'tellp'
cout << "Current file position is: " << iofile.tellp() << endl;
// output a different character at the current file position
    iofile << '!';
// declare another array to receive input from the file
    char string2[80];
    i = 0;
    char temp_char;
    iofile.seekp(0);
// read characters using 'put' until the end of file (using 'ios::eof()')
    while(!iofile.eof())
    {
        iofile.get(temp_char);
        string2[i] = temp_char;
        i++;
    }
// display the modified string
    cout << "String is: " << string2 << endl;
}
```

The program outputs the following messages:

Current file position is: 21
String is: File handling advice ! don't hold it by the sharp end

Object i/o using overloaded operators

So far we have looked at how stream operators may be overloaded to work with objects, and how files are handled. In the next example, we draw together these two aspects to show object attributes being written to and from disk via a file stream. Like class 'Person' in the previous example, the 'Box' class, representing a three dimensional object, is handled by overloaded insertion and extraction operators. In this example, however, they are not used for keyboard input and screen output but for streaming to and from a file object.

Overloaded operators as 'friend functions'

In the 'Person' example, the insertion and extraction operators were separately defined functions (not members of any class) taking 'Person' objects as parameters. This approach has two drawbacks:

1. Inside the functions, the parameter objects could only be accessed in terms of their public interfaces (lots of 'get' and 'set' methods required).
2. There is no evidence in the class body itself that the operators have been overloaded for 'Person' objects. This does not help the readability of the code.

We can overcome both of these problems by making the operators 'friend functions'. A 'friend' is a function (or method, or class) that is not actually a member of a given class, but nevertheless has direct access to its attributes, just as if it was a member. A function is declared as a friend simply by putting it in the class body, preceded by the keyword 'friend'. In the next example, the operators are friends of class 'Box', and appear in the class body like this:

```
friend ostream& operator << (ostream& out, Box& box);
friend istream& operator >> (istream& in, Box& box);
```

Using delimiters in the file

When we write data to a file, we have to format it in such a way that it can be easily read back in again. Since input stream objects are naturally whitespace delimited (that is, a space is seen as a separator between two items of data) we can write out object attributes to a file separated by spaces, and easily read them in again.

In the 'showData' method the attributes are displayed on screen using the 'setw' format specifier.

This is the 'Box' class:

```
/*
    BOX.H definition of the 'Box' class
*/
class Box
{
private:
//   a 'Box' has three integer attributes defining its dimensions
    int height;
    int width;
    int depth;
public:
// methods to set and display the state of the object
    void setData();
    void showData();
// overloaded '<<' and '>>' operators for use with 'Box' objects,
// declared as friends to allow them to appear in the class definition
    friend ostream& operator << (ostream& out, Box& box);
    friend istream& operator >> (istream& in, Box& box);
};
/*
    BOX.CPP  method definitions for the 'Box' class
*/
#include <fstream.h>      // for all streams, including file streams
#include <iomanip.h>      // for the 'setw' format specifier
#include "box.h"
// method for setting all the data attributes from the keyboard
void Box::setData()
{
    cout << "Enter height: ";
    cin >> height;
    cout << "Enter width: ";
    cin >> width;
    cout << "Enter depth: ";
    cin >> depth;
}
// method to display all the attributes on screen
void Box::showData()
{
```

```
// note how the 'setw' method is used to format the numeric data
// '\t' is used to align the text to tab stops
    cout << "Height: " << setw(5) << height;
    cout << "\tWidth: " << setw(5) << width;
    cout << "\tDepth: " << setw(5) << depth << endl;
}
// overload the output operator '<<' for use with 'Box' objects
// this example includes the operators as 'friend' functions, which
// allows them direct access to the attributes of the 'Box' object
// a space is output between each attribute as a delimiter to enable
// us to read the data back in correctly
ostream& operator << (ostream& out, Box& box)
{
// output the attributes to the stream, and return it to allow chaining
    out << box.height << " " << box.width << " " << box.depth << endl;
    return out;
}
// overload the input operator '>>' for use with 'Box' objects. having
// also declared this function as a 'friend' of class Box we have direct
// access to the attributes. for input, this avoids having to read data
// into temporary variables and using 'set' methods
istream& operator >> (istream& in, Box& box)
{
// because the input stream is delimited by whitespace, we can
// input all three attributes at once
    in >> box.height >> box.width >> box.depth;
// return the stream to allow chaining
    return in;
}
```

The following program demonstrates the 'Box' data being written to and read from a file, with the attributes of one array of boxes being used to set the attributes of a second array. This underlines the fact that it is not the object identity that is being made persistent, simply the object's state data. Notice that in this program the same file is used for both output and input.

```
/*
    BOXMAIN.CPP    program to test the file streaming of 'Box' objects
*/
#include <fstream.h>    // for all streams, including file streams
#include "box.h"
void main()
{
// instantiate 5 boxes
    Box boxes[5];
// instantiate an 'fstream' file object and open the file for I/O,
// replacing any previous data in the file
    fstream io_file;
    io_file.open("BOXES.DAT", ios::trunc | ios::in | ios::out);
//  set the 'Box' attributes and write them out to file
    for(int i = 0; i < 5; i++)
    {
        boxes[i].setData();
        io_file << boxes[i];
    }
// reset the file pointer to the beginning of the file
    io_file.seekg(0);
// instantiate a new 'Box' array, read the cube data back in from file and
```

325

```
    // display. although these boxes have a different identity, their state is
    // the same as the original boxes
        Box new_boxes[5];
        for(i = 0; i < 5; i++)
        {
            io_file >> new_boxes[i];
            new_boxes[i].showData();
        }
    // the file will automatically close when it falls out of scope
    }
```

Running the program, we are asked to enter the dimensions of the first five boxes:

Enter height: 100
Enter width: 150
Enter depth: 200
Enter height: 3
Enter width: 4
Enter depth: 5
Enter height: 23
Enter width: 45
Enter depth: 67
Enter height: 12
Enter width: 11
Enter depth: 1
Enter height: 44
Enter width: 55
Enter depth: 33

At this point, the data file has been written; 'boxes.dat' will contain the following data, with the three attributes of each object separated by spaces:

100 150 200
3 4 5
23 45 67
12 11 1
44 55 33

The program then reads this data back into a second array of 'Box' objects that display their attributes on the screen:

Height:	*100*	*Width:*	*150*	*Depth:*	*200*
Height:	*3*	*Width:*	*4*	*Depth:*	*5*
Height:	*23*	*Width:*	*45*	*Depth:*	*67*
Height:	*12*	*Width:*	*11*	*Depth:*	*1*
Height:	*44*	*Width:*	*55*	*Depth:*	*33*

A further example: handling data with embedded spaces and methods for stream handling

This example explores some more aspects of streaming object data to and from a file, principally handling data that contains embedded spaces, and using stream handling methods that are true members of the class.

Streaming data with embedded spaces

When the data for 'Box' objects was streamed to and from file, using the space as the delimiter was an appropriate means of separating out the numeric attribute values. Since numbers do not have embedded spaces, they are easy to handle. We encounter difficulties, though, if we need to handle data that does contain embedded spaces. In the next example, objects of the 'DirectoryEntry' class (representing entries in a telephone directory) have three attributes that may all contain spaces; name, address and telephone number. To ensure that this data can be successfully read from file, we must use the version of 'get' that reads in all characters until a terminating character, rather than the space delimited extraction operator. You may recall that the default terminating character is the newline ('\n') character. So that the data can be read back form the file using '\n' as the terminator, each attribute is written on a separate line in the file. An alternative strategy would be to use some other separator character between each attribute.

Methods for stream handling

In previous examples, we have seen two ways of overloading the stream operators:

1. Separate functions taking objects of the class as a parameter and interfacing with their public methods. These cannot appear as members of the class.

2. Separate functions declared as friend functions and accessing the parameter object's private attributes. These appear in the class but are not actually methods of it, which to some extent breaks encapsulation.

Neither of these is ideal. An alternative approach is to provide the class with its own methods that take stream objects as parameters. This means that the methods are proper members of the class rather than just friends, accessing private attributes without compromising encapsulation. These methods can still be used by overloaded operators if required, as well as being useable with any objects of stream classes. The 'DirectoryEntry' class (modelling entries in a telephone directory) has two such methods, 'readFrom' and 'writeTo':

```
void writeTo(ostream& out);
void readFrom(istream& in);
```

The parameters passed to these methods can be either objects of the ostream or istream classes (e.g. 'cout' or 'cin') or equally objects of the file stream classes, ofstream and ifstream.

In this example, the DirectoryEntry class is used in two separate programs; one that creates objects and stores their attributes in a file and another that retrieves this data to recreate the objects.

This is the class definition:

```
/*
    DIRENTRY.H   Class definitions for the 'DirectoryEntry' class, to demonstrate object
                 streaming methods and handling data with embedded spaces.
*/
// the 'DirectoryEntry' class has methods to write to and read from streams.
#include<fstream.h> // for all streams, including file streams
class DirectoryEntry
{
private:
    char name[20];
```

```
        char address[25];
        char telno[15];
public:
    void setData();
    void showData();
    void writeTo(ostream& out);
    void readFrom(istream& in);
};
/*
    DIRENTRY.CPP   Method definitions for the 'DirectoryEntry' class
*/
#include <string.h>  // for 'strncpy'
#include "direntry.h"
// methods for setting and displaying all data
void DirectoryEntry::setData()
{
// local variable to clear the terminating character from the input stream
    char temp_char;
    cout << "Enter name: ";
// get the name from the stream
    cin.get(name, 20);
// clear the '\n' from the stream
    cin.get(temp_char);
// and the same for the other inputs...
    cout << "Enter address: ";
    cin.get(address, 25);
    cin.get(temp_char);
    cout << "Enter Telno: ";
    cin.get(telno, 15);
    cin.get(temp_char);
}
// display the entry on screen (on a single line, separated by tabs)
void DirectoryEntry::showData()
{
    cout << "Name: " << name;
    cout << "\tAddress: " << address;
    cout << "\tTelno: " << telno << endl;
}
// method for writing out attributes as separate lines. the parameter
// object class is 'ostream', but it may also be 'ofstream' in practice
// because 'ostream' is a base class of 'ostream'. this means that this
// method can be used to write to either screen or output file stream
void DirectoryEntry::writeTo(ostream& out)
{
    out << name << endl;
    out << address << endl;
    out << telno << endl;
}
// method for reading back lines representing individual attribute
// values. again, although the parameter is of the 'istream' class,
// it can equally apply to 'ifstream' objects, to allow input from
// either keyboard or input file stream
void DirectoryEntry::readFrom(istream& in)
{
// local variable for the terminating character
// (same principle as the 'setData' method)
    char temp_char;
    in.get(name, 20);
```

```
        in.get(temp_char);
        in.get(address, 25);
        in.get(temp_char);
        in.get(telno, 15);
        in.get(temp_char);
}
```

This program writes objects of the 'DirectoryEntry' class to file, using the stream handling method 'writeTo'. The parameter is an object of the 'ofstream' class.

```
/*
    DIRCTOUT.CPP    Program to write 'DirectoryEntry' object data to file
*/
#include "direntry.h"
void main()
{
// instantiate five directory entry objects
    DirectoryEntry phone_book[5];
//    set their attributes
    for(int i = 0; i < 5; i++)
    {
        phone_book[i].setData();
    }
// open an output file stream object
    ofstream out("DIRECTRY.DAT");
// write the objects to the file
    for(i = 0; i < 5; i++)
    {
// use the file object as the parameter to the 'writeTo' method
        phone_book[i].writeTo(out);
    }
// close the output file (in fact this would be automatic as 'out' falls out
// of scope and its destructor is called)
    out.close();
}
```

After a test run of this program the data file ('directry.dat') might look something like this. Notice how the file is 'long and thin' compared to the 'boxes.dat' file because the newline character is being used as the terminator for each individual attribute. Each object therefore writes three separate lines to the file:

John Jones
10 High Road
234 456
Joan T Smith
12 Newlands
134 456
Archimedes
Parthenon
111
Simon Says
100 Old Ave.
223 444
Harry Harris
14 New Street
23 2341

This program uses the stored attribute data in the file to recreate the 'DirectoryEntry' objects instantiated in the previous program. Thus the objects appear to be persistent between runs of the two programs.

```
/*
    DIRECTIN.CPP    Program to read DirectoryEntry object data from file
*/
#include "direntry.h"
void main()
{
// instantiate 5 entries
    DirectoryEntry phone_book[5];
// open an input file stream object
    ifstream in("DIRECTRY.DAT");
// check that the file has been opened successfully
    if(in)
    {
// read the attribute data back in from the file, use it to set the states of
// the objects and display their attribute values
        for(int i = 0; i < 5; i++)
        {
// as in the previous program, the streaming method of the class is used:
            phone_book[i].readFrom(in);
            phone_book[i].showData();
        }
    }
    else
    {
        cout << "unable to open file" << endl;
    }
// the input file will automatically close when it falls out of scope
}
```

The screen output from the program shows that the file data has been read into the objects:

Name: John Jones	Address: 10 High Road	Telno: 234 456
Name: Joan T Smith	Address: 12 Newlands	Telno: 134 456
Name: Archimedes	Address: Parthenon	Telno: 111
Name: Simon Says	Address: 100 Old Ave.	Telno: 223 444
Name: Harry Harris	Address: 14 New Street	Telno: 23 2341

Using overloaded operators with stream handling methods

Although the 'writeTo' and 'readFrom' methods provide all the functionality of overloaded operators, it may be useful to also have these operators available for our classes. This is very easily achieved. All we have to do is to implement overloaded operators that call our own object methods. We would add the function prototypes to the header file as normal; not as 'friends' here because we already have methods in the class, but as separate functions. Then we can define the operators as simple calls to our own methods.

```
// the overloaded insertion operator calls the 'writeTo' method
ostream& operator << (ostream& out, DirectoryEntry& entry)
{
    entry.writeTo(out);
    return out;
}
```

```
// the overloaded extraction operator calls the 'readFrom' method
istream& operator >> (istream& in, DirectoryEntry& entry)
{
    entry.readFrom(in);
    return in;
}
```

We now have the option of using either our own methods or the overloaded operators. We could replace the following line from the first program:

```
phone_book[i].writeTo(out);
```

with this:

```
out << phone_book[i];
```

and the effect would be exactly the same. Similarly, in the second program we could replace:

```
phone_book[i].readFrom(in);
```

with:

```
in >> phone_book[i];
```

In these examples, we have seen different ways in which the attribute data of objects may be stored in a file, and how this data may be used to recreate the objects. This allows us to have objects which at least appear to persist between different runs of the same program, and between different programs which have access to the same class definitions. The syntax used here is not very elegant, since it relies on the small set of standard iostream/fstream facilities which are mentioned by Stroustrup. Specific compilers will no doubt provide a wider range of classes and methods to enhance the stream and file handling processes.

Summary of key points from this chapter

1. Objects may need to persist beyond a single program run time, perhaps between different programs.

2. Storing objects is difficult because both data and processes need to persist, ideally together.

3. Object data can be stored in traditional file formats, but an object-oriented database is a preferable storage medium since it maintains the integrity of objects.

4. Object-oriented databases store objects 'whole', and come in two main types – those which are relational but have an object 'shell', and those which are fully object-oriented.

5. File handling in C++ is done via streams, which are also used for keyboard and screen I/O with similar syntax.

6. The stream classes are in a hierarchy based on the 'ios' class. This and its derived classes provide the objects, methods and overloaded operators necessary for I/O.

7. To handle objects of our own classes in stream I/O, we can overload the 'istream' and 'ostream' operators to work with user-defined types, or create our own file handling methods. Attributes may be written out as fields in larger records or as single data records.

Exercises

1. Overload the insertion operator to output objects of the 'Point' class (from Chapter 11, page 192). Test that it works with a 'main' function.

2. The 'Person' class described in this chapter is used with an overloaded insertion operator that includes text labels for output and an overloaded extraction operator that includes prompts for user input. Clearly these operators will not work with file streams. Modify the operators so that they can be used with file streams by removing the prompts and labels. Test the operators with a main function that writes a 'Person' to file and reads the attribute data back into a second 'Person' object.

3. Given that the demands of console i/o and file i/o are somewhat different, we might use overloading to provide more than output stream method for a class, for example:

   ```
   void streamOut(ostream& out);
   void streamOut(ofstream& out);
   ```

   Using the technique suggested above, provide two versions of a stream output method for the 'Point' class; one including text labels that can be used for screen output (using an 'ostream' parameter) and one that only writes the attribute values for output to a file (using an 'ofstream' parameter).

4. Add insertion and extraction operators as 'friends' of your 'String' class (from Chapter 11, exercise 5). Because a string has only one attribute, a single implementation should suffice for both console and file I/0.

18 Object-oriented analysis and design

Overview

This chapter introduces some approaches to analyzing and designing an object-oriented system. The fundamental elements of design methods are summarised, and a number of different activities within the overall analysis and design cycle are identified. A simple example using notation from Rumbaugh, Booch and Jacobsen's 'Unified Modelling Language' (UML) is worked through from design to implementation.

'The screw'
'If you concentrate on it, think about it, stay stuck on it for a long enough time, I would guess that in time you will come to see that the screw is less and less an object typical of a class and more and more an object unique in itself. Then with more concentration you will begin to see the screw as not even an object at all but as a collection of functions...you aren't interested in what it is...you are interested in what it does and why it's doing it.'

from 'Zen and the Art of Motorcycle Maintenance' by Robert Pirsig.

The need for analysis and design methods

In the first chapter we discussed the software crisis and the need for some means to handle the development of large and complex systems. Object-oriented programming alone is not enough; it has to be used in the context of a coherent overall design which can integrate all the objects identified in a system together. Indeed, object-oriented programming alone can only add to the problem if it is not applied in the context of a semantically appropriate systems analysis. We need object-oriented analysis and design methods because we could not to create large and complex object-oriented systems without them:

'The distinguishing characteristic of industrial-strength software is that it is intensely difficult, if not impossible, for the individual developer to comprehend all the subtleties of the design. Stated in blunt terms. the complexity of such systems exceeds the human intellectual capacity....we may master this complexity, but we can never make it go away'

[Booch 1994, p.4]

We can only master complexity by putting it into a formal framework that allows us to concentrate on small parts of a system while being confident that each part will relate appropriately to the other system components.

One problem with trying to introduce these methods is that they are difficult to contextualise when using very small scale examples:

'There is a tendency for the textbooks on OOD to describe systems in which identifying the objects is very easy, or at least to present the description of a design in such a way that it is made to look easy'

[Blair et al p. 220]

The example in this chapter is no exception, so it is wise to remember that ultimately we need methods because real problems are not so easy to solve.

Components of an object-oriented analysis and design method

While there are many different methods for object-oriented analysis and design, they all have to address the fundamental components of all object-oriented systems. Any method must address (at least) the following:

1. Identifying objects.
2. Identifying classes (classifying the objects).
3. Defining object behaviours (methods).
4. Structures using generalisation and specialisation (inheritance).
5. Structures using aggregation (composition, containers).
6. Object state representation (attributes, and events that change state).
7. Message passing between objects (association and visibility).

The means we use to tackle these problems can vary between methods, and there are two schools of thought; one that stresses the behaviour of objects (e.g. Wirfs-Brock, Gibson et al) and another that stresses state (Rumbaugh et al). This divide between the 'responsibility centred' and 'data centred' approaches mirrors in some ways the traditional divide between process driven and data driven structured methods. However, there are many common elements between the approaches advocated by different authors, and users can often 'mix and match' elements of different methodologies.

The difference between analysis and design

One of the claims which is made for object-orientation is that it smooths the transition between analysis and design, and between design and implementation. Coad and Yourdon in their analysis and design texts use a simple 'chasm' diagram to imply that in traditional approaches, each of these three stages is discrete, to the point where the transition from one to another is difficult (Fig. 18.1).

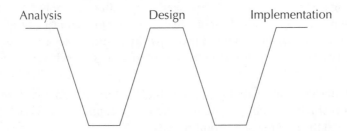

Fig. 18.1: 'Chasm' diagram adapted from Coad and Yourdon – traditional analysis and design techniques make it difficult to move from one phase to another.

With an object-oriented approach, the analysis and design cycle can be seen as a single process, albeit one which has different concerns at different levels of detail. We may contrast traditional analysis and design approaches which use different models at different stages of development with the object-oriented approach which progressively expands the same model of a system. Booch talks about the process as being a 'round-trip gestalt', a continuous iteration through the stages of analysis and design, including the use of prototyping and refinement of the existing design as necessary.

In object-oriented analysis, we are attempting to create a model of the problem by identifying the objects (and by extension the classes) which exist in the problem domain. In the design phase, we are defining how these abstractions can be made to exist and interact in software by creating an overall framework for the system. Depending on the scale of the problem, these activities may merge into a seamless process.

'For small to medium projects there often is no distinction made between analysis and design: These two phases have been merged into one. Similarly, in small projects there often is no distinction made between design and programming'

[Stroustrup, 1995 p.368]

Classifying objects

Since the first step in any analysis must be to identify objects which must belong to classes, then the way in which classification is done is important. As Booch explains, there are only three general approaches to classification [Booch, 1994, pp.150–155]:

1. Classical categorization.
2. Conceptual clustering.
3. Prototype theory.

In all three we look for common properties and behaviours, but in increasingly abstract ways. In classical categorization for instance It is important that the properties of objects are measurable, so that it is clear to which category an object belongs, but conceptual clustering involves less easily measured similarities (style rather than content perhaps). Occasionally we come up against abstractions which cannot be clearly defined either in terms of their properties or concepts. A game is an example of this – what exactly defines a game? This is the area of prototype theory, where we can only look for 'family resemblances' between one abstraction and another. All forms of categorisation are, of course, always going to be domain specific, since nature does not categorise; it is purely a human activity which attempts to make sense of our environment. Therefore something which is a valid category in one context may not be in another.

The relevance of these theories to object-oriented analysis is the connection between levels of abstraction in classification theory, and levels of abstraction in classification hierarchies. The more abstract the classification, the higher up the hierarchy it is likely to appear.

Identifying classes

When we come to analyze an object-oriented system we have to identify the classes and objects in the problem domain. This is not always a simple task;

'Some of the classes and objects we identify early in the life cycle will be wrong, but that is not necessarily a bad thing'   [Booch, 1994 p.237]

When we analyze a system, we will make immediate assumptions that may need to be re-appraised later. Therefore it is important that any assumptions we make about the classification of objects are identified and, if necessary, challenged. Remember that our final model of the system is not necessarily right or wrong, but simply one way of analyzing the problem. Any classifications we apply might equally be replaced by different but equally valid ones. Certainly when we reach the later stages of design and maybe have to decide whether to use classes in complex hierarchies, delegations, mixins and aggregations, then we may well find that a number of different classifications are possible.

Defining system boundaries

The first step in any analysis must be to define the system boundaries, to exclude from our design any aspect of the overall application which is not directly part of the system. A 'user' is a typical example of an 'object' which is clearly outside the system we are trying to build. Although we will need to be aware of the messages being sent to and from a 'user', there is no reason to model the user as an object (an exception to this general rule is the 'actor' class described by Jacobson [Jacobson, 1993 p.129], but such classes are specifically intended to model behaviours outside the main system.) Before we can begin to successfully analyze a system, we should understand that some of the 'objects' which we talk about in the analysis are external and will therefore not become objects in the implementation.

Domain analysis

Given that one of the primary elements of an object-oriented design method is to encompass re-use, it is important that this aspect should be emphasised at an early stage. Whether or not we are able to reuse software components at the implementation stage, there is no reason why reuse should not be applied at the analysis and design stages. Domain analysis simply a detailed study of the problem area. One aspect of this involves looking at similar systems to the one we are analyzing and finding out what objects have been identified in them. Since there are not so many different types of application, the chances of finding a useful precedent are quite high. It would be re-inventing the wheel, for example, to approach a bank cash machine application without reference to the many existing similar systems. Other sources of information may be developers, users and libraries. A domain analysis might take the following steps [Booch 1994, p.157]:

1. Consult with domain experts to get a general model of the system. A 'domain expert' is not necessarily a software engineer but someone who knows the application area, perhaps as a user. A domain expert in cash machine systems might simply be someone who spends a lot of cash!

2. Look at existing systems in the problem domain.

3. Compare existing systems for similarities and differences.

4. Refine the original model in the light of this comparison.

How much access we might have to existing systems depends on a particular context. Some developers may have access to other similar applications written in the same company or organisation, in which case a great deal of information can be accessed. In other cases, very little domain information may be available.

Domain analysis does not have to depend on information supplied by people – written sources can be equally useful. Coad & Yourdon recommend the following approach:

> 'Go to Encyclopedia Britannica's Macropedia for a 10–12 page professionally-written description of the problem space under consideration; this is an excellent way to learn the terminology and fundamentals of a topic'   [Coad, Yourdon, 1990, p.61]

We can also make a distinction between vertical and horizontal domain analysis. Vertical domain analysis means looking across similar applications (as above). In contrast, horizontal domain analysis means finding similar abstractions within a single application, so that we can understand the common elements between them, such as identifying the similarities between all the different reports in an accounting system.

At the detailed design stage, we may usefully study design patterns, such as those documented by [Gamma et al, 1995] that may provide reusable approaches to designing various elements of the system. The Unified Modelling Language (UML) integrates such patterns into its notation.

Actors and use cases

Many object-oriented analysis methods start from the problem statement, but do not suggest how that problem statement might be arrived at. Therefore we need to be aware of how to approach requirements analysis from an object-oriented perspective. A useful approach is the 'use case' model (originally described by Jacobson and now part of the UML method) which is based on scenarios provided by 'actors' at a very early stage of the analysis and describes what the system is intended to do. An actor represents something outside the system which interacts with it, and is generally a role adopted by an end-user. These scenarios are then analyzed using 'storyboards' to identify the objects in the system, their responsibilities and how they collaborate with other objects.

Class, Responsibility and Collaboration (C.R.C.) cards

A similar approach to the use-case storyboard is the CRC card, used by a number of authors including Wirfs-Brock and Beck & Cunningham. CRC stands for 'Class/ Responsibility/Collaboration', and is a useful way of 'brainstorming' the application. A CRC card is simply an index card or sticky note divided into three sections: the name of the class, its responsibilities and its collaborators (Fig. 18.2). A responsibility is written as a short verb phrase containing an active verb, such as 'turn on the pump', or 'print the account balance'. A collaborator is an object that will send or be sent messages when responsibilities are carried out (perhaps 'pump' as the receiver of the message 'turn on').

C.R.C. (Class, Responsibility & Collaboration) Card

Class: AIRCRAFT	
Responsibilities:	Collaborators:
Take Off Land	Airport Pilot

**Fig. 18.2: A typical CRC card. Layout (and media) may vary,
but the fundamental information remains the same.**

Because CRC cards can be moved around, torn up, replaced and written on, they are a very flexible tool for analysis. Developers can 'anthropomorphise' the behaviours of objects by 'becoming' a particular card and walking through scenarios.

'It is not unusual to see a designer with a card in each hand, waving them about, making a strong identification with the objects while describing their collaboration'

[Beck & Cunningham, 1989 p.3].

By defining what an object does, and when it needs to do it, we can begin to define the required behaviours (methods) of an object, and the contexts in which it needs to send or receive messages to and from other objects. The use of CRC cards can be easily integrated into other methods, alongside, for example, text analysis (described later).

The approach also allows cards to be physically arranged so that inheritance and aggregation hierarchies begin to arise naturally from the physical location of cards. Cards representing closely collaborating objects can be overlapped, parts of an aggregation can be arranged below the enclosing object, and generalisations at the higher levels of a hierarchy can be placed at the top of a pile of cards containing the specialised objects. Again, detail is added to the design by acting out scenarios identifying object behaviour in particular situations.

Interviewing

One important aspect of analysis, particularly in the context of domain analysis, is the interviewing of users of the system. One method which lays emphasis on this phase is 'Object Behaviour Analysis' [Gibson, 1990]. This approach stresses the way in which interviewing should be handled, particularly to identify behaviours important in the system. Strategies such as using open rather than closed questions, avoiding multiple choice in favour of simple one-part questions and 'active listening' (clarification and summarisation of answers) are all recommended. Throughout the analysis, the importance of identifying behaviour rather than state is emphasised, partly to overcome a natural inclination to do the opposite;

> 'Looking into the research on how people form concepts and categories showed that the aspect of objects that people notice most readily has to do with state'
>
> [Gibson 1990 p.250].

High level scenarios known as 'scripts' are used to walk through typical system interactions with the interviewees, recording actions and results. As part of this process, the agents and recipients of behaviours and messages are also identified. After notating some initial behaviours of the system, and the objects performing them, OBA uses 'modelling cards' (basically the same as CRC cards) to begin modelling the objects themselves.

Text analysis

A general approach first suggested by Abbott [Booch, 1994 p.159] is the textual analysis of a problem description. This approach is used as part of a number of methods, since it can be done early in the analysis phase. All that is required is some kind of initial problem description which some authors suggest may be as small as a single paragraph. The initial problem description may have been arrived at by some other analysis tool, such as interviewing, or may simply be a specification provided by a domain expert or end-user. Rumbaugh emphasises that the problem description should be:

> 'a statement of needs, not a proposal for a solution...The problem statement is just a starting point for understanding the problem, not an immutable document'
>
> [Rumbaugh et al, 1991 p.150].

In a text analysis, any nouns identified correspond to objects or attributes, and verbs correspond to associations or operations (Fig. 18.3). An 'operation' in the analysis phase is what we call a method in the implementation; strictly speaking, a method is the implementation of an operation.

A much deeper textual analysis than the simple 'noun vs. verb' approach is possible, but to some extent limited by the vagaries of English (Ian Graham [Graham, 1991] suggests that Chinese might be a better tool for this kind of analysis!). One problem is that, as Booch says, *'any noun can be verbed, and any verb can be nouned'* [Booch, 1994 p.160]. We might equally find the verb phrase 'to report' or the noun phrase 'a report' in a problem description referring to the same thing, so is it an object or an operation? This potential ambiguity might seem to invalidate the process entirely, but it is a useful first step in identifying candidate objects and their behaviours, perhaps to build into some initial scenarios for use with CRC cards or use-case storyboards.

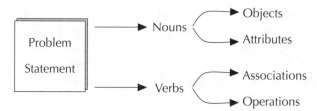

Fig. 18.3: A text analysis derives objects, attributes, associations and operations from the nouns and verbs in the problem statement.

Identifying abstractions

There are, as Booch notes, two processes in the identification of the abstractions in a system; 'discovery' and 'invention' [Booch 1994, p.162]. Discovery is the identification of objects that are found in the problem domain, perhaps referred to by domain experts and whose descriptions are part of the problem itself. In contrast, we have to invent other abstractions, those that allow us to implement the solution. We might say that we discover objects in the analysis phase and invent objects in the design phase. As we noted in the very first chapter, Stroustrup refers to 'artifacts of the implementation', objects like databases, stacks and screen managers that belong to the application rather than the problem.

What is an abstraction?

It is easy to think of objects as 'things', but of course only some of the objects in an analysis turn out to be 'things' in the real world, which is why the term 'abstraction' is perhaps rather more appropriate than 'object'.

> 'Many of the objects in an OO design do not correspond to any thing in the real world. A mouse button click is not a thing; neither is a transaction. What about a print buffer, an event dispatcher or an interaction mode?'   [Blackwell, 1993 p.30].

What we are doing is modelling behaviours of a system at different levels of abstraction, and many of these behaviours are to do with the way computers work rather than application domain objects. As we move from the initial analysis to design, we may find that the abstractions we are working with move from real world objects to user interface components (windows and other similar components, but also smaller elements of the display such as single data fields) to low level abstractions which manage or implement all the other parts of the program. These abstractions are 'invisible' to the user; they do not appear on the screen and do not persist outside the program, but at some point must be identified, either for creation or reuse from existing components. Many of these may be low level 'building blocks' (re the 'system interface layer' of Corbett's class framework described in Chapter 9) which devolve responsibility for managing object components to the components themselves.

Refining abstractions

Once an abstraction has been identified, it must be refined until its behaviours and role in the overall system have been clearly defined. Any object we identify will have to be seen in relation to other abstractions, in terms of class hierarchies, associations and aggregations. Given that some classes are abstract, and simply exist to provide generalisations of other classes, the appropriate level of abstraction must be found. A class that is too abstract may lead to large differences between it and the next level down in the hierarchy. In contrast, classes that are too specialised may lead to duplication and redundancy. In the end, the 'granularity' of abstractions (i.e. how big each class should be) is based on the best models available for high cohesion and low coupling. In addition to these two qualities (discussed in Chapter 1) we might also consider three others [Booch, 1994 p.138]:

Sufficiency: Does the abstraction do enough to be sufficient for its purpose?

Completeness: Does its interface cover enough aspects of the abstraction for it to have common usage?

Primitiveness: Do all aspects of its interface have to access the underlying representation in order to be implemented?

The optimum level for all of these characteristics is to a degree subjective. Ultimately, developers have to apply their own judgement.

Naming conventions

One important aspect of refining abstractions is to name them appropriately. As Beck & Cunningham state *'The class name of an object creates a vocabulary for discussing a design'* [Beck & Cunningham, 1989 p.2]. Clearly, if an inappropriate name is chosen then this may cause problems in understanding the role of that class in the system and in relation to other classes. This principle applies right through from the initial naming of classes to the design and implementation stages. At a lower level of detail, Booch suggests the following approach to naming all aspects of classes and objects [Booch, 1994 p.164]:

1. Name objects with proper nouns
   e.g. *the_bank_branch, the_checkout, fuel_tank,* etc.

2. Classes should be named with common nouns
   e.g. *BankAccounts, GraphicsObjects, FuelTanks,* etc.

3. Modifier methods should be named with active verbs
   e.g. *draw, fillTank, applyBrakes, setColour,* etc.

4. Selector methods should imply a query, or named with verbs of the form 'to be'
   e.g. *currentFuelLevel, isEmpty, getBalance* etc.

Following these or similar guidelines should ultimately lead to more readable code which relates easily to the design, e.g.

```
FuelTanks fuel_tank;
if(fuel_tank.isempty())
{
    fuel_tank.fillTank();
    // etc.
}
```

You might have noticed that this convention has not been entirely followed in this book in that class names are singular rather than plural. After all, you should not take everything that methodologists say as gospel!

Names are particularly important when deciding on the semantics of inheritance and aggregation. If the names of our classes in an inheritance hierarchy do not easily suit the 'is a kind of' relationship, then we need to decide if either the names or the hierarchy may be inappropriate. To suggest a simplistic example, we might have a class called 'Rectangle' inheriting from a class called 'Line'. However, the statement 'a rectangle is a kind of line' does not read too easily. Perhaps we need an intermediate class called 'Polygon', and another more abstract base class called 'GraphicsObject' from which both it and 'Line' inherit. Clearly, the appropriate model depends on the requirements of the problem, but thinking about names in this way can help to clarify the issues involved in defining abstractions.

Similarly, if an aggregation does not easily fit with an 'a part of' description, then again either the names or the structure may need revision. Relationships which have been modelled as aggregations but are better expressed as associations (or vice versa) might be revealed by such analyses. To say that 'a trailer is a part of a lorry' might appear valid, but we may find that in fact different trailers and tractors combine together at different times to make a 'Lorry' and that both tractors and trailers are objects in their own right. Again, we might need to rethink either the names of the classes, or their roles in the aggregation/association, or both.

Associations and mechanisms

Objects that do not send messages to each other cannot combine to create a useful system, so the associations that provide the routes for these messages are a crucial part of the analysis and design. Booch uses the term 'mechanisms' to describe the way that objects collaborate together to provide some high level behaviour required by the system. Without mechanisms, a software system has no organisation, so it is important that the developer is able to identify situations in which objects must collaborate. These can be analyzed via scenarios, identifying which objects collaborate in a particular process and which methods each object requires in order to do so. The UML provides us with a series of tools for this process, described in the case study that follows this chapter. Although there are some differences in emphasis between methodologists in the way that these links between objects are defined (some stressing behaviour, some stressing state), they must ultimately provide the means for objects to communicate with one another.

Summary of key points from this chapter

1. Object-oriented programs of any scale require object-oriented analysis and design.
2. Many methods exist, some stressing behaviour and some stressing state. However, they all have many common aspects.

3. The transition from analysis to design is to an extent a seamless process, but analysis is in general terms looking at the problem, and design is providing a framework for the solution.

4. Analysis methods often centre on interactions with the system, identified in domain analyses and described in scenarios and 'use cases'.

5. One of the key activities in analysis is classifying objects. A number of techniques may be applied to this process including text analysis and CRC cards.

6. Having defined abstractions (objects) we have to look at the way they interact with each other in associations and/or mechanisms.

7. As well as a static model of objects in the system, we have to model them dynamically over time to define the sequences of the messages which pass between them, and the events which change their states.

Case study: a UML design

The Unified Modelling Language (UML) is primarily the work of Rumbaugh, Booch and Jacobson who joined together in 1995 to produce a single object-oriented modelling tool. The UML version 1.0 was published in January 1997 and a subset of it is used as the basis for the notation in the case study. The process described, however, is still to some extent based on Rumbaugh's original method [Rumbaugh et al, 1991].

This case study is intended to convey some of the basic steps involved in an object-oriented analysis, design and implementation. It is, of necessity, extremely simplistic, but allows us to work through some of the key stages in the analysis and design cycle. The scenario is based on a rather simplified electronic course prospectus system. A few sample stages of the design process are demonstrated, though this is not intended to be a full lifecycle and many design elements are not included.

The initial problem statement

We might assume that the initial problem statement has been derived from some kind of domain analysis involving interviews with domain experts and end users. As it stands, it contains relatively little detail but provides us with a basis for some initial analysis.

As part of the college's I.T. strategy, the 'electronic prospectus' is intended to provide a means of viewing course information for staff, students and managers.

Courses at the college comprise a number of units at two levels, with students normally taking level one units in the first year of their course and progressing level two units in the second. Part time students may take two or more years to complete all their units at a given level. Level one units are assessed on course work grades, but level two units are assessed with examinations. Some courses also include a compulsory foundation unit where particular technical skills need to be established.

The system will provide lists of lecturers, courses and units, and access to more detailed information about which units are taught on which courses. Individual lecturer records may be queried for information such as their office room number, e-mail address and subject specialisms, as well as reporting the units that a lecturer teaches. Each course in the prospectus can be identified by a unique course code, and consists of a number of units at each level. Every course has one lecturer acting as course leader, who is responsible for administering that course and updating unit descriptions. Management functions of the prospectus allow lecturers and courses to be added to or removed from the system.

Use cases

In order to determine the system boundaries and high level requirements for the system, a use case diagram is drawn to show the actors in the system and the general services they require. Use cases come originally from the work of Jacobsen who is one of the three authors of the UML.

A use case diagram shows the 'actors' as stick people, and the services as ellipses. In this simple system the actors are managers, lecturers, course leaders and students. The services of the system come into three general types, 'view prospectus', 'modify prospectus' and 'update unit descriptions'. All actors may view the prospectus but only managers are able to generally modify it. Lecturers in the role of course leaders can update unit descriptions. Fig. CS.1 shows the use case diagram.

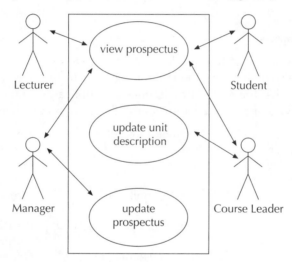

Fig. CS.1: A use case diagram showing the actors, use cases and system boundary.

Textual analysis

In a larger system, each use case would be modelled in detail to provide a number of textual descriptions of the system before attempting a text analysis. For a small example like this, however, the whole system can be generally described in one document. We might therefore usefully do a textual analysis of the problem statement to identify candidate objects, associations, operations and attributes. In order to find candidate objects, we look for nouns (or noun phrases) in the problem statement. A noun phrase may be a name consisting of more than one word, or a noun preceded by a verb or adjective such as 'electronic prospectus' in the problem statement.

Identifying nouns as candidate objects

At this point, all the nouns and noun phrases are underlined. This is a largely mechanical process, where we are not trying to make value judgements about whether or not these nouns are likely to be useful object classes in the system:

As part of the <u>college's I.T. strategy</u>, the '<u>electronic prospectus</u>' is intended to provide <u>a</u> <u>means</u> of viewing <u>course information</u> for <u>staff</u>, <u>students</u> and <u>managers</u>.

<u>Courses</u> at the <u>college</u> comprise a number of <u>units</u> at two <u>levels</u>, with <u>students</u> normally taking <u>level one units</u> in the <u>first year</u> of their <u>course</u> and progressing <u>level two units</u> in the <u>second</u>. <u>Part time students</u> may take two or more <u>years</u> to complete all their <u>units</u> at a given <u>level</u>. <u>Level one units</u> are assessed on <u>course work grades</u>, but <u>level two units</u> are assessed with <u>examinations</u>. Some <u>courses</u> also include a <u>compulsory foundation unit</u> where <u>particular technical skills</u> need to be established.

The <u>system</u> will provide <u>lists</u> of <u>lecturers</u>, <u>courses</u> and <u>units</u>, and access to more detailed <u>information</u> about which <u>units</u> are taught on which <u>courses</u>. <u>Individual lecturer records</u> may be queried for <u>information</u> such as their <u>office room number</u>, <u>e-mail address</u> and <u>subject specialisms</u>, as well as reporting the <u>units</u> that a <u>lecturer</u> teaches. Each <u>course</u> in the <u>prospectus</u> can be identified by a <u>unique course code</u>, and consists of a number of <u>units</u> at each <u>level</u>. Every <u>course</u> has one <u>lecturer</u> acting as <u>course leader</u>, who is responsible for administering that <u>course</u> and updating <u>unit descriptions</u>. <u>Management functions</u> of the <u>prospectus</u> allow <u>lecturers</u> and <u>courses</u> to be added to or removed from the <u>system</u>.

List of candidate objects

From our initial analysis of the problem statement, we have a set of nouns and noun phrases which may or may not be suitable objects. In order to examine them more closely, we simply list them all, but eliminate all duplications and plurals. We do not, after all, need to write 'prospectus' four times! The list of nouns then looks like this:

College's I.T. strategy	Electronic Prospectus	Means
Course information	Staff	Student
Manager	Course	College
Unit	Level	Level one unit
First year	Level two unit	Second (year)
Part time student	Year	Course work grade
Examination	Compulsory foundation unit	Particular technical skills
System	List	Lecturer
Information	Individual lecturer records	Office room number
E-mail address	Subject specialism	Unique course code
Course leader	Unit description	Management function

Eliminate inappropriate candidate objects

Given that a number of our nouns will not necessarily be appropriate object classes, we must examine each in turn to see whether or not it should be modelled as a class. Rumbaugh [Rumbaugh et al, 1991, pp.153-4] suggests a set of criteria for candidate objects which should be eliminated from the list, as follows:

Redundant classes Where two words mean the same thing, choose the more descriptive.

Irrelevant classes Those which have nothing directly to do with the problem.

Vague classes If classes are not specific enough, they need to be more closely defined before they can be used.

Attributes	Since attributes are described by nouns, we are likely to find a number of nouns in our list which are in fact attributes of other objects.
Operations	Some nouns are in fact the names of dynamic processes which may be operations rather than objects in their own right.
Roles	Role names are appropriate to the way in which objects interact, but are not good names for objects.
Implementation constructs	Any object that is an artifact of the implementation (i.e. is part of the intended system rather than the problem) should be discarded, or perhaps renamed. Anything which refers to a data structure for instance is part of the implementation, but may be replaced by the name of an object which is being represented by that data structure.

We should also eliminate the 'actors' i.e. roles which interact with the system but are not part of it. These will be important in terms of sending messages to objects, but are not themselves objects. It is important to note that 'Lecturer', although an actor, is also an object within the system (e.g. a lecturer can view lecturer details).

Eliminated candidate objects

Our lists of candidate objects contains some which may be eliminated on the following grounds:

College's I.T. strategy	External to the scope of the given problem.
Means	Too vague, a general term for the system itself.
Course information	Too vague, but specified later.
Staff	This is a redundant class, because the staff referred to are in fact lecturers, which is a more descriptive name.
Student, part time student	Irrelevant classes. Students are clients of the system but are not part of it.
Manager	An 'actor', outside the system but interacting with it.
College	Irrelevant. The college is the client, not part of the system.
Level	Redundant in the sense that the more specific 'level one unit' and level two unit' also appear in the list of candidate classes.
First year, second (year)	Redundant. Synonymous in practice with levels one and two.
Course work grade, examination	Relate to attributes of level one and two units.
Particular technical skills	Vague, but implies a set of attributes relating to the foundation unit.
System	This is a redundant class, because it refers to '(electronic) prospectus', which is a more descriptive name.
List	List of lecturers etc. may appear to be a noun phrase, but on closer inspection is a verb phrase. Operations that can provide these lists should become apparent at the dynamic modelling stage.
Information	Too vague, but clarified in the rest of the sentence as a set of attributes specific to lecturers.
Individual lecturer record	An implementation construct. From the point of view of the analysis, it is the same as a 'Lecturer' object.

Office room number *E-mail address* *Subject specialism*	} All attributes of a 'Lecturer'.
Unique course code	An attribute of courses. May also be used to qualify an association in the implementation.
Course leader	A role played by a 'Lecturer'.
Unit description	An attribute of a unit.
Management function	Operations described later in the sentence.

Revised list of candidate objects

Our revised list of candidate objects is shown below. By enclosing them in rectangles, we are providing the first element of the class diagram. As we know, each object class is represented in the UML by a divided rectangle showing the class name, attributes and methods. Having established the names of classes, the attributes and methods may be added later.

Prospectus	Course	Unit

Level one unit	Level two unit	Foundation unit

Lecturer

The data dictionary

Having established a set of classes, we should begin to maintain a data dictionary which describes each class. A data dictionary is simply a textual definition of classes, which may include such details as scope, associations, attributes and operations. These are continually developed throughout the analysis and design process. An example data dictionary entry for the 'Lecturer' object might appear as follows:

> *Lecturer* A lecturer teaches a number of units and may act as a course leader. Lecturer attributes include office room number, e-mail address and subject specialisms.

This initial entry will become more closely defined as the object's role in the system is further investigated.

Identifying associations

An association occurs where classes depend on, or refer to, one another. Associations are important because they define the routes for message passing between objects, and therefore relate to the operations which objects must have to meet their responsibilities. We can derive a candidate list of associations by identifying verbs and verb phrases in the problem statement, although this is often less clear cut than identifying nouns. Since we already have an idea of which objects we are interested in, it is relatively easy to spot phrases that refer to these objects, and might therefore be associations (including aggregations):

> *'Courses...comprise a number of units'*
> *'Some courses also include a compulsory foundation unit'*

'The system will provide lists of lecturers, courses and units'
'units are taught on...courses'
'units...a lecturer teaches'
'Every course has one lecturer acting as course leader'
'course leader...is responsible for...updating unit descriptions'
'lecturers and courses...added to or removed from the system.'

From this list, we can see that courses have an aggregation relationship with units and foundation units. Lecturers associate with units, and some also associate with courses as course leaders. Some verb phrases are actions rather than associations, such as providing lists, updating unit descriptions and adding/removing items. These action phrases will be operations on the class diagram.

Adding associations to the class diagram

These associations can now be added to the class diagram. Each association is represented by a line between the objects involved, and should be named appropriately. If roles can be defined for the objects, they should also appear on the association, near the object to which that role name applies. In this example, the lecturer class has the role 'leader' in its association with the course class.

All associations should describe their multiplicity (i.e. the number of objects involved in an association). The notation for multiplicity between classes in the UML is shown in Fig. CS.2. See also Fig. 9.1. Some associations describe aggregation, in which case the 'diamond' notation is used, but multiplicity should be shown both for ordinary associations and for aggregations.

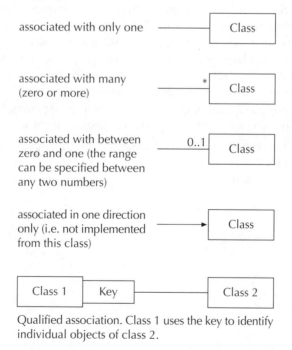

associated with only one — Class

associated with many
(zero or more) —* Class

associated with between
zero and one (the range
can be specified between
any two numbers) 0..1 Class

associated in one direction
only (i.e. not implemented
from this class) → Class

Class 1 | Key — Class 2

Qualified association. Class 1 uses the key to identify
individual objects of class 2.

**Fig. CS.2: The notation for multiplicity in the UML.
This notation is used for object associations.**

If an association has a 'many' side in terms of its multiplicity, then there may be an appropriate way of specifying how each individual object can be identified. If this is the case, then it is known as a 'qualified association', and is denoted by an appropriate identifer enclosed in a box applied to the object that uses the identifier (also shown in Fig. CS.2). In the example, courses have unique course codes that allow them to be referenced by the prospectus.

Identifying attributes

We already have a few attributes from the problem statement, and some others may be fairly obvious from our knowledge of the problem domain. However, we should not place too much stress on finding attributes at this stage, since they exist largely to support object behaviours, not vice versa. Some attributes are known as 'derived attributes' because their values may be derived from other attributes. A simple example of this might be the number of units on a particular course, which may be derived by counting the number of associated 'Unit' objects. Other attributes may be 'link attributes', those that are properties of a link between objects rather than properties of the objects themselves. Although there are no link attributes specified in the text description of the system, it might be appropriate to consider a more detailed system where part time lecturers are contracted to teach particular units. An 'hourly pay rate' might then be modelled as a link attribute between objects of the 'Lecturer' and 'Unit' classes, since it would not be appropriate to make it a permanent attribute of either of the two classes.

Refining with inheritance

By looking at the classes in our system, we may find examples where generalisation or specialisation is possible. In our scenario, there are clearly similarities between level one units and level two units. Whether a level two unit is a specialised type of level one unit, or whether level one and level two units are derived types of 'unit' depends largely on a closer investigation of the features of the two types of unit. In the example, we will model both as derived classes of an abstract 'unit' on the rather arbitrary assumption that their assessment mechanisms constitute different behaviours. In reality we would need to look a bit more closely at the requirements before leaping to this conclusion!

Fig. CS.3 shows the class diagram with associations (including an aggregation) and inheritance shown for types of unit. Attributes and operations already identified in the text analysis are also shown.

#36   09-13-2009 2:10PM
Item(s) checked out to Shriver, Edward L

TITLE: The UNIX programming environment
BARCODE: 35150002045708
DUE DATE: 10-04-09

Waynesburg University
Eberly Library   (724) 852-3278

#36   09-13-2009 2:10PM
Item(s) checked out to Shriver, Edward L

TITLE: Object-oriented programming with
BARCODE: 35150002289868
DUE DATE: 10-04-09

Waynesburg University
Eberly Library   (724) 852-3278

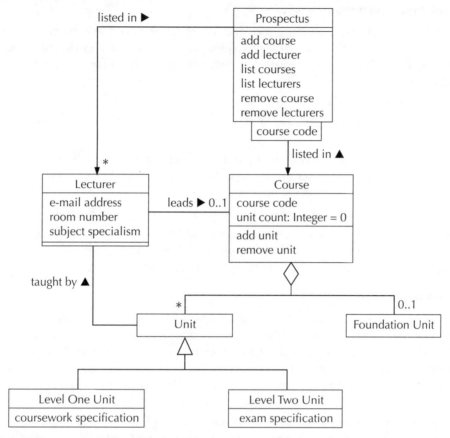

Fig. CS.3: The class diagram showing associations and their multiplicity, also aggregations, inheritance and some attributes and operations.

Dynamic modelling

The class diagram gives us a static view of the classes in the system and the relationships between them, but does not give us any information about how the system behaves dynamically, i.e. what happens over time as the system runs. Four types of 'behaviour diagram' are available for dynamic modelling in the UML, but we do not necessarily need to use all of them in a given design. The diagrams are:

- *sequence diagrams*
- *collaboration diagrams*
- *state diagrams*
- *activity diagrams*

Sequence diagrams and collaboration diagrams are different ways of showing the messages that pass between objects over time. State diagrams show how objects of a class change state in response to events. Activity diagrams are similar, but more appropriate to systems (like vending machines) that change state as a result of internal processes rather than external events. These diagrams are drawn in conjunction with the existing use cases to design dynamic processes and refine the class diagram.

Use cases and operations

Having identified objects, associations and attributes, we need to determine the behaviours of the objects in the system by examining what happens to them in various use case contexts. The following sequence of events can be used in constructing a dynamic model:

1. Take a single use case.
2. Prepare text based scenarios of typical interactions with their possible alternate flows.
3. Draw sequence and/or collaboration diagrams for the use case. Sequence diagrams are better able to represent more complex scenarios, while collaboration diagrams more closely reflect the class diagram.
4. Draw/update state diagrams for any classes with complex behaviours.

This process, repeated for each use case, should highlight the required behaviours of objects, and therefore the operations to appear on the class diagram. It also assists us in designing the processes involved in implementing a given use case.

Modelling a use case

Each use case has an associated text description of the possible events that take place, including the 'alternate flows' (different events that depend on different circumstances). Use case scenarios are simple dialogues between users and the system, defined as a sequence of events. We should start with the 'normal' scenario, then move on to more exceptional cases such as error conditions. The following scenario is a simple 'normal' case of a manager adding a course to the prospectus:

> The prospectus creates a new course, and asks the manager to enter a code and name for the course. The prospectus then asks for the identity of the course leader to be selected by the manager from a list of existing lecturers. The prospectus assigns the course to the course leader and then a number of units are created and added to the course. For each unit the manager enters the unit description and the prospectus assigns the unit to the course. The process ends when the required number of units has been created and added to the course.

Alternate flows may then be added to show different sequences of events, such as:

> alternate flow:
> The manager enters a course code that is already in the system. The manager is asked if s/he wishes to enter a different code before continuing or to abort the operation.

Similar alternate flows might be added where other constraints are breached, such as providing the wrong number of units for a course, or assigning too many course leadership roles to a particular lecturer (these are not stated in the text description, but there would no doubt be many practical constraints to build into the system.) After describing a number of scenarios, we can summarise this information on one or more sequence diagrams showing all the messages being passed between the objects. Fig. CS.4 shows a sequence diagram for this use case, describing the 'normal' flow of events. The objects appear along one axis of the diagram and the time sequence along the other. A dotted line shows where an object is in existence, becoming a bar where the object has focus of control. Objects created during the process (course and units) appear at the point where they are created. Messages are shown as arrows from one object (or actor) to another.

To show the alternate flows, either the same diagram could be expanded or other sequence diagrams could be drawn. Notice that the 'Prospectus' class takes the role of a 'controller'; a class that manages the control interface between the user and the other objects in the system, not unlike the 'Hotel' object in the example program that follows Chapter 9.

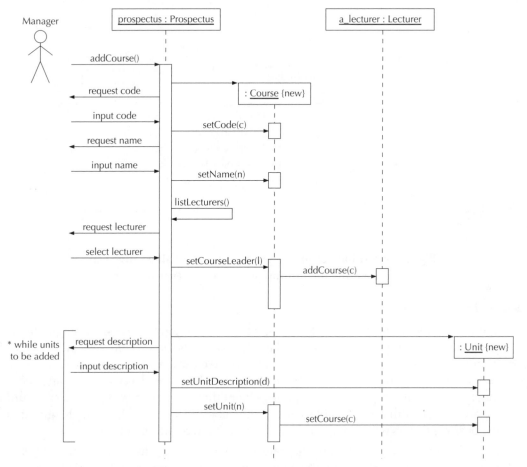

Fig. CS.4: A sequence diagram showing the messages passing between objects in the system.

An alternative diagram is the collaboration diagram, which also shows the messages passed between the objects in the system but relates more closely to the class diagram (Fig. CS.5). Messages are numbered to show the sequence of events, using 'nested' numbers to show where some events are components of more general events (e.g. the events that together make up 'create unit'). To simplify this diagram, the interaction with the 'actor' is not shown, but it otherwise mirrors the sequence diagram.

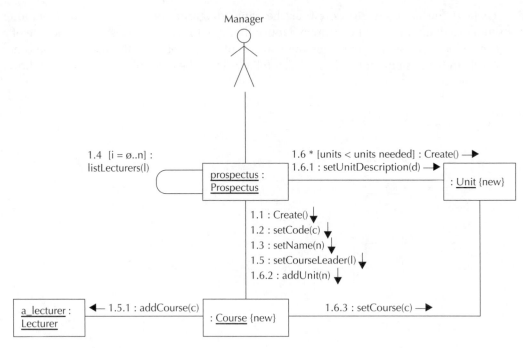

**Fig. CS.5: A collaboration diagram provides an alternative way
of representing the information on a sequence diagram.**

State diagrams

Unlike the other dynamic modelling diagrams, a state diagram refers to a single class. A state diagram is only necessary where the behaviour of objects is complex, and is derived from the events that refer to objects of that class. We can start with one use case, extract all the events in it that affect our object, and define how the object's state is affected by those events. We can continue this process by adding in more and more use cases until we are confident that all possible states for the object have been defined, along with all the possible events which may cause a transition between different states.

Fig. CS.6 shows a partial state diagram for the 'Course' class. States are shown as rounded rectangles, containing the name of the state and any operations that take place in that state. Transitions from one state to another are shown as arrows, labelled with the events that trigger the transition. In this example, the course is assumed to be in a state of initialisation until the minimum set of information is provided, namely a course code, a name, and a course leader. Once this information is entered, there is an automatic transition to the 'adding units' state. This does not have to be labelled since there is no external event triggering the transition. The course is then 'adding units' state until the condition 'units added = units required' is met. The number of units in a particular course is the kind of information that one would expect to be readily available at the analysis stage. Each time a unit is added a message has to be sent from the course object to create a new unit object (hence the 'send create unit' label). Once all the necessary units have been added the course moves to its 'fully defined' state until it is eventually closed.

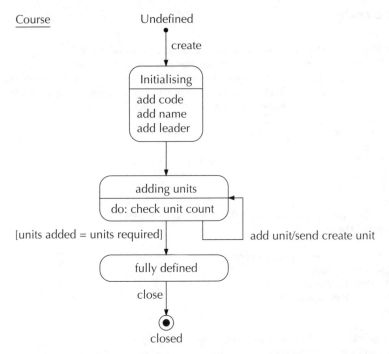

Fig. CS.6: A state diagram shows all the possible states, events and transitions for objects of a single class. This one is for the 'Course' class.

Implementation

Having described the structure of classes and how they behave, we need to move from analysis and design to implementation of their inner workings; turn operations into methods. The general approach is that we can apply use cases to the point where the methods are easily implementable. Actors do not have to be external to the system; they can be objects within the system itself. This means that a high level use case may send a message to an object that in turn sends messages to other objects that are described in a lower level use case. Once object interaction has been described, then it is up to the programmer to apply the appropriate algorithms to provide the required object behaviours. At an implementation level many other types of non-application object can come into play here, such as container classes and predefined algorithm objects.

From the class diagram and the dynamic modelling we have done so far, we can write the outline C++ classes for the system, model their associations using pointers and arrays and add some attributes and methods. Our dynamic modelling so far has described the 'addCourse' method of the 'Prospectus' class, so a 'quick and dirty' implementation is provided here, supported by some other methods in other classes (mainly 'get' and 'set' methods). Although a number of short cuts are taken here to keep the code short and simple, you should be able to see the relationship between the class diagram and the class definitions in the code, and also the relationship between the 'addCourse' method and the dynamic modelling diagrams.

C++ source code

```
/*
        HEADERS.H   Contains skeletons for the classes 'Lecturer', 'Unit',
                    'LevelOneUnit', 'LevelTwoUnit' and 'FoundationUnit'
                    This file contains the skeletons of classes that so far have very little
                    implementation. As they are developed, they will be separated out
                    into separate header and method files.
*/
// forward declaration to enable 'Lecturer' to compile
class Course;
// at this stage, no methods are implemented for the lecturer class
class Lecturer
{
public:
// association with up to 2 courses in the role of course leader
    Course* leader_of[2];
private:
// the attributes identified in the text analysis
    char* email_address;
    int room_number;
    char* subject_specialism;
public:
};
// the 'Unit' class has the very basic functionality of being able
// to get and set its description
class Unit
{
private:
// association with the lecturer who teaches the unit
    Lecturer* taught_by;
// the description attribute
    char* unit_description;
public:
// get and set methods
    void setUnitDescription(char*);
    char* getUnitDescription();
};
// the other unit classes are at this stage totally undeveloped
class LevelOneUnit : public Unit
{
private:
    char* coursework_specification;
public:
};
class LevelTwoUnit : public Unit
{
private:
    char* exam_specification;
public:
};
class FoundationUnit
{};
/*
        UNIT.CPP        method definitions for the 'Unit' class
*/
#include "headers.h"
#include <string.h>
```

```
// set the description using a parameter
void Unit::setUnitDescription(char* description)
{
    int len = strlen(description) + 1;
    unit_description = new char[len];
    strcpy(unit_description, description);
}
// return the description
char* Unit::getUnitDescription()
{
    return unit_description;
}
/*
    COURSE.H    class definition for the 'Course' class
                The course class has been developed enough for it to follow some of the
                processes described in the state diagram. We can set some of its attributes
                and add units to it. 'listUnits' is just for testing at this stage, and
                might well be replaced later by more flexible methods
*/
#include "headers.h"
class Course
{
private:
// a course may associate with a foundation unit
    FoundationUnit* foundation;
// it will associate with a number of units
    Unit* units[20];
// it also has an association with a lecturer acting as course leader
    Lecturer* course_leader;
// attributes
    int course_code;
    char* course_name;
    int unit_count;
    int units_required;
public:
    Course(int);
    void setCourseCode(int code);
    void setCourseName(char* name);
    void setCourseLeader(Lecturer* lect);
    int getCourseCode();
    char* getCourseName();
    Lecturer* getCourseLeader();
    void addUnit(Unit* unit);        // not implemented yet
    void removeUnit(Unit* unit);     // not implemented yet
    void listUnits();
};
/*
    COURSE.CPPmethod definitions for the 'Course' class
*/
#include "course.h"
#include <string.h>
#include <iostream.h>
// constructor
// although the 'units_required' attribute is set to allow the condition
// on the state diagram to be implemented, it is not actually used in the
// simplified methods provided here
Course::Course(int required)
{
```

```
    units_required = required;
    unit_count = 0;
    course_leader = NULL;
}
// straightforward 'set' methods
void Course::setCourseCode(int code)
{
    course_code = code;
}
void Course::setCourseName(char* name)
{
    int len = strlen(name) + 1;
    course_name = new char[len];
    strcpy(course_name, name);
}
void Course::setCourseLeader(Lecturer* leader)
{
    course_leader = leader;
}
// 'get' methods
int Course::getCourseCode()
{
    return course_code;
}
char* Course::getCourseName()
{
    return course_name;
}
Lecturer* Course::getCourseLeader()
{
    return course_leader;
}
// this method implements the aggregation relationship between
// courses and units
void Course::addUnit(Unit* add_unit)
{
    units[unit_count] = add_unit;
    unit_count++;
}
// this is useful for testing during development. later on we would probably
// be better off removing interface methods like this and replacing them with
// iterators that return the necessary data to separate interface objects
void Course::listUnits()
{
    cout << "Unit descriptions:" << endl;
    for(int i = 0; i < unit_count; i++)
    {
        cout << units[i] -> getUnitDescription() << endl;
    }
}
/*
    PROSPECT.H Class definition for the 'Prospectus' class
*/
#include "course.h"
// 'Prospectus' has two methods ('addCourse' and 'listCourses') implemented
// at a basically functional level.
class Prospectus
{
```

```
private:
// associations with courses and lecturers
    Course* courses[50];
    Lecturer* lecturers[50];
// attributes
    int course_count;
    int lecturer_count;
public:
    Prospectus();
    void addCourse();
    void addLecturer();   // not implemented yet
    void listCourses();
    void removeCourse();    // not implemented yet
    void removeLecturer();  // not implemented yet
};
/*
    PROSPECT.CPP  Method definitions for the 'Prospectus' class
*/
#include "prospect.h"
#include <string.h>
#include <iostream.h>
Prospectus::Prospectus()
{
    course_count = 0;
    lecturer_count = 0;
}
// this method cuts a few corners but demonstrates that a course can be
// created and units added to it. It matches (with some details fudged) the
// sequence and collaboration diagrams in the dynamic model
void Prospectus::addCourse()
{
// local variables for input
    int temp;
    char buffer[160];
// the constructor here hard codes a small number of required units
// this could be done more flexibly
    courses[course_count] = new Course(5);
    cout << "Enter course code ";
    cin >> temp;
    courses[course_count] -> setCourseCode(temp);
    cout << "Enter course name ";
    cin >> buffer;
    courses[course_count] -> setCourseName(buffer);
// this is a complete fudge because we have not yet implemented
// the 'addLecturer' method! Instead, we hard code in a lecturer object
    Lecturer* lect = new Lecturer;
    courses[course_count] -> setCourseLeader(lect);
// now we add some units
    for(int i = 0; i < 5; i++)
    {
        cout << "Enter unit description ";
// to input some text with embedded spaces, clear the input stream
// and then get the data using two versions of the 'get' method
// (see Chapter 17)
        char ch;
        cin.get(ch);
        cin.get(buffer, 160);
// create a new unit, give it a description and add it to the course
```

357

```
            Unit* temp_unit = new Unit;
            temp_unit -> setUnitDescription(buffer);
            courses[course_count] -> addUnit(temp_unit);
        }
// increment the course count ready for the next one
        course_count++;
}
// 'listCourses' displays a limited set of information to prove
// the system has some functionality
void Prospectus::listCourses()
{
    for(int i = 0; i < course_count; i++)
    {
        cout << "Course code: " << courses[i] -> getCourseCode() << endl;
        cout << "Course name: " << courses[i] -> getCourseName() << endl;
        courses[i] -> listUnits();
    }
}
/*
    TESTMAIN.CPP   This 'main' is purely a test of the two prospectus
                   methods implemented so far. One useful exercise would be to
                   build a proper interface object to interact with the user
                   and remove all keyboard and screen i/o operations from the
                   application objects.
*/
#include "prospect.h"
void main()
{
// create a prospectus
    Prospectus prospectus;
// add a course to it
    prospectus.addCourse();
// display the results
    prospectus.listCourses();
}
```

This is an interactive run from the test program:

Enter course code 100
Enter course name Computing
Enter unit description maths for computing
Enter unit description assembly language
Enter unit description object-oriented analysis and design
Enter unit description programming with C++
Enter unit description knitting patterns
Course code: 100
Course name: Computing
Unit descriptions:
maths for computing
assembly language
object-oriented analysis and design
programming with C++
knitting patterns

Continuing the process

What we have seen so far has been a single brief iteration through the cycle of analysis, design and implementation, which needs to be followed by many other iterations before the program is complete. It is beyond the scope of this book to attempt to describe a full analysis, design and implementation cycle or to fully explain the UML notation. The reader is advised to refer to the appropriate books by the various developers of the methodology, and check the UML web site at *www.rational.com*.

At this stage we have introduced some of the elements of object-oriented analysis and design and outlined a simple example using a single notation. Hopefully this will have given a general impression of the issues involved and put the preceding chapters on programming into a wider context.

Exercise

Continue the design process and implement further methods for the classes. Consider object persistence in your system and add appropriate functionality to stream objects to and from disk.

Appendix: answers to exercises

Chapter 3 Part 1

Exercise 1

```
/*
        C3P1_EX1.CPP   Chapter 3, part 1, exercise 1
*/
#include <iostream.h>
void main()
{
    int x = 1;
    x++;
    x *= 5;
    int y = --x;
    cout << "x = " << x << endl << "y = " << y << endl;
}
```

Exercise 2

```
/*
        C3P1_EX2.CPP   Chapter 3, part 1, exercise 2
        This program uses the escape sequence character \"
        to embed speech marks inside a string of characters
*/
#include <iostream.h>
void main()
{
    cout << "C++ is an \"Object-Oriented\" language";
}
```

Exercise 3

```
/*
        C3P1_EX3.CPP   Chapter 3, part 1, exercise 3
*/
// the 'pass by value' version of the square function
int Square1(int value_in)
{
    return value_in * value_in;
}
// the 'pass by reference' version
void Square2(int& value_in)
{
    value_in *= value_in;
}
#include <iostream.h>
// 'main' calls both versions in turn
void main()
{
// declare and initialise an integer variable
    int x = 4;
// square it using the 'pass by value' function. Because it returns
// a value it can be placed directly in a 'cout' statement
    cout << "Square by value = " << Square1(x) << endl;
```

```
// the 'pass by reference' version does not return a value.
// it operates directly on the parameter argument
    Square2(x);
// 'x' has now been changed by the function
    cout << "Square by reference = " << x << endl;
}
```

Chapter 3 Part 2

Exercise 1

```
/*
    C3P2_EX1.CPP    Chapter 3, part 2, exercise 1
                    This program sorts an array of integers
*/
// the 'swap' function is as it appears in the text, using
// 'pass by reference' to swap the parameters
void swap (int& first, int& second)
{
    int temp;
    temp = first;
    first = second;
    second = temp;
}
// a constant is declared to size the array
const int SIZE = 10;
#include <iostream.h>
// 'main' sorts the array and displays the result
void main()
{
// the array is declared with an unordered collection of integers
    int sort_array[SIZE] = { 8, 23, 4, 7, 33, 1, 8, 9, 55, 100 };
// the classic 'bubble sort' algorithm (slow but simple!) is used
// to sort the array into order
    for(int i = 0; i < SIZE-1; i++)
    {
        for(int j = 0; j < SIZE-1; j++)
        {
// if this pair of numbers is in the wrong order, call the 'swap' function
            if(sort_array[j] < sort_array[j+1])
            {
                swap(sort_array[j], sort_array[j+1]);
            }
        }
    }
// the sorted array is displayed
    for(i = 0; i < SIZE; i++)
    {
        cout << sort_array[i] << ", ";
    }
    cout << endl;
}
```

Chapter 4

Exercise 1

The suggested attributes and methods for the 'coffee cup' abstract data type are as follows:

Coffee Cup
colour
temperature
fill level
manufacture
fill
drink from
carry
wash
break

Note the relationships between certain attributes and methods – the attribute 'fill level' for example is affected by the modifier methods 'drink from' and 'fill'.

As well as the above which appear in the text, we might add 'position' as an attribute, since it relates to the 'carry' method – i.e. when the cup is carried its position changes. Perhaps 'cleanliness' could be added to relate to the 'wash' method.

'Manufacture' and 'break' are special methods which define the beginning and the end of an object's existence, and will be investigated in later chapters. A method which creates an object is known as a 'constructor', and a method which destroys an object is known as a 'destructor'.

Exercise 2

The wallet / purse abstract data type might look like this:

Wallet/Purse
cash
credit cards
count cash
take out cash
put in cash
use credit card

There may be lots of other things in yours! The interesting thing about this example is the way in which cash and credit cards may be handled. For example, are we only going to count our credit cards, or do we need more complex attributes and methods which allow us to see what credit cards we have and choose to use a particular one. In a programming context, such questions raise issues of what internal data structures are required to adequately provide an object's behaviour.

Exercise 3

```
/*
    C4_EX3.H       Chapter 4, exercise 3
                   ('Person' class and methods)
*/
#include <string.h>   // for 'strncpy'
class Person
{
private:
    char name[20];
    int year_of_birth;
    float height_in_metres;
public:
// simple 'set' methods
    void setName(char* name_in);
    void setBirth(int year_in);
    void setHeight(float height_in);
// simple 'get' methods
    char* getName();
    int getBirthYear();
    float getHeight();
// more interesting methods to return 'derived attributes'
    int getAge(int current_year);
    float getHeightInCM();
};
// 'set' methods
void Person::setName(char* name_in)
{
    strncpy(name, name_in, 19);
    name[19] = '\0';
}
void Person::setBirth(int year_in)
{
    year_of_birth = year_in;
}
void Person::setHeight(float height_in)
{
    height_in_metres = height_in;
}
// 'get' methods
char* Person::getName()
{
    return name;
}
int Person::getBirthYear()
{
    return year_of_birth;
}
float Person::getHeight()
{
    return height_in_metres;
}
// 'getAge' returns the approximate age by subtracting the year of birth
// attribute from the parameter and returning the result
int Person::getAge(int current_year)
{
    return current_year - year_of_birth;
```

```
    }
    // 'getHeightInCM' multiplies the height in metres by 100 to get
    // the appropriate return value
    float Person::getHeightInCM()
    {
        return height_in_metres * 100;
    }
```

Chapter 5

Exercise 1

In this example, we assume that 'bankacct.h' contains the definition for the parameterised constructor as described on page 73.

```
/*
        C5_EX1.CPP  Chapter 5, exercise 1
                        (test the parameterised constructor and copy constructor)
*/
#include <iostream.h>
#include "bankacct.h"
void main()
{
// instantiate a BankAccount object with a parameter (start balance)
    BankAccount account1(50.00);
// set its attributes
    account1.setAccountHolder("Fred");
    account1.setAccountNumber(2);
// test the copy constructor
    BankAccount account2 = account1;
    cout << "Holder: " << account2.getAccountHolder() << endl;
    cout << "Number: " << account2.getAccountNumber() << endl;
    cout << "Balance: " << account2.getCurrentBalance() << endl;
}
```

Exercise 2

```
/*
        C5_EX2.CPP  Chapter 5, exercise 2
                        (testing the methods of 'BankAccount')
*/
#include <iostream.h>
#include "bankacct.h"
void main()
{
    BankAccount account1(0.00), account2(0.00), account3(100.00);
    account1.setAccountNumber(1);
    account2.setAccountNumber(2);
    account3.setAccountNumber(3);
    account1.setAccountHolder("Tom");
    account2.setAccountHolder("Dick");
    account3.setAccountHolder("Harry");
    account1.deposit(50.00);
    account2.deposit(75.00);
    account3.withdrawal(75.00);
    cout << "Details of Accounts" << endl;
    cout << "_____" << endl << endl;
    cout << "Holder: " << account1.getAccountHolder() << endl;
```

```
        cout << "Number: " << account1.getAccountNumber() << endl;
        cout << "Balance: " << account1.getCurrentBalance() << endl << endl;
        cout << "Holder: " << account2.getAccountHolder() << endl;
        cout << "Number: " << account2.getAccountNumber() << endl;
        cout << "Balance: " << account2.getCurrentBalance() << endl << endl;
        cout << "Holder: " << account3.getAccountHolder() << endl;
        cout << "Number: " << account3.getAccountNumber() << endl;
        cout << "Balance: " << account3.getCurrentBalance() << endl;
    }
```

Chapter 6

Exercise 1

```
/*
        C6_EX1.CPP  Chapter 6, exercise 1
                        (convert program on page 98 to dynamic object syntax)
*/
#include <iostream.h>
#include "bankacct.h"
void main()
{
// the bank account is created using a pointer and the 'new' operator
    BankAccount* an_account = new BankAccount;
// the arrow operator is used to send messages to a dynamic object
    an_account ->setAccountNumber(100);
    cout << an_account -> getAccountNumber();
// dynamic objects should be deleted when no longer needed
    delete an_account;
}
```

Exercise 2

This example shows the BankAccount pointers being passed by reference, though they could also be passed by value and de-referenced.

```
/*
        C6_EX2.CPP  Chapter 6, exercise 2
                        (swapping dynamic objects by reference)
*/
#include <iostream.h>
#include "bankacct.h"
// the 'swap' function passes the pointers by reference
void swap (BankAccount* &first, BankAccount* &second)
{
    BankAccount* temp;
    temp = first;
    first = second;
    second = temp;
}
// in 'main', two dynamic bank accounts are swapped
void main()
{
// create the bank accounts
    BankAccount* account_pointer1 = new BankAccount;
    BankAccount* account_pointer2 = new BankAccount;
    account_pointer1 -> setAccountNumber(1);
    account_pointer2 -> setAccountNumber(2);
```

```
    // call the 'swap' function
        swap(account_pointer1, account_pointer2);
    // display the account numbers to show the objects have been swapped
        cout << "Number of first account: " << account_pointer1 -> getAccountNumber()
        << endl;
        cout << "Number of second account: " << account_pointer2 ->
    getAccountNumber() << endl;
    }
```

Exercise 3

```
    /*
        C6_EX3.CPP   Chapter 6, exercise 3
                     (declare and initialise an array of BankAccount pointers)
    */
    #include "bankacct.h"
    void main()
    {
    // declare an array of 20 pointers to 'BankAccount'
        BankAccount* accounts[20];
    // initialise all the pointers to NULL
        for(int i = 0; i < 20; i++)
        {
            accounts[i] = NULL;
        }
    }
```

Chapter 7

Exercise 1

```
    /*
        C7_EX1.H     Chapter 7 exercise 1
                     (class attributes and methods for the 'Object' class)
    */
    // the class has two class attributes and two class methods
    class Object
    {
    private:
        static int object_count;
        static char class_name[10];
    public:
        Object();
        static int getObjectCount();
        static char* getClassName();
    };
    // reserve memory for the class attributes.
    // the default for 'object_count' will be zero
    int Object::object_count;
    char Object::class_name[] = "Object";
    // the constructor increments the count by one
    Object::Object()
    {
        object_count++;
    }
    // the two 'get' methods return the attributes
    int Object::getObjectCount()
```

```
    {
        return object_count;
    }
    char* Object::getClassName()
    {
        return class_name;
    }
```

Exercise 2

This example assumes that 'C7_EX1.H' contains the class definition from exercise 1

```
/*
    C7_EX2.CPP  Chapter 7, exercise 2
                    ('main' function to test the 'Object' class)
*/
#include "c7_ex1.h"
#include <iostream.h>
void main()
{
    Object object1, object2, object3, object4;
    cout << "The total number of objects is: " << Object::getObjectCount()
        << endl;
    cout << "The name of the class is: " << Object::getClassName() << endl;
}
```

Exercise 3

Although this question is rather open ended, we might suggest a range of possible class attributes that are common to all objects of the class. Perhaps the number of bananas that will fit in a box, or how many weeks it takes a banana to ripen. We might contrast these with object attributes like 'ripeness' (each banana will have its own state) or 'colour' (anything from green to yellow to black). The example program contrasts a class attribute recording the weight of all the bananas with an object attribute recording the weight of each single banana.

```
/*
    C7_EX3.CPP  Chapter 7, exercise 3
                    (Class 'Banana' and test program. These are
                    suggestions for possible class attributes,
                    contrasted with a possible object attribute)
*/
class Banana
{
private:
// class attributes
    static int banana_count;
    static float crate_weight;
// an object attribute
    float weight;
public:
    Banana(float banana_weight);
    static int howManyBananas();
    static float whatDoesTheCrateWeigh();
    float whatDoesThisBananaWeigh();
};
// reserve memory for the two class attributes
// (default values will be zero)
```

```
int Banana::banana_count;
float Banana::crate_weight;
// the constructor takes the weight of this banana as a parameter
Banana::Banana(float banana_weight)
{
// add to the count
    banana_count++;
// set the attribute value using the parameter
    weight = banana_weight;
// add the weight of this banana to the class attribute
    crate_weight += banana_weight;
}
// class method to return the number of bananas
int Banana::howManyBananas()
{
    return banana_count;
}
// class method to return the weight of all the bananas
float Banana::whatDoesTheCrateWeigh()
{
    return crate_weight;
}
// method to return the weight of this banana
float Banana::whatDoesThisBananaWeigh()
{
    return weight;
}
// the 'main' function tests the various methods
#include <iostream.h>
void main()
{
// note how the class method can be used even if no objects of the
// class have been instantiated
    cout << "Total Bananas = " << Banana::howManyBananas() << endl;
// four bananas are instantiated
    Banana banana1(10.00), banana2(7.5), banana3(8.00), banana4(9.25);
// the counting and weighing of the bananas.....
    cout << "Total Bananas = " << Banana::howManyBananas() << endl;
    cout << "The crate of bananas weighs " << Banana::whatDoesTheCrateWeigh()
<< endl;
    cout << "This banana weighs " << banana1.whatDoesThisBananaWeigh()
        << endl;
}
```

Chapter 8

Exercise 1

In this example, the added methods are simply constructors and get/set methods.

```
/*
    PUBLISH.H    Chapter 8 exercise 1
                 (add base class and methods to 'Book' and 'Magazine' classes.
                 This header file contains the class bodies.
                 C8_EX1.CPP contains the method definitions)
*/
// this base class has been added to generalise parts of the 'Book'
// and 'Magazine' classes
```

```
class Publication
{
private:
// shared attributes for both derived classes
    char title[30];
    char publisher[30];
public:
// 'set' methods added
    void setTitle(char* title_in);
    void setPublisher(char* publisher_in);
// 'get' methods added
    char* getTitle();
    char* getPublisher();
};
// 'Book' now derives from 'Publication, and only has two attributes.
// the other two are inherited.
class Book : public Publication
{
private:
    char author[30];
    char ISBN[20];
public:
// 'set' methods added
    void setAuthor(char* author);
    void setISBN(char* ISBN);
// 'get' methods added
    char* getAuthor();
    char* getISBN();
};
// the 'Magazine' class inherits from 'Publication and adds one attribute
class Magazine : public Publication
{
private:
    char editor[30];
public:
// 'set' method added
    void setEditor(char* editor_in);
// 'get' method added
    char* getEditor();
};
/*
    C8_EX1.CPP  Chapter 8, exercise 1
                    (definition of methods for publication classes)
*/
#include "publish.h"
#include <string.h>
// definitions of 'Publication' methods
void Publication::setTitle(char* title_in)
{
    strncpy(title, title_in, 29);
    title[29] = '\0';
}
void Publication::setPublisher(char* publisher_in)
{
    strncpy(publisher, publisher_in, 29);
    publisher[29] = '\0';
}
char* Publication::getTitle()
```

369

```
        {
            return title;
        }
        char* Publication::getPublisher()
        {
            return publisher;
        }
        // definitions of 'Book' methods
        void Book::setAuthor(char* author_in)
        {
            strncpy(author, author_in, 29);
            author[29] = '\0';
        }
        void Book::setISBN(char* ISBN_in)
        {
            strncpy(ISBN, ISBN_in, 19);
            ISBN[19] = '\0';
        }
        char* Book::getAuthor()
        {
            return author;
        }
        char* Book::getISBN()
        {
            return ISBN;
        }
        // method definitions for the 'Magazine' class
        void Magazine::setEditor(char* editor_in)
        {
            strncpy(editor, editor_in, 29);
            editor[29] = '\0';
        }
        char* Magazine::getEditor()
        {
            return editor;
        }
```

Chapter 9

Aggregation exercise 1

```
        /*
            C9_EX1.CPP  Chapter 9, exercise 1
                        (test the methods of the 'Bike' class)
        */
        #include "bike.h" // class definitions from page 159
        #include <iostream.h>
        void main()
        {
        // create a bike with wheels of size 24
            Bike my_bike(24);
        // test the wheel size methods of the 'Bike' class
            cout << "Wheel 1 size is: " << my_bike.getFrontWheelSize() << endl;
            cout << "Wheel 2 size is: " << my_bike.getBackWheelSize() << endl;
        }
```

Aggregation exercise 2

```
/*
    C9_EX2.H      Chapter 9 exercise 2
                  (class and method definitions for the 'Rider' class)
*/
#include <string.h>
class Rider
{
private:
    char name[30];
public:
    Rider(char* name_in);
    char* getName();
}
// constructor
Rider::Rider(char* name_in)
{
    strncpy(name, name_in, 29);
    name[29] = '\0';
}
// method to return the rider's name
char* Rider::getName()
{
    return name;
}
```

Association exercise 1

```
/*
    C9ASCEX1.H      Chapter 9, association exercise 1
                    (Header file for 'Telephone' and 'Desk' classes)
*/
// forward declaration of 'Telephone' to allow 'Desk' to compile
class Telephone;
// definition of class 'Desk', associated with a 'Telephone'
class Desk
{
private:
    char name[80];
    Telephone* telephone;
public:
    Desk(char* name_in);
    char* getName();
    void addTelephone(Telephone* phone);
    Telephone* getTelephone();
};
// definition of class 'Telephone', associated with a 'Desk'
class Telephone
{
private:
    int telephone_number;
    Desk* desk;
public:
    Telephone(int number);
    int getTelephoneNumber();
    void putOnDesk(Desk* location);
    Desk* getDesk();
```

```
};
#include <string.h>
// method definitions for the 'Desk' class
Desk::Desk(char* name_in)
{
    strcpy(name, name_in);
}
char* Desk::getName()
{
    return name;
}
void Desk::addTelephone(Telephone* phone)
{
    telephone = phone;
}
Telephone* Desk::getTelephone()
{
    return telephone;
}
// method definitions for the 'Telephone' class
Telephone::Telephone(int number)
{
    telephone_number = number;
}
int Telephone::getTelephoneNumber()
{
    return telephone_number;
}
void Telephone::putOnDesk(Desk* location)
{
    desk = location;
}
Desk* Telephone::getDesk()
{
    return desk;
}
/*
    C9ASCEX1.CPP   Chapter 9, association exercise 1
                   (Test program for desk/telephone association)
*/
#include "c9ascex1.h"
#include <iostream.h>
void main()
{
// create a desk and a telephone
    Desk* desk1 = new Desk("reception desk");
    Telephone* phone1 = new Telephone(9991);
// make the link between the desk and the telephone
    desk1 -> addTelephone(phone1);
// make the link between the telephone and the desk
    phone1 -> putOnDesk(desk1);
// display the details of the association from both objects
    cout << "The " << desk1 -> getName() << " is on extension ";
    cout << desk1 -> getTelephone() -> getTelephoneNumber() << endl;
    cout << "Extension " << phone1 -> getTelephoneNumber()
        << " is for the ";
    cout << phone1 -> getDesk() -> getName() << endl;
}
```

Chapter 10

Exercise 1

```
/*
    C10_EX1.CPP     Chapter 10, exercise 1
                    (using casts to find the ASCII value of characters)
*/
#include <iostream.h>
void main()
{
// display headings for the data
    cout << "ASCII" << '\t' << "character" << endl;
// loop from ASCII code 97 ('a') to ASCII code 122 ('z')
    for(int i = 97; i < 123; i++)
    {
// use a cast to force 'cout' to display the code as a character
        cout << i << '\t' << char(i) << endl;
    }
}
```

Chapter 11

Exercise 1

Only the modifications to the existing class are included here. First, the prototype is added to the class definition:

```
Point operator + (const Point& point);
```

Then the overloaded operator is defined. The addition operator returns an object containing the result:

```
Point Point::operator + (const Point& point)
{
    Point temp;
    temp.x = x + point.x;
    temp.y = y + point.y;
    return temp;
}
```

Exercise 2

Only the modifications to the existing class are included here. First, the prototype is added to the class definition:

```
int operator > (const StudentGrade& grade_in);
```

Then the overloaded operator is defined. The 'greater than' operator returns an integer representing true (1) or false (0):

```
int StudentGrade::operator > (const StudentGrade& grade_in)
{
// use temporary variables to work out which object has the highest grades
    int is_greater, total1, total2;
    total1 = maths_grade + english_grade;
    total2 = grade_in.maths_grade + grade_in.english_grade;
// compare the local integer values to return 'true' (1) or 'false' (0)
    if(total1 > total2)
```

```
        {
            is_greater = 1;
        }
        else
        {
            is_greater = 0;
        }
        return is_greater;
    }
```

Chapter 12

Exercise 1

```
/*
    C12_EX1.CPP      Chapter 12, exercise 1
                     (overloaded 'getMax' functions)
*/
#include <iostream.h>
// fix the array sizes with a constant
const int SIZE = 10;
// this version of 'getMax' returns the largest integer in an array
int getMax(int integer_array[SIZE])
{
// 'max' is initialised to zero
    int max = 0;
// iterate through the array
    for(int i = 0; i < SIZE; i++)
    {
// if the current integer is larger than 'max', replace the value in 'max'
        if(integer_array[i] > max)
        {
            max = integer_array[i];
        }
    }
// return the result
    return max;
}
// this version of 'getMax' returns the largest letter character in an array
// if there are no letter characters then zero is returned
char getMax(char char_array[SIZE])
{
// 'max' is initialised to zero
    char max = 0;
// iterate through the array
    for(int i = 0; i < SIZE; i++)
    {
// if the current character is either an upper case or lower case letter...
        if((char_array[i] >= 65 && char_array[i] <= 90) ||
        (char_array[i] >= 97 && char_array[i] <= 122))
        {
// if that letter is larger than 'max', replace the value in 'max'
            if(char_array[i] > max)
            {
                max = char_array[i];
            }
        }
```

```
    }
// return the result
    return max;
}
// a test 'main' function
void main()
{
// put some values into an integer array
    int integers[SIZE] = {4, 67, 43, 99, 2, 1, 45, 86, 9, 2};
// put values into two 'char' arrays, one with numbers and one with letters
    char chars1[SIZE] = {'a', 'x', 'h', 'k', 'n', 'p', 'y', 'b', 's', 'w'};
    char chars2[SIZE] = {34, 2, 78, 130, 98, 145, 44, 23, 22, 3};
// test the integer version of 'getMax'
    cout << "Maximum integer is " << getMax(integers) << endl;
// test the char version of 'getMax' using both char arrays
    cout << "Highest ASCII character (from letter array) is "
        << getMax(chars1) << endl;
    cout << "Highest ASCII character (from number array) is "
        << getMax(chars2) << endl;
}
```

Chapter 13

Exercise 1

```
/*
    C13_EX1.CPP      Chapter 13, exercise 1
                     (statically bound polymorphic methods
                     in derived classes of 'Pump')
*/
#include <iostream.h>
// the base class 'Pump', with an empty 'turnOn' method
class Pump
{
public:
    void turnOn() {}
};
// the derived class 'FuelPump' implements 'turnOn'
class FuelPump : public Pump
{
public:
    void turnOn();
};
// 'WaterPump' implements its own version of 'turnOn'
class WaterPump : public Pump
{
public:
    void turnOn();
};
// the polymorphic definitions of 'turnOn' in the derived classes:
void FuelPump::turnOn()
{
    cout << "pumping fuel" << endl;
}
void WaterPump::turnOn()
{
    cout << "pumping water" << endl;
```

```
    }
// 'main' tests the 'turnOn' methods
void main()
{
// source code from page 217
    FuelPump fuel_pump1;
    WaterPump water_pump1;
    fuel_pump1.turnOn();
    water_pump1.turnOn();
}
```

Chapter 14

Exercise 1

```
/*
    C14EX1.CPP  Chapter 13, exercise 1
                (dynamically bound polymorphic/virtual
                methods in derived classes of 'Pump')
*/
#include <iostream.h>
// the base class 'Pump', with an abstract 'turnOn' method
class Pump
{
public:
    virtual void turnOn() = 0;
};
// the derived class 'FuelPump' implements 'turnOn'
class FuelPump : public Pump
{
public:
    virtual void turnOn();
};
// 'WaterPump' implements its own version of 'turnOn'
class WaterPump : public Pump
{
public:
    virtual void turnOn();
};
// the polymorphic definitions of 'turnOn' in the derived classes:
void FuelPump::turnOn()
{
    cout << "pumping fuel" << endl;
}
void WaterPump::turnOn()
{
    cout << "pumping water" << endl;
}
// 'main' tests the 'turnOn' methods with dynamic binding
void main()
{
// source code from page 232/233
    Pump* a_pump;
    int pump_type;
    cout << "Enter 1 for a fuel pump, 2 for a water pump ";
    cin >> pump_type;
    if(pump_type == 1)
```

```
        {
            a_pump = new FuelPump;
        }
        else
        {
            a_pump = new WaterPump;
        }
    a_pump -> turnOn();
}
```

Chapter 15 Part 1

Exercise 1

```
/*
        C15P1EX1.CPP    Chapter 15, part 1, exercise 1
                        (class and method definitions for the 'CD' class,
                        with declaration and initialisation of an array of
                        pointers)
*/
#include <string.h>
class CD
{
private:
    char artist[30];
    char title[30];
public:
// constructor
    CD(char* artist_in, char* title_in);
// 'get' methods
    char* getArtist();
    char* getTitle();
};
// constructor definition
CD::CD(char* artist_in, char* title_in)
{
    strncpy(artist, artist_in, 29);
    artist[29] = '\0';
    strncpy(title, title_in, 29);
    title[29] = '\0';
}
// method definitions
char* CD::getArtist()
{
    return artist;
}
char* CD::getTitle()
{
    return title;
}
// in 'main' we declare and initialise an array of pointers
#include <iostream.h>
void main()
{
// declaration of an array of pointers
    CD* cabinet[50];
// initialisation of pointers to NULL
```

```
        for(int i = 0; i < 50; i++)
        {
            cabinet[i] = NULL;
        }
// instantiate an object to test the methods
        cabinet[0] = new CD("The Stroustrups", "Brain on Fire");
        cout << cabinet[0] -> getArtist() << ", " << cabinet[0] -> getTitle()
            << endl;
    }
```

We declare pointers rather than objects because this is not a fixed aggregation (like the hotel rooms in the example program) but a container. Therefore we need to be able to handle dynamic objects that come and go (in and out of the container) as the program runs. Pointers should, of course, be initialised to NULL.

Chapter 15 Part 2

Exercise 1

This example assumes that the definition of the template 'Stack' class (pages 276 to 278) is in 'tstack.h'

```
/*
        C15P2EX1.CPP    Chapter 15, part 2, exercise 1
                        (test the template 'Stack' class, in this example
                        with dynamic arrays of type 'char')
*/
#include "tstack.h"
#include <iostream.h>
#include <string.h>
// this 'main' function tests the template stack with dynamic strings
void main()
{
// local variables for user input
    int stack_size, choice;
    char buffer[80];
// pointer to instantiate dynamic strings
    char* string;
// instantiate a 'Stack' object with dynamically allocated size
    cout << "Enter size of stack required ";
    cin >> stack_size;
// because the template stack always handles pointers, we use 'char'
// rather than 'char*' as the type when creating the stack object
    Stack <char> a_stack(stack_size);
// the menu iterates until the user chooses to exit
    do
    {
        cout << "Enter 1 to push, 2 to pop, 3 to exit ";
        cin >> choice;
        switch(choice)
        {
// push a string onto the stack
            case 1 : cout << "Enter a string ";
                     cin >> buffer;
// dynamically allocate the string and copy from the array
                     string = new char[strlen(buffer) + 1];
                     strcpy(string, buffer);
```

```
        // if 'push' returns zero, then it was unsuccessful
                        if(!a_stack.push(string))
                        {
                                cout << "No room on the stack" << endl;
                        }
                        break;
        // pop a string from the top of the stack. If 'pop' fails (ie the stack
        // is empty) then it returns NULL
                case 2 : if(string = a_stack.pop())
                        {
                                cout << string << endl;
                        }
                        else
                        {
                                cout << "Nothing on the stack" << endl;
                        }
                        break;
                }
        }
        while(choice != 3);
}
```

Chapter 16

Exercise 1

```
/*
        C16_EX1.H       Chapter 16, exercise 1
                        (Class and method definitions for 'TemperatureGauge',
                        'Switch and 'Thermostat')
*/
#include <iostream.h>
// the 'TemperatureGauge' class and method
class TemperatureGauge
{
private:
        float temperature;
public:
        float getTemperature();
};
float TemperatureGauge::getTemperature()
{
// this is a fudge to pretend we have a temperature being measured!
        cout << "Enter current temperature ";
        cin >> temperature;
        return temperature;
}
// an enumerated type for the state of the switch
enum status{on, off};
// the 'Switch' class and methods
class Switch
{
private:
        status switch_status;
public:
        void turnOn();
        void turnOff();
```

```
};
// methods to turn the switch on and off
void Switch::turnOn()
{
    switch_status = on;
    cout << "Switch is on" << endl;
}
void Switch::turnOff()
{
    switch_status = off;
    cout << "Switch is off" << endl;
}
// the 'Thermostat' class multiply inherits from both 'TemperatureGauge'
// and 'Switch'
class Thermostat : public TemperatureGauge, public Switch
{
private:
    float required_temperature;
public:
    void setRequiredTemperature(float temp);
    void monitorTemperature();
};
// methods of 'Thermostat'
void Thermostat::setRequiredTemperature(float temp)
{
    required_temperature = temp;
}
void Thermostat::monitorTemperature()
{
    if(getTemperature() < required_temperature)
    {
        turnOn();
    }
    else
    {
        turnOff();
    }
}
/*
    C16_EX1.CPP     Chapter 16, exercise 1
                    (Test program for the 'Thermostat' class)
*/
#include "c16_ex1.h"
void main()
{
// create a thermostat object
    Thermostat therm;
// local variables for user input
    int choice = 0;
    float temp;
// iterating menu
    do
    {
        cout << "Enter 1 to set temperature, 2 to monitor, 3 to quit
            << endl;
        cin >> choice;
        switch(choice)
        {
```

```
// set the temperature
            case 1 : cout << "Enter required temperature ";
                     cin >> temp;
                     therm.setRequiredTemperature(temp);
                     break;
// monitor the temperature (the method actually asks for input
// from the keyboard)
            case 2 : therm.monitorTemperature();
        }
    } while(choice != 3);
}
```

Chapter 17

Exercise 1

Only the modifications to the existing class are included here. First, the prototype of the 'friend' is added to the class definition:

```
friend ostream& operator << (ostream& out, Point& point);
```

Then the overloaded operator is defined. The operator sends the attribute values (with text labels) to the output stream:

This overloaded operator is tailored for screen output with text labels. It would not be very helpful for writing to file because the labels would have to be read in as well as the data.

```
ostream& operator << (ostream& out, Point& point)
{
    out << "x: " << point.x << " y: " << point.y << endl;
    return out;
}
```

Glossary

Many terms are introduced in this book, but this is a summary of the most fundamental.

Abstract data type A user defined data type, including its attributes (the data representation of its state) and its methods (its behaviours). An abstract data type acts like a 'blueprint' for all objects of that type.

Aggregation Objects which are composed of other objects are known as aggregations. They may involve containment (the contained objects are components of the larger object) or containership (see 'container class').

Attribute A characteristic of an object. An object attribute contains state data about the object.

Class The definition of objects of the same abstract data type. In C++, 'class' is the keyword used to define such types, some of which may be abstract base classes, not intended to instantiate objects.

Container Class A class defining objects which are able to contain other objects. Objects of container classes are used to manage collections of objects of other classes.

Dynamic (late) binding The identification at run time of which version of a polymorphic method is being called. When the class of an object cannot be identified at compile time, it is impossible to statically bind object methods, so dynamic binding must be used.

Encapsulation The combining together of attributes (data) and methods (processes) into a single object type with a public interface and a private implementation.

Genericity The ability of a class, method or function to apply the same implementation to different data or object types.

Inheritance The derivation of one class from another so that the attributes and methods of one class are part of the definition of another class. Derived classes are always 'a kind of' their base classes.

Metaclass The 'class of a class' – the metaclass contains those parts of a class which are not part of objects.

Method The implementation of some behaviour of an object.

Object An instance of a class. Objects have state, identity and behaviour.

Operator overloading Giving new meanings to the existing operators available in C++, allowing them to be used with objects of user-defined classes.

Overloading Allowing the same function or method name to be used for more than one implementation, the various versions distinguishable by differences in their parameter lists.

Polymorphism In general terms, the ability of different classes of object to respond to the same message in different, class-specific ways. Polymorphic methods are those which have one name but different implementations for different classes.

Static (early) binding The identification at compile time of which version of a polymorphic method is being called. In order to do this, the compiler must identify the class of an object.

Bibliography

Where references appear in the text, the name of the author and date of publication appears in square brackets (in the format used here) along with the page reference numbers.

Books

[Blair et al, 1991]
'Object Oriented Languages, Systems and Applications'
Gordon Blair, John Gallagher, David Hutchison and Doug Shepherd
Pitman, London 1991

[Booch, 1991]
'Object Oriented Design With Applications'
Grady Booch
Benjamin/Cummings, Redwood City, Calif. 1991

[Booch, 1994]
'Object-Oriented Analysis and Design With Applications' (2nd Edition)
Grady Booch
Benjamin/Cummings, Redwood City, Calif. 1994

[Coad/Yourdon, 1990]
'Object-Oriented Analysis'
Peter Coad and Edward Yourdon
Yourdon Press, Prentice-Hall, New Jersey 1990

[Coplien, 1992]
'Advanced C++ Programming Styles and Idioms'
James O. Coplien,
Addison-Wesley, 1992

[Cox, 1986]
'Object-Oriented Programming – An Evolutionary Approach'
Brad J. Cox
Addison-Wesley, Reading, Mass. 1986

[Gamma et al, 1995]
'Design Patterns: Elements of Reusable Object-Oriented Software'
Erich Gamma, Richard Helm, Ralph Johnson and John Vlissides,
Addison-Wesley, 1995

[Graham, 1991]
'Object Oriented Methods'
Ian Graham
Addison-Wesley, Wokingham 1991

[Holmes, 1992]
'Convert to C and C++'
B.J.Holmes
DP Publications, London 1992

[Jacobson, 1992]
'Object-Oriented Software Engineering – A Use Case Driven Approach'
Ivar Jacobson, Magnus Christerson, Patrik Jonsson & Gunnar Overgaard
Addison-Wesley, Wokingham 1992

Bibliography

[Kernighan & Ritchie, 1988]
'The C Programming Language' (2nd edition)
Brian Kernighan and Dennis Ritchie
Prentice-Hall, New Jersey 1988

[Lafore, 1991]
'The Waite Group's Object-Oriented Programming in Turbo C++'
Robert Lafore
The Waite Group Press, Emeryville, Calif. 1991

[Meyer, 1988]
'Object-oriented Software Construction'
Bertrand Meyer
Prentice-Hall, Hemel Hempstead, 1988

[Naughton, 1996]
'The Java Handbook'
Patrick Naughton,
Osborne McGraw Hill, Berkeley 1996

[Pirsig, 1974]
'Zen and the Art of Motorcycle Maintenance'
Robert M. Pirsig
Corgi, London, 1978 (originally published 1974)

[Rumbaugh et al, 1991]
'Object-Oriented Modeling and Design'
James Rumbaugh, Michael Blaha, William Premerlani, Frederick Eddy and William Lorenson
Prentice-Hall International, New Jersey, 1991

[Shlaer & Mellor, 1988]
'Object-Oriented Systems Analysis – Modelling the World in Data'
Sally Shlaer, Stephen J. Mellor
Yourdon Press, New Jersey, 1988

[Stroustrup, 1991]
'The C++ Programming Language' (2nd Edition)
Bjarne Stroustrup
Addison-Wesley, Reading, Mass. 1995

Articles

[Beck & Cunningham, 1989]
'A Laboratory For Teaching Object-Oriented Thinking'
Kent Beck and Ward Cunningham
Sigplan Notices, Vol 24, No. 10, October 1989 (pp 1–6)

[Blackwell, 1993]
'Bottom-Up Design and This Thing Called an Object'
Alan Blackwell
EXE magazine, Vol 8, Issue 7, December 1993 (pp 28–32)

[Brooks, 1986]
'Essence and Accidents of Software Engineering'
Frederick P Brooks
Computer magazine, April 1987 (pp 10–19)

[Chaudhri, 1993]
'Object Database Management Systems – An Overview'
Akmal B. Chaudhri
BCS OOPS Group Newsletter 18 (pp 6–15)

[Collinson, 1991]
'What Dennis says'
Peter Collinson
EXE magazine, Vol 5, Issue 8, February 1991 (pp 14–18)

[Corbett, 1993]
'A Framework for Application Class Design'
Eric Corbett
EXE magazine, Vol 7, Issue 10, April 1993 (pp 12–16)

[Cox, 1990]
'There Is a Silver Bullet'
Brad J. Cox
BYTE magazine, October 1990 (pp 209–218)

[Drake, 1990]
'History of a Useful Illusion'
Richard Drake
EXE magazine, Vol 4, Issue 11, May 1990 (pp 18–24)

[Flower, 1993]
'Objects by Design'
Alan Flower
EXE magazine, Vol 8, Issue 7, December 1993 (pp 12–20)

[Gibson, 1990]
'Objects – Born and Bred'
Elizabeth Gibson
Byte magazine, October 1990 (pp 245–254)

[Harmon, 1990]
'Object-Oriented Systems'
Paul Harmon
Intelligent Software Strategies Newsletter, (Cutter Information Corp) September 1990

[Kesterton 1997]
'The Role of Use Cases in the Unified Modelling Language'
Anthony Kesterton,
Proceedings of 'Object Technology 97' conference, Oxford 1997

[McCausland, 1996]
'Implementing Associations in C++'
Campbell McCausland,
Proceedings of the 'Object Technology 96' conference, Oxford 1996

[Parnas, 1972]
'On the Criteria To Be Used in Decomposing Systems Into Modules'
in 'Classics in Software Engineering', ed. E.Yourdon, Yourdon Press, New Jersey 1979
(pp 141–150)

[Rumbaugh, 1996]
'Models for Design: Generating Code for Associations'
James Rumbaugh,
Journal of Object-Oriented Programming, February 1996

[Smith, 1989]
'The Man Who is C++'
Paul Smith
EXE Magazine, Vol 4, Issue 7, December 1989 (pp 12–17)

[Stroustrup, 1988]
'A Better C?'
Bjarne Stroustrup
Byte magazine, August 1988 (pp 215–216D)

[Stump, 1993]
'Multiple Inheritance: When? and When Not?
Laine Stump
EXE magazine, Vol 7, Issue 8, February 1993 (pp 49–55)

[UML, 1997]
UML documents at http://www.rational.com/
Rational Corporation, 1997

[Watts (1), 1992]
'Yet More Bjarne'
Will Watts
EXE magazine, Vol 6, Issue 9, March 1992 (pp 30–36)

[Watts (2), 1992]
'La Resistance'
Will Watts
EXE magazine, Vol 6, Issue 11, May 1992 (pp 28–35)

[Wegner, 1989]
'Learning the Language'
Peter Wegner
Byte magazine, March 1989 (pp 245–253)

[Wirth, 1990]
'OOP meets Modula–2'
Niklaus Wirth
EXE magazine, Vol 4, Issue 11, May 1990 (pp 12–16)

[Yourdon, 1990]
'Auld Lang Syne'
Edward Yourdon
BYTE magazine, October 1990 (pp 257–263)

Index

#include, 17, 32, 39, 63
'\0' (escape sequence), 38, 39
'\n' (escape sequence), 22, 32, 327

absolute value, 208–9
abstract class, 117–8, 119, 123, 139, 217, 218, 231–3, 238
abstract data type, 4, 8, 10, 53, 54–5, 57, 58, 62
abstract method, 218, 219, 221–2, 237–8
abstraction, 7, 8, 54, 139, 339–40
activity diagram, 349
actor, 135, 336, 343, 345, 350
'address of' operator (&), 44
agent, 135
aggregation, 8–9, 133, 136–48, 159–60, 161–2, 244, 292, 293, 334, 341
    fixed, 140, 141, 143–5, 244
    partial, 140
    recursive, 140
    variable, 140, 147–8, 244
AKO (a kind of), 111–2, 284, 341
ALGOL (ALGOrithmic Language), 14, 15, 18
alias, 27
ancestor, 110, 286
ANSI, 14, 16, 21, 39, 211
antisymmetry, 139
APO (a part of), 112, 136, 341
applet, 11
application class framework, 142–3
arithmetic operator, 24–6, 181–2, 186, 192, 194, 201
array, 36, 246, 248
    as function parameter, 37
    bounds checking, 36, 40
    declaration, 36
    dynamic allocation, 163–4, 207
    initialisation, 36
    of chars, 38
    of integers, 36
    of object pointers, 95, 154
    of objects, 127, 196
    of objects – initialisation, 210
    of two dimensions, 36
arrow operator (–>), 87, 88
'artifact of the implementation', 1, 339, 345
ASCII character, 21, 22, 49, 222–4, 314, 315
assignment operator (=), 23, 39, 40, 88, 187, 190–1, 197–9
association, 133–5, 148–58, 341, 346–8
associative array, 250
AT&T, 15
attribute, 56, 99–101, 140, 310–1, 348
automatic object, 77, 78–9, 83

B (language), 13–4
Backus Naur Form, 14
bag, 250
base class, 110, 111, 220, 232–3
BCPL (Basic CPL), 13, 14, 15, 20, 34
Beck & Cunningham, 337, 340
Bohm & Jacopini, 45
Booch, Grady, 246, 293, 335, 339, 340
bool (data type) 21, 165, 211
Boolean, 46
brace, 26, 93
break (keyword), 45, 47

C, 13–4
C++, 7, 13, 15–19
callback function, 252
Cardelli & Wegner's taxonomy, 179
casting, 182–5, 197, 275
character constant, 22
child class, 110
cin, 33–4, 313–4
cin.get (method), 269, 314
class, 2, 55, 58–60, 65–7
    attribute, 101, 105
    based programming, 9
    declaration, 59
    diagram, 162, 349
    keyword, 58
    libraries, 246
    methods, 102, 105
    reservation of memory, 107
classical categorisation, 335
classification hierarchy, 110, 111, 117, 179, 181, 285
cleanup, 82, 89, 94, 278
CLOS, 17–18
close (ofstream method), 320
Coad/Yourdon, 61, 334
coercion, 177, 179, 181–2
cohesion, 5
collaboration diagram, 349, 351–2
colon operator (:), 120–1, 145–6, 294
comment syntax, 34–5
Common Object Request Broker Architecture (CORBA), 11
composition hierarchy, 137
conceptual clustering, 335
const (keyword), 24, 28, 74–5, 192
constant, 24
constructor, 68–9, 71–2, 87–8, 93, 128
    copy, 69–70, 74–5, 187
    default, 69, 71
    overloading, 209–11
    parameterised, 73–4